DISCARDED

W9-CZT-961

DISCARDED

TEN MEN
AND HISTORY

Books by Don Cook

TEN MEN AND HISTORY
FLOODTIDE IN EUROPE

TEN MEN
AND HISTORY

Don Cook

DOUBLEDAY & COMPANY, INC.
Garden City, New York 1981

Upsala College
Library
East Orange, N. J. 07019

920.04
C771t

Library of Congress Cataloging in Publication Data

Cook, Don, 1920–
Ten men and history.

Bibliography.
Includes index.
1. Heads of state—Europe—Biography.
2. Statesmen—Europe—Biography.   3. Europe—
Politics and government—1945–   4. Europe—
Economic conditions—1945–   5. Cook, Don,
1920–   I. Title.
D839.5.C66   920'.04

ISBN: 0-385-14908-5
Library of Congress Catalog Card Number 80-1062

Copyright © 1981 by Don Cook
ALL RIGHTS RESERVED

PRINTED IN THE UNITED STATES OF AMERICA
FIRST EDITION

For seven Americans
born and reared in Europe

174071

Contents

Contents

Author's Note

MEN AND EVENTS ARE THE DAILY FARE OF JOURNALISM AND THE warp and woof of history. The framework for these ten biographical sketches and the reconstruction of key events with which the ten men are associated has been my own reporting as a foreign correspondent in Europe from 1945 to 1965 with the now defunct New York *Herald Tribune* and since then with the Los Angeles *Times*. I have watched and written about all these men in action, and some of them I have known personally. I have also covered all the events in this book, some more continuously and intensively than others, but all of them at some point in their unfolding.

I arrived in Britain as a war correspondent early in 1945 and continued on in London in the postwar period of the Marshall Plan and the origins of the Cold War until 1949. I was then transferred to West Germany, where my assignment began as the Berlin blockade was coming to an end and the Bonn Republic was formed. In 1952 I moved on to Paris and a roving assignment that included covering General Dwight D. Eisenhower at the newly formed Supreme Headquarters, Allied Powers Europe (SHAPE) and the European Coal and Steel Community, which was starting up under Jean Monnet. I returned to London at the end of 1955 for five years that began with the Suez crisis, and in 1960 I moved back to Paris on a European diplomatic beat, with General Charles de Gaulle as the centerpiece. By the luck of assignments, therefore, I was covering much of the decision making and formative events of the vital period from roughly 1947 to 1953, when the institutions were established that shape Europe today: its economic recovery, its security and its unity. I have been

close at hand since those great years for most of the key developments and turns through which Europe has evolved and built on
those original strong historic foundations.

In going back over these thirty-five years of journalism, I
have of course taken full advantage of much else that has come
out in autobiographies, biographies, memoirs, histories, articles,
and documentary writings to round out my own reporting and recollections. I have also gone back to numerous old friends and colleagues and participants at the time to reconstruct details and re-
fresh my impressions and judgments. In particular in these
sketches I have sought to keep alive the element of journalism:
how things happened. Too often, histories written at a distance by
authors who were not there seem to stop with simply recording
what happened. Historians will probably dispose of the student
uprising in Paris in May 1968, which began the downfall of
General de Gaulle, in a few paragraphs, but this occupied reporters
and newspaper headlines for weeks. What happened in those
weeks can readily be summarized, but *how* it all happened is a
considerable story.

These sketches are not definitive biography or history, but I
hope that, as a journalistic synthesis, they will portray the essential
qualities of character and leadership of Europe's key postwar political figures and will accurately recount the challenges and
problems they have faced, and the vitality and achievements
of what to me has been the most interesting continent in the
world.

L'Étang la Ville
France
August 1980

1

Ernest Bevin

ERNEST BEVIN, ONE OF THE GREAT FOREIGN SECRETARIES OF British history, was born in 1881 and drove a cart and horse delivering mineral water to the pubs and hotels of the port city of Bristol, in the West of England, until he was twenty-nine years old. His father died before he was born, and his mother died before he was seven. His formal education ended when he was eleven. He died in 1951, and a plaque in Westminster Abbey commemorates his service to his nation.

For the last five years of a prodigious life, in the decisive period immediately following World War II, Bevin shaped and directed British foreign policy—and by extension the policies of Europe and the Atlantic Community—with a strength and personality unmatched by any foreign secretary in this century. Anthony Eden was at the Foreign Office longer than Bevin (ten years with two interruptions) but left less of a stamp on the institution or on history. Nor do any other notable foreign secretaries of the century come near to Bevin's stature or achievements: Lord Lansdowne, Sir Edward Grey, Lord Curzon. Many have held the office. Bevin filled it.

The most difficult and truest test of a great general is the ability to conduct a skillful and successful retreat, and it fell to Bevin to set the main lines of British foreign policy at a time of historic decline in the power and fortunes of the Empire. It was much easier to be a Palmerston in the nineteenth century, dispatching gunboats and taking up the white man's burden for the glory of Queen Victoria. Of course, British prestige at the end of World War II was never higher in history, but British resources were the reality with which Bevin had to deal. Playing a weakening hand, his contribution to the revival of Europe and the stability of the West was profound.

"I haven't got a ton of coal or a pound of cotton to negotiate with," Bevin cried out in anguish in 1946 at the annual rally of the Durham miners, one of the great traditional events of the British trade-union movement, to which he devoted his life. But if Bevin was short on economic means with which to conduct foreign policy, he was not lacking in resources of character, deeply rooted democratic principles, and a great sense of history and British values. No less than Winston Churchill, he was an epitome of the English and an authentic if much less elegant, more colloquial voice of Britain. In personality as well as appearance, Bevin had all the rugged, knotty, gnarled qualities of English oak. He exuded power. His learning was untutored but his intelligence was far-ranging, his grasp of issues and fundamentals acute, his mind intuitive, his vision of the world wide, his common sense sound, and his self-confidence complete. He was not an easy man. He could be ruthless and vindictive, rough and crude and thoroughly undiplomatic. He was egotistical, but he was not vain and he scorned flattery. "Me and you—we can't 'elp but being prima donnas, can we?" he once joshed a cabinet colleague. He also had humor and warmth, which commanded extraordinary loyalty and affection from men in all walks of life who worked with him. Loyalty, in fact, was a touchstone of Bevin's character. He gave it and he expected it, and it was much better to have him on your side than wind up opposing him. There was nothing devious about him, and he was instantly suspicious of deviousness in others. In particular this applied to Communists, fellow travelers, and left-wing intellectuals, against whom he fought many a skirmish in the trade-union movement and the British Labour Party for more than forty years. As a union leader, he was never Marxist or revolutionary but simply democratic and a determined fighter for social justice—and he was the same as British Foreign Secretary.

Bevin became Foreign Secretary in the middle of the Potsdam Conference in July 1945. He had been Minister of Labour in Churchill's coalition War Cabinet, and being well aware of the economic problems that Britain was facing, he sensed that a power vacuum of grave implications was materializing in the world in the guise of peace. It was by no means as certain in 1945 and 1946 as it all seems to have been today that the United States would grasp the realities in time and be ready to fill up the gap or know how to fill it. Bevin therefore directed everything to maintaining the wartime Anglo-American partnership and intimacy and increasing the active involvement of the United States in the destiny of Europe. At three vital points in postwar history, Bevin acted decisively to bring the United States on stage to fill the role in world affairs that had to be filled and that Britain could no longer sustain.

The first came in February of 1947, when Bevin abruptly informed Washington that Britain could no longer afford the burden of economic and military support for the tottering Greek Government in its civil war against the Communists. It was, as Walter Lippmann later put it, the point at which full realization of its European responsibilities was forced on the United States. The second moment of history came four months later, when General George C. Marshall made his historic speech at Harvard University in June 1947 offering aid to Europe if Europe would join in collectively dealing with its economic problems. Bevin immediately "grasped with both hands" the initiative of response. The third occasion came in 1948, when Bevin initiated through secret diplomacy the question of an American security guarantee for Europe, out of which the North Atlantic Treaty emerged, in 1949.

Bevin was less successful, less perceptive, in charting the right long-term course for Britain in its relations with Europe, on its doorstep. And of course, for some the memory of his handling of the Palestine question and the whole Arab-Jewish explosion of 1947–48 remains a botch and a blot that obscures his greatness. But if Bevin was less than adroit and frequently downright insensitive and inept over Palestine, at least he was not devious. He thrashed around, openly trying to find a basis for Arab-Jewish agreement over the future of what was British mandated territory, but it was a climate of totally irreconcilable political emotions. When he could not get agreement, he packed up and walked away from the problem. The struggle is still going on, more than thirty years later. Whatever mistakes Bevin made, it cannot be said that he failed where somebody else might have succeeded.

In the meantime, in the most crowded and decisive peacetime years of this century, Ernest Bevin was a rocklike figure of certitude and common sense in Europe. He was no man to be blown off course, and even though he appeared most of the time to be sailing in the American wake, this should not obscure the fact that he did an extraordinary amount of the navigating.

Bevin was born in the village of Winsford, in Somerset County. His father, unnamed on the birth certificate, had been a landless farm laborer at a time of abject agricultural poverty in England. His mother kept the family going by taking domestic jobs and working as the village midwife. She was intensely religious and of strong, independent radical character—a Methodist dissenter against the established Church of England. She fell ill when Bevin was six, and his last recollections of her were reporting to her bedside on Sunday evenings to recount what the preacher had said in church. Later, in his twenties, he became a lay preacher for a time himself.

When his mother died, he went to live with a sister who worked as a domestic servant and was married to a railway workman. He had a two-mile walk to a country school each morning after household chores, which included cleaning all the family shoes. He continued to shine his own shoes most of his life, and once, at a foreign ministers' conference, he remarked somewhat puckishly to Vyacheslav M. Molotov: "I had a thought this morning while I was polishing me boots . . ." and went on to make some proposal for a way out of one of the obscure deadlocks that constantly plagued four-power deliberations. The Soviet Foreign Minister took the bait and began his reply by expressing surprise that the British Foreign Secretary had to shine his own shoes. Not at all, Bevin responded; he had always found it a congenial task which was helpful to constructive and objective thinking in the morning, and Mr. Molotov should try it. There is no evidence that Mr. Molotov ever did.

In 1892, when Bevin was eleven, it was time for him to find work and relieve his sister and her husband of the burden of his upkeep. He was taken on as a farm boy a few miles from his sister's home, with a bed and his meals and a shilling a week in wages. At that, he was more comfortably off than boys of his age in the factory towns of Victorian England. As he was just out of school, he would read aloud in the evening to the farm family the main news articles and editorials from the leading newspaper in the West of England, the Bristol *Mercury*. But after two years of farm work he headed for Bristol himself, where a brother was living. Over the next years, he worked variously as a kitchen boy in a restaurant (a shilling a day and one good meal), a grocery errand boy, a hotel porter, a streetcar conductor, and a dray-horse driver. Finally, when he was eighteen, he went to work for a man named John Macy who had a mineral-water business, and stayed there for the next eleven years doing the rounds of Bristol with a horse and cart for a wage of eighteen shillings—not much more than four dollars a week, plus tiny commissions on sales.

"It sounds hard when you look back on it, but you've got to remember that conditions were very different then," Bevin told a friend in later years. "I hadn't anything to complain about. They were good people I worked for and they treated me well. You had to take what was going. You got a job and you lost it and you picked up something else and made do with whatever came along."

His wages in the mineral-water business crept up to two pounds weekly, and he married, and he and his wife, Florence, had a daughter, their only child. He was a teetotaler and strongly religious still, but in the social and economic conditions of his life in Bristol, his intellectual interest began to shift from religion and the pulpit to the more active appeal of the Bristol Socialist Society. This was a political group, rather like the Fabian Society, and by 1908 Bevin was one of its leaders at a time of depression, when at least twenty thousand men, women, and children in Bristol were existing on the barest of paupers' handouts. Pressure on the Bristol City Council for relief was getting little response, and Bevin now organized his first social action.

On a Sunday morning, a great crowd of unemployed assembled under Bevin's leadership, dressed and cleaned and combed as best they could, and marched quietly to morning church service at the Bristol Cathedral. They silently filled the empty pews alongside the wealthy of the city, stayed to sing and pray, then mutely filed out when the service was over and dispersed without disturbance. The psychological impact was profound. Some of Bevin's regular customers responded by boycotting his mineral-water service, but his employer, a liberal man, stood by him. The City Council was roused to more positive action, and at Bevin's proposal it set aside public funds to build a lake in one of the city parks to make work for the unemployed.

Cart drivers and delivery men such as Bevin had no trade union in Bristol at that time. But organizers were active. On August 27, 1910, Bevin became a founder-member of the Bristol Carmen's Branch of the Dock, Wharf, Riverside and General Laborers' Union. The certificate of membership was hanging on the wall of the Foreign Secretary's official residence at Carlton House Terrace, in the heart of London, when Bevin died.

The first twenty-nine years of Bevin's life had been unremarkable except from the standpoint of the development of character in facing difficulties and meeting challenges: his ability to cope for himself before he was out of knee pants, an uncomplaining acceptance of hard work in the harsh economic conditions of the time, and a strong strain of independence. In his mineral-water job he was on his own from the time he loaded his cart and started out in the morning, and that is why he stayed at it for eleven years. But now his religion was transforming into the democratic fight for social justice.

Six months after the Bristol Carmen's Branch was founded, the organizers decided that a full-time secretary was needed. Bevin gave up his two pounds weekly and commissions selling mineral water for two pounds weekly as a paid union official. Three years later, after he had built up his branch and successfully sustained its morale and resources following a crippling strike in the West-of-England ports, Bevin was called to London and made assistant national organizer. He quickly came to dominate his job, and in 1915 his chief died and he became national organizer for the British Dock Workers Union, at the age of thirty-four.

The First World War had broken out, and despite the enormous demands it was making on manpower, Britain did not even have a ministry of labor. It fell to Bevin and other union leaders to help evolve a kind of ad hoc labor scheme to shift dockers and other

workers from port to port to handle convoys and troop movements. Prime Minister David Lloyd George, bowing to trade
union and Labour Party pressures, finally established a labor ministry when he formed a coalition cabinet in 1916. Bevin then
finished out the war as the trade-union representative on an inter-
ministerial Port and Transit Committee, involving the Admiralty,
the War Office, the Board of Trade, and other departments as well
as the employers' organizations. It was his first but by no means
last experience of the problems and techniques of large-scale government decision making and administration.

After ten years of union work, he was the most powerful man
in his organization but relatively unknown outside. He now propelled himself unexpectedly and dramatically into the public eye.
At the end of the war, legislation had been passed giving the
Minister of Labour the power to set up an industrial court of inquiry to examine the evidence in labor disputes, but the unions
had been suspicious and wary of putting the machinery to use.
Bevin, with considerable difficulty, finally persuaded his own
union to apply for a court of inquiry into a dockworkers' claim
for a new basic minimum wage of sixteen shillings a day—approximately four dollars at that time. Union militants would have preferred strike action, but Bevin believed that there was more to be
gained by exposing the case to public opinion through the inquiry
machinery. The inquiry began in February 1920, under Lord
Shaw, a High Court justice, and Bevin became famous almost
overnight.

The shipowners employed a battery of distinguished and highly
paid King's Counsels to put their case. Bevin, with vast self-
confidence, decided to do without lawyers and represent his union
himself and quickly became known as "the dockers' K.C." He
opened with a speech that lasted eleven hours over two and a half
days, and by the time he concluded he was acclaimed and
discussed in every newspaper in the country. He began with the
background of the claim, its moral and economic justification, and
swept on through a review of wartime profits reaped by the shipowners and their ability to meet the dockers' claim. But he went
on then to evolve a broad case for wholesale reorganization of the
dock labor system, and he covered all of this with the kind of

comprehensive analysis of relevant statistics and records and economic reports that nobody in Britain had ever heard from a trade-
union leader before. His peroration, at the end of two and a half
days alone in the well of the court, is still a classic in British trade-
union annals:

"I challenge Counsel to show that a family can exist in physical
efficiency on less than I have indicated. I say that if the Captains
of Industry cannot organize their concerns to give labour a living
wage then they should resign from their captaincy. If you refuse
our claim then I suggest you must adopt an alternative. You must
go to the Prime Minister. You must go to the Minister of Education, and tell them to close down our schools and teach us nothing. We must get back then to the purely fodder basis. For it is no
use to give us knowledge if we are not to be given the possibility
of using it, to give us a sense of the beautiful without allowing us
ever to have a chance to obtain the employment of it. Education
creates aspirations and a love of the beautiful. Are we to be denied the wherewithal to secure these things? It is a false policy.
Better to let us live in the dark if our claims are not to be met."

Greater courtroom drama was to follow. The lawyers for the
shipowners unwisely put an eminent Cambridge economist on the
stand to show that a wage of £3.17s. per week was adequate to
feed, clothe, and house a dockworker's family. Bevin and his secretary left the court that afternoon and went out to Canning Town
market, in the East End of London, and bought the amount of
food they could get for a family dinner on the "budget" of the
economist. They cooked it that night and produced it in court next
morning, cut up and served on five plates, the average size of a
docker's family. The effect was devastating—particularly when
Bevin went on to establish in cross-examination of a shipowner
that British dockers in those days were expected to manhandle on
their backs loads totaling up to seventy-one tons a day.

"And do you know the average haulage for a horse for a
week?" the ex-cart driver asked the shipowner.

"No."

"Fifty tons."

Bevin won his case hands down. The tribunal ordered a daily
minimum wage of sixteen shillings a day for a forty-four-hour

week. But reorganization of the dock labor system had to wait another twenty years, until Bevin was Minister of Labour.

"This has been something bigger than an inquiry into sixteen shillings a day," Bevin told a union rally at Albert Hall when it was all over. "It has been a platform on which it has been possible to open a page of history, and unfold the great human tragedy of men and women fighting year in and year out against terrible economic conditions with which they have been surrounded. When the time comes, if it ever does, for a great struggle between capital and labour, I want it to be for something bigger than a penny an hour. It won't be worth it. I don't want a blind struggle. I want it to have the objective of achieving for those who toil the mastery of their own lives."

All the same, when the traumatic experience of the general strike worked itself to a complicated climax in Britain in 1926, Bevin misjudged the force of public opinion, which he had brought to his side so effectively in the dockers' inquiry. The general strike evolved out of support for minuscule and pitiful claims to sustain starving coal miners. The Tory government of the day, headed by Stanley Baldwin, pulled the rug from under the trade-union leaders, who were verging on a last-minute settlement to avoid the worst. When the strike was on, Bevin was its chief organizer, but in the public and political backlash, it had to be called off more or less ignominiously after only five days. The Tories exploited their victory to the fullest. The trade unions retreated, crippled and harassed, into the Great Depression of the 1930s. Union membership fell off by almost half a million, and the strike weapon had to be sheathed. In the seven years before the general strike, an average of nearly 28 million working days a year had been lost in Britain through strike actions, while in the seven years following, this dropped to only 4 million a year. Bevin himself concentrated his energies on consolidating his own union from a loose association of small units into the integrated, massive Transport and General Workers Union (TGWU), which then became his power base in the Trades Union Congress and the Labour Party. In this he showed both his skill as a careful and patient negotiator and his ruthlessness in giving the shove to older men above him who had served the movement far longer. As a democrat, Bevin had his limits. He certainly imposed a "consensus view" on his union more often than negotiating one, and he brooked no challenge to his authority. He now turned increasingly to political activity to achieve the social ends and the justice for labor that strike action could not attain.

In the general election of 1929, the Labour Party emerged with a small majority over Baldwin and the Tories, with the Liberals holding a balance in the House of Commons. Nevertheless, Ramsay MacDonald formed a Labour government. But his majority was insecure, and his political strength and judgment even more so. It ended in disaster for Labour in 1931, when MacDonald double-crossed the party overnight and set himself up as Prime Minister of a national coalition government with Conservative support, pledged to drastic deflationary measures to meet the economic crisis. In a national election that followed, the Labour Party was swamped—including Bevin, who ran out of loyalty rather than hope for a seat, at Gateshead, in the Northeast of England, and was defeated along with hundreds of other Labour candidates.

But meanwhile he had extended his prominence and influence in the labor movement by reorganizing the Labour Party newspaper *Daily Herald,* transferring its management to a publishing house that was sympathetic to the Left and turning it into a mass-circulation daily that continued to enliven Fleet Street right through the Second World War. Bevin and three other directors from the Trades Union Congress served on the paper's board, controlling its editorial policy and naming the editor but leaving its journalism to good professionals. It remained "my newspaper" for Bevin the rest of his life, and faded and died not long after he did.

One of the few notable actions of the MacDonald Labour government apart from the nature of its demise was the establishment of a committee of inquiry into the causes of the country's economic depression. It was headed by Lord Macmillan, and Bevin served as one of the trade-union members. The hearings, which droned on for weeks, were noteworthy for only one reason: the emergence of an unexpected and unusual intellectual alliance between Bevin and the famous Cambridge economist John Maynard Keynes, who was also a committee member.

Both agreed that one of the iniquitous causes of the depression had been the return to the gold standard, engineered by Winston Churchill during his tenure as Chancellor of the Exchequer in 1925. Between them, passing the lead in questioning back and forth, Keynes and Bevin politely slaughtered the governor of the Bank of England, Sir Montagu Norman, when he took the witness stand. They pulled his economic theories to shreds and drew from him the most damaging and callous statements of moral and political philosophy. The practical results of the Macmillan Committee were nil as far as its effect on British policies, but it established Bevin, untutored though he was, as one of the country's intellectual peers. This then somewhat lessened Bevin's natural suspicions about elitists such as Keynes.

In the demoralized condition of the Labour Party after the MacDonald defection and the election disaster of 1931, Bevin, with his powerful union base, became increasingly strong in party affairs. But he always kept his distance from the party leaders, some of whom he openly disliked. Once, when somebody remarked in Bevin's presence that Aneurin Bevan, the fiery Welsh leftist, was "his own worst enemy," Ernie growled: "Not while I'm alive, 'e ain't." In Bevin's book, the union and not the Labour Party came first. Party decisions at the annual conferences are taken by block votes, and the massive vote of the Transport and General Workers Union continues to be a major sledgehammer in pounding out policies. Bevin enjoyed the independence of lumbering up to the platform from his seat among the delegates and laying down the law to the party leaders on the dais. It was in this fashion that he committed one of the most ruthless, brutal power acts of British political history—a one-man public political execution of George Lansbury as leader of the Labour Party, at the annual party conference held in Brighton in 1935.

Lansbury, an intense pacifist who had gone to prison rather than accept military service in the First World War, succeeded to the party leadership when MacDonald deserted. But his pacifist views had become increasingly difficult for the Labour Party to swallow in the climate of rising Fascism and Nazism of the 1930s.

In 1935 the issue before the party conference was a motion of support for League of Nations sanctions against Mussolini over his invasion of Ethiopia. Lansbury took the rostrum to deliver what turned out to be his last pacifist sermon to the party, ending: "If mine were the only voice in this conference, I would say in the name of the faith I hold, the belief I have that God intended us to live peaceably and quietly with one another, that if some people do not allow us to do so, I am ready to stand as the early Christians did and say: This is our faith, this is where we stand, and if necessary this is where we will die."

He sat down to a tumult of applause and cheers and tears welling up in Labour Party eyes as the delegates sang "For He's a Jolly Good Fellow." But Bevin sat ominously on his hands, and the TGWU delegates massively followed their leader. He then signaled that he wished to speak, and made his way to the rostrum with the odd, rolling gait of a short, stout, powerful man, rather like one of those old First World War tanks lumbering into firing position. Totally unimpressed by the scene he had just sat through, Bevin began harshly and never let up.

"I hope this conference will not be influenced by either sentiment or personal attachment. I hope you will carry no resolution telling a man with a conscience like Lansbury's what he ought to do with it. If he finds that he ought to take a certain course, then his conscience should direct him."

Brushing aside cries of objection and indignation from the floor, Bevin turned on Lansbury personally, and contemptuously accused him of "placing the Labour Party executive and the movement in an absolutely wrong position by trailing your conscience round from body to body and asking to be told what to do with it." And then he roared above the hubbub: "There is one quotation from the Scriptures which George Lansbury ought to apply to himself: Do unto others. . . . I have had to sit in conference with him as leader and come to decisions, and I am a democrat and I feel we have been betrayed."

In one speech, Bevin swung the conference around completely. The resolution supporting sanctions was carried, and George Lansbury was even denied the traditional right of reply after Bevin's speech. He resigned as party leader immediately after the conference ended—to be succeeded by Clement R. Attlee. Bevin had shown the harshest brutality and vindictiveness in his handling of Lansbury, but his only comment afterward to those who ventured to remonstrate with him was: "Lansbury has been going about dressed in saint's clothes for years waiting for martyrdom. All I did was set fire to the faggots."

He had also single-handedly altered the top leadership and political image of the Labour Party. The party now stood clearly and firmly committed to opposing the rise of Fascism. For Bevin the issue was overly simple. Mussolini and Hitler had destroyed the trade-union movements in Italy and Germany as initial acts after seizing power, and therefore their systems had to be opposed. The Labour Party record was not always as clear in the 1930s on rearmament and other aspects of the policy of opposing dictators, but at least it was clearer in history and the public image than the record of Neville Chamberlain and his government. And it was the record on which the Labour Party joined Winston Churchill's coalition government to fight the war.

Poland was attacked by Germany at dawn on September 1, 1939. On April 9, 1940, the Germans invaded Denmark and Norway. On May 10, a Friday, the Nazi armies rolled into the Netherlands, Belgium and northern France, and the center of the city of Rotterdam was destroyed by air attack. On that day, Neville Chamberlain at last resigned and King George VI asked Winston Churchill to head a new government. The leaders of the Labour Party had made it clear for some weeks that Churchill was their only choice for Prime Minister if a national coalition was to be formed. Churchill moved with all due constitutional niceties but no delay. He conferred immediately with Attlee and offered him the deputy prime ministership in a new, inner War Cabinet of five (later six). Churchill also proposed Bevin for the Ministry of Labour, Herbert Morrison for the Ministry of Supply, and A. V. Alexander to take over at the Admiralty. Both the Labour Party and the Trades Union Congress were assembling for annual conferences in Bournemouth that tumultuous weekend, and Attlee gave Churchill a prompt acceptance, after first conferring with the party executive. Bevin took a little longer. On May 12 he accepted the Ministry of Labour with the blessing of the T.U.C. general council, telling his fellow union leaders: "I take no job that ends with the war. I take a ministry whose value will be permanent to our people."

On Tuesday morning, May 14, he left Bournemouth by train for London and on the way jotted down on a sheet of foolscap paper the main principles of a scheme of manpower mobilization in which he would take unprecedented authority over the entire labor force of the country. He walked into his new office at two-thirty in the afternoon and handed his sheet of paper to the top officials of the ministry, a number of whom he already knew from his union activities. He went on Wednesday to his first meeting with the War Cabinet and swiftly obtained agreement in principle on his manpower plans.

By Friday the legal experts had completed the draft of an emergency powers (defense) bill for circulation to the other government departments involved. On the following Wednesday, May 22, as Churchill flew to France to confer with the tottering French Government and the Nazi *Blitzkrieg* turned north and headed for the English Channel ports, the emergency powers legislation was moved in the House of Commons by Attlee. (Bevin did not yet have a seat in the House. A by-election was held in the London district of Wandsworth to elect him several months later.) As a matter of urgency, the bill was rushed through all its stages in the House of Commons and the House of Lords that same afternoon. Democracy has seldom functioned with greater speed—and in any circumstances but Britain at war the legislation that was so swiftly approved would have been a terrifying act of a police state.

It required "all persons to place themselves, their services and their property at the disposal of His Majesty so far as might appear to be necessary or expedient for security of public safety, the defense of the realm, the maintenance of public order or the efficient prosecution of the war, or for maintaining supplies or services essential to the life of the community." And it vested in the Minister of Labour and National Service "the control and use of all labour by giving him the power to direct any person in Great Britain to perform such services as may be specified by directions issued by the Minister, to require persons of any class or description to

register particulars about themselves, and power to enter and in-
spect premises and to require employers to keep and produce such
books, documents and records as might be necessary."

This was total mobilization with a vengeance. Bevin had more
direct power and authority over the lives of Britons than any one
man on the island since Oliver Cromwell. Paradoxically, of
course, only a man of true democratic principles could make such
power work.

There were 1.3 million unemployed in Britain when the war
began, and there were still 700,000 out of work when Bevin
became Minister of Labour. On the afternoon that his new emergency powers bill was being rushed through parliament, he called
both union and employer representatives to the Ministry of Labour and in a round-table discussion asked for and got immediate
agreement by both sides to set aside for the duration of the war a
whole network of established union and industry practices on hir-
ing and job assignments, so that the flow of unemployed into munitions factories and the engineering industries could be speeded.
Large numbers could now flock to the factories with no previous
technical training, and learn on the job.

As Churchill wrote in his war memoirs with typical flourish:
"All the workers were ready to take his direction. The trade unionists cast their slowly-framed, jealously-guarded rules and privileges upon the altar where wealth, rank, privilege and property
had already been laid."

This was the hectic first week of a democratic mobilization unmatched by any nation in history. Yet, throughout it all, the number of Britons who refused or resisted labor direction never even
came near 1 percent of the total being directed. By mid-1943 the
number in the armed forces had risen from 477,000 when the war
broke out to 5.1 million; in civil defense services from 80,000 to
384,000; in munitions industries from 3.1 million to 5.2 million.
When the war started, there were 4.8 million women working in
Britain and by 1943 this had risen to 7.2 million. Total mobilization of men and women in all forms of service and employment
under the direction and control of the Minister of Labour rose
from 18.5 million in 1939 to 22.3 million in 1943.

Bevin himself never stopped. He worked a seventy-hour week,

up and down the country visiting labor exchanges, addressing production rallies, conferring with employers and union leaders, eating in canteens, drinking in pubs, laughing and singing at entertainment breaks that he organized in the factories, patting horses and discussing crops with farm workers, always prodding, explaining, negotiating.

"Not on your life am I imposing dictation from above on an unwilling people," he told an interviewer at the time. "All I am doing is putting the form to what people want. This is a People's War. We are all in this war together, and the people who know it best of all are those who are now being directed to jobs all over the place."

At the same time, Bevin looked constantly ahead to the long-range social aims and objectives of his own Labour Party and the trade-union movement. There was nothing devious or hidden about this. These were, after all, the things for which labor was fighting the war. Bevin told the War Cabinet at the outset: "You cannot in the middle of a war with the enemy at your gates be too nice as to the methods you adopt, but I feel that it would be unfair and unwise and psychologically wrong to ask me to appeal to the working men to give a bigger output unless at the same time you agree immediately to a policy that no other citizen can profit as a result of that increased output." The War Cabinet heard and got the message—and so did the working people of Britain.

Again, to a farm-labor rally he said: "I have told the government that this difference between public employees and those in the factories and the people in rural England must be obliterated and the old conception that agriculture is an industry of servitude must go, and go for all time. I hope not only to make a contribution to produce the necessary food but to remove a grievance which as a country lad myself has always burned in my bones."

In September of 1940, at the height of the Battle of Britain, Churchill took Bevin into the inner War Cabinet, where he remained a member until the coalition government was dissolved, after victory in Europe, in May 1945. The two men had great mutual respect and great loyalty to each other and to the wartime coalition. It never translated into friendship, however—in part because their backgrounds and interests differed so widely, and in part because Bevin gave friendship very sparingly even among his own people in the Labour Party and the trade unions. He was not exactly a loner, but in the exercise of power, which was his life, he preferred to have colleagues rather than cronies. Churchill recognized in Bevin a man with a power base of his own, the most powerful man in the War Cabinet aside from himself. Bevin could deliver to the war effort in ways that Churchill could not. For all of Churchill's genius of leadership and eloquence, it was Bevin who made it "The People's War" for Great Britain.

On the eve of D day, Churchill and Bevin went together on a tour of the Channel ports where British troops were embarking to lead the assault on the Normandy beaches—Bevin, who had drafted the men; Churchill, who commanded them. There were cheers everywhere, of course, for Winston in his bowler hat with a cigar sticking belligerently from a corner of his mouth, his walking stick, his watch chain draped across an ample waist and his V-for-Victory sign. Then some men in uniform drafted from the Transport Workers Union recognized Bevin standing on the dock and called out as their landing craft cast off and headed out to the Channel on that June evening of 1944: "See they don't let us down when we come back this time, Ernie."

After the wartime coalition government was dissolved, Churchill fixed Thursday, July 5, 1945, as the polling date for the first general elections in Britain in ten years. But actual counting of the ballots was delayed for three weeks to permit the soldier vote to be cast all over the world, including men still fighting the Japanese in the Far East. The locked ballot boxes sat like a time bomb under the unsuspecting Churchill when he flew off to the Potsdam Conference with President Truman and Marshal Stalin at Berlin on July 15, prudently taking Attlee with him as a member of the British delegation, however, in case there should be a change of government. They returned to London on the evening of July 25, and when counting began, next morning, it was clear in a matter of hours that Churchill and the Conservatives had been swamped by Labour in one of the most startling election upsets in democratic history. Churchill tendered his resignation that evening to King George VI, who immediately sent for Attlee and commissioned him to form a Labour government. The only thing the British ever do in a hurry is change governments.

The following morning, a Friday, Attlee, working by telephone from an office at Labour Party headquarters with only three or four people even knowing where he was, consulted with Bevin first, and then Herbert Morrison and Hugh Dalton. Bevin told Attlee that he would like to go to the treasury as Chancellor of the Exchequer, where he reasoned he would have the greatest influence over shaping the economic and social policies of a socialist Britain, for which he had fought for thirty-five years. Dalton, meanwhile, told Attlee that he would like the Foreign Office—and Attlee concurred with both. He had already decided that he wanted Morrison, an adroit parliamentarian and politician, to become leader of the House of Commons and steer the new government's legislative program, which would be controversial and vast. So things stood on Friday morning, and then a curious and surprising change took place.

Attlee, who could get on a London bus without anybody noticing, but who in fact was an exceptionally strong and much underrated Prime Minister, slipped off to Buckingham Palace again to have lunch alone with the King. During their talk, which was an easy reestablishment of relations from the War Cabinet days, King George told his new Prime Minister that he felt that the country's biggest problems would lie in the field of foreign policy and that he hoped therefore that "you will put your strongest man at the Foreign Office." There was no doubt that the King meant Bevin. It was an unusual, probably unprecedented royal intervention, but Attlee at that point had not made any formal submission of ministerial nominations to the King, so no constitutional precedents were breached. But he went away from lunch and telephoned Bevin and told him in the abrupt, matter-of-fact way in which he usually took decisions that he had been thinking it all over and now wanted Bevin to take the Foreign Office and Dalton to go to the treasury, so would Bevin please pack and be ready to leave for Potsdam next morning. Years later, Attlee said that his discussion with the King had nothing to do with the switch—that he had already come to the conclusion that there would be too much Cabinet friction if Bevin and Morrison were both working on domestic problems. Bevin disliked Morrison—detested might not be too strong a word. On the other hand, since the days of the Lansbury affair, Bevin's feelings for "Little Clem" had ripened from moderate respect into deep and genuine regard and friendship, about the only real political friendship of Bevin's life. He accepted Attlee's decision without discussion, and the two men flew back to Potsdam on Saturday before Bevin even had time to set foot in his new domain.

For Ernie Bevin and the British Foreign Office, it was love at first sight. The instinctive apprehensions of the diplomatic elite at finding themselves suddenly under the direction of the former head of the Transport and General Workers Union evaporated almost at once in a cloud of wonderment, discovery, amusement, and admiration that grew day by day for Bevin and his intellect and the way his mind worked. It began at Potsdam when he first gave his delegation a wide-ranging recital of his own view of the world and its problems. He listened to a briefing from carefully prepared notes about a particular issue he was about to have to discuss with Truman and Stalin, and then said: "Now, can you put that in dockers' language for me." The Foreign Office man took a deep breath and said: "Well, Secretary of State, if you wish me to call a spade a bloody shovel I will." From then on it was a relationship that the Foreign Office still recalls with warmth and wonder.

"For him, no matter of foreign policy that came to him for decision ever stood alone," wrote Sir William (later Lord) Strang, who was permanent undersecretary and professional head of the Foreign Office for the last two years of Bevin's tenure. "He would call his advisers together and go round the map with them and look at the question at issue from the point of view of each of the other governments concerned. Again and again he would perceive connections which none of us had thought of, and if, as was sometimes the case, they were invalid he would expect us to tell him so. He had no ordered method of procedure, but when the preliminaries were exhausted he would gather himself together and come to his conclusion. It might not always be very accurately formulated, but we knew his mind well enough to interpret it and to translate it into executive terms. Some secretaries of state stimulate; others devitalize. Bevin nourished."

The breadth of his vision and his intuitive feel for the problems of the world, and of diplomacy and foreign policy, took the Foreign Office professionals by surprise. Of course, Bevin had been reading Foreign Office telegrams and following global issues for five years in the War Cabinet, and his trade union and Labour Party horizons had never been limited to the British Isles. All the same, his grasp and the sureness of his touch were unexpected by those who had worked for the preceding ten years under two men who were the ultimate of upper-class elitism: Anthony Eden and Lord Halifax. Bevin brought an enormously rich, earthy quality to Foreign Office deliberations, an ability to relate automatically the abstract of what he was doing to the lives of people. He once remarked that the aim of his foreign policy was "to be able to go down to Victoria Station and buy a ticket and travel wherever the hell I want to go without a visa," and he saw to it that Britain took the lead in eliminating visas in Europe after the war. He had years of negotiating experience behind him, and he treated every problem that came before him with unvarnished common sense—no ideological hang-ups, and prejudices that were usually pretty sound, such as a suspicion of almost anything emanating from the Communists or others on the extreme Left. He had another quality that the Foreign Office usually values above all others in its chief: his weight in the Cabinet, the trust and confidence of the Prime Minister, the absolute certainty that when Bevin decided on a policy it would become government policy as well and not get diluted or reversed by his colleagues. He was scrupulous in his relations with Attlee, and his loyalty to the Prime Minister was complete. On at least two occasions he squashed plots in the Labour Party to oust Attlee. Once, one of the plotters foolishly approached Ernie direct with a proposal that he replace Attlee, and Bevin simply growled: "Tell you what—let's go across Downing Street and discuss it with Clem right now," and practically threw the man out of his office.

Bevin was a voracious reader of Foreign Office telegrams and minutes—beginning his day with the dispatch boxes around five or six in the morning, for he remained an early riser all his life from

his days as a farm boy. But his handwriting was crabbed, almost
undecipherable, with a schoolboy's look to the way the letters
were formed. He held a pen oddly, between the second and third
fingers of his right hand, and confined his written notes on official
documents to a minimum, usually nothing more than a scrawled
"EB" indicating that it had been read and approved. The officials
all got to know how his mind worked, and would leave a discussion with him to translate his mixed metaphors and trade-union
English into officialese, usually chuckling at some new Bevinism.
Of a particular proposal that he did not like, he growled: "You
open up that Pandora's box and you'll find a lot of Trojan 'Orses
inside." On another occasion an official got his instructions on
something and then had to return ten or fifteen minutes later to
take up another telegram that had come in, and when he walked
in Bevin said jovially: "So, the ink is scarcely dry on the words
out of me mouth and you're back!" He was warm with people, utterly without side, class consciousness, or snobbism inverted or
otherwise. He always insisted that Foreign Office typists and
clerks got their share of invitations to the diplomatic parties at
conferences, because "they do most of the hard work and ought to
have some of the fun." To a young official who once caused a
public upset in Anglo-American relations with an indiscreet
speech at a critical juncture, Bevin cabled: "Don't worry. What
are old men for but to help young men over their mistakes."

Dean Acheson, whose affection and admiration for Bevin were
total, later wrote: "Life with Ernie was gay and turbulent, for his
temper could build up as suddenly as a summer storm, and could
flash and thunder as noisily and then disappear as the sun broke
through." Bevin called Acheson always "me boy," and of course
he was "Ernie" to America's patrician Secretary of State.

On one occasion, unforgettable for me, he asked half a dozen
American correspondents in London to the Foreign Office for a
background briefing, and I found myself unwittingly in one of
those storms. Bevin had announced to the House of Commons
that afternoon that Britain would be giving up its mandate over
the Palestine territory—hoping that by this action the impossible
would happen and it might help force an Arab-Jewish agreement
about the future of the land. Bevin was hunched behind his desk,

and we distributed ourselves in comfortable, low leather armchairs in front of him. As the discussion developed, I asked if he was not concerned over the possibility of the Russians trying to grab the mandate in the United Nations and "cut across the throat of the Empire"—using a phrase Bevin had used many months before in denouncing the Russians for trying to pick up a mandate over the old Italian territories of Libya and Tripolitania. I lit a short fuse, and Bevin's fist came down on his desk and he seemed to bellow: "It's BOTH our throats—that is what I have been trying to tell your people for two years—it's BOTH our throats." He went on with a passionate defense of his Palestine policy and the dangers to the West and the opportunities to the Soviet Union if the Arab-Jewish question could not be peaceably resolved. I slumped lower and lower in the deep leather armchair, but there was no place to retreat. Then it got quiet, and a few additional desultory questions were asked and we got up to file out. After that came the sudden sunshine. Bevin came out from behind his desk, clamped a massive arm around my shoulders and grinned warmly and said: "Well, now, that was just the price of admission, wasn't it?" It seemed high at the time, but it was no bad price to have paid.

There could scarcely have been a greater contrast when Attlee and Bevin replaced Churchill and Eden at the Potsdam table. In the opening half of the conference, Churchill consistently took the lead for the British in the discussions, with Eden backing him up from time to time. Now it was Bevin taking the British lead and Attlee more in the backup role. (The intimacy and confidence between the two men, and Attlee's own self-effacing sureness of himself and his role as Prime Minister was very English and very difficult, always, for anybody outside the British Cabinet to sense or understand.) Straightaway, Bevin impressed and even alarmed the Americans by the blunt and pugnacious attitude he took toward Stalin and Molotov. A number of key issues were still unresolved at Potsdam—among them a Soviet demand for reparations from Italy; the question of whether the Ruhr, in the British occupation zone of Germany, was to be treated separately from the rest of Germany; size and delivery of German reparations to Russia, which would come largely from the British zone; and the map-

ping of Poland's revised borders and arrangements for the administration of German territory that was being transferred to Polish
authority to compensate for what the Russians were annexing on
Poland's eastern exposure. Bevin plunged into all these discussions almost as if he were dealing with a Communist faction in the
Transport and General Workers Union. At the very outset his instinctive attitude toward the Russians was to halt, to check, to
limit, to contain, to resist any further encroachments or demands
in the West. In this, he was little different from Churchill in the
earlier Potsdam stages, but he was more openly suspicious and
more blunt in his expressions and attitudes. It is difficult to recapture or reconstruct the atmosphere of Potsdam, but Bevin did not
exactly fit in with President Truman's overriding preoccupation,
and that of the United States military commanders at that time,
which was to ensure that Stalin and the Soviet Union would not be
put off from entering the war against Japan.

Other political and psychological factors were at work against
the British as well: Truman had inherited from President Roosevelt the idea that it was a bad tactic to be seen to be trying to gang
up with the British against Stalin. Then there was the old-
fashioned latent anti-British isolationist political feeling in the
United States, anti-imperialism, anti-colonialism, opposition to
pulling British chestnuts out of the fire, and all that. Harry Hopkins had advised Truman, despite his own difficult meetings with
Stalin before Potsdam, that "no major source of conflict between
Russian and American interests exists in any part of the world." If
Hopkins meant "conflict" to be war, he was narrowly correct, but
as the ensuing decades have continued to show, the Russians have
been able to rewrite Clausewitz and pursue diplomatic objectives
by Communist means. The prevailing American attitude at Potsdam, therefore, was that accommodation with the Russians could
and should be reached, that it would of course be tough, but that
in the end the United States and the Soviet Union would work out
a peaceful world—and in the meantime let's not upset Stalin or
he might decline to go to war against Japan. Bevin, however,
instinctively took a different view of Soviet aims and the Communist threat that Europe was facing. The Americans had seen this
coming from Churchill, but it took them by surprise when it sur-

faced so quickly at Potsdam from Bevin and Attlee as well—leaders of a new leftist, socialist government in Britain. The initial American reaction was not to look at the realities as Bevin saw them but to treat Bevin as if he were simply blustering around trying to play a weak hand to preserve British interests and a role in the world. He certainly was trying to play a weak hand as best he could, and he knew it. But it took almost two years, until the spring of 1947, for the United States to accept that it was not just British interests he was seeking to preserve but indeed "BOTH our throats."

President Truman, before even heading for Potsdam, had abruptly canceled Lend-Lease aid for the British and other American allies in Western Europe. The United States Navy was shifting wholesale from the Atlantic to the Pacific, and United States forces in West Germany were ultimately run down in 1947 to barely two divisions, which acted more like the New Jersey State Police than a fighting army. Roosevelt, insofar as he thought about the postwar occupation of Germany, figured that it would be over in a handful of years, and if Truman had a longer-range concept in 1945 he didn't show it. Meanwhile, the new Labour government, with its economic back to the wall, sent John Maynard Keynes to Washington to extract, in arduous and difficult negotiations, a postwar American loan of $3.75 billion, which Britain will be repaying until the end of this century. Under these conditions, Britain was desperately holding the world's pressure points in 1945, 1946, and 1947—Greece, Turkey, Trieste, Iran, Iraq, Syria, Lebanon, Palestine, Transjordan, Egypt, the Suez Canal, Ethiopia and the horn of Africa, India, Burma, Ceylon, the forward occupation zone in Austria, the major occupation zone of West Germany—the major navy in the Atlantic. There was no lack of realization in London that the nation was weakened and historically overstrained. The desperate problem was what to do about it—how to pull back without leaving a vacuum everywhere.

It is significant that on the same day that Bevin framed his devastating message to Washington informing the United States that Britain could no longer carry the burden of military and economic support for Greece and Turkey—February 20, 1947—Attlee also announced in the House of Commons that Britain was withdrawing from India in one year and giving full independence to the subcontinent whether the India-Pakistan problem was resolved by then or not. In laying down the burden of Greece and Turkey, the British could not be accused by American opinion of trying to hang on to imperial relics.

Of course, by early 1947 the mood and attitude toward the Soviet Union had hardened considerably in Washington, too. General Marshall had succeeded James F. Byrnes as Secretary of State, and although there was nothing "soft on Communism" about Byrnes, there was a new depth and vigor to analysis and policy making at the Department of State with Dean Acheson as undersecretary and George F. Kennan and Charles E. Bohlen as top Soviet-affairs advisers. Bevin and the British had held the torch in Greece and Turkey as long as they could, and now at last there was someone to catch it when they had to let it fall. In June of 1947, then, came Bevin's big opportunity to act for Europe with the Marshall Plan speech at Harvard.

But Bevin continued to think another long step ahead: to the security of Europe, and not just her economic revival. He began the building of a postwar European security system with the signing of the Treaty of Dunkirk, in January 1947, creating a new, fifty-year defense alliance between Britain and France. Then, after the Marshall Plan machinery was in place and beginning to operate, he raised the whole security question in a private conversation when General Marshall visited London in early 1948. Bevin told Marshall that despite the start of economic recovery, with the Soviets maintaining swollen forces in East Germany and Russian intransigence over any diplomatic progress toward solution of Europe's future, no country on the continent had any confidence in its security. He asked what, if anything, the United States could do in the face of Soviet armed might. Marshall replied that the only formula he could think of was the one that was being successfully applied in the field of economic recovery: for the Europeans to get together and see what they could do in their own defense and then turn to the United States.

Bevin now moved to open discussions with the French on enlarging membership in the Treaty of Dunkirk to include Belgium, the Netherlands and Luxembourg, and set up a treaty organization and secretariat to be known as the Western European Union. It was also to have an integrated military command. This enlarged security pact was completed and signed in Brussels in March 1948. Its military headquarters was then established at Fontainebleau under Field Marshal Viscount Montgomery. This was the forerunner of NATO Supreme Headquarters, Allied Powers in Europe (SHAPE), under General Dwight D. Eisenhower—but that was still three years away.

In mid-March, as the Brussels treaty was being readied for signature, events developed for Bevin from an unexpected quarter. The Norwegian Government secretly informed the British that Norway was coming under heavy Soviet pressure to sign a treaty of mutual assistance of the kind that had been imposed on Finland shortly before. Norway was determined to refuse and resist, but this could well lead to Soviet demands for territory or even military action against Norway's common frontier with Russia in the extreme North. What help, Norway asked, might she be able to expect from Britain and the other wartime Allies if she were attacked? On March 11, Bevin passed this extremely serious message to Washington with an aide-mémoire in which he proposed a firm course of action to General Marshall. He was acting in line with Marshall's ideas to create an embryo European security system, and the aide-mémoire stated:

"Mr. Bevin considers that the most effective course would be to take very early steps, before Norway goes under, to conclude under Article 5 of the Charter of the United Nations a regional Atlantic Approaches Pact of Mutual Assistance, in which all countries directly threatened by the Russian move to the Atlantic could participate."

The next day, March 12, 1948, General Marshall, with a soldier's grasp of the strategic importance of the Norwegian situation and a diplomatic grasp of the need for prompt action, replied through the British embassy in Washington: "Please inform Mr. Bevin that we are prepared to proceed at once in the joint discussion on the establishment of an Atlantic security system."

Thus began the secret negotiations for the North Atlantic Treaty—and at the same time the concurrent talks between the

Truman administration and leaders of the United States Senate on the need for such a far-reaching American undertaking. Almost exactly one year later, Bevin journeyed to Washington for the historic signing, along with other foreign ministers of Western Europe, on April 4, 1949. When he lumbered up to the table where the leather-bound treaty texts were awaiting his scrawl, the applause was warm and prolonged, greater than was accorded any other, for his fellow foreign ministers knew better than anyone else what his role and achievement had been.

The last two years of Bevin's life were even more exacting and arduous and his place in history grew. Global travel to endless meetings had now become the lot of foreign ministers of the world. His health in all his years at the Foreign Office was never stable—a heart condition with which he lived on the brink of daily extinction, and emergency pills to pop into action constantly. He was a reasonable drinker, but he had a workingman's capacity, and it was difficult to rein him in. "I know, I know," he said impatiently to the doctor who attended him constantly, "if I do your don'ts I'll be in trouble."

By the end, he was failing and he knew it, but he was still hurt and bewildered when the Prime Minister, his great friend Little Clem, finally informed him that he was relieving him of his arduous office and replacing him with the man he liked least in Labour politics: Herbert Morrison. He was to continue in the Cabinet in the nondepartmental office of Lord Privy Seal.

His last day at the Foreign Office was his seventieth birthday, April 14, 1951. Everybody had been invited to make a contribution limited to a sixpence for a party—everyone from the permanent undersecretary down to the code clerks and the doormen.

"It was a very jolly party," Bevin told a friend a few days later. "We all stood together and enjoyed ourselves and blew out the candles and had a good time. I don't think it has ever happened before. You know—it was really a wonderful thing."

After the party, he left his office for the last time. Five weeks later, his heart gave up and he died.

2
The Marshall Plan

"It is logical that the United States should do whatever it is able to do to assist in the return of normal economic health in the world, without which there can be no political stability and no assured peace. Our policy is directed not against any country or doctrine, but against hunger, poverty, desperation and chaos. . . . It is already evident that before the United States government can proceed much further in its efforts to alleviate the situation, and help start the European world on its way to recovery, there must be some agreement among the countries of Europe as to the requirements. . . . The initiative, I think, must come from Europe. . . ."

General George C. Marshall
Harvard University
June 5, 1947

ERNEST BEVIN WAS AT HOME IN HIS APARTMENT IN THE BARONS Court section of southwest London and had gone to bed early on the evening of Thursday, June 5, 1947, but he turned on his bedside radio to listen to a news broadcast before going to sleep. That is how he heard that the American Secretary of State had delivered a speech in Boston on the subject of American economic assistance for Europe which appeared to be of special significance. In Washington earlier that day, the British embassy had decided inexplicably not to cable the text of the Marshall speech to London. But the Washington correspondent of the BBC, Leonard Miall, struck by the potential importance of what General Marshall had said, persuaded the BBC news editors in London to make it the opening item of the regular 9 o'clock evening news broadcast.

Otherwise the Harvard speech might have been largely unnoticed in London, and certainly Bevin's historic reaction to it would have been slower.

But in Washington, General Marshall, before departing for Harvard, where he was to receive an honorary degree along with General Omar Bradley, nuclear scientist J. Robert Oppenheimer, and poet T. S. Eliot, had ordered a complete ban on any special press briefings on what he was going to say. It was a time of deepening uncertainty and despair in Europe, and there was only one country to turn to for resources and leadership. Marshall had been pondering the situation continuously ever since a meeting in Moscow in April with Joseph Stalin, and now he was ready to act. But there was to be no visible preparation for a surprise attack. His speech would distinguish him as one of the great tacticians of democracy as well as war.

Ever since the British had been forced to dump the problem of sustaining Greece and Turkey on Washington in February, four months earlier, the Department of State had been churning with incoming diplomatic cables, internal study memorandums, statistical analyses, policy-planning papers, and staff discussions on the onrushing economic crisis in Europe and what to do about it. All of this had begun to focus in recommendations for action as the time also approached for General Marshall to confirm an invitation he had tentatively accepted much earlier from Harvard University. On May 28, he telegraphed Harvard that he would definitely be coming. He then turned to Charles E. Bohlen, his close adviser on Soviet affairs, who had served as his interpreter at the meeting with Stalin, and asked him to prepare a draft of a speech based on the various policy studies, on the need for action in Europe, that had reached the top. Bohlen completed the draft in two days. Marshall then asked for comments from Dean Acheson, who at that time was Undersecretary of State. Acheson was all for action, but he advised Marshall against using the Harvard commencement as a platform on the grounds that such an academic occasion would not command sufficient press coverage or public attention. Marshall, as was his long habit and method, simply listened and held his counsel. But he had a better feel than Acheson for the domestic political problems the speech would raise. He did not want to begin with a long process of congressional lobbying, with all its explanations and pitfalls. The reaction he wanted was from Europe—not home. He wanted Congress to respond to Europe, respond to the problem, and not just get locked into an internal political debate over policy with the Secretary of State. Hence there was to be no prior warning of what was coming, no domestic political buildup, no consultations or seeking of advice or support in advance with leaders on the Hill.

In fact, there is no evidence that Marshall even consulted in advance on the text of the speech with President Truman. There is no reference in Truman's own memoirs or in his papers to his having seen the speech in advance, nor to any role he might have played in its timing. This is not necessarily surprising, for Truman and Marshall were on a wavelength of total trust and confidence, and Truman, who had just signed the Greek-Turkish aid bill, was well aware of the acuteness of the situation in Europe and the recommendations for action in the accumulation of government studies. Most probably, Marshall, with his complete punctiliousness, simply told the President what he had in mind, but the ultimate shaping and timing of the Marshall Plan speech was Marshall's alone. When he left by plane for Boston on the afternoon of Wednesday, June 4, all the copies of the Bohlen draft went with him, and he made important key changes in the text on the way. The State Department got the final text by telephone dictation from one of Marshall's aides a few hours before he spoke, next afternoon.

Meanwhile, Acheson, still worried that the speech might pass unnoticed, was given an opportunity to breach discreetly Marshall's instructions about no press briefings or advance buildup on what he was going to say. He had accepted a luncheon invitation from Miall, of the BBC, and two other British correspondents in Washington, Malcolm Muggeridge, who was then with the *Daily Telegraph,* and René MacColl, of the *Daily Express,* on Tuesday, June 3. During the lunch, Acheson talked with the three British journalists about the general idea of a "continental plan" for American assistance for Europe, but emphasized over and over again that the initiative for such a plan had to come from Europe itself. Loyal to the letter of General Marshall's instructions, Acheson never even mentioned the forthcoming Harvard speech during the lunch, but when Miall saw the text of the speech, two days later, he realized instantly that this was what Acheson had in fact been talking about. Above all, the three British journalists were thoroughly aware, as Miall later put it, "of the importance of the next move coming from the other side of the Atlantic—Acheson seemed desperately anxious for such a sign." Miall accordingly got the BBC in London to schedule a special commentary, which he then broadcast from Washington after the 9 o'clock news, and it was this that Bevin heard in his bedroom in London. Muggeridge, meanwhile, did what the British embassy had failed to do and cabled the full text of the speech to the *Daily Telegraph,* persuading his editors of its importance on the basis of the Acheson lunch. Bevin then read the text when he woke, as was his lifelong habit, around 6 o'clock next morning.

Two years after these events, Bevin told a National Press Club audience in Washington:

"I remember, with a little wireless set alongside the bed, just turning on the news, and there came this report of the Harvard speech. I assure you, gentlemen, it was like a lifeline to a sinking man. It seemed to bring hope where there was none. The generosity of it was beyond our belief. It expressed a mutual thing. It said: 'Try and help yourselves, and we will try to see what we can do. Try and do the thing collectively and we will see what we can put into the pool.' I think you understand why, therefore, we responded with such alacrity and why we grasped the lifeline with both hands, as it were. To us it meant the beginning of Europe's salvation, and Europe will go on until it has restored itself and reestablished its culture, its influence, and in turn that gift will become an investment, because in the years to come we will return to the United States, for all of the gifts you have made, the blessings that Europe can still give."

When Bevin reached the Foreign Office, around nine-thirty as usual, one official said later that "it was astonishing the way in which he, with his elephantine frame, sprang into action." The first adviser to see him was Sir William Strang, then an assistant undersecretary. Strang's proposal was typically Foreign Office. He suggested that since there had been no official communication

from Washington about the speech, the embassy there should be
instructed to inquire at the State Department what General Marshall had in mind, what he meant.

Bevin reacted like a dockers' leader. "Look 'ere, Bill," he said
(and nobody but Ernie at the Foreign Office would have dreamed
of calling Sir William "Bill"), "we know what he *said,* don't we?
If you ask questions, you get answers you don't want. Our problem is what *we do*—not what *he meant.*"

Bevin fully understood the difference between motion and action. A cable was promptly drafted after his morning staff meeting
with instructions to the embassy to inform the State Department
that Mr. Bevin had noted with great interest the speech of the Secretary of State and that he was initiating immediate consultations
with the French Government on an appropriate European response
to Mr. Marshall's suggestion for an initiative. He hoped that this
would be coordinated in the shortest possible time, and he trusted
that this course of action in Europe would be welcomed in Washington. In barely twenty-four hours, General Marshall had the
response he wanted and needed. The Marshall Plan was underway.

Like many great historic initiatives or actions, the Marshall Plan
speech in itself was a relatively unadorned, straightforward expression of a simple idea whose time had come. But the seemingly
offhanded or even innocent manner in which Marshall said that
"the initiative, I think, must come from Europe" gave rise subsequently to a feeling, particularly in the Foreign Office, that, as
Strang later put it, "he had not perhaps fully realized the poten-
tiality of his words." Marshall knew perfectly well what he was
getting into, or trying to get into. State Department studies had already shown a need for minimum assistance for Europe on
the order of $5 billion. The fact that Marshall avoided using
any figure in his speech did not at all mean that he was unaware
of the size of the burden that America might be called upon
to shoulder. According to Bohlen, while considering the draft of
the speech he expressed concern that he might be accused of making some Santa Claus offer to Europe that would raise a storm of
protest particularly from the isolationist Midwest. Hence he

wanted the impression that he was being a little offhanded. That was why he ordered that there be no advance publicity or puffing up of what he was going to say. Much later, Marshall wrote that "it is easy to propose a great plan but exceedingly difficult to manage the form and procedure so that it has a fair chance of political survival." With his acute sense of the American democratic processes, and his enormous personal prestige with Congress from his days as wartime Chief of Staff, Marshall managed by his low-key tactics to avoid stirring up feelings that he had gone out to offer a Santa Claus giveaway. Instead, thanks to Bevin and subsequent developments in Europe, the debate in the United States quickly focused not on what Marshall had said but on what the Europeans were doing—not on the politics but the economic problem.

The Marshall Plan speech was also deliberately framed in both concept and language to redress or refocus the approach that had been whipped into shape in the form of the Truman Doctrine to deal with the Greek-Turkish problem in February. Curiously enough, the British communication on Greece and Turkey reached Washington on a Friday when General Marshall had just departed to another university to make a speech: to Princeton, which was celebrating the bicentennial of its founding. The Greek crisis was not entirely unforeseen at the State Department, for a memorandum on the situation had reached Marshall's desk the day before he left, based on dispatches from both Athens and London. Nevertheless, the Administration was not prepared for the full force of the "shocker," as Dean Acheson called it. The British gave the Americans six weeks' notice that they would be ending all aid and pulling out all military forces, warning that in their own estimate the Greek Government could not then survive the civil war in which it was engaged, and that a Communist takeover of the country would be inevitable unless the United States came to the rescue. During the weekend, Acheson started crash studies on what emergency funds and personnel could be made immediately available and what the longer-term needs would be, as well as the military and strategic implications of a Greek collapse. When Marshall returned from Princeton, a first step was to implore the British to hold on a little while longer, which Bevin agreed to do.

An action plan was approved by Truman on Wednesday, and on Thursday, February 27, 1947, congressional leaders were called to the White House to get the full blast of crisis treatment. Acheson, in fact, took the lead, writing later in his memoirs that "my distinguished chief, most unusually and unhappily, flubbed his opening statement." Marshall had relied on soldierly logic and orderly presentation of facts to make his points and convince his interlocutors, rather than sweeping eloquence or crisis imagery. So Acheson asked for the floor and gave it to the assembled legislators in patriotic language that would have had Tom Paine cheering.

When Acheson concluded, the redoubtable Senator Arthur H. Vandenberg turned to Truman and said: "Mr. President, if you will say that to the Congress and the country, I will support you and I believe that most of its members will do the same."

Marshall, meanwhile, was due to depart the following week for Moscow for a Council of Foreign Ministers meeting on Germany and other postwar problems with Bevin, Molotov and France's Georges Bidault. Acheson drew up the first draft of the speech that was to become the Truman Doctrine. George Kennan, who had been recalled from the American embassy in Moscow by Marshall to head a newly created Policy Planning Staff in the Department, felt that Acheson's draft was too sweeping in its declaration of what amounted to a universal American commitment to support free peoples everywhere, but his objections did not carry much weight. The draft went to the White House, where Clark Clifford took over to get it more into Truman's style. Clifford, who was Truman's key political adviser, regarded the speech as "the opening gun in a campaign to bring people to the realization that the war isn't over by any means." Meanwhile a draft was cabled to Marshall in Paris, where he had stopped off on his way to Moscow. He and Bohlen talked it over and commented in a cable back to Washington that "there was a little too much flamboyant anti-Communism in the speech and that Truman was using too much rhetoric." They got back a cable saying that in the opinion of the White House the Senate would not approve a Greece-Turkey aid program without all the emphasis on the Communist danger.

Accordingly, Truman went before Congress on March 12 with a speech that in effect shaped American policy all the way through the Vietnam War.

"We shall not realize our objectives unless we are willing to help free peoples to maintain their free institutions and their national integrity against aggressive movements that seek to impose upon them totalitarian regimes. This is no more than a frank recognition that totalitarian regimes imposed upon free peoples, by direct or indirect aggression, undermine the foundations of international peace and hence the security of the United States," the President said. Then came his hard-line kicker using Acheson's draft: "I believe that it *must* be the policy of the United States to support free peoples who are resisting attempted subjugation by armed minorities or by outside pressures."

It echoed in President John F. Kennedy's 1961 Inaugural Address ("We shall help any friend, fight any foe"), and it continues to echo in the rhetoric of American politics today.

Yet in throwing down the gauntlet in this fashion, Truman ran into strong liberal opposition in the United States and elsewhere. The Greek civil war seemed to American public opinion to be a muddled political affair. It was not automatically clear in the public mind that this was a Communist attempt to subvert democracy. Many liberals regarded the Greek Government as a reactionary rump, installed by Winston Churchill, that deserved to be overthrown. Mrs. Eleanor Roosevelt wrote Truman in her waspish style complaining about "taking over Mr. Churchill's policies in the Near East in the name of democracy," and others shared this view.

Revisionist historians have since sought to rip it all out of the context of the times to show that America was thus responsible for launching the Cold War against peaceable Joseph Stalin. But it *was* a Communist-directed civil war, supported from bases in Yugoslavia and Bulgaria, which did not finally peter out until Tito broke with Stalin in 1948. Without Truman's rhetoric, the facts of the situation remain the same. Marshall chose a different tactic and a low-key style when he came to deliver his great speech three months after the Truman Doctrine—but without the earlier impact

of the Greek-Turkish crisis there almost certainly would have
been no Marshall Plan.

While America debated the Truman Doctrine, General Marshall
was away from Washington for six weeks of frustrating and futile
negotiations in Moscow with Molotov. The Moscow meeting was
concerned primarily with an attempt to draft a German peace
treaty, and there was a total-stonewall Soviet attitude: an insatiable demand for more reparations from the Western occupation
zones and a blanket refusal to cooperate in any way on matters of
four-power control and the administration of Germany as one
country through the Allied Control Council. But in side discussions with Bevin, Marshall at least laid the groundwork for an
economic improvement of the British and American occupation
zones so that a beginning could be made on changing Germany
from an economic liability in the heart of Europe to standing on
her own feet. At the end of the six weeks, Marshall went to the
Kremlin for a meeting with Stalin that lasted an hour and a half,
with Bohlen doing the interpreting. The date was April 18, 1947.
    Marshall had no hope of getting any last-minute agreement
after all his arguments with Molotov, but he did want to impress
on Stalin how dangerous and impossible it was to leave Germany
in a chaotic and divided state. It quickly became clear that Stalin
couldn't care less. He was detached, relaxed, and indifferent to
what Marshall had to say, doodling wolves' heads with a red pen-
cil on a pad of paper, according to Bohlen. But his very
indifference impressed Marshall deeply, who now came to feel
clearly that Stalin's whole strategy for advancing Soviet aims was
to let Germany and Europe wallow in economic ruins, crisis, uncertainty, and despair.
    He stopped in Berlin on the way back to Washington to confer
with General Lucius D. Clay, the American occupation commander, and go over with him the economic program for the combined British and American zones that had been discussed with
Bevin. Then, all the way across the continent and the Atlantic, he
talked endlessly with Bohlen about the problem of finding an
American initiative to avert a complete collapse of Western
Europe.

The entire basic balance of Europe's economy had been destroyed by the war. Once, it had imported food and raw materials and paid for this by exporting industrial goods. But now, in 1947, not only was industrial production only two thirds or less of what it had been before the war. The elements, as well, were conspiring against the old continent. The winter of 1946–47 had been the worst of the century. In Britain, where I was then living, snow fell in early January and did not thaw until April. The Thames froze so that coal barges could not get up to the power stations. The sun was not seen in London for twenty-eight continuous days of freezing gray winter haze. Coal was rationed at one hundred *pounds* per week per household, electricity was cut off to homes two hours in the morning and two hours in the afternoon, factories were simply shut down completely during the worst of the power shortage. Bread was rationed—something that had not happened even during the war—and the weekly rations of butter, cheese, and bacon were cut below wartime levels.

Already in 1946 Western Europe had imported 17 million tons of American coal at twice the price per ton of its own coal. In West Germany, coal production in 1947 was only 144 million tons, against 221 million before the war, and steel production, at 4 million tons, was less than a quarter of the prewar figure. In France, the 1947 harvest after that terrible winter was only half what it had been in 1946. In Norway, the daily food ration in 1947 was cut from twenty-five hundred calories to twenty-two hundred, while in Germany for a time it was all the way down to one thousand calories.

In Marshall's absence, Acheson had launched the first broadscale study of probable foreign-aid requirements using the machinery of what was then called the State-War-Navy Coordinating Committee. A first preliminary report from this group was ready when Marshall got back to Washington. The Secretary of State went on the air to report on the Moscow deadlock, and tell the American people that Europeans were "crying out for help, for coal, for food, for most of the necessities of life. . . . The patient is sinking while the doctors deliberate."

Next day, Marshall sent for George Kennan, and instructed that the Policy Planning Staff begin work immediately to produce rec-

ommendations for a program of American action on aid to
Europe. Marshall told Kennan that he wanted a succinct memorandum in the shortest possible time, and to "avoid trivia."
Meanwhile, Acheson, at Truman's request, had accepted a speaking engagement as a substitute for the President at Cleveland, Mis-
sissippi, on May 8, 1947, the second anniversary of the victory in
Europe. Acheson, with Truman's enthusiastic support, decided to
use the occasion to pull together the whole picture of the onrushing European economic crisis—as he later wrote, "not the trumpet
note which General Marshall sounded a month later, but perhaps
it is not too much to say that it was reveille which awoke the
American people to the duties of that day of decision."

The Acheson speech outlined the problem in stark details:
Europe taking $16 billion in imports from the United States in
1947 with only enough exports to cover about half this sum, the
prospect of bankruptcy and starvation if the United States could
not find a solution in aid, loans, or grants. But where Acheson's
speech posed the problem, Marshall's speech posed the action.

By May 23, Kennan was ready with a thirteen-page memorandum, from the Policy Planning Staff, in which he laid down the key
element in what was to become the Marshall Plan in these words:
"It would be neither fitting nor efficacious for this government to
undertake to draw up unilaterally and to promulgate formally on
its own initiative a program designed to place Western Europe on
its feet economically. This is the business of the Europeans. The
formal initiative must come from Europe and the Europeans must
bear the responsibility for it. The role of this country should consist of friendly aid in the drafting of a European program and of
later support of such a program."

Redrafted by Bohlen and then modified and edited by Marshall,
this paragraph by Kennan became the heart of the speech.

As to the American determination that the Europeans should
come up with a joint plan, Kennan later succinctly summarized
the political and economic wisdom and logic in his memoirs: "Had
this not been insisted upon, the United States would have been
confronted with a whole series of competing national demands, all
padded and exaggerated for competitive purposes, all reflecting attempts to solve economic problems within national frameworks

rather than on an all-European basis. This would have forced us
to make choices bound to be politically unpopular in many quarters, with the respective European governments in a position to
shift onto our shoulders the blame for any features of the program
that were particularly disagreeable to sections of their electorate.
But beyond this, we had serious doubts about the success of any
movement toward European recovery that rested merely on a series of uncoordinated national programs; we considered that one
of the long-term deficiencies of the European economy as a whole
was its excessive fragmentation, the lack of competitive flexibility
in commercial exchanges, the lack, in particular, of a large consumer's market. By insisting on a joint approach, we hoped to
force the Europeans to begin to think like Europeans, and not like
nationalists, in their approach to the economic problems of the
continent."

The key question in the final stages before Marshall went to
Harvard lay in whether the call should be addressed simply to
Western Europe, as was implied in the Kennan memorandum, or
to all of Europe. Here the brief discussions that Marshall had with
his advisers came down quickly on the premise that the United
States must not take the responsibility for dividing Europe, even
though it was clear that Russian acceptance of an American aid
offer would scuttle the whole thing politically in Congress. Bohlen,
mindful of the objections to the hard-line Truman Doctrine speech
that he and Marshall had cabled from Paris three months before,
had already produced a draft that set out deliberately to downplay
the ideological struggle. American policy, the draft said, "is
directed not against any country or doctrine, but against hunger,
poverty, desperation and chaos." The changes that Marshall made
on the way to Harvard were aimed primarily at removing anything
from the speech that might by implication appear to be closing the
door to Russian participation. The initiative, he said in the final
text, should come "from Europe" and not Western Europe, and
he added a phrase that a program should be a joint one "agreed to
by a number, if not all" of the European nations. And in the only
sentence in the speech that in fact committed the United States to
anything, Marshall included an important conditional to avoid any
Santa Claus charges from Congress: "The role of this country

should consist of friendly aid in the drafting of a European program and of later support of such a program *so far as it may be
practical for us to do so.*"

Acheson, who had drafted the Truman Doctrine speech, would
have liked a sharper ideological hard line from Marshall. He
later wrote: "If General Marshall believed, which I am sure he
did not, that the American people would be moved to so great an
effort as he contemplated by as platonic a purpose as combating
'hunger, poverty, desperation and chaos' he was mistaken. In the
last analysis, it was how the Marshall aid operated to block the
extension of Soviet power."

But Marshall was a man who listened far more than he talked,
and when he left for Boston, neither Acheson nor Bohlen nor anybody else in the State Department knew precisely how he would
handle these nuances in what he was going to say. Will Clayton,
the undersecretary for economic affairs, had even urged that the
tactic should be to make it look as if the initiative was coming
from Europe but the United States must run the show. It would
have been justifiable for Marshall to have invited "like-minded
governments" to join in working out an economic recovery program, and it would probably have been more popular with the Republican Congress if he had not gone out of his way to say that
American policy was NOT directed against any country or doctrine. But, in the end, he chose not the limited appeal of politics
but the broad appeal of the statesman; and integrity was rewarded.

So short had been the time in which the speech was drafted and
discussed, in the midst of all the other pressures of State Department business, that it was not until after his return from Harvard
that Marshall asked both Bohlen and Kennan their assessments as
to whether the Russians would now accept the open invitation to
join. He would be facing a press conference later that day, and of
course he would have to say that the Soviet Union was not being
excluded. Bohlen and Kennan both agreed that it would be entirely contrary to all of past Russian behavior under Stalin to accept any American verification over the use of aid or funds, as
would certainly be required in an aid program, and moreover
that Russia risked losing control over Eastern Europe if it permit-

ted those countries to join. Their judgment was that Russia would stay out, and they were quickly proved right.

Bevin telephoned Georges Bidault in Paris on Friday, June 6, the day after Marshall spoke, which also happened to be the third anniversary of the D-day landings in Normandy. It was quickly arranged that he would go to Paris ten days later, after the two foreign ministries had worked out some practical ideas for a European initiative. It was part of Bevin's quality as a Foreign Secretary that he was perfectly prepared to have the French take the public lead in hosting and arranging the meetings even though he himself was urging the initiatives. As if to underscore the problems of "hunger, poverty, desperation and chaos," France was in the throes of a Communist-led railway workers' strike that had brought practically the whole national transport system to a halt, when Bevin telephoned Bidault.

Stalin was moving also. From Sofia, as Marshall spoke, came an announcement that a counterrevolutionary movement in Bulgaria had been "crushed" by the alert Communists. And that same weekend a similar squeeze got underway in Hungary against non-Communist leftists who had reluctantly joined a coalition government earlier in the year. There was a cabinet purge, and the first of these leaders managed to get out to Vienna. It was not yet the complete Communist takeover, which came later, but it was clear how things were heading. The United States and British governments fired off protests to Moscow, as members of the Armistice Control Commissions for Bulgaria and Hungary, and the response came two days later in Pravda, with the first signal also of the Kremlin attitude toward the Marshall speech.

"As soon as a country like Hungary purges its government bodies of conspirators convicted by a court, there resounds the bossy shout of the United States," Pravda said. "Now comes the speech of the American Secretary of State, Marshall, which is only a repetition of the Truman Plan for political pressure with the help of dollars, a plan for the interference in the domestic affairs of other countries."

Bevin crossed to Paris on June 17, where Bidault had assembled a strong team of Foreign Ministry advisers headed by

Hervé Alphand, later French ambassador to Washington. The two men agreed rapidly on the framework of how Europe should respond to Marshall's call, and as a first step they issued an invitation to Molotov to come to Paris on June 27 to join in working out the European reply. Both the British and the French were as aware as the Americans of the risks of Russia scuttling the whole affair, and they determined, therefore, in advance that the door would be open to Russian cooperation, but they would not get trapped in Russian obstruction. On Sunday, June 22, despite the growling noises from Pravda, word came from Moscow that Molotov was accepting. Bevin, back at the Foreign Office, had a brief moment of Hope that maybe, after all, Europe would not wind up divided. To another cabinet minister who had come to see him in his office on a problem involving British food supplies, Bevin kept repeating: "Perhaps they *will* play, after all. Perhaps they *will* play."

Molotov arrived in Paris with an enormous delegation: some eighty people in all, which, again, seemed to indicate that they would play. But after an initial four-hour meeting in the Salon Bauvais, at the Quai d'Orsay, it was pretty clear that they were prepared to play, as usual, only on their own terms. The response to Marshall, as Molotov saw it, was very simple. Each country should make known to the Americans its individual requirements, and the United States should then provide the necessary aid "without any interference with internal sovereignty or with internal plans for recovery."

Bidault, on the other hand, opened with a long statement, coordinated with Bevin and the British, that sketched the framework for a multilateral approach under a special European steering committee.

The debate went on for three days in dialogue-of-the-deaf form, with Molotov repeating endlessly that "it is not the function of a conference to draw up an all-embracing program for the European countries, since this would inevitably result in the imposition of the will of the strong and would constitute intervention in the domestic affairs of states and a violation of their sovereignty"—to which Bevin or Bidault endlessly replied that "the idea of cooperation does not imply any interference in the internal affairs of European states, nor any infringement on their sovereignty."

This turgid argument finally came to a break on Wednesday, July 2, in circumstances that Bevin later recounted to Acheson:

"It seems that Molotov has a bump on his forehead which swells when he is under emotional strain. We were debating away, and Molotov had raised relatively minor questions or objections at various points when a telegram was handed to him. He turned pale and the bump on his forehead swelled. After that his attitude changed, and he became much more harsh. I suspect that Molotov must have thought the instruction sent him was stupid. In any case the withdrawal of the Russians made operations much more simple."

Before gathering up his papers and his delegation to walk out, Molotov, in typical Stalinist Soviet behavior of those times, took the floor to deliver a final warning of "grave consequences" for Britain, France and Europe if the Marshall offer was accepted in the fashion in which they had proposed. Bevin immediately replied, having watched the bump on Molotov's forehead: "My country has faced grave consequences and threats before, and it is not the sort of prospect which will deter us from doing what we consider our duty. I want Mr. Molotov to know that I profoundly regret this threat."

Molotov flew back to Moscow, and the next day, Bidault and Bevin quickly cleaned up the business at hand. On July 3 they issued a joint invitation to twenty-two European countries (the exceptions being Russia, Franco's Spain, and ex-enemy states) to come to Paris on July 12 to work out a joint response to the American Government. Poland hesitated until July 9 and then declined. Czechoslovakia, where Jan Masaryk was still foreign minister, accepted on July 7 and then rescinded, on Stalin's direct orders, on July 10. The Finnish Government rather skillfully replied that as the Marshall Plan was "a matter of serious disagreement between the great powers," Finland wished to remain outside the conflict "but will make its needs known and wants to contribute to cooperation in Europe." In effect the Finns were saying that they wanted to take part but could not join. In the end, sixteen nations accepted and sent delegations to Paris: Austria, Belgium, Denmark, France, Greece, Iceland, Ireland, Italy, Luxembourg, the Netherlands, Norway, Portugal, Sweden, Switzerland, Turkey and the United Kingdom.

With Molotov's departure from Paris, Europe in July 1947 rapidly split in two. The last vestiges of hopes or ideas about bridge-building or cooperation across the ideological frontiers and military boundaries where the Red Army held total sway now evaporated totally. As the democratic governments of Western Europe prepared for the Paris conference, Stalin moved with equal speed to consolidate the grip on his helpless client states. On July 10, the Bulgarians signed a trade agreement with the Soviet Union. The Czechs, who had been refused permission to join the Marshall Plan, were then forced to follow with a trade agreement on July 11. Hungary signed on July 14, Yugoslavia (later to break away) on July 25, Poland on August 4, and Romania on August 26. This was the nucleus around which Comecon was later formed—the Communist economic cooperation organization.

Meanwhile on July 14, the United States cut off any further food relief shipments to Czechoslovakia. Perhaps it was an unnecessarily brutal act at that point in history, but the fate of Czechoslovakia was already being decided in Moscow, and American food would have made no difference to the outcome.

Then Stalin summoned Communist Party representatives from all the Eastern European states as well as France and Italy to a meeting in Warsaw on September 22, where it was agreed to set up the Cominform—Communist Information Bureau. This, of course, was simply a revival of the old Comintern of 1919, the Communist International, which had been the Soviet Union's worldwide instrument of propaganda, espionage, terror, and political control of the Communist movement everywhere. Stalin had suppressed the Comintern back in 1943 as a gesture of goodwill to the wartime alliance, but now it was back with a new label. It was to be headquartered in Belgrade, and the Yugoslavs quickly went to work to build a headquarters building. But in 1948 came Tito's historic break with Stalin before the building was even completed, and it was later converted into a much-needed hotel to attract Western tourists to Yugoslavia.

As was the case with the Truman Doctrine, revisionist historians continue to pick over the record of these events in the hope of establishing that the blame or responsibility for the great East-West divide lies with the West and not with Stalin. It will not wear. Of course the West could have avoided a split by doing nothing, sliding further and further into chaos while Stalin simply waited. But the record shows that both Bevin and Bidault went out of their way in Paris to try to accommodate the Russians by tying any Marshall Plan organization into the United Nations, or by making the cooperative arrangements as loose and as flexible as they could possibly be. And of course Marshall had ensured that no doors were slammed against the Russians in his offer. But there were simply no terms at all for Western aid that would have been acceptable to Stalin.

If there was relief in Washington and elsewhere at Molotov's walkout, the speed with which Stalin moved to pull Eastern Europe into line and form Comecon and the Cominform should be sufficient proof of his intentions all along. Had the Marshall Plan offer never been made, then Stalin could of course have adopted different tactics, but his strategic political objective and the strategic outcome would have remained the same. The Europe that the world had known for a century and a half, the Europe of the Congress of Vienna and the Peace of Versailles, was now gone forever. Regrets, resentments, revulsions were great —but so, too, was the relief in Western Europe that it could get on with the job.

The sixteen original "subscribers" to the Marshall Plan gathered in Paris with Bevin in the chair, and quickly agreed to set up a Committee of European Economic Cooperation (CEEC). They decided to approach the task of responding to the Marshall offer by preparing crash studies on Europe's across-the-board needs in four key areas: food and agriculture, iron and steel, fuel and power, and transport. Britain's Sir Oliver Franks, a university intellectual with broad wartime experience as a civil servant and economist, became the CEEC's chairman. They set mid-September as a target date for completing their initial report.

Meanwhile, with the initial organizational steps to implement the Marshall Plan now well underway, the United States began stepping up its discreet but strong involvement in shaping the program as well as its policy objectives. Will Clayton, the undersecretary of state for economic affairs, was the key personality as well as the key policy figure. Well over six feet tall, with a courtly southern manner, Clayton had been a successful cotton broker in private life. He led the charge of American officials who were determined that the objectives of the Marshall Plan not be confined to recovery alone, but encompass free trade and European integration as well.

The Franks Committee was ready with a draft of its report in mid-September, when Clayton arrived in Paris to confront the Europeans with the first of a long-running series of what might be called "constructive crises." Clayton found the report to be "too much of a shopping list," without enough high-minded far-reaching policy objectives and commitments to impress Congress and set the sights in Europe for the future. He insisted on a commitment to establish some kind of organization of the Europeans to continue after the CEEC had completed its work. He said that there had to be a recommendation from the committee for more steps to relax European trade barriers, and he wanted a better statement of general principles of what Europe saw itself trying to achieve with recovery. A foreign ministers' meeting to consider the report was postponed for a week while Franks and his committee went back to work to produce a draft to suit the Americans. It was completed and signed on September 22, the same day the Cominform was being set up at Warsaw.

The report estimated that Europe would have a combined trade deficit from 1947 to 1951 of around $22.5 billion of which $15.8 billion would be with the United States. It did not try to define what the American aid burden should or would be, but simply laid out the problems. It fixed targets for a one-third increase in European coal production by 1951, a 40 percent increase in electricity, and an 80 percent increase in steel.

Meanwhile back in Washington a similar series of studies were underway to galvanize congressional and public opinion behind the Marshall aid offer. In late July, a nineteen-man House of Representatives study committee began a tour of Europe under the chairmanship of Christian Herter, of Massachusetts, later Secretary of State in the Eisenhower administration. Then a joint Senate-House committee went to work on the problem under former Senator Robert La Follette, Jr. For the executive branch, the most important study of all was done by a committee working under the chairmanship of Commerce Secretary Averell Harriman, later Marshall Plan administrator in Europe.

For all the speed with which plans and programs were taking shape on both sides of the Atlantic, the economic crisis itself would not wait. In October, Truman called Congress into special session and asked for an immediate appropriation of a little over half a billion dollars in emergency aid for France, Italy, and Austria. The full-dress European aid program, based on the Harriman Committee report, went to Congress from the White House in early December. The Economic Cooperation Act became law on April 3, 1948, ten months almost to the day after Marshall's Harvard speech.

Truman initially thought of placing Dean Acheson at the head of the new European Cooperation Administration (ECA). But both Acheson and Senator Vandenberg advised the President that Paul Hoffman, president of the Studebaker Corporation and a prominent Republican who had served on the bipartisan Harriman Committee, would be a better political choice. Hoffman was reluctant, but Truman forced his hand with a premature leak that he had accepted. He was sworn into office on April 9, and two weeks later the first freighter sailed from Galveston, Texas, with nine thousand tons of Marshall Plan wheat for Europe. Meanwhile Harriman agreed to give up the Commerce Department, and he arrived in Paris late in April to set up European headquarters for the ECA. Marshall Plan missions now sprang up at every American embassy in Europe where governments were receiving aid. For a brief period of three or four years, these heads of Marshall Plan missions were often more important than the ambassadors—involving themselves deeply in the spending, taxation, budgeting, trade, monetary, agricultural, and even housing and labor policies of the countries to which they were assigned.

Behind all this was an almost evangelical American fervor for European unity, which at that time was always ahead of what the

Europeans themselves were ready to do or believed they could do. Two major interventions by the United States in this period are worth detailing due to their bearing on history.

The first intervention concerned the establishment of a European economic organization. Will Clayton had insisted on including such a recommendation in the Franks Committee report, but even this was watered down with a proviso that it would "cease to exist when the special assistance necessary for the recovery of Europe comes to an end." For some reason or other, still trying to avoid any blame for the division of Europe, the Western Europeans were reluctant to have it appear that they were setting up some rival to the United Nations or were joining in some exclusive power bloc. It was here, in fact, that Bevin's shortsightedness about Europe contrasted with his vision and vigor and imagination of wider Atlantic Community and world issues. Having taken the initiative in setting up the CEEC, the British were now dragging their feet in turning this into a permanent European cooperative venture.

In the end, in January 1948, the United States literally laid down the law to all sixteen governments that were receiving Marshall aid. Notes were simultaneously transmitted, through all the American embassies, that in effect demanded that a permanent organization be formed if Marshall aid was to continue. By April, a charter for the establishment of the Organization for European Economic Cooperation (OEEC) was finally agreed on. The British, with their usual panache when they finally see the way the wind is blowing, installed their man as the first chairman of the OEEC permanent council, while an acute and lively Frenchman, Robert Marjolin, became its first secretary-general. Marjolin was to go on to play a key role in setting up the European Common Market a decade later. Then, in 1961, thirteen years after it was formed, the OEEC went through another metamorphosis appropriate to the changing times and became the Organization for Economic Cooperation and Development (OECD), which today numbers twenty-four members including Japan, Australia, New Zealand, Yugoslavia, and Finland as well as all Western Europeans and the United States and Canada. It is the central cooperation machinery of the industrialized world.

With a permanent European organization finally in place, the United States now set about hammering it into an instrument of genuine European integration and unity. On June 5, 1948, the first anniversary of the Marshall speech, Averell Harriman announced to a stunned OEEC council that the United States would no longer be responsible for allocating Marshall Plan aid among the various nations and that this would now have to be decided collectively by the receiving states themselves. Naturally, the habit and expectation of each had been that it would be free to lobby its own case and its own needs in Washington—but now the Europeans were being told abruptly and without either warning or recourse or discussion that they would have to sort the whole thing out themselves. Moreover, the 1948–49 Marshall Plan appropriation by Congress was going to be only around $500 million, well short of Europe's hopes and requests. Finally, after ten days of wrestling with the problem, the Europeans decided to appoint a group of four senior national civil servants, from Britain, France, Italy and the Netherlands, to examine all the aid requests and come back with the pie cut up. The four men then literally disappeared to a French château near Chantilly, north of Paris, but when they came back with their proposals, something close to diplomatic pandemonium broke out at the OEEC Council. After weeks of recrimination and argument and bargaining, a division of the American aid package was finally agreed on, and of course accepted by Harriman. The following year, there was a bigger aid appropriation to divide, and the percentages of the original package were used as the starting point for cutting up the pie. And of course it got easier from year to year. Thanks to the American hardheadedness, mainly of Clayton and Harriman, cooperation and integration of effort were imposed upon Europe to a degree the governments at that time had never even contemplated. Much the same approach, of starting with multinational experts' studies and then thrashing out a wider consensus, remains the basis of cooperation in the OECD today.

The formal period of Marshall Plan aid lasted four years, from 1948 to 1952, although individual aid programs for some of the more impoverished nations in Europe continued beyond that time —and continue in other parts of the world today. The speed with which results begin to flow, once confidence and economic security were assured, was little short of amazing. Intra-European trade between 1947 and 1950 more than doubled, reaching prewar levels in 1949, two years ahead of expectations. By the summer of 1951, Western European industrial production was 43 percent above prewar, and farm production was 10 percent above prewar. Across the whole of the four-year period of Marshall aid, two thirds went for food, feed, fertilizers, raw materials, and semifinished products. Fuel, mainly coal, accounted for 16 percent of the aid, and machinery and vehicles for 17 percent. Above all, the groundwork was laid from 1948 to 1952 for an unparalleled twenty years of European economic growth, which was finally brought to a halt only by the 1973 Middle East war and the oil crisis and oil price rise that followed.

Marshall Plan aid for Europe cost the American taxpayers $13.1 billion from 1948 to 1952, in addition to appropriations of $9.5 billion for aid through the United Nations Relief and Rehabilitation Administration and aid to occupied countries such as Germany and Austria, which had been funded separately in the immediate postwar years. At the end of the program, Great Britain and her dependencies had received $3.1 billion, France $2.7 billion, Italy $1.5 billion, and West Germany $1.4 billion. Winston Churchill called it "the most unsordid act in history." It was also the greatest bargain in history.

3

Konrad Adenauer

ACROSS A CENTURY OF HISTORY, GERMANY MORE THAN ANY NA-
tion in Europe has adapted or adjusted its national character and
sense of values to follow the image and personality of one man.
Britain can produce a Winston Churchill and France can turn to a
Charles de Gaulle in national crisis, but these leaders were quin-
tessential products of deep traditional strengths and the long history of the nations they served. They did not take power in order
to erase the past or alter the character of the people they were
leading. Their greatness lay in the fact that they were giving renewed expression and leadership to values and virtues that had
long been tested and defended. Churchill would have been perfectly at home in one of Queen Victoria's governments, and de
Gaulle could have been Louis XIV. Not so in Germany. There has
been Bismarck's Germany of blood and iron, Hitler's Germany of
the police state, concentration camps, and national *Götterdäm-
merung,* and today there is Adenauer's Germany of democracy,
European integration, and *Ostpolitik.* Except for geography and
language, and the high price for war, there is little interchangeable
in the historic experiences of these three Germanies, their governing philosophies, political principles, or national images. The dividing lines and cutoffs that separate one German epoch from another are about as complete as if it had all happened in three
different countries. Even the continuity of Prussian military tradition and influence from Bismarck through the Kaisers and the
Weimar Republic to Hitler was finally extinguished with the unconditional surrender of the Third Reich. Only in the lives of Germans who lived across all this history was there at least a continuity of experience and survival. One of those was Konrad

Adenauer, who emerged from this turbulence in the autumn of his
life to become the greatest German statesman of the century.

Adenauer was born in 1876, in the aftermath of the Franco-
Prussian War, when Bismarck was at the height of his power. He
died only nine years short of a century later, having guided his nation out of the most complete moral, spiritual, intellectual, and
physical destruction any country has ever experienced onto a new
historic plateau of successful and stable democracy—a land which
although divided is largely at peace with itself. It is perhaps paradoxical, but a peculiarly German paradox, that the building of
democracy in Germany, when it finally came about, should have
been so much the achievement of one man. Of course, democracy
by definition can never be a one-man affair, and many took part in
the fashioning of the Bonn constitution and rallied to make the
political institutions of the new federal system work. Nevertheless,
in the final analysis it was the Federal Chancellor who brought it
all together and, for a remarkable fourteen years, gave the new
republic its image, its direction, its sense of being governed, its
force and its power and its place in Europe. A lesser man than
Adenauer could easily have missed the great opportunity and allowed the same constitution and the same institutions to slide and
drift into a repeat of the Weimar Republic. But Adenauer, having
lived through the Weimar days as well as those of Bismarck, Kaiser Wilhelm, and Hitler, was no man to repeat past mistakes and
allow things to drift. His greatness lay in the fashion in which he
was able to ensure that the essentials of the new German democracy functioned openly, honestly, and effectively, while at the
same time applying a rather grandfatherly authoritarian leadership, which the sickened and ruined German nation also badly
needed as it emerged bewildered and uncertain from the physical
and moral ashes.

The most important measure of Adenauer's greatness is the record of early vital choices that he and he alone made for the
emerging West German republic. There was a constitution and
there was a cabinet, but it was a government whose competence
was limited, by the Allied occupation, to internal affairs. There
was a fragmented Bundestag holding wild and confused democratic debates on the banks of the Rhine. There was no consensus

about foreign policy, because Bonn was not supposed to have a foreign policy in those early days. There was no foreign ministry, and as for a ministry of defense, this was unthinkable and unmentionable. In the beginning, there was Konrad Adenauer and there were three or four key advisers who drafted papers to carry out his decisions.

He could have chosen at the outset to form the first Bonn government in coalition with the Social Democrats, as many of his own Christian Democratic supporters were urging. But he had seen enough of coalitions in the Weimar days, and he decided firmly that the new democracy was going to get clear and undiluted rightist government with a clear and undiluted opposition on the left. He could have appealed to German nationalism by picking fights and doing constant political and propaganda battle with the British, French, and American occupation authorities instead of following a line of broad cooperation. He could have opted for tighter economic controls instead of the market economy that was allowed to prevail. When the French proposed the Schuman Plan for creation of the European Coal and Steel Community, forerunner of the Common Market of today, he could have tried to extract concessions or preconditions, but he accepted it openly and without reservations.

As his foreign policy began, he could have attempted the traditional German balancing act between East and West. He could have taken a more neutralist line instead of devoting all his efforts and political skills to merging West Germany with the European and Atlantic communities. He could have decided not to seek membership in the North Atlantic Treaty Organization, because it would be incompatible with ultimate German reunification, and he could have refused to allow West Germany to be rearmed. He could have flirted with the Soviet Union, dreamed up another Rapallo Pact, tried to play off one side against the other to Germany's advantage, kept the Western Allies suspicious and uncertain about where the new Germany really stood. All these alternatives were open to Adenauer, and there were prominent West German politicians in Bonn who could and would have played this way. But Adenauer chose none of these games. Clearly, unambiguously and as permanently as he possibly could, he lined up the

Federal Republic with the West at every conceivable turn without
ever looking back or even hinting that there could be any other
course. Today, with the Bonn Republic in its fourth decade and its
place in Western Europe and a consensus on its foreign policy
secure, the original choices facing Adenauer may seem to have
been easy and obvious. But they were not that simple or without
political risk at the time, and it would have been easy for him to
equivocate, avoiding having to choose. It is a simple measure of
Adenauer's greatness to ask what Europe would be like today if
he *had* equivocated or chosen differently.

Adenauer was seventy-three when he became the first Chancellor
of West Germany, in September 1949. There was little to mark
him at that time and at that age as much more than a good interim
choice to get the Bonn government started while younger men
found their political feet. But he remained at the helm until 1963
—longer than the entire twelve-year history of Hitler's Thousand
Year Reich. He was in fact far better equipped for the postwar
challenges and the role of a statesman than any younger man
emerging from the Hitler era could have been. In a rather prosaic
career as a provincial politician and *Oberburgermeister* of the city
of Cologne, until he was removed from office by Hitler in 1933,
Adenauer had accumulated the practical experience of living and
coping with everything from Bismarck's time: the victories and
defeats, the glory and the decadence, the euphoria and the chaos,
the inflation and deflation, the debts and credits, the destruction
and rebuilding, the advances and retreats, the reparations and the
occupations, the heroes and the wounded, the mistrust and the
hatreds, the separatists and the unifiers, the Catholics and the
Protestants, the prisons and the monasteries, the good Germany
and the bad. He had been hailed and jailed, he had lost two wives,
he had fathered eight children, and he had been fired from the
same job by both the Nazis and the British. In the sixteen years
before he became Bonn chancellor, he had lived in uneasy retirement, marked by the Gestapo, without a profession or a salary,
and his life could easily have ended in obscurity. But it did not,
and he brought to the task and opportunity of 1949 a serenity of
age and a stamina of youth, a political capacity and psychological

staying power, a calm sureness of himself and his judgment and his role which no younger man in postwar Germany could possibly have emulated. All of these qualities he was fortunately able to transfer into the stability and sense of values of the new West German republic simply by remaining its head and making its decisions for such a formative epoch of history.

"My first and strong impression of the Chancellor was of his conservative and prudent use of energy," Dean Acheson wrote of Adenauer. "The control is absolute; not an unnecessary erg is spent on movement, gesture, voice or facial expression. He moves slowly, gestures sparingly, speaks quietly, smiles briefly and chuckles rather than laughs when amused. It is not surprising that a man more given to chuckles than laughter is given, too, to irony rather than broad humor or sparkling wit. As an example, his remark that God made a great mistake to limit the intelligence of man but not his stupidity. His whole appearance and manner is of stiffness and inscrutability, enhanced by a hint of the Orient in the eyes set wide apart and the flatness of the bridge of his nose. But a first sense of cold aloofness goes if, after due deliberation, he gives his confidence and friendship."

My own remembrances of Adenauer, when I was living in Bonn and reporting the nascent years of the Federal Republic, center on his great dignity and old-fashioned courtesy and composure. Dignity was rare in Germany in those days, when attitudes often varied from sullen arrogance to insufferable obsequiousness. With Adenauer it was much more than just a dignity of age. It was a dignity of character and intellect as well. You felt the presence of a great man, even in the most banal or undignified settings or circumstances. Nobody has ever spoken of Adenauer losing his temper, for there was never any visible display of emotion with him. In the most irritating or provocative or hurtful or trying conditions, his dignity and composure were unchanged. He once remarked that "in politics, patience is of major importance and I have a great deal of patience." He lived his whole life in an attitude of calm persistence and fortitude, and the rewards of patience for himself and his nation were great.

His origins were completely plebeian, rooted in the Catholic Rhineland as opposed to Protestant Prussia, from which Germany

was ruled until he became its Chancellor. Adenauer's father was
the son of a baker in Bonn and worked as a farmhand and in a
brick works before enlisting in Bismarck's army, just before the
outbreak of the Austro-Prussian War in 1866. The Iron Chancellor was out to humble the Austrian Empire, which he did in six
weeks at a cost of thirty thousand dead. Adenauer's father wound
up in the climactic Battle of Königgrätz, where he was wounded
and literally buried beneath a heap of corpses. He emerged a picture of nineteenth-century military heroism, clutching the torn colors of his unit in his hands. For this he won a battlefield promotion
from the enlisted ranks to an officer's commission—most unusual in
the Prussian Army of the times. But on his return from the war he
met and fell in love with the daughter of a Cologne bank clerk and
decided to marry. Prussian regulations also laid down that the parents of a bride must supply her officer husband with an adequate
dowry to enable them to live in suitable state on his menial pay.
This was out of the question, so the senior Adenauer left military
service but used it as a back door to obtain state employment as
the clerk of a district court in Cologne.

Here Konrad Adenauer was born, one of three sons and a
daughter, with a sister who died in infancy, into a household of
strict discipline, Catholic piety, and limited if adequate means. It
was, moreover, a time of one of Bismarck's blood-and-iron campaigns to mold Germany to his own Protestant beliefs: the *Kul-
turkampf,* in which he sought for more than a decade to curb the
power and influence of the Catholic Church. The Jesuit Order was
banned by Bismarck, and its members expelled from the country.
Priests had to be German and were limited in numbers. Catholic
education was curtailed and civil marriage made compulsory. Bismarck even arrested the Catholic archbishop of Cologne, in 1874,
and imprisoned six bishops as well.

In this atmosphere, the young Adenauer learned his catechism
and prepared for his first Communion. Eventually Bismarck retreated, but it was not until 1886 that state examinations for
priests were dropped and control of the priesthood returned exclusively to the Church. Meanwhile, his display of the mailed fist had
only increased political support in the Rhineland for the Catholic
Center Party. When Adenauer eventually began his career in Co-

logne politics, his allegiance went automatically to the Center Party. His childhood memories of what Prussian rule had meant to his family and life in the Rhineland were never forgotten, and can probably be said to have had a decisive influence on German history.

Adenauer's father obtained money from a Cologne scholarship foundation to send his son to Freiburg University, in southern Germany, when he turned eighteen. In the German educational tradition of the times, he moved on to Munich University and finally back to the Rhineland to Bonn University, where he graduated with a law degree in 1899, at the age of twenty-three. He won an appointment almost immediately to the staff of the state prosecutor's office in Cologne, but two years later he left to enter a private law firm headed by a member of the Cologne City Council who was also one of the leaders of the Center Party. Then, in 1906, a place on the City Council became vacant, and Adenauer was well situated to mount a successful campaign for the vacancy. At the age of thirty, he began a municipal career in Cologne that lasted twenty-seven years, until the Nazis came to power, in 1933.

Meanwhile he had married in 1904, and his wife, Emma, bore two sons and a daughter. But her health was weak and she was in and out of hospitals and sanatoriums with curvature of the spine and chronic kidney difficulties and died tragically, after only twelve years of marriage, in 1916. The following year, Adenauer was elected Lord Mayor of Cologne by his fellow city councilors.

During the First World War, from 1914 to 1918, Cologne was the key communications hub through which the Kaiser's gray-clad legions and their equipment, supplies, and ammunition flowed across the Rhine to the battlefields of northeastern France and Belgium. It fell to Adenauer, first as a city councilor and later as Lord Mayor, to requisition the buildings, organize the billets and supplies, and eventually the hospital facilities and even the burial grounds for the endless troop movements forward and the ghastly return of the wounded and the dead. At last, in October 1918, the Kaiser's Reich began to crumble with a mutiny of sailors at Kiel. Then the Kaiser abdicated, slipping away from his military headquarters at Spa, in Belgium, sixty miles west of Cologne, and heading across the Dutch border to exile and refuge in Holland, where he died in 1940. On November 11, the Armistice was signed and the fighting ended, but Germany was already plunged into chaos. The Kiel mutineers descended on Cologne by train from the North, and for days the city was practically in the hands of roving mobs and looters waving red flags. Adenauer was a lone figure of authority doing what he could to sustain order, as four full field corps of the defeated army began pouring back through the city for demobilization and home. One of his most important actions was to require, in the absence of any other orders or organization by the military authorities, that soldiers give up their arms before they were granted discharge papers or railway tickets or pay or ration vouchers. He managed to avoid the worst for Cologne, compared to the violence that struck Berlin with the Spartacus uprising, as well as Munich, Hamburg, Leipzig, and elsewhere.

Then, on December 6, 1918, three days after the last of the Kaiser's retreating soldiers marched through Cologne and across the bridge over the Rhine, a British infantry brigade entered the city, and its first Allied occupation began.

The *Oberburgermeister* formally handed over to the British a German Army barracks that he had requisitioned from the retreating Reichswehr, and then requested that the British brigade be paraded through the city so that its presence would be felt. The commanding officer said his men were tired, but he would stage the march after they had rested and cleaned up.

Adenauer now had his first polite brush with British authority. He was handed a set of occupation regulations to be promulgated on behalf of the British forces, which included among other things a proviso requiring all male citizens to "salute" British officers in public by raising their hats to them. Adenauer objected that "he could not imagine that an English gentleman would wish to humiliate a vanquished people in this way." The British officer simply shrugged and said that his orders were to hand the proclamation to the Lord Mayor and what he did with it was then up to him. Adenauer replied that he would carry out British orders "as far as my conscience permits," and the British general responded that "we shall treat you correctly, as is our duty." That was the end of it. The proclamation was never posted or published.

On the whole, Adenauer's relations with the British during the occupation of 1918 to 1926 were good. It was an occupation with a light hand, compared to what was to follow the Second World War. The real problem for Adenauer and the Rhineland in those years was the French, who were doing everything in their power— which was plenty—to agitate for and finance and promote the creation of a separate, breakaway independent Rhenish republic as a means of dismembering and further weakening the old Reich. For six years this agitation went on, with the French constantly pressuring and even threatening Adenauer to throw his weight behind the separatists. They knew him to be a figure of growing importance in Rhineland politics, but Adenauer played his own game.

His objective for the Rhineland was quite clear: a federal solution in which the right of separate states to their own identity and existence would be recognized, but "we should remain united with our fellow nationals in the Reich." In a speech to a major conference of mayors and political leaders from all over the Rhineland, held in Cologne on February 1, 1919, Adenauer laid down a prophetic policy that he was finally able to carry out thirty years later:

"Is there any solution available which could satisfy the claims of France and yet avoid such damage to Germany as would necessarily be caused by a cession of the left bank of the Rhine? It is the creation of a federated state. In the opinion of our former enemies, it was Prussia who drove the world into this war. They believe that Prussia is dominated by a military and Junker caste and that Prussia in turn dominates the rest of Germany including the peoples of Western and Southern Germany with whose general outlook and temperament the Entente nations are basically in sympathy. Public opinion abroad now therefore demands: Prussia must be partitioned. If this were done, if the western provinces of Germany were joined together in a federated state, it would no longer be possible for Prussia, in the opinion of other countries, to dominate Germany. If there were a Rhineland-Westphalia state within a new German Reich, it would play a considerable part in its affairs and correspondingly it would be able to guide Germany's foreign policy along peaceful and conciliatory lines. This could, and should, satisfy France."

But the French at that time were far from satisfied with the way Adenauer was playing. He was going along with French separatism only for his ends, not theirs. Georges Clemenceau, the wartime Premier, later wrote in his memoirs in exasperation over the results of that Cologne meeting:

"The Mayor of Cologne had taken over the leadership of the separatist movement, and the purpose of the meeting was the solemn proclamation of the foundation of the Rhenish Republic. But what happened? Under the influence of Adenauer the meeting contented itself with electing a committee charged with preparing plans for the establishment of a self-contained Rhineland within the constitutional frame of the German Reich. And how often did this committee meet? Not once!"

The French were nothing if not persistent. They kept spending money and pushing agitators forward, and on June 1, 1919, a shadowy French-puppet leader named Dr. Josef Adam Dorten proclaimed in Mainz, in the French occupation zone, the establishment of a "Rhineland Republic" with a "seat of government" in Wiesbaden. He called, of course, for the rest of the cities of the Rhine to rally to the new state's colors.

Adenauer was summoned to British Military Headquarters at Cologne by General Sir Sidney Clive, head of the political affairs section. Appraised of the situation and asked for advice, Adenauer thought for a moment and then replied: "Your Excellency, my advice is that you issue an order forthwith to the effect that constitutional changes in British-occupied territory are prohibited unless prior permission has been obtained from the occupation authorities."

Clive not only issued the order; he drove immediately to Paris, where Prime Minister David Lloyd George was involved in the Versailles peace-treaty negotiations, and got assurances that British policy was against any dismemberment of the Rhineland in favor of France.

Still the French kept at it. In October 1923, the separatists under Dr. Dorten went into action again, this time in the city of Aachen, where they seized the town hall and once more proclaimed the establishment of a Rhineland Republic. Again the French put the pressure on Adenauer for support. The French president of the Inter-Allied Commission, in Coblentz, met the Cologne mayor and first reported positive results to Paris but later changed his tune to declare that Adenauer was being "obstructionist." The French had by now badly overplayed their hand. German nationalism was thoroughly aroused against separatist agitation coming on top of the terms of the Versailles Treaty. Vicious police action against the separatists now erupted all over the Rhineland. Finally, in Paris, a Socialist administration under Édouard Herriot replaced the revanchist Poincaré government, and French support for the separatists waned and the movement died. Dr. Dorten took off from the Rhineland for Nice, where he was duly rewarded with French citizenship.

These events had little lasting historic importance, but they were of considerable importance to Adenauer's experiences of dealings with British and French occupation authorities with differing mentalities and interests, and finally the root problem of getting peace and security out of all this between Germany and France for Europe. In 1945, when the British entered Cologne and the occupation of Germany began all over again, for Adenauer it was like playing an old, scratchy record: the British still preoccupied about saluting and correctness, the French agitating for separatism, dismemberment, decentralization, this time focusing on the Saar, installing a puppet governor named Johannes Hoffman, who was practically indistinguishable from Dr. Dorten, and doing everything short of permanently annexing the territory to France.

In 1919, in the face of separatist agitation, the Weimar Constitution had been promulgated with neither a strong central government nor the federal solution for Germany's future that Adenauer had advocated. By virtue of his position as Lord Mayor of Cologne, he found himself with an unsolicited seat in the Prussian Diet in Berlin—the upper chamber of the legislature, which was powerless to influence events but which nevertheless brought Adenauer to center stage. All the same, his interest and his role remained peripheral, and he was never much tempted by the national scene, which he regarded largely as an unwelcome distraction from his beloved Cologne.

Still, he was now a prominent national figure in the Center Party, and in 1926 the other party leaders approached him to see if he would form what would have been the thirteenth Weimar government in seven years. In mid-May he spent two days in Berlin negotiating with the Social Democrats and the People's Party as well as his own Center Party on a possible cabinet, but he abruptly decided that the cards were stacked against him. He packed his bag and caught a train back to Cologne with no regrets. He had neither his heart nor his stomach in it.

In any case, he had every reason to be content with his situation in Cologne, far from the turmoil and confusions and impossible problems of the national scene in Berlin. By 1929 he was not only at the height of his political power and influence in the city. He was also probably the highest-paid public official in the whole of Germany, making more in salary and expenses and perquisites than Reich President Otto von Hindenburg. His gross income from the city at that time was estimated at around eighty-five thousand marks, or about thirty thousand dollars, a very handsome income in Germany in those days. Moreover, he sat on a variety of boards of directors involved in public utilities, public transport, real estate, and construction. He was successful, and life was good.

He had remarried after the war, a bride eighteen years younger than himself, Auguste (Gussi) Zinsser, who, as it happened, was a distant cousin of the wife of the future American High Commissioner in West Germany after World War II, Mrs. John J. McCloy. Gussi bore three sons and a daughter, after the death of a first-born child in infancy, while also looking after Adenauer's children from his first marriage. She was a gayer person than his first wife, and Mrs. McCloy later wrote to an Adenauer biographer that "she was a very remarkable woman—more aggressively anti-Hitler and anti-Nazi than Adenauer himself, although both were put in prison."

Whatever the contentments of Cologne at the end of the 1920s, Germany was sliding rapidly into economic and political chaos. Hitler's Nazi Brownshirts marched the streets of German cities beating up and intimidating opponents at will. The enfeebled Weimar regime practically ceased to govern. In the 1930 elections, the Nazis increased their seats in the Berlin Reichstag from twelve to

107. In 1931, more than fifteen thousand German citizens were injured in political street fighting, 182 being killed. In January 1933, Hindenburg finally sent for Adolf Hitler and asked him to form a government. The Reichstag was dissolved and new elections were fixed for March 5, 1933.

There now occurred an incident that was decisive to Adenauer's future. During all of the preceding years, he had refused to have anything to do with the Nazi Party, and as Mayor of Cologne had struggled as best he could to preserve law and order. Maybe he could or should have done more, but as far as the Nazis were concerned, since he was not for them he was clearly against them. Adenauer sealed this when Hitler scheduled a visit to Cologne on February 17, 1933, to address a rally and the Lord Mayor decided not to go to the airport to meet him because he was there to campaign and not in his capacity as the newly installed Reich Chancellor. Adenauer sent a city councilor in charge of police affairs to the airport. Hitler ignored him and drove off in a rage to the Hotel Dreesen, in Bad Godesberg, where he was to headquarter five years later in his last round of appeasement meetings with Prime Minister Neville Chamberlain. Meanwhile in Cologne more was to follow. While Hitler slept at the Dreesen, Nazi Party workers hoisted two huge swastikas on the pylons of the bridge across the Rhine into Cologne, which he would be crossing next morning. But this was municipal property and Adenauer had given instructions that no party flags or emblems were to be displayed during the election campaign from any municipal building. Municipal workers were sent to take down the Nazi banners under police protection. Adenauer made a final concession to the Nazi organizers. He allowed them to fly their flags in front of the municipal fair ground building, where Hitler would be speaking, but not on the building. As far as Hitler was concerned, this was open defiance. Adenauer's days as Cologne mayor were numbered.

In the March 5 elections, the Nazis failed to capture a national majority, but with 44 percent of the vote it was enough to snuff out the last vestiges of Weimar democracy. Adenauer was warned in Cologne that there was a plot to liquidate him by throwing him out of his town hall office window. It seems to have been Nazi intimidation rather than intention. In any case, the Nazi government in Berlin announced his removal from office on March 13, 1933.

Adenauer was now a marked man as far as the Nazis were concerned, and he began twelve years of perilous existence, at best living quietly and lying low, at worst hiding out from the Gestapo or in jail. He left Cologne surreptitiously on the day of his removal from office and traveled to Berlin to seek an interview with Hermann Göring, then Reich Minister of the Interior. The most that can be said was that it was at least courageous, but all that he learned was that things were worse than he thought.

Göring kept him waiting three days and then informed him that the affair of the Nazi banners would not be forgotten and that he was under investigation for embezzling city funds. His salary of course had stopped, and his bank account had been frozen. At this point a wealthy American Jew named Daniel Heinemann, whom Adenauer had gotten to know back in the early 1920s, suddenly appeared out of nowhere in Berlin, handed Adenauer ten thousand reichsmarks in cash, and disappeared. On this money, Gussi and the Adenauer children lived for months in Cologne. But Adenauer was barred from the city by the Nazi edict firing him from his job. He turned for help to an old school friend who had become the abbot of a Catholic monastery at Maria Laach, in a remote region of the Eifel Mountains between Cologne and the Belgian frontier. In May, as the charges against him were taken up in Cologne, he disappeared behind the monastery walls, where he remained in seclusion except for occasional circumspect visits from members of his family for the next eight months.

But the family did stage a Christmas reunion at a small country hotel, which did not pass unnoticed. The abbot received a letter of complaint from the Nazi governor of the region about Adenauer's presence at Maria Laach, and although he replied with a dignified rejection, Adenauer decided not to worsen things for his religious hosts, so he took his leave. He still could not go back to Cologne to join his family, but friends now lent him a house on the outskirts of Berlin, in a secluded suburb called Neubabelsberg, where the Soviet checkpoint into the city now stands. Here he was picked up by the Gestapo on the "night of the long knives," in June 1934, when Hitler launched his purge of Ernst Röhm, the homosexual Brownshirt leader, which became a bloodbath involving hundreds of other enemies real and imagined. Adenauer was released after a few days of questioning, and then he simply kept on the move, from one small German hotel to another, for weeks.

Once this period was over, things quieted down for Adenauer. Nothing had been uncovered by the Nazis in their investigation of his financial management of Cologne, and even a trumped-up effort to charge him on false evidence failed when his accuser admitted under cross-examination that he was lying. The whole affair was quietly dropped, and at this point his brother, a lawyer in Cologne, began action to get his pension rights restored. In 1935 he was granted a pension by the city, and at the same time, he got compensation for two houses in Cologne that the Nazis had seized when they exiled him from the city. With this little bit of capital, he bought a property on the east bank of the Rhine at the town of Rhöndorf, southeast of Bonn, and built a home high up on a bluff overlooking the river valley, where he lived the rest of his life.

When war broke out, in September 1939, he prudently took Gussi on a holiday in Switzerland in the event of a Gestapo roundup, but he was now sixty-three years old, and nothing happened. His three sons were called up for military service to fight in a war in which they had no belief. His youngest daughter, Libeth, says that, from the first, her father "told us that the Nazis could not win and believed that they should not—he made this clear to all of us. We prayed for the war to be lost by Germany, not our Germany but Hitler's Germany." But, at the same time, Adenauer eschewed any contact with anti-Nazi resistance and chose to survive as a non-Nazi rather than risk martyrdom. He was approached in a roundabout, third-party way by those who were organizing the July 20, 1944, plot to assassinate Hitler, but he brushed the overtures aside, partly out of fear of the risks he would be taking with his family, mainly because he did not believe that the leader, Dr. Karl Goerdeler, mayor of Leipzig, was discreet or strong enough to make it a success.

The Gestapo was at his doorstep almost at once when the July

20 plot failed, but a search of his home turned up nothing. Three weeks later, they returned, and he was arrested and taken to a temporary detention center at the Cologne fairgrounds, where the flag incident with the Nazis had cost him his job eleven years before. He was locked up with a local Communist, who, with conspiratorial experience, knew everything a prisoner could know about what was going on. He learned that Adenauer was listed for transfer to Buchenwald, and with the help of a prisoner-doctor a sudden "illness" was contrived and Adenauer was transferred to a hospital instead. The Communist, Eugen Zander, had saved his life. Next, a friend of the family who was an officer in the Luftwaffe made a daring foray into the hospital with forged release papers and an official car and whisked Adenauer to a secret hideout at an old mill in the mountains behind Cologne.

Now his wife was picked up by the Gestapo, roughly interrogated, and threatened with reprisals including imprisonment of sixteen-year-old Libeth if she did not disclose where her husband was. She finally broke, and the Gestapo quickly flushed Adenauer out of his hiding place and locked him up in Brauweiler prison, at Cologne. Gussi was meanwhile released from the same prison in poor health from a bone disease, from which she later died. But still there were no charges against him, and he now asked his daughter on one of her prison visits to contact her brother, Max, a lieutenant in the German Army and have Max intercede at Gestapo Headquarters, in Berlin. Max made the plea that it was impossible for army morale to have fathers locked up without any charges and without having done anything, and somehow an order reached Cologne for his release.

He returned to Rhöndorf—without shoelaces, belt, tie, or suspenders—on November 27, 1944, just before Hitler's last big gamble: the Battle of the Bulge. Then, in March of 1945, the Allied armies broke out of the Eifel Mountains and the Hürtgen Forest and advanced to the Rhine. In one of the most dramatic episodes of the war, the 9th Armored Division, of the U.S. First Army reached the town of Remagen and found a bridge across the Rhine only partly destroyed. The leading company commander never hesitated. Calling for reinforcements, he took a platoon in a dash across the bridge in the face of defensive fire from a German reserve unit of older men who had failed to blow their demolition charges on time. In less than an hour the bridge was securely in American hands. Remagen was only five miles south of Rhöndorf, where Adenauer and his family, joined by five escaped French prisoners of war, were huddled in a garden dugout shelter waiting for shelling to cease. Finally, in the Rhöndorf streets below, a German Tiger tank got orders to pull out, and on March 14, 1945, the guns fell quiet. The war was over for the Adenauers.

A few days later, a U. S. Army jeep arrived at the foot of the long flight of steps up the hill to Adenauer's home, and an American major entered his garden. The military authorities wished him to resume his duties as Lord Mayor of Cologne. Would he accompany the American officers to the city immediately?

The American decision to reinstate Adenauer was not the result of any master plan or any "whitelist" of anti-Nazis whom the military authorities had been told to seek out. Adenauer was not known to Allied authorities, nor was he on anybody's anti-Nazi list at all. When the Americans captured Cologne, they simply asked who the last mayor had been before Hitler, whether he was still alive, and where he could be found. They did the same thing in cities all over Germany.

Adenauer returned to a scene of utter, harrowing, total destruction and desolation. It is a moot question which German city suffered the most in the war, but Cologne certainly suffered the longest. It was the first city to be hit by the Royal Air Force "thousand-plane raids," and it was hit again and again and again, since it conveniently lay in the path of bombers heading for almost all the other target cities in central and southern Germany. At the end came the artillery, as the German Army pulled back across the Rhine. Not even streets were visible when Adenauer entered the city, and every church had been damaged or destroyed. Out of a population of 750,000, barely 30,000 were scratching around in the rubble in March of 1945.

The restored Lord Mayor set up offices in a couple of rooms in a partly destroyed suburban office building and began organizing gangs of men to clear rubble and open ration depots and repair water lines and get the sewers open. Then, in mid-June, after the unconditional surrender had taken effect, the various Allied armies withdrew to the permanent occupation zones fixed by the Potsdam Agreements. The Americans pulled out of Cologne and headed south to their zone, centered on Frankfurt. The British took over where they had been occupiers twenty-five years before.

Adenauer had gotten along perfectly satisfactorily with the Americans during their three months of occupation of Cologne, but when the British arrived things stiffened markedly. The British military by nature and training are often stiffer and more precise about correctness and orders than their American counterparts, and by the end of the war all the victorious armies were full of martinets anyway. There now occurred an incident in which a no-nonsense British brigadier can fairly be said to have changed the course of history by firing a mayor instead of firing a shot.

The British occupation authorities quickly came to feel that the sixty-nine-year-old Lord Mayor of Cologne, whatever his anti-Nazi past, was a little too peremptory in the tone of requests he was constantly putting forward for food or coal or building materials for his city, and not doing enough on his own to get rebuilding and relief moving. Things reached something of a head when the occupation authorities ordered trees to be cut down in the Cologne Green Belt, of parks and woods around the city, to stockpile wood for what was going to be a difficult winter. But the Green Belt had been one of Adenauer's creations from his earlier days as Lord Mayor, and he insisted, rightly, that those trees were a long-term investment, which would do little to keep Cologne warm anyway. He refused the order, and he also then gave an interview to a couple of British journalists in which he openly criticized the occupation authorities for failing to provide sufficient fuel. He even went on to discuss in prophetic terms foreign policy questions that Germans were not supposed even to think about.

"If Russia is unwilling to cooperate in the unification of the whole of Germany, the best thing by far would be to unite at least the three western zones in a federal state, the sooner the better," Adenauer told the London *News Chronicle* and *Daily Express*. "In order to satisfy French security wishes with regard to such a federal state, the economy of this West German territory should be integrated with that of France and Belgium as intimately and closely as possible. Common economic interests are the best foundations for a rapprochement between the nations and the safeguarding of peace."

These statements from a German mayor in October 1945 were not only remarkable but sensational—too sensational for the British authorities.

At this same time, the Director of Military Government for the British occupation zone, General Sir Gerald Templer, paid a visit to Cologne on inspection. Templer, later a field marshal, was one of the superior products of the British Army in every sense of the word, which also meant that those below him listened respectfully to catch every nuance of the General's wishes. He was not very happy about the state of rebuilding and cleanup in the city, even with due allowance for the extremes it had suffered. When the Lord Mayor was discussed, Templer seems to have muttered something akin to King Henry II remarking of Thomas à Becket: "Who will free me of this turbulent priest." In any case, on October 6, 1945, the chief administrative officer for military government for the North Rhine, Brigadier John Barraclough, who had accompanied Templer, summoned Adenauer to his headquarters in Düsseldorf and summarily fired him.

Barraclough acted without any reference to higher headquarters or to any British civilian political advisers. Allied officers who wore stars in Germany in those days were gods where they commanded, and they knew it. Barraclough's superior, a corps commander, endorsed his decision immediately and unquestioningly. Adenauer was simply an old man who wasn't up to the job, in Barraclough's judgment, and that was that.

The firing was bad enough, but totally unnecessary was a punitive order that Barraclough also imposed on Adenauer, again banning him from Cologne, as he had been banned by the Nazis, and even denying him visits to his wife, who was in a Cologne hospital, except by special permission. And he was prohibited in the same order from taking part in any political activity in the British zone of occupation. Such was the mentality and such were the occupation orders of 1945—neither unusual nor exceptional in the temper of the times.

Adenauer returned in dignity, composure, and fortitude to his rose garden in Rhöndorf. Barraclough did not have a clue of the man he had fired, let alone any inkling of the effect his action would have on the future of Germany. Had Adenauer remained at the helm in Cologne, his time and energies would have been absorbed completely in the postwar problems of the municipality, and having devoted his early life to the city, there is little doubt that he would have devoted his last years to it as well. As it was, relieved of all the tedium of dealing with occupation authorities over rations and coal and de-Nazification and building materials and school books and local newspapers, he now turned his attention automatically to building a political role for himself in shaping the German future.

The British political authorities realized at once that their brigadier had bloopered, and they sought to get things back on an even keel with Adenauer, but they could not act too obviously or hastily. In early December an experienced, German-speaking political officer was sent to Rhöndorf to talk things over with the former Lord Mayor. But Adenauer, with complete punctiliousness and an ironical sense of humor, pointed out that he was forbidden to talk politics in the British zone. So he suggested that he and the British officer drive to a riverside *Weinstube* three miles up the Rhine, in the town of Bad Honnef, which was just over the zonal border, in French occupation territory, where the ban did not apply! There they settled down for more than three hours. The officer returned to British headquarters, and shortly after, the ban on Adenauer's political activity was lifted.

To this day, the British continue to debate the obvious question about whether Brigadier Barraclough's impetuous, martinet action in October 1945 did not seriously damage British interests with Konrad Adenauer in later years—as witness his fundamental indifference toward British entry into the European Common Market when they finally got around to making the effort.

Certainly the Barraclough affair did not help, but there was nothing petty about Adenauer, and he always talked of it as something of an ironic joke. Still, his son Paul did believe that "it rankled him a bit," even though he got plenty of conversational and political mileage out of the story for the rest of his days. But it did harden Adenauer's conviction that the British Labour government of the day was out to maneuver the Social Democrats into national political dominance at the expense of the Christian Democrats. In fact, the British were more inept than adept. As for their relations with Europe over the Schuman Plan and the Common Market, the British created more than enough stumbling blocks of their own in the years ahead, without Adenauer's needing to add to their difficulties and penchant for impeding themselves.

In the meantime, relief from the responsibility for running postwar Cologne was a blessing without much disguise. Surveying the political as well as the physical ruins of Germany from the heights above Rhöndorf in 1946, Adenauer had time and opportunity to widen his sphere of operations and influence. The manner of his departure from Cologne had given him a cachet unique among German politicians. He had been dismissed from the same job by both the Nazis and the British—clearly, nobody could accuse him of being anyone's political tool.

Along with time and opportunity, he had vision, patience, and the political experience and adroitness and agility of an old fox. For a man of seventy, his physical endurance and energy were astounding. Now, in the ruins of his country, he was fired with real ambition and with an opportunity for political achievement never open to him before. The rest of his life was inextricably bound up with the creation and coming of age of the Bonn republic.

4

The Bonn Republic

AT THE CENTER OF THE EUROPEAN CONTINENT LIES GERMANY, and at the center of Germany lies Berlin. The power politics and diplomacy of postwar Europe went hand in hand with its geography. Central to everything—economic recovery, political stability, military security, European unity, and the wider strategic balance of power between East and West—was the future of Germany. And central to the German question first of all was the fate of Berlin.

At Potsdam the victorious Allies had decreed that Germany was to be treated as one country, one economic entity, under a four-power Allied Control Council to coordinate policy in four separately administered occupation zones. Similarly, Berlin, inside Soviet occupation territory, was divided into British, French, American, and Russian occupation sectors under an Allied Kommandatura. Eventually, in a future that never came, a central German government was supposed to be revived in Berlin, when a peace treaty was negotiated. But the amity of Potsdam, such as it was, barely survived Stalin's return to Moscow and Truman's voyage home on the cruiser *Augusta*.

From the outset, Soviet policy toward Germany was little more than a ruthless and insatiable demand for delivery of reparations from the productive wealth of the British, American, and French occupation zones, while at the same time refusing any cooperation to restore even minimal health to the German economy, or any four-power Control Council agreements that might lend a semblance of unity to the treatment of the defeated nation. Meanwhile, of course, the Russians were proceeding with the brutal incorporation of the eastern half of Germany into the Soviet satellite system. It was perfectly clear to the Western Allies what was happening in Germany. All the same, they were reluctant to take the onus for any breakup of the four-power control machinery, which remained at least nominally intact until the Berlin blockade.

From the start of the year 1948, events gathered speed. Molotov had warned Bevin and Bidault of "grave consequences" when he walked out of the Marshall Plan conference in Paris in July 1947, and now these began to multiply into a dramatic challenge to the strength, nerves and political will of the Western democracies. While the West Europeans proceeded with organizing for the Marshall Plan, the last vestiges of democracy were snuffed out in Poland and Hungary. Non-Communists were purged from the government and jailed, and Stalin puppets installed as dictators.

In February 1948, it was the turn of Czechoslovakia. Red Army reinforcements moved into the Soviet occupation zone of Austria, taking up stations along the Czech border within a few hours' advance on Prague. One of the most vicious of Stalin's hatchet men, Valerian Zorin, arrived in the city to mastermind and direct the final coup. On February 21, a vast Communist workers' militia staged a rally of two hundred thousand in Wenceslas Square. Backed by this display of power, the Communist premier, Klement Gottwald, demanded that President Eduard Beneš install a new cabinet with Communists in complete control. Students flocked to the streets in counterdemonstrations, and for two days things teetered on the brink of civil war. But the Czech Army was confined to barracks, and the Communist-controlled gendarmes and security police moved in to crush the students. Five truckloads of "armed workers" seized the Social Democratic party headquarters in Prague, and on the evening of February 25, Beneš gave way to Gottwald's demands. Two weeks later, on the morning of March 10, 1948, the pajama-clad body of Jan Masaryk, who had stayed as foreign minister, was found in the courtyard pavement outside the windows of his apartment in Czernin Palace, headquarters of the Foreign Ministry. It looked like a suicide, but today there is no longer any doubt that he was murdered on Stalin's orders.

In my memory of those days, no single event had as much emotional, spiritual and intellectual impact in political and government circles as the death of Jan Masaryk. London and Paris had watched Warsaw and Budapest go under, and Bucharest, Sofia and Belgrade had already gone, but the death of Masaryk and the snuffing out of democracy in Prague now suddenly transformed all that was happening into a stab of personal pain and anguish. Masaryk was a man of the world, of intellectual sophistication, charm and great humor in many languages, with a host of friends in Europe and the United States. He had lived the war years in London as Czech Foreign Minister in the exiled government, and of course the fate of his nation after the Munich pact weighed heavily on the consciences of the British and the French. He had worked tirelessly after the war to assuage Stalin and preserve his country's independence, and now it was all over and he was gone. Those who knew Masaryk well could not believe that this buoyant spirit could take his own life, but it was not until twenty years later, during the Prague Spring, of 1968, before the Soviet tanks moved into Prague to wipe out the short-lived Dubček reform regime, that clear evidence that he had indeed been murdered finally emerged. In 1948, whether it was murder or suicide, Masaryk's death produced a shocked realization that this was no longer a civilized political contest between competing systems. It was a moment of truth when it suddenly became clear that democracies were facing a power that would stop at nothing.

That same week, the Norwegian Government sent its secret message to London that it was coming under heavy Russian pressure to sign a "friendship treaty," which it would resist even if it meant war, and Bevin passed the message urgently to General Marshall in Washington with his proposal to start negotiations on what became the North Atlantic Treaty.

Ten days after the death of Masaryk and consolidation of the Communist coup in Prague, on March 20, 1948, Marshal Vassily Danilovich Sokolovsky stormed out of a four-power Allied Control Council meeting in Berlin without fixing a date for another session. The intent was clear: After Prague, only Berlin remained free of complete Communist domination and control in all of the territory east of the Elbe River. Berlin was to be next. The fate of Germany now hung in the balance.

A few weeks earlier, in February, General Marshall had met

with Bevin and Bidault in London to discuss the future of Germany and its relation to the Marshall Plan—and this provided Sokolovsky and the Russians with the pretext for staging the Berlin walkout. The Soviet commander opened the meeting with a demand that the other members of the Control Council—General Lucius D. Clay, General Sir Brian Robertson and General Pierre Koenig—inform him of what had transpired in London. He went on to accuse the Western powers of "treating quadripartite authority in Germany as a suitable screen behind which to hide unilateral actions in the Western zones directed against the peace-loving people of Germany." When the Western generals objected to Sokolovsky's "using the meeting for propaganda purposes," he then launched into reading a prepared statement of denunciation at such a rapid pace that the interpreters could not keep up with him. At the end, he swept up his papers, rose to his feet, and declared: "I see no sense in continuing today's meeting and announce that it is adjourned." The Control Council never met again.

In London, the Western foreign ministers had taken several key decisions on Germany's future. The French finally agreed, under the impetus of the Marshall Plan, at last to merge their zone economically with the British and American zones, which had been joined as one since December 1946. It was also agreed to work out some kind of currency reform with or without Russian cooperation and to begin studies on the ultimate formation of a West German government if Soviet obstruction continued.

With Sokolovsky's walkout, all this now became not merely urgent but imperative. Early in the morning hours of Thursday, April 1, the Soviets made their first move in what was to become the Berlin blockade. The regular American Army overnight sleeping-car train from Frankfurt to Berlin was halted at Marienborn, just inside the Soviet zone, and surrounded by armed military police, who announced that on Marshal Sokolovsky's orders the travel papers of every single passenger aboard would have to be checked and cleared before the train would be allowed to continue to Berlin. The American train commander flatly refused and informed the Russians that if they attempted to board the train, his American MPs would shoot. A Soviet engine was then connected to the train and shunted it to a siding, where British and French military trains had also been halted. Fourteen hours later, after frantic exchanges between American headquarters in Berlin and the Pentagon, in Washington, the train was ordered back to Frankfurt. From then on, it was one harassment for the Allies after another on an ever-rising scale of confrontation until the full blockade descended, in late June.

Meanwhile, the Allied economic experts had decided that the only way to cope with inflation and the black market in Germany was through an entire new currency issue. At one point, earlier on, there had been discussions with the Russians about a joint currency reform for all four zones, with the new banknotes to be printed at the old German State Printing House, in the American sector of Berlin—but Sokolovsky had blocked this along with all the other efforts at any four-power economic policies. Now, after his walkout from the Control Council, the Western powers were ready at last to act on their own. The printing presses were at work at the Bureau of Printing and Engraving, in Washington. By early June, the new bills were airlifted to Frankfurt in close security and deepest secrecy.

Although the Allied Control Council was dead, the Allied Kommandatura for Berlin continued to function as the noose tightened around the city. The American member was a wiry, graying forty-five-year-old cavalry officer, an Irishman with the appearance and personality of a fighting cock, Colonel Frank "Howlin' Mad" Howley, military commander in the American sector. Kommandatura meetings had been getting steadily longer and more and more acrimonious and on Wednesday, June 16, the four commanders met for the last time. When Colonel Alexei Yelizarov, the Soviet deputy commander, turned up in place of General Alexander Kotikov, it seemed probable to the Allied officers that something was up, because Yelizarov was known as the military intelligence officer who called the shots. Howley had already raised with the Russians charges that a black market in the American sector was causing all the trouble, and the agenda that day included the usual tedious topics such as organization of the Berlin city courts, the employment of personnel at Spandau Prison, and licensing of nonpolitical organizations. From midmorning through late afternoon and into the evening this dragged on and on, until Yelizarov asked, at around 10:30 P.M., that the commandants should discuss a Soviet proposal of "fourteen points for the amelioration of workers' conditions in Berlin." Howley tried to get agreement on an adjournment at 11 P.M., but Yelizarov refused. At 11:15 Howley got up and announced that he was tired and going home and his deputy would take over. He walked out and headed for the American Press Club, where he habitually turned up to have a drink and to brief correspondents.

Howley had barely closed the door on the Kommandatura meeting when Yelizarov was on his feet denouncing "hooligan behavior" by the American commandant, demanding an apology and heading for the door shouting: "As far as I'm concerned there won't be a next meeting."

At the Press Club, Howley had just settled down to a large midnight martini with Marguerite Higgins, of the New York *Herald Tribune,* and John Thompson, of *Newsweek,* when he was called to the phone by General Clay ordering him to "get over here and get here fast." He drove to Clay's residence, about ten minutes away, and found Clay in a cold fury. Howley's deputy had phoned Clay to tell him what had happened.

"Your job was to sit there and take it; you have done a terrible thing," Clay raged. Howley, standing at attention, replied that the Russians could always find an excuse, anytime they wanted to, for a walkout—as they had walked out on the Control Council. Clay rasped that this had nothing to do with it; Howley had blundered into handing them an excuse. Finally, knowing that Howley's heart was in the Berlin struggle, he dismissed him with the remark: "Well, get some sleep. I guess you've had your quota of conferences for one day."

Clay's great worry was that, with the currency reform ready to go, he did not want the onus for a break in the Kommandatura until that had been accomplished. In the end, it was certainly true, as Howley had said, that the Russians could break the Kommandatura anytime they chose, but in the tensions of the moment Clay was certainly right to rage at his subordinate for providing the excuse.

The next day, June 17, Clay and the Western zone commanders

issued the final secret orders for currency reform, and on the evening of Friday, June 18, after the banks had closed for the weekend it was announced that all reichsmarks would be exchanged for new deutsche marks, starting at 7 A.M. Monday, at a whopping deflationary rate of one new for ten old.

On Sunday, Clay received a letter from Sokolovsky protesting against the currency reform and declaring ominously: "With respect to Greater Berlin, I consider it to be economically integrated with the Soviet Zone."

The Allies had deliberately omitted West Berlin from the first stage of the currency reform, and Clay now countered by proposing to Sokolovsky that the economic advisers of the Control Council meet to discuss the situation. The Russians accepted, but they were only stalling for time, having been taken by surprise by the Allied move, while they prepared to counter. The economic advisers met on Tuesday to discuss currency reform for Berlin and, predictably, got nowhere. Next day, Wednesday, June 23, the Berlin City Council convened at the City Hall, in the Soviet sector, and the Russians tried to ram through a decree that only Soviet currency would be valid throughout the city. A Communist rabble was turned loose to intimidate the 130 city councilors, but at the end of a wild and stormy meeting a counterresolution was approved, 106–24, specifying that the currency question was a matter for the individual occupation authorities and not the Berlin city government. Only the Communists voted against.

That evening, at 11 P.M., the news agency in the Soviet zone clattered out a teletype message: "The transport division of the Soviet Military Administration is compelled to halt all passenger and freight traffic to and from Berlin tomorrow at 0600 hours because of technical difficulties." The Berlin blockade had begun.

Much debate has since been expended over the question of whether the Allies could or should have forced a military convoy through to Berlin instead of launching the airlift. In fact, General Clay had given secret orders to American Army headquarters at Heidelberg some weeks before, after the Sokolovsky walkout on the Control Council, to form a task force and make contingency plans for pushing a military force of infantry, tanks, support troops, and bridging equipment up the autobahn. But that was as far as the project ever got. As Dean Acheson later wrote, General

Clay's confidence "was not based on the belief that the Russians could not stop a convoy but that they would not."

Clay flew to Heidelberg as the blockade began, to talk to army commanders on the convoy question, and when he returned to Berlin, a few hours later, General Sir Brian Robertson went to confer with him. When he heard what Clay had in mind, he was appalled.

"If you do that, it will be war—it's as simple as that," Robertson told Clay. He then added with British soldierly exactitude: "In such an event I am afraid my government could offer you no support and I am sure that Koenig and the French will feel the same."

In Washington, Undersecretary Robert Lovett met with congressional leaders at the State Department at about this same time, and both Senator Arthur Vandenberg and Senator Tom Connally emphatically rejected any action that would make the United States look like an aggressor. From a simple military standpoint, the Joint Chiefs of Staff reasoned that the bridge across the Elbe at Marienborn could be blown by the Russians either ahead of the convoy or after it had crossed, and going to the rescue of an ambushed American force halfway down the autobahn to Berlin would indeed be going to war. Both Clay and his political adviser, Robert Murphy, continued to argue long after that a convoy should have been used, but it was never seriously considered. The Allies would not back it, and the risks were too great.

Robertson immediately proposed to Clay that Berlin should be supplied by air, as the only course open, and disclosed that a Royal Air Force contingency plan for such an operation had already been prepared. The British were ready ahead of the Americans, and the first RAF planes of the Berlin air lift flew from Britain the next morning and made the first deliveries into Gatow Airfield, in Berlin, later that same day, June 25. Clay was skeptical, but there was little open to him except to get on the scrambler phone to Air Force General Curtis Lemay at Wiesbaden and say: "Curt, have you any planes that can carry coal?"

Up to this time, the German people and their political leaders had been little more than pawns in a chess game moved and directed by other hands, watching and waiting tensely as the postwar

power struggle that would decide their fate was joined by the Soviet Union and the Western Allies. But if the pawns had been
taken or lost, the game could never have been played even to a
draw. With the Berlin blockade, the three-year Potsdam era for
Germany was finished. In the Western zones, the clear and urgent
task was to begin replacing military occupation with democratic
government. The Germans were to be pawns no longer. Two great
men had been watching and waiting along with all the rest: Ernst
Reuter in Berlin and Konrad Adenauer in Bonn.

Reuter was the antithesis of Adenauer. In his youth, in the First
World War, he was taken prisoner by the Czarist forces on the
Eastern Front, and came back to Germany a Communist. Adenauer was the epitome of conservative order in Cologne in those
days, while Reuter, in Berlin, was in the "vanguard of the revolution." But he broke with the Communists in the early 1920s, as
true socialist intellectuals always seem to do, and joined the Social
Democratic Party. He entered the Berlin city administration and
wound up as a director of public utilities—experience that would
serve him well in the blockade days a quarter of a century later. In
1933, he was seized and imprisoned by the Nazis, along with
dozens of other Socialist leaders, but he was then released, somewhat surprisingly, in 1934. He left Germany and made his way to
Turkey, where he remained for the next thirteen years, teaching
school. Returning to Berlin in 1947, his political experience, his
intelligence, and his record quickly put him back in the top echelons of his old party. In June of that year, the Socialist-dominated
Berlin City Council, sitting in the Rathaus, in the Soviet sector,
elected him *Oberburgermeister*. But as an ex-Communist he was
anathema to the Russians, and they imposed a veto in the Allied
Kommandatura to prevent his taking office.

The Socialists on the City Council responded by blocking the
election of a Communist candidate, and as a result when the
blockade began, there were two "acting mayors," dividing the job.
Reuter had an office in the City Hall, and as the leader of the Social Democrats he was the dominant figure on the council floor.
The Soviets could veto him, but they could not get rid of him.
There are no fighters against communism to equal ex-Com-
munists, who understand the mentality and know all the tactics,

and the Russians had good reason not to want to see Reuter mayor of greater Berlin. He was sixty years old at the time, a man with a long, lean face and sad eyes, rather like a bloodhound, habitually wearing a black beret, which became his personal trademark. He was altogether a more sympathetic and philosophical man than Adenauer, warmer, less distant and more human, a personality born out of an entirely different outlook, life and experience. For the Berliners, it was Reuter who infused the coming struggle with determination, courage and passion.

On June 25, the day after train traffic into the city was halted, the exchange of the new deutsche marks for the old reichsmarks began in the Western sectors of Berlin at 7 A.M. The Russians swiftly completed the rest of the blockade measures, cutting off food shipments from their occupation zone into West Berlin, milk in particular, halting barge and river traffic and blocking the last road access between the city and the outside world. But they could not block the air lanes without shooting down planes, and these began to roar into Tempelhof and Gatow and Tegel airfields in a tempo that literally increased by the hour. Nor did the Russians then halt intercity traffic between East and West Berlin—that was to come thirteen years later, when they built the infamous Berlin Wall. But on July 1, they declared the Allied Kommandatura to be dissolved, using as the final excuse the introduction of the Western currency into the American, British, and French sectors of the city.

On that day of the Berlin drama, the Allied military governors left the city and flew to Frankfurt, where they had summoned the minister-presidents of the eleven separate West German *Länder* (states) for a meeting of decisive importance to Germany's future. They handed the Germans three documents, which had been drafted by a six-nation conference that had met in London during May and June. Taking part in the London conference were America, Britain and France, along with the three Benelux countries, which also had a vital interest in Germany's future. One document dealt with some problems of boundary revisions among the West German states. The second was an outline of certain "reserve powers" which the occupation authorities intended to go on exercising in the Western zones. And finally, the third and by far the most important was an invitation to the minister-presidents to organize and convene a constituent assembly to draft a new democratic constitution for a West German federal state, which would then take over all the powers and administration not reserved by the allies. They asked that the assembly be convened by September 1 and complete its work by the end of 1948. This vital business out of the way, the military governors flew back to the Berlin crisis.

As a first step, the eleven minister-presidents set up a working party of law professors and constitutional experts from various German courts and universities to sketch the outlines of a constitution. They then held a preparatory meeting with these experts for two weeks in mid-August at the vacation resort of Herrenchiemsee, a large lake in Bavaria east of Munich. At this meeting they decided to set up a "Parliamentary Council" of sixty-five members to be selected by the state parliaments on an arbitrary seat allocation of twenty-seven Christian Democrats, twenty-seven Social Democrats, five Free Democrats and two delegates each from the Communist Party, the Catholic Center Party and the right-wing German Party.

In order to remove the constitutional deliberations as far as possible from the physical and psychological presence of the occupation authorities, the German leaders ruled out meeting in Frankfurt and decided to convene the Parliamentary Council in Bonn. There the delegates gathered in September in a white modernistic building on the banks of the Rhine that had housed a teacher-training college. Today it remains the home of the West German Bundestag.

Adenauer, as a party leader who held no public office, played no direct role in these preliminaries, but he had no trouble making his views known and felt, and his influence was certainly clear in the selection of Bonn instead of some equally available town in Bavaria or Baden or Westphalia or Hanover.

In the three years following his dismissal from Cologne City Hall, Adenauer had worked quietly, steadily, tirelessly to gather into his hands the reins of leadership of the Christian Democratic Party. At the outset he had a deft tactic of using even his age to further his objectives. He would turn up for meetings, affable and patriarchal, and then when proceedings were about to begin he would slide into the chair and announce briskly that since he was elder to everybody else present in both age and past political service in Germany he assumed there was no opposition to his presiding. There seldom was. He also had won an important early tactical victory in the CDU by maneuvering an agreement among its leaders to remove the party headquarters from Berlin to Düsseldorf. Berlin was not only deep inside Soviet territory, but it was also dominated by the Social Democrats—and of course it was Prussian. For Adenauer these were all good reasons to anchor the CDU in West Germany. Meanwhile he had made several trips abroad to modest European political gatherings, and in May of 1948, just before the blockade, he led the German delegation to a big European congress at The Hague, where he met Winston Churchill, Paul-Henri Spaak and others with whom he would soon be working. It was this congress that launched the creation of the Council of Europe, in Strasbourg.

When the Parliamentary Council convened on Adenauer's home territory, in Bonn, he again automatically took over the presiding officer's chair—this time by virtue of the fact that he was the only delegate who had been a member of the old Prussian State Diet, the upper chamber of the Weimar legislature before democracy was wiped out by Hitler.

As Adenauer moved to the political helm in West Germany at the beginning of September, Reuter faced his biggest test and finest hour in Berlin. Although the Allied Kommandatura was dead, and with it any four-power administration of the city, the Berlin City Council was still in being in the Soviet sector of the city, with its big Social Democratic majority. But tensions were escalating daily in the city. The tempo of the airlift mounted, and the West Berliners refused utterly to knuckle under to Russian threats or enticements—no matter how far they had to tighten belts to live on meager handouts. As the U. S. Air Force flew in C-54 four-engine workhorse transports from all around the globe to feed Berlin, President Truman in July also ordered sixty B-29 bombers transferred from the United States to World War II air bases in Britain. Capable of delivering nuclear bombs to Soviet territory, they were an ample warning to Stalin that the Western Allies would not be forced out of Berlin. At the end of July in the city itself, the Western commandants took another essential step. They sanctioned the withdrawal of the West Berlin Police Force from the administrative control of a Communist police chief for all the city, who had been imposed on the City Council by the Russians early in the occupation. In this situation, city-wide government of greater Berlin clearly was not going to last much longer.

In the early days of September, Reuter went to see Colonel Howley to warn that it looked as though the Communists were about to force a complete disruption of the City Council in the Soviet sector—and in such an event could the democratic rump of the city government set up in West Berlin? Howley (perhaps with his own experience of June 16 in the Allied Kommandatura in mind) told Reuter that the Social Democrats should stick it out and make sure that the onus for any breakup of the city government would lie clearly with the Communists. Howley later had doubts about the wisdom of his advice, as this clearly risked that the Soviet authorities might simply seize and imprison all the Social Democrats when the City Council next met. In any event, the die was cast, and Reuter and his fellow party members were not lacking in courage. The City Council was to meet on September 6, and as it assembled, a Communist mob was turned loose on the Rathaus, whipped to a frenzy of violence on party orders. Rioters broke through the thin police ranks, stormed the building, burst into the assembly chamber and with brute force broke up the meeting. Reuter and the Social Democrats stoically made their way out of this howling, jeering vicious mob and decamped to West Berlin. Meanwhile the Russians grabbed and jailed nineteen West-sector policemen who had crossed into the Soviet sector to protect the Social Democrats.

Three days later, on the afternoon of Thursday, September 9, a hot, sunny day, the city fathers of West Berlin staged an enormous rally in front of the destroyed shell of the old Reichstag Building, in the Tiergarten, at the edge of the Soviet sector. The British had secretly deployed a heavily armed battalion of the Royal Norfolk Regiment in the building in case of trouble from the Soviet side. A vast throng of three hundred thousand Berliners gathered to hear

Reuter declare from the steps of the Reichstag like some impassioned apostle:

"We cannot be bartered, we cannot be negotiated, we cannot be sold. Whoever would surrender this city, whoever would surrender the people of Berlin, would surrender a world. More, he would surrender himself. On this day, if they could, the people of Leipzig, of Chemnitz, of Dresden, of Weimar, of all the cities in the East Zone, would stand like us in their public squares and listen to our voices. People of the world, look upon this city! You cannot, you must not forsake us! There is only one possibility for all of us: to stand jointly together until this fight has been won."

It was the seventy-fifth day of the airlift, and as Reuter spoke, a record 3,392 tons of food, coal and other supplies landed at Tempelhof. American technical competence and organizational genius under a new airlift commander, Major General William Tunner, were rapidly overcoming the difficulties and dispelling the doubts about sustaining two million people with airplanes—doubts that General Clay and even senior Air Force commanders had openly expressed when the airlift began. By October the daily average coming into the city had risen to 4,000 tons. By November 5, the cumulative total reached 300,000 tons, and by December 15 it was 640,000 tons. In January the daily average passed 6,000 tons despite appalling weather and then rose to 8,000 tons in April and hit high figures above 9,000 tons daily during May as the end finally neared.

After the breakup of the City Council, Reuter moved into offices in the Rathaus in the West Berlin borough of Schöneberg, and a separate city administration for the British, French and American sectors quickly took shape. On December 5, 1948, West Berliners went to the polls to elect new city councilors. It was supposed to have been a city-wide election, scheduled before the blockade began, but the Russians were taking no chances with the voters of East Berlin and they had canceled the election in their city sector. A vast Soviet propaganda campaign was mounted to disrupt the election: posters warning that "those who vote will be noted," and threats of dire consequences to the life of the city, which the Russians were now clearly failing to strangle. This attempt at intimidation also failed totally. Of the registered electorate, 86 percent turned out to cast ballots, on a cold, dull, damp Sunday. The Social Democrats under Reuter's leadership captured 64 percent of the vote. Democratic government had a clear mandate, and democratic will had been firmly expressed and established in West Berlin as the city settled down to the harsh test of winter weather and a grim and uncertain future.

Stalin's power play had failed, but how long would it be before he shifted ground or pulled back? The blockade ground remorselessly on, but an Allied counterblockade against all trade with the Soviet bloc was making itself felt in the economic conditions of 1948. The Western Allies made several attempts at direct contact with Stalin and Molotov in Moscow, and at the United Nations General Assembly, which met that year in Paris, but the only basis for ending the blockade amounted to capitulation. Then, in January of 1949, a chink of light appeared in the tunnel. In those days, one of the ways of getting occasional information out of the Kremlin was to write a letter to Stalin. He seldom answered, but when he did it was almost always for some significant political or propaganda purpose. Kingsbury Smith, then the European manager of the Hearst International News Service, sent off one of these routine missives with some questions about the blockade that Stalin clearly wanted to answer. The answers came back on January 31, 1949—and the most significant aspect of the replies lay not in what he said but in what he did *not* say.

He did not reiterate a demand that the Western powers withdraw their new, Western currency from Berlin, which had been the Soviet excuse for the blockade in the first place. Ignoring the currency issue, Stalin said that the blockade could be lifted if the Allied counterblockade was lifted at the same time and if the Allies agreed not to proceed with forming a West German government pending another meeting of the defunct Council of Foreign Ministers. At the State Department, Charles E. Bohlen, the Soviet-affairs adviser, told Secretary of State Dean Acheson at once that this could be a signal but would have to be explored very carefully and secretly. Acheson began the probe by telling a press conference three days later that "I hope the press will not take it amiss if I point out that if I on my part were seeking to give assurances of seriousness of purpose I would choose some other channel than the channel of a press statement." Next, the American ambassador to the United Nations, Philip Jessup, was called to Washington to be briefed alone by Acheson and Bohlen, to avoid any transmission in writing of the instructions for the next move. He was told to make a completely casual approach to the Soviet representative at the UN, Jacob Malik, and ask in an offhanded way if the omission by Stalin of the currency question had been intentional and whether it had any significance. On February 15, Jessup found his moment to catch Malik "accidentally" in the delegates' lounge at the old UN Headquarters at Lake Success, on Long Island. (It was not in the men's room, as was later reported.) Malik said he did not know whether the omission had been intentional or not. Jessup said that if Malik found out anything he would be grateful if he would pass it on. For some weeks, nothing happened, and Jessup was transferred to Washington as ambassador-at-large. Then, in mid-March, he got a telephone call from the Soviet Mission in New York asking him to come up to see Malik. No, Malik said, the omission was not accidental. Thus the secret channel was opened to Stalin for negotiations to bring the blockade to an end.

But if Stalin had given up on the currency question, it was a tactical shift to try to achieve the same strategic objective: a disruption of Allied plans and policies for reviving West Germany, while he, of course, would proceed with his own integration of East Germany into the Soviet system. Stalin's policy was still "hunger, poverty, desperation and chaos," which the Marshall Plan was fighting. Had the Western Allies accepted his new price for lifting the blockade, and suspended the constitutional deliberations in Bonn, they would have been walking right back into the same trap or dead end of the Potsdam era. They would have been handing back to Stalin the power to veto or disrupt what they were attempting to achieve in the Western occupation zones. This, Dean Acheson, Bohlen and company were not about to do.

The Jessup-Malik talks were still a closely held secret even from the Western Allies when Malik flatly asked, in the second exchange they held, toward the end of March, that the Bonn deliberations be suspended as a price for lifting the blockade. Jessup simply replied smoothly that the constitutional preparations would

take some time anyway, and that therefore there would be no *fait
accompli* and no bar to a prompt lifting of the blockade while proceeding with a Foreign Ministers meeting, if the Russians meant
business.

In Bonn, under Adenauer's chairmanship, the Parliamentary
Council was indeed making haste slowly, but it was not entirely
the fault of the Germans. The original deadline of the end of the
year for completing work, which the Allied military governors had
fixed when they gave the green light on establishing the council,
had long since passed. But the Allies themselves had not yet
agreed on the exact terms of the "occupation statute" concerning
the reserve powers they would continue to hold, which was supposed to be promulgated simultaneously with the new federal constitution. So the Germans were working in at least half-dark.

Moreover there were tedious differences among the Allies (with
the French often being legalistically difficult) over the division of
powers between the states and the central government in the new
federal system. The French, of course, wanted to limit strong central government in Germany, and this extended into such matters
as the banking system, collection and division of tax revenues,
budgeting and finance. Allied liaison officers kept a discreet but
constant watch on the Bonn deliberations, and Adenauer and
other party leaders conferred frequently with the military governors along the way. It was a slow process, and on top of this there
was a fair share of disruptive tactics from the Communist delegates in Bonn.

The Allied foreign ministers gathered in Washington in early
April for a meeting of historic importance. The first order of busi-
ness was the signing of the North Atlantic Treaty, on April 4,
1949, by twelve states of Western Europe and North America: the
United States, Canada, Britain, France, Italy, Norway, Denmark,
Belgium, the Netherlands, Luxembourg, Portugal and Iceland.
(Greece, Turkey and West Germany joined later.)

The NATO treaty signing was a potent message to Stalin that
the blockade could not halt the building of recovery and mutual security in the West. Acheson next moved in secret talks with
Bevin and Robert Schuman (who had replaced Georges Bidault at
the Quai d'Orsay) to speed things up in West Germany. He in-

formed them of the secret Jessup-Malik exchanges, and they all agreed on the necessity for a three-power message to Stalin, via Malik, accepting a foreign ministers' meeting to discuss Germany but again refusing to suspend the Bonn deliberations. Stalin was to be given no opportunity to try to play the Allies off, one against the other. Next, they agreed on a simplified and more liberal version of the occupation statute. This was duly transmitted to Germany and handed to Adenauer and the Parliamentary Council on April 10—the same day the three-power message went to Stalin.

With this firm demonstration of Allied resolution, events moved to a climax. In Bonn, the tempo picked up in the Parliamentary Council. Some key differences between the Allies and the Germans were worked out, in Germany's favor, and article-by-article approval of the 147-article constitution draft got underway. On April 25, from Tass came an announcement of the readiness of the Soviet Union to lift the blockade in return only for a meeting of foreign ministers—no scuttling of the Bonn constitution. Jessup and Malik now got together to work out final details and quickly agreed that all road, rail and barge traffic into Berlin would be lifted in two weeks, on May 12. The Allied counterblockade would be lifted at the same time. It would be back to *status quo ante,* but with the city divided. The blockade lasted six weeks short of a full year and cost the American and British governments an estimated $200 million. If it ended in a stalemate, it is difficult to see what more could peacefully have been won.

In Bonn, toward midnight on May 8, 1949, the fourth anniversary of the unconditional surrender of the Third Reich, the Basic Law, as the constitution was termed, for a new German Federal Republic was voted by the Parliamentary Council, 53–12. The military governors gave it their formal approval on May 12, the day the blockade was lifted, and at the same time, they promulgated the new occupation statute, which defined the powers the Allies would continue to exercise when the new government was formed, and took over responsibility for internal affairs.

Thus, the Bonn constitution was a *fait accompli* by the time the Big Four foreign ministers met in Paris on May 23. Stalin had been outmaneuvered, to a large degree by his own ruthlessness. The Paris talks lasted a futile six weeks and produced, as the Allies intended, nothing but an uneasy *modus vivendi*. Democratic govern-

ment, economic recovery and Western security would go forward
in Bonn and West Berlin unimpeded by any hamstringing agreements with the Soviets.

At the Helmstedt checkpoint, on the autobahn to Berlin,
promptly at 12:01 A.M. on Tuesday, May 12, a grinning Russian
soldier raised the barrier across the highway in the glare of camera
floodlights as casually as if he had been doing it every day for a
year. A gaggle of newsmen set out in a wild automobile race to be
the first into the city. It was won by Walter Rundel, of United
Press, who covered the 110 miles in one hour and forty-six minutes and was pelted with flowers when he crossed the line, as if he
had won the Monte Carlo rally. It was my good fortune to have
been transferred from London in late April to a new assignment
as correspondent in West Germany for the New York *Herald
Tribune.* I boarded the first American military train to clear the
Helmstedt checkpoint that night and rode into Berlin and into a
new era in Germany.

The great Berlin drama was over, although it was another twenty-
three years before the Russians finally agreed to negotiate a
formal four-power accord on access to the city, which was
completed and signed in 1972. Minor Soviet harassment of West
Berlin continues even to this day. But, with the end of the blockade, the Allied presence in the city was firmly fixed for all time.
The political focus in Germany now swung to Bonn and the creation of the West German state.

Immediately after the constitution was voted, Adenauer won his
first political victory of the new era with a vote by the Parliamentary Council to put the capital permanently in Bonn. The only
other city in the running was Frankfurt, but Adenauer got a large
assist from the British authorities, who announced that if the capital was placed in Bonn, in their zone, they would withdraw all occupation forces and personnel from the city and derequisition the
property they held there for the benefit of the new government.
The Americans were not about to move out of their headquarters,
in the Farben Building, in Frankfurt. So Bonn it was, a pleasant
provincial university town lying hot and humid in the summer on
the banks of the Rhine.

West Germany went to the polls on August 14, 1949, for its first national election since 1934, and out of an electorate of approximately 32 million voters, an astounding 79 percent turned out to cast democratic ballots. The Social Democrats, with the cachet of their strength and success in Berlin, entered the campaign strong and confident, and the outcome was fairly close. But the Christian Democrats and their Bavarian wing, the Christian Socialists, emerged with 7.36 million votes, against 6.93 million for the Social Democrats, and this translated into 139 Bundestag seats against 131. The remainder of the 402 seats in the lower house of the new legislature were divided among seven parties, ranging from the liberal Free Democrats to the Communists on the left and the German Party on the ultra right.

One week later, Adenauer convened an informal meeting of CDU/CSU party leaders at his home at Rhöndorf for a discussion on forming a government. His own mind was made up: he wanted an undiluted coalition of the parties to the right, leaving the Social Democrats in undiluted opposition on the left. But he ran into strong and logical counterarguments from Peter Altmeier, minister-president of Rhineland-Palatinate, in the French occupation zone, who held that it was vital to tie the Social Democrats into government decision-making. Otherwise, he said, they would be using nationalist arguments to attack every agreement or understanding that the government made with the occupying powers as being insufficient and no good. This would not only put the CDU/CSU constantly on the defensive; it would be politically unwise for the German people.

Adenauer countered: "There is a great difference of principles between ourselves and the Social Democrats and there is an unbridgeable gap in the matter of economic structure. There can be a planned economy or a social market economy. The two will not mix. We could never get things moving. We have got to steer a steady course. Only then can there be a good parliamentary opposition."

Adenauer then sketched out how a rightist coalition could be put together with the Free Democrats and the German Party with a solid, 208-seat working majority. The informal caucus agreed that the leader of the Free Democrats, Professor Theodor Heuss, would make a suitable president of the new Federal Republic, and there was little doubt who should be the coalition Chancellor. The new Bundestag gathered in Bonn on September 7 and first elected its speaker and then Heuss as Federal President. The election of the Federal Chancellor was held on September 15, and Adenauer took office by the narrowest of margins: only one vote—his own. Asked later if he voted for himself, he replied: "Naturally. Anything else would have been hypocrisy."

Adenauer in a way was fortunate in the personality of the opposition leader of that time, Dr. Kurt Schumacher. As a result of twelve years in Hitler's concentration camps, Schumacher had lost an arm and a leg on opposite sides of his gaunt frame. His political makeup was a strange mixture of intense German nationalism interwoven into his own view of how Social Democracy should bring Germany a new future. He was neither adroit nor flexible, nor very self-controlled. It was as if he were constantly stoking fires of burning emotion in what was left of his wracked body. In fact, whatever the philosophical political reasons that Adenauer voiced against a "grand coalition," it is impossible to see how he and Schumacher could ever have worked in harness to run a government. Schumacher died in 1952, leaving a curious record of having opposed to the hilt both the challenges of Stalin and the Communists and all the steps Adenauer took to regain West German sovereignty and integrate the Federal Republic into the West.

True to Altmeier's forecast, Schumacher's politics consisted of little more than blind, nationalistic, breast-beating opposition to practically everything Adenauer produced out of negotiations with the Western Allies. Dean Acheson visited the new West German capital in November 1949, soon after the government was formed, and he subsequently summarized his meeting with Schumacher: "He at once launched into an unrestrained attack against Adenauer, who he apparently hated, on the grounds that Adenauer was working smoothly with the British, American and French occupation authorities. I pointed out what immense benefits this had brought to the German people, and wondered what sensible alternative he thought possible. Apparently the Russians were to be induced to reunite Eastern and Western Germany by a German policy of aloofness to the west, which almost ten years later became known as disengagement—the removal of all foreign troops from the soil of a neutralized Germany. The clear demonstration that the Soviet Union was not prepared to make any agreement about Germany which would weaken Soviet control in the Eastern zone was immaterial to him. I broke off this futile interview as soon as politeness permitted."

Of course with an opposition leader like Schumacher, the Allied high commissioners (no longer military governors after the Bonn government was formed) gave thanks regularly that political fortune had given them Adenauer to work with. Not that Adenauer was any pushover, for he showed himself from the first to be a formidable negotiator of phenomenal staying power for a man of seventy-three. He was clear about broad objectives, the first of which was to bring the occupation status of West Germany to an end as rapidly as possible and restore full sovereignty to the Bonn government. This required concessions by the Allies, which meant confidence in Adenauer—and it did Adenauer no political harm to have Schumacher as the "democratic alternative" in unbridled opposition.

Within three months after the Bonn government was formed, Adenauer was well on his way to achieving his political goals for the new state. The first big fundamental problem to be resolved between the Allies and the West Germans was the old Potsdam policy, still being carried out, of dismantling German heavy industrial plant for reparations and on security grounds. By this time, with the Marshall Plan in full swing, there was something obviously contradictory about pumping money into West German recovery at one end while cutting up and destroying Germany's productive capacity at the other. In November 1949, the Allies therefore proposed a bargain: an agreement to cut the list of plants to be dismantled and bring it all to a prompt halt in return for voluntary acceptance by the Germans of certain security restrictions and production limits. As part of the agreement, the Bonn government would be permitted to join the Marshall Plan organization in Paris as a full member, to join the Council of Europe in Strasbourg, and to open consular offices in Paris, London and Washington as a first step toward diplomatic sovereignty.

Generous as the Allied offer seemed to the Allies, the only
thing the Germans could focus on was the number of factories
that would still be dismantled and the security restrictions they
were being asked to accept. It was therefore a very tough negotiation, in which Adenauer fought long and hard, telling the high
commissioners: "I'm not only anxious to have my actions approved by a majority in parliament. I'm even more anxious to
have the support of the majority of the German people, and you
are asking of us some very heavy things to carry." To which the
French high commissioner, André François-Poncet, responded
with a heavy sigh: "It is a very hard task making presents to the
Germans and a very thankless task." But in the end it was done
and approved despite a riotous scene in the Bundestag staged by
Schumacher.

The next big breakthrough for Adenauer came only six months
later, in May of 1950, when French Foreign Minister Robert
Schuman, at the instigation of Jean Monnet, launched his historic
plan for the pooling of the entire coal and steel industry of Western Europe under the direction and control of a single supranational high authority. Here at last was the true basis for historic
Franco-German *rapprochement,* which Adenauer had been waiting for ever since the First World War. He saw at once that this
was the great leap across the pettifogging gulf of nationalist revanchist political attitudes about security, level of industry, balance of
power, and all the rest. Above all, it was a way around the Saar
problem, for at that time the future of that wretched little industrial valley was the biggest single bar to any kind of real Franco-
German understanding. Moreover, the French invitation to West
Germany to join the Schuman Plan meant that the Federal Republic would take its place as a sovereign power at a negotiating table
in Europe immediately, even though sovereignty was still in the
distance. Adenauer embraced the Schuman Plan at once.

In June of 1950, war broke out in Korea. In an instant, the perilous condition of Europe's defenses became a matter of urgency,
and with it the question of German rearmament. Just as it was impossible to create a prosperous Europe with Germany wallowing
in economic depression in the middle, neither could Germany be
omitted from any effective system of Western defenses. No

amount of hand-wringing or historic emotion about German militarism could change the problem. The basis for a security system was firmly established in the North Atlantic Treaty, and the United States was ready to put its weight behind establishing a Supreme Allied Headquarters and was prepared to send General of the Army Dwight D. Eisenhower back to Europe to take command. But Washington insisted that a way must be found quickly for Germany to be rearmed and play her fair share and role. In principle, this was agreed by the Allies, but in fact it was five years before a German put on a uniform.

The French, as a means of containing this traumatic prospect, came up with the concept of creating a European army, to which the Germans would contribute units no larger than brigades, which would be mixed up with formations of other Europeans and never come under German independent command. It was a kind of military counterpart to the Schuman Plan for coal and steel. But coal and steel are inanimate, and armies are not. A European-army treaty was negotiated by the end of 1951, and then endless foot-dragging on ratification ensued in Paris as one Fourth Republic government succeeded another. General Charles de Gaulle pronounced his total opposition from sulky retirement at Colombey-les-Deux-Églises, and it is debatable whether any French government could have mustered votes for its passage. In any case, when Pierre Mendès-France became Premier, in 1954, he first extricated France from its plight in Indochina and then finally ended the long hiatus over the European army by standing aside and letting the National Assembly kill the treaty.

John Foster Dulles had become American Secretary of State, and he had openly threatened "agonizing reappraisal" of America's defense commitment to Europe if the treaty was not approved. Britain's Anthony Eden then stepped into the breach, and in the finest achievement of his long career, seized the moment to catch the French on a kind of diplomatic rebound and get their agreement to limited rearmament of Germany without the European-army features, by bringing Bonn into the Western European Union, which had been Ernest Bevin's creation in 1946. At the same time, West Germany would also be admitted to full membership in NATO. It was altogether a more sensible and workable solution than the European army. Meanwhile, the Western Allies gave up their last residual occupation powers, replacing them with a series of "contractual agreements" by the Bonn government. They then declared an end to the occupation status of West Germany in April 1955.

In six short years, Konrad Adenauer had transformed West Germany from a defeated nation into a respected ally and key member of the Atlantic Community. On foreign policy questions in the 1950s, he lined up solidly behind Dulles on East-West matters while playing wholeheartedly the role of a constructive European integrationist.

Moreover, the stability of government at the top in Bonn was steadily translated into a growing stability of voting patterns from one election to the next. The multiplicity of nine political parties and four independent members elected to the Bundestag in 1949 shook down to six parties in the election of 1953, four parties in 1957, and three parties ever since 1961: the CDU/CSU, the Social Democrats and the Free Democrats. As Adenauer had foreseen, by avoiding the false allure of a grand coalition, democracy in West Germany steadily matured into the most stable of all systems: a strong government with a strong opposition as a democratic alternative.

The last act of Adenauer's remarkable octogenarian service to Germany was fitting to his entire life: the signing in Paris with President Charles de Gaulle of the Franco-German Treaty of Friendship and Cooperation, on January 22, 1963. The fact that the treaty was deliberately timed by General de Gaulle as an act of maximum confusion and consternation to the United States and the rest of Europe should not in the end obscure its fundamental importance. De Gaulle, at a famous press conference the week before the treaty was signed, had vetoed British entry into the European Common Market and rejected overtures from President John F. Kennedy for cooperation in the field of strategic nuclear weapons. Therefore, coming at this juncture, the Franco-German treaty looked suspiciously like some kind of cornerstone for a Gaullist "grand design" for Europe, to replace the Atlantic Alliance with a purely continental system built around French leadership. Something along these lines was certainly in the General's mind, but it didn't work out that way with the Germans, and de Gaulle was soon sulking and complaining about lack of response to his leadership in Bonn.

For Adenauer, the treaty with France was the culmination of efforts to wipe clean a century of tragic Franco-German history, to which he had been a lifetime witness. He did not see it as replacing or superseding Germany's other interests and commitments—but de Gaulle did, and was open in his resentment that the Bonn government continued to place its relations with Washington as high as if not higher than its relations with Paris. In any case, the treaty existed, and long after both Adenauer and de Gaulle had disappeared from the scene, the fundamental amity between the two nations finally came into its own when Valéry Giscard d'Estaing became President of France and Helmut Schmidt became Chancellor of West Germany.

Adenauer had just passed his eighty-seventh birthday when he came to Paris for the treaty signing, in 1963. Younger men were restive and more than ready to see him out of office, and the election of 1961 had fundamentally shifted the balance of forces in the Bundestag and undermined his grip on the reins of power. In order to remain Chancellor after his fourth election campaign, Adenauer had been forced to give a pledge in writing to the coalition partners that he would go at the end of two years, halfway through the life of the 1961 Bundestag. In October of 1963, to his visible and painful resentment, the political promissory note was presented for payment. His going was not his most dignified hour, and his treatment of his successor, Ludwig Erhard, was considerably less than generous or gracious.

From a suite of offices in the Bundestag, he dispensed interviews and wisdom and recollections and wrote his memoirs and kept up a stream of caustic comments on how things were being run by his successors. He died on April 19, 1967, three months into his ninety-second year. Statesmen came from all over the Western world to attend his funeral at Cologne Cathedral.

In West Germany today it can well be said of Konrad Adenauer, as is said of Sir Christopher Wren on the walls of St. Paul's Cathedral, in London: "If you would see his monument, look around."

5
Jean Monnet

AMONG THE MEN WHO HAVE MOLDED THE HISTORY OF WESTERN Europe since World War II, Jean Monnet is unique. He never exercised high political power, and he was never a cabinet minister or even a member of a legislature. A complete internationalist among Frenchmen, he never belonged to a political party, never ran for public office, never was elected to anything. He was not a trained economist and never even went to a university. He was not a civil servant; he was not a career diplomat. In fact, in a tremendously active and varied and independent life on three continents, switching back and forth between private business and public affairs, Monnet seldom remained in any one place or at any one task for more than three or four years. Yet he had a personal impact and left his particular stamp of success everywhere he went and on practically everything he did, and his influence on history at key times and in key places across nearly three quarters of this century was remarkable.

"First have an idea, then look for the man who can put it to work," Monnet wrote in his *Memoirs*. "Sometimes there have to be intermediaries, who may well be little known, although they are very much aware of the responsibilities they are taking on. Each time that I personally have been convinced of the need for action, I have proposed it to men in power, leaving them to take the political responsibility and reap the reward. Men in power are short of new ideas. They lack the time and the information. And they want to do good so long as they get credit for it."

Yet, to picture Jean Monnet or to think of him simply as the Western world's most successful *éminence grise* is to miss completely the quality of the man: his personality, his intellect, his vision, his mind, his conversation, his forcefulness with its mixture of assertiveness and selflessness, his human understanding, his integrity, his strength, his greatness.

Of course everybody from journalists and editorial writers to corporation executives and think-tank directors has ideas to thrust at men of power. What, then, was unique about Jean Monnet? In the first place, there was the quality, one might almost say the purity, of his ideas. He did not peddle petty proposals. He concentrated on global solutions to fundamental problems, and when he proposed an idea it automatically required attention—it would not go away, it would not lie down, it could not be dismissed. Monnet himself constantly contrived to see that his ideas stayed alive in men's minds until they got action. He was self-effacing, but also the most persistent of men. He was both patient and incisive in argument and discussion, and never superficial. More often than not, his big proposals were simple and obvious, but, then, great ideas are usually like swords cutting Gordian knots. The Marshall Plan was a simple idea and so was the Schuman Plan. It is the empirical quality of simple proposals that gives them force, and Monnet always put forward his ideas with a great distillation of practical experience, logic, close examination of hard facts, a wealth of preliminary exploration and political wisdom, and finally a careful sense of timing. Politicians faced with new proposals usually do not worry much about how good they are but whether they will work—and Monnet seldom made a suggestion without at the same time charting how it could be made to work. To do this, he drew on a lifetime of meeting and working with people all over the world.

He was equally at home in Paris, London and Washington, and he probably commanded the widest international circle of acquaintances, contacts, associates, admirers and close friends of any man of his time. He drew from everybody, just as he gave, and he would prepare his ground carefully and reconnoiter his support thoroughly. A man of independent though modest means, he traveled constantly to corridors of power everywhere, wherever the pursuit of his ideas took him. Doors were open to him, and he was listened to not only for what he had to propose but also for

what else he had to say, the pleasure of his mind and his company
—and because his advice was independent and disinterested.

For the last twenty years of his active life, no longer holding
any public function, Monnet acted as a kind of one-man catalyst
and lobbyist to speak for Europe. He formed a remarkable multinational, multiparty organization of European political leaders
and trade unionists, a group of men at the top, which he kept
small and elite, called the Action Committee for the United States
of Europe. He directed its affairs from an apartment-office at the
end of the Avenue Foch, overlooking the Bois de Boulogne. From
here the telephone calls would go out to London, Brussels, Bonn,
The Hague, Rome, Washington, to friends and supporters behind
the scenes in de Gaulle's France. Visitors would arrive from all
over Europe and from across the Atlantic, and Monnet would talk
and listen and ponder and reflect—always seeking to fit the issues
and problems of the day into the advancement of the unending,
unfinished, permanent quest for the unity of Europe. Federalism
was his goal, and whatever he proposed or attempted was always
designed to build, step by step, a federated Europe.

"A federal authority of the mind" was how a French political
commentator described Monnet's Action Committee. It would
meet only once or maybe twice a year for no more than two days,
to discuss and approve working papers on specific goals or political proposals that Monnet would have worked out in careful advance preparation by telephone calls and endless back-and-forth
letters. These might concern some aspect of getting Britain into
Europe, action on Europe's agricultural problem, the development
of a European monetary system, direct election of a European
parliament, trade and economic relations with the United States, a
unified approach to the energy problem. Since the committee was
composed of men who were party leaders in home legislatures—
Socialists, Liberals, Christian Democrats, Conservatives, etc.—
its positions would then automatically translate into legislative support when governments were ready to act. Of course, getting
governments to act was another matter, a different problem—particularly when President Charles de Gaulle was dominating the
European scene. But Monnet used those fallow years to prepare

the ground ahead and mobilize parliamentary support in advance
each step of the way.

As European issues ebbed and flowed, like other journalists I
would periodically go to talk with Monnet at the Avenue Foch,
usually around five o'clock in the afternoon. He would settle in a
worn, comfortable little armchair, his back to a french window
opening out onto the trees, a late-afternoon sun often filling
the room. I would be motioned to a sofa to his right, and his faithful assistant of many years, Jacques van Helmont, usually took
another armchair. The conversation would open slowly. I would
bring up this or that current problem with the British or de Gaulle
or the Americans, and Monnet would respond briefly at first, tap-
ping the tips of his fingers, sometimes closing his eyes, and Van
Helmont would interject a remark to keep things moving. I had
learned from past sessions that this was not any indifference on
Monnet's part, but simply the care with which he collected his
thoughts for any visitor.

At the time of one of my visits, the British were involved in one
of their periodic arguments with the rest of the European Common Market members in Brussels—this time a demand that they
be allocated a far larger sum from Common Market funds for regional development of depressed areas of Britain than was available in the current budget. This meant that money would have to
be taken from other Common Market activities to give to the British, and this the other eight members were not prepared to do. At
one point the argument had seemed to threaten Britain's continued
presence in Brussels, and as we talked I remarked to Monnet: "I
don't see why the Common Market doesn't just go out and borrow
the money, sell bonds, and turn the proceeds over to the British.
They don't have to operate a balanced budget in Brussels, and the
Common Market ought to be a pretty good credit risk for any
investor. Anyway, debt was one of the things that unified the
American states."

Monnet's interest was instantly piqued, not by the idea of borrowing money to help the British but by my offhanded remark
about debt and the American states. What was this, he said, what
was I referring to? I said that I couldn't recall the details, but I did
know that Alexander Hamilton had insisted in the early days that

the federal government take over all the state debts of the former colonies, and this then became one of the great unifying forces of the federal system of the United States.

"Is it in *The Federalist Papers?*" Monnet asked, getting up to go to the phone. He spoke to his secretary, and a minute or two later a hefty volume of a French translation of that work was plunked down on the coffee table. "Find it," he said. I leafed through, looking at authors and dates, and realized that these had all been written before the American Constitution came into force and Hamilton's action would have come later. Well, said Monnet, where could I get more detail about this for him? I said that perhaps I had an American history at home that would help.

Next morning I dropped a history volume at the Avenue Foch. The story is a true vignette of the federal process at work. Early in 1790, Hamilton introduced in the First Congress, then meeting in New York, legislation to transfer the state debts to the federal government. But, in one of the early constitutional arguments over states' rights, he was opposed by the influential Virginians Thomas Jefferson and James Madison, and the bill was defeated. Hamilton persisted, perceiving clearly that there would be no strong central American government without federal control of the monetary system, of which borrowing was of course a key element. He embarked on a shrewd political deal with the Virginians to get his way. They wanted the federal capital to be placed permanently in Virginia, so Hamilton proposed to Jefferson that he would deliver the New York State votes to move the government to the banks of the Potomac if Jefferson would deliver Virginia's votes on a new bill, which he would reintroduce on taking over the state debts. Jefferson agreed and the deal was done. Debt was successfully used to strengthen the federal system, and the capital is in Washington, D.C.

The following week, I was in Brussels and went to see a friend on the British delegation to the Common Market to find out how things stood on the budget fight. In the original Schuman Plan treaty for the Coal and Steel Community, Monnet in fact had seen to it that there was provision for the High Authority of the new Community to issue bonds and borrow money to finance modernization and rationalization of Europe's heavy industry, but this had not been carried forward in the operations of the Common Market. I asked my British friend if any thought had been given to the possibility of solving the problem by borrowing, and he smiled and said: "Jean Monnet has been on the telephone all over Europe trying to sell that one. But as far as we are concerned it won't work, because the Common Market would simply borrow the money on the London market, and we want currency coming into Britain from the outside, across the foreign exchanges."

Nevertheless, somewhat later, when Britain's Roy Jenkins, a "Monnet man," left the Labour government to become president of the Common Market Commission, in Brussels, in 1977, one of the first things he began to press for was authority from governments to borrow money to finance Community development projects, instead of having to do it out of Community revenues. Much had changed economically for both Britain and Europe by that time, but it took Jenkins nearly eighteen months to convince governments that this was an equitable and practical way to proceed. The first borrowing was limited to $600 million, and the bonds were sold in Frankfurt, Amsterdam and elsewhere as well as on the London market. This has now become a regular, fixed Common Market practice for the benefit of Europe.

Jean Monnet was born in the town of Cognac on November 9, 1888. His grandfather had founded a brandy business early in the century, and J. G. Monnet was a respected and thriving house even though Cognac was (and still is) dominated by the big Martell and Hennessy interests. Cognac, as Monnet later wrote, was a town that had to look outward, to the markets of the world.

"We knew that our existence depended on the prosperity and the tastes of people all over the world. Our concerns took us a long way from Cognac; but never far from the cognac it produced. From the days of my childhood, while French society stagnated in its own parochialism, I was taught to realize that we lived in a world of vast distances, and it was natural for me to expect to meet people who spoke other languages and had different customs. To observe and take account of these customs was our daily necessity. But it did not make us feel different or dependent. We avoided the proud or defensive nationalistic reactions that were beginning to permeate French politics. In later years in my relations with other people, I have never had to fight against reflexes that I have never acquired. So my upbringing may have given me some aptitude for what I have done."

At the age of sixteen, not having done very well in school, which he did not like, Monnet decided that he did not want to face the chore of study for the second half of the famous *baccalauréat* examination, which all French students still take to be admitted to a university. Instead he asked his father if he could go straight into the family business. His father, a worldly man who spoke several languages and had traveled widely to build up Monnet sales, decided that his son should go immediately to London to master English. It was arranged for him to work a kind of office apprenticeship with a City financial house for two years. Monnet not only spoke English to perfection; André Fontaine, the editor of Le Monde, found that he was stronger in expressing himself in English, with more force and depth, than in his native French. He returned to Cognac at the age of eighteen, and then in 1906 he set out immediately for Canada and the American West. He sold Monnet cognac to the Hudson Bay Company ("we needed furs; the trappers liked cognac"), to railroad hotels along the Canadian Pacific, the Union Pacific and the Northern Pacific, to bars in San Francisco and Scandinavian immigrants in Minnesota and the Dakotas. Then he went to Sweden, to Russia, to Egypt, to Greece and often back to London.

By the time the First World War broke out, in August 1914, Monnet, not yet twenty-six, had behind him a wealth of travel and exceptional experience for any Frenchman. He had also acquired an abundance of worldly self-confidence, even brashness. He knew about business contracts, finance, prices, ships, markets, banking and trade, and he had absorbed with an open mind how other people perform and think and do business, the British in particular. Due to a kidney ailment, he was temporarily deferred from military call-up—but he was obsessed with a central idea that it would be necessary for France and Britain to organize their economic cooperation in order to win the war, and he was determined to find a way to serve.

Within two months, as the Kaiser's armies swept forward to the climactic Battle of the Marne, France lost two thirds of its iron and steel industry and half of its coal. The French Government, under Premier René Viviani, withdrew from Paris to Bordeaux. While these tumultuous events unfolded, twenty-six-year-old Jean Monnet squirmed and fretted in his native Cognac about the need to organize—in particular shipping, which was the key to everything from the price of wheat to the movement of troops. By chance a lawyer in Cognac who handled Monnet affairs was also a close personal friend of Viviani's, and he arranged a meeting between Monnet and the Premier in Bordeaux. Monnet recounted the highlights of their talk.

"We need to set up joint bodies to estimate the combined resources of the Allies, share them out, and share out the costs."

"But we already have machinery for inter-Allied cooperation, and I'm told that it works well."

"That's nothing more than a communications system. It doesn't take decisions or make choices. We're beginning to suffer from shortages, and we must devote our resources to the most rational ends. All our resources—our joint resources—it's this that is not understood. Allied solidarity must be total, neither side free to use its men, its supplies or its shipping in ways that haven't been agreed by both."

"I see what you mean—but you must realize that we are talking about two governments and two sovereign parliaments. Can you imagine these joint decisions being taken simultaneously?"

"I know the British well enough to be sure that we can reach a real agreement with them if we appeal to their loyalty and if we play fair."

Viviani was sufficiently impressed to send Monnet next to see the Minister of War, and in November 1914, he arrived in London as French member of an amorphous "International Supply Committee." But it was a place to begin.

The British, too, had produced a bright young man to work on supply problems, who was Monnet's exact contemporary: Arthur Salter, more conservative, less politically venturous and idealistic than Monnet, but no less convinced about the proper approach and the need for joint machinery to handle the mounting economic problems of the war effort. Together they made a highly effective behind-the-scenes Allied team, and formed a close personal friendship, which was renewed in action on the same supply problems all over again when the Second World War broke out, a quarter of a century later.

But it was the economic realities, rather than the logic and argument and persuasion of Monnet and Salter, that eventually forced the solution of a combined effort. First steps were taken with a wheat supply agreement—but the French continued to buy wheat on the world market for civilian needs and operated the purchase agreement only for military requirements. Price fluctuations and shipping problems remained. A sugar agreement came next, but, like the wheat agreement, it was only peripheral to the central problem, which was shipping. Things dragged on with half measures, half allocations, half determination and half success until 1917. In the first two years of the war, the Allies lost about 4 million tons of shipping to German submarines, but then, in 1917, after the United States entered the war and unrestricted torpedoing began in earnest, the loss soared to 6 million tons in the single year. It was now painfully clear that the only way to win the war was to pool Allied shipping. Once the ships were under central direction and control, it automatically followed that priorities and controls had to be established for the cargoes that went into them—in effect, economic direction of the entire war effort. It was finally done at a climactic conference at the Foreign Office in London in November, 1917—just in time to organize the ships for the flood of 2 million American doughboys who crossed the Atlantic to France before the guns fell silent, in November 1918.

By the end of 1917, Monnet, not yet thirty years old, was head of the London mission of the French Ministry of Commerce and Maritime Transport, and delegate in London of the French Ministry of Supply. And he was France's representative—as was Salter for the British—on the key Allied Maritime Transport Executive. As the war drew to a close, Monnet launched a brief but foredoomed effort to preserve and adapt the wartime machinery to the economic problems of the peace.

"The Armistice will find France and Belgium greatly weakened economically," he wrote in a minute to the French Government. "It would be a negation of our whole war effort and of the ideals for which we fought if we did not continue to put into practice the principles that have enabled the Allies to bring the struggle against the common enemy to a successful conclusion—mutual aid, the sharing-out of raw materials in proportion to the most urgent needs. Arbitration and unity are two essential elements in the present economic order, in which goods and transport are deployed not in accordance with legal ownership, but under agreements ensuring that recognized needs are met as of right."

Whatever the logic of Monnet's views, they were much too far in advance of the times and much too at odds with traditional American thinking and *laissez-faire* outlook to stand any chance of winning general Allied acceptance. The Americans could see nothing in this approach but a ruse that would strengthen British dominance of world shipping and raw-materials markets. They abruptly withdrew from all the Allied economic cooperation groups two months after the end of the war, declaring the American objective to be that "prewar methods of trade should be restored as soon as possible."

The war was over, and the threat to survival which had brought the Allies together no longer operated. No less than the Americans, the British—and indeed the French, apart from Monnet and a few likeminded men—wanted a return to the traditional outlook of sovereign nations, and no politician anywhere in Europe was tempted to see things Monnet's way or take up his ideas about organizing the economics of the peace. It would be another thirty years and another World War before Europe would be receptive and ready for such an effort. But, as Monnet has remarked: "I can wait a long time for the right moment. In Cognac they are good at waiting. It is the only way to make a good brandy."

The Allied Supreme Economic Council held its last meeting in London in April 1919, but Monnet was not long without public duties. In Paris, President Woodrow Wilson was busily constructing the League of Nations at the Crillon Hotel, and in July, Prime Minister Georges Clemenceau asked Monnet to join the League's embryo international staff as deputy to its British secretary-general, Sir Eric Drummond. He was chosen due to his inter-Allied wartime experiences in London. Not only was the League a new institution, with no previous guidelines of either organization or action; it was also crippled from the outset by the abrupt withdrawal of the Americans when the League treaty failed in the United States Senate—and it became a kind of wastepaper basket for the festering sores of the aftermath of the First World War: The Silesian question between Poland and Germany, the Saar question between France and Germany, the Danzig question, problems of artificially reshaped countries such as Czechoslovakia and Austria, currency problems exacerbated by reparations and inflation with no international monetary system. When statesmen failed—and rampant nationalism made failures inevitable—they "referred it to the League" as a reflex, which in practice meant the League's small, hard-working Secretariat.

Monnet remained at the League, in Geneva, only two years, but in that brief and crowded span he played an instrumental organizing role behind the scenes in evolving the League solutions for the Silesian dispute, the Saar problem, and the free-city constitution for Danzig. But then, of course, Hitler went to war over Danzig. Poland finally achieved its territorial ambition by annexing the Silesian territory after World War II. The Saar problem continued to bedevil Franco-German relations until Monnet solved it once and for all with the Schuman Plan. Intensive and absorbing as his period with the League was, he simply did not take to the League's abstractions, its lack of any firm mandate or authority, the necessity to seek power from diverse and competing governments to accomplish the most obvious tasks. In 1921 his family asked him to return to Cognac.

His father had aged—and was guarding the family brandy stocks like the Bank of France looking after its gold. A somewhat painful family struggle followed, like a chapter out of Balzac. The father was dedicated to quality. The son was dedicated to quantity and sales. But it took the son long discussions and finally harsh decisions to overrule the father and release the brandy stocks to blend and produce more bottles for sale. Not that Monnet brandy ever became inferior or cheap—but if Monnet's father had had his way it would probably have simply remained a connoisseur's product headed for bankruptcy. Fortunately, the world market also began to pick up as Monnet moved to increase the release of stocks and push more of the family product onto the market. He reorganized the business, and then turned to other things.

In 1925, Monnet was approached by one of the big American investment banking houses, Blair and Company, to organize a Paris subsidiary and extend its operations to Europe. In those days, private banking houses played a far greater role in government financial transactions and currency matters than is the case today. There was no International Monetary Fund and no mechanism among central banks for exchange-stabilization operations. When governments got into difficulties, they would turn to private investment houses for credit. Monnet's first big operation for Blair and Company was a $70-million stabilization loan for the Polish Government in 1926 to strengthen the zloty, guaranteed against Polish customs revenues. Next he went to Romania, in 1928, and in months of negotiation back and forth to Bucharest he arranged a $100-million loan to support the Romanian leu.

In 1929 Monnet moved to New York as Blair and Company negotiated a merger with the Bank of America. Monnet became vice-president of the Bancamerica-Blair Corporation in San Francisco only a few months before the Wall Street crash. The bank's founder, Amadeo Giannini, had been persuaded to take a vacation for the good of his institution, and Monnet now pushed through a reorganization of the bank holding company, Transamerica, which the Blair people felt was seriously overvalued even without the Wall Street crash. But in 1932 Giannini returned to San Francisco from a lengthy sojourn in Austria and campaigned among the shareholders to regain control. Preaching that "the men in Wall Street have robbed me and are out to ruin honest Californians," he won a stockholders fight, and Monnet departed to return to Europe—where he had been asked to sort out and clean up an even worse tangle.

Ivar Kreuger, the enigmatic, power-mad, fraudulent Swedish Match King, had committed suicide in his Paris apartment in March of 1932, leaving behind a safe full of forged Italian Government bonds, and a towering mass of international debts based on frantic borrowings and lendings in which Kreuger's control of state match monopolies all over Europe were supposed to have been security and cover. Monnet was brought in by the Swedish

Government to sort out the real Kreuger assets from the fraudulent and liquidate the mess.

Meanwhile, he had met in Paris an Italian diplomat named Emilio de Bondini with a beautiful and talented wife, Silvia, a painter. De Bondini was planning to found a bank in New York and proposed to Monnet that he become his partner. Instead Monnet proposed to Silvia—twenty years younger than he. They had fallen in love instantly and became totally devoted, but under Italian law divorce was impossible. Monnet finally solved the problem in a most unorthodox way. He found out that a quickie divorce would be possible under Soviet law, so he and Silvia journeyed to Moscow in November 1934, obtained the divorce and immediately married, just after Monnet's forty-sixth birthday. They then continued on across Siberia to China, where Monnet spent the next two years in Shanghai working on financial problems with the Chiang Kai-shek entourage. He established a China Finance Development Corporation to inject mixed Chinese and foreign capital into industrial concerns and finance the railroads.

In 1936 he was back in New York, where he formed a private partnership to advise on international finance and business deals, but he was getting bored with private business. The dangers were clearly mounting in Europe, and he returned to Paris to position himself once more for action. It was 1938—the year of Munich.

First Hitler swallowed Austria, and next the Nazis turned on Czechoslovakia. A German minority living in the Sudeten border areas was readily whipped into a frenzy of demands against the Prague government. Monnet by now was in close contact with Édouard Daladier, France's Minister of Defense and later Premier. In late September, Daladier went to Munich to negotiate the Sudeten "settlement" with Hitler, with a hand tied firmly behind his back. Before he left Paris he received a memorandum from the French Air Staff advising him that the country had only six hundred combat aircraft, all inferior to German planes, and that the Germans could bomb Paris whenever they chose. Although the Munich pact was received with almost hysterical relief in Paris and London, Daladier returned in a state of total anguish and remorse. He knew the realities, and he sent immediately for

Monnet and the American ambassador to Paris, William C. Bullitt. At the end of the meeting, Bullitt cabled President Franklin D. Roosevelt in Washington that the French Government wished to send Monnet to the United States on a secret mission of the highest importance to discuss the purchase of aircraft. Roosevelt fixed October 19, 1938, for the meeting. Monnet sailed for New York and inconspicuously boarded a train for Hyde Park. For several hours, with Bullitt present, he and Roosevelt talked about French orders to build up American productive capacity, and ways to get around the Neutrality Act. Monnet then continued on to Washington at the President's instigation to meet Secretary of the Treasury Henry Morgenthau and discuss how French assets might be mobilized for a major financial effort.

He returned to Paris in early November, but now the French Treasury objected to what Daladier was trying to do, afraid to risk the country's reserves on such a large overseas order. In Washington, the burly chief of the Army Air Corps (as it then was), General Henry H. Arnold, was causing difficulties by flatly refusing to allow the French even to look at the Air Corps's latest fighter and bomber models.

In January, Monnet was back in Washington, ready to place an order. But first it took a direct written order to General Arnold from the Commander-in-Chief to let the French test-fly what they wanted to purchase. News of what was going on became public in a totally unexpected manner. At the Douglas factory in Los Angeles, a plane crashed on a test flight with a French pilot aboard, and reporters at the scene heard French spoken as another man in civilian clothes rushed to help free the two men in the plane. Isolationists in the Senate whipped up a storm of protest, but Roosevelt brazened it out by declaring that it was good business to sell to the French with the aircraft industry still wallowing in the Great Depression—and besides it was cash-and-carry. Monnet finally placed a firm order for six hundred American aircraft to be delivered in 1939, and another fifteen hundred on option for delivery in 1940. Alas, they did not arrive in time for the Battle of France, but the order was then switched to the British, and they did begin to come into action by the time of the Battle of Britain. At least the French had helped turn on the tap of American pro-

ductive capacity, which was stalled by isolationist anti-war sentiment until then.

In March 1939, Hitler snuffed out what remained of Czechoslovakia, and it was now only a question of time when war would
come. Monnet continued to operate in the background in Paris on
supply and armament problems, and then, at the end of August,
Hitler's armies rolled into Danzig and Poland and the war was on.
On September 3, 1939, Monnet sent a note to Daladier briefly re-
capitulating the struggles to organize inter-Allied supply and economic machinery in the First World War, and crisply concluded:
"This lesson ought to convince the French and British governments
that the same decisions need to be taken now and the same machinery needs to be set up—and that this time it should be done
immediately."

Two weeks later, Daladier wrote along the same lines to Prime
Minister Neville Chamberlain, and sent Monnet to London to see
what the British were prepared to do. This time there was no
delay on the necessity and the principles of a combined Allied
supply effort, although, as Monnet later said, "habits were another
matter." Still, it was quickly agreed to establish an Anglo-French
Coordinating Committee for the war effort, with separate executives for food, armaments, raw materials, petroleum, aircraft and
shipping. The committee headquarters would be in London, and it
then fell almost automatically that the Allied chairman would be
Monnet—who would report directly to the Prime Minister in London and the Premier in Paris. Sir Arthur Salter, well up the political ladder since the First World War, returned to work alongside
Monnet. At the same time, a joint Anglo-French Purchasing Mission was established in Washington to avoid overlapping or competition between the two countries on American supply orders,
which clearly would determine the outcome of the war.

At least some of the lessons of World War I had been learned.
But although the machinery of economic direction of the new war
was organized and in place, it was only getting geared up and had
scarcely made much of an impact when Hitler's armies grabbed
Denmark and Norway and then unleashed the *Blitzkrieg* on the
Netherlands, Belgium and France on May 10, 1940.

Winston Churchill replaced Chamberlain at No. 10 Downing Street that same day, and Monnet had no hesitation about promptly using his right of access to the new Prime Minister in his Allied capacity. In fact, Monnet had a direct private phone line from the apartment where he and his wife were living, on Mount Street, in the Mayfair section of London, to the Cabinet Office, in Whitehall. But his first personal appeal to Churchill must have irritated rather than impressed—for it concerned more British planes for France.

In barely two weeks, the famous Nazi Panzer commanders Heinz Guderian and Erwin Rommel tore through the center of the French Army in northern France and then turned north to the English Channel to encircle the British forces, which fell back to the port of Dunkirk. On June 3 the British completed their heroic evacuation from the beaches (337,000 troops, including 110,000 French), while the German Army crossed the Seine at Rouen, captured Le Havre and headed for Cherbourg. On June 10, Premier Paul Reynaud declared Paris an open city, and the government departed, heading first for Orléans, then Tours and finally Bordeaux. At the height of these events, as Churchill shuttled across to France to try to bolster a dazed and tottering government, Monnet sent him a personal appeal, on June 6:

"The Allied aircraft now operating in France are outnumbered by several to one. But if we combine the two countries' air forces, the ratio becomes about two to one-and-a-half, and with our proven superiority when evenly matched, we should then have a chance of winning. In a word, victory or defeat may be determined by an immediate decision to use our respective aircraft and pilots in the present battle as a single force. If that in turn requires a unified command for our two air forces, then this position should in my opinion be studied and studied now."

But Churchill had already once overruled his own Chiefs of Staff in sending more RAF planes to the continent as France fell, and Monnet on this occasion was out of his depth in dealing with a military matter. It was not a simple matter of two plus two making four. It involved spare parts and maintenance, pilots, tactics and communications. None of this could be solved in the middle of a battle by suddenly conjuring up a unified command. Churchill was under similar pressure for more planes from the French Government, but a firm British decision had already been taken to hold a minimum of twenty-five squadrons for home defense, in what was to become the Battle of Britain.

Nevertheless, behind Monnet's appeal to Churchill lay the consistency of his simple conviction, the root of practically everything he attempted in public and private life from his first interview with Premier Viviani in 1914 to the last meeting of his Action Committee for the United States of Europe: the need for international unity in all things great and small. The next time he tried, only days later in the darkest moment in French annals, he came close to turning the course of history.

As the debacle spread in France, Monnet sat down with his old friend and associate Arthur Salter to discuss what could be salvaged and how it could be salvaged. Together they drafted a memorandum, titled "Anglo-French Unity," which urged that consideration be given to "a dramatic declaration by the two governments on the solidarity of the two countries' interests, and on their mutual commitment to restore the devastated areas, making clear also that the two governments are to merge and form a single Cabinet and to unite the two Parliaments."

They completed the document on Thursday, June 13, 1940, but when Monnet first attempted to talk to Churchill about the concept, the old bulldog growled: "I am fighting a war, and you come to talk about the future." Nevertheless, Monnet persisted with other British ministers and senior officials at the Foreign Office and elsewhere. Thanks to his behind-the-scenes lobbying, the document was circulated as a Cabinet paper and put on the agenda for an emergency War Cabinet meeting Saturday—by Neville Chamberlain, of all people.

Meanwhile, events in France gathered speed. On Saturday, the French Government of Paul Reynaud reached the end of the road at Bordeaux, and that same day Brigadier General Charles de Gaulle arrived in London at Reynaud's direction, ostensibly to ask the British for transport to move French troops to North Africa. De Gaulle sought out Monnet immediately, as the most important Frenchman in town with direct access to Downing Street. All was over in France, he said, and he had decided to stay in England.

Monnet seized the instant to press de Gaulle to support the plan for Anglo-French union. De Gaulle was no more enthusiastic than Churchill had been. Much later, he ridiculed Monnet's plan as "integrating King George VI with President Lebrun and the Garde Republicaine with the Horse Guards," and his subsequent record as an anti-integrationist in Europe is as clear as Monnet's long record as an integrationist. Nevertheless, for a brief moment that fateful weekend in London they were united on a course in which each might differ about the ultimate outcome but both had the same primary aim: saving France or diverting France from surrender.

On Saturday afternoon, the Anglo-French-unity-paper discussion opened in the War Cabinet. Churchill still thought little of it, and in his war memoirs he admits his surprise "to see the staid, solid, experienced politicians of all parties engage themselves so passionately in an immense design whose implications and consequences were not in any way thought out. I did not resist, but yielded easily to these generous surges." Thus, by Saturday evening, the War Cabinet had approved in principle, and de Gaulle had approved as Reynaud's emissary.

Sunday, June 16, was for Monnet and France "a day of lost opportunities." In the morning, Monnet got through to Reynaud in Bordeaux by telephone to tell him cryptically that "something very important is being prepared" and to hold out against any government changes or basic decisions until later in the day. Monnet and de Gaulle then went into a meeting with British officials and spent the rest of the morning putting together an agreed text of a "Proclamation of Anglo-French Unity" for formal approval by the War Cabinet and transmission to Bordeaux. Churchill took de Gaulle to lunch, along with French Ambassador Charles Corbin, at the Carlton Club, citadel of the British Conservative Party, where the Prime Minister no doubt thought it would be good for Tory morale to be seen dining casually like an ordinary member with distinguished guests.

They returned to Downing Street together, and at a short meeting of the War Cabinet, the text of the proclamation was read and approved. They then telephoned Reynaud in Bordeaux from the Cabinet room, which also serves as the Prime Minister's office. De

Gaulle told Reynaud what had been done and read him the proclamation, a simple, straightforward document of barely five hundred words. Churchill got on the phone immediately after to assure Reynaud of Britain's full support, and told him that de
Gaulle would leave immediately to fly to Bordeaux with the text
and he would follow on Monday morning, bringing with him Clement Attlee, the Labour Party leader and deputy Prime Minister, to
seal the historic pact. The telephone conversation ended in excitement and exhilaration in both London and Bordeaux—but not for
long.

Around five o'clock on that rare June Sunday afternoon, de
Gaulle left Downing Street for a waiting aircraft at Hendon
Airfield, not far from the center of the city. Monnet drove to the
airfield with him to see him off. Meanwhile Reynaud went into a
fateful Cabinet meeting in Bordeaux with his notes on the Anglo-
French Unity proclamation in his hands—but Pétain waiting. Monnet returned to London after de Gaulle took off, to prepare his
own departure with the British Government party. They were to
travel by special train to Plymouth, where a Royal Navy destroyer
would be waiting to speed them to Bordeaux. Churchill and Attlee
would fly to join them. Just as the special train was about to leave,
at 9 P.M. came a call from Downing Street to the station canceling
the trip. The Reynaud government had fallen, and Pétain had
taken over. Monnet went back to his office, and by some miracle
of telephone communications, he managed to reach de Gaulle in
Bordeaux. The General told him briefly that it was all over and he
would be returning to London.

And so, Monnet's great project of Anglo-French unity blew
away as some passing cloud of history. De Gaulle spent Monday
in Bordeaux and flew back to London in a British plane early on
the morning of Tuesday, June 18, to begin his long march to the
liberation four years later. At midday, Pétain broadcast his announcement that he was seeking armistice terms from the Germans.

Monnet, who was in continuous touch with Churchill, now proposed a last mission to attempt to bring out political leaders who
would continue the struggle outside France. Churchill assigned for
Monnet's use a large seaplane with room for thirty passengers and

plenty of range. Monnet then saw de Gaulle and asked him if he would go back to Bordeaux once again to help. But de Gaulle, fresh from the defeatist atmosphere of the city, with a military arrest order already issued against him, judged the mission to be hopeless and was already shaping his famous appeal to France over the BBC to place himself at the head of the resistance.

Accordingly, Monnet set out on the morning of Wednesday, June 19, with one of his close associates, René Pleven, and Lord Lloyd from the War Cabinet to put British weight behind the mission, in a seaplane that was practically empty. But it was a far different Bordeaux to which Monnet returned in 1940 than it was when he visited Viviani there in 1914. In the First World War, the withdrawal of the government to Bordeaux at the height of the Battle of the Marne was an act of defiance, a show of determination not to succumb, but to fight on. In 1940 it was an act of retreat, hopelessness and defeat. Monnet, whose faith in the human spirit was always constant, was appalled by the degradation of French morale that he found in Bordeaux in the brief hours he spent there vainly seeking the true France.

The seaplane landed in the Gironde estuary, and Monnet and his party made their way to the center of Bordeaux. It is a small city with some elegant and impressive nineteenth-century buildings, and all the activities of the defeated government were going on in offices and hotels in a walking radius of twenty minutes or half an hour. He first sought out Paul Baudouin, who had become Pétain's Foreign Minister. They talked for about half an hour, with Baudouin assuring Monnet in routine fashion that Pétain would give consideration to the Anglo-French-unity plan. He even talked about moving to North Africa, but he would not leave. Next they tried without success to locate President Lebrun. Then they went to see Édouard Herriot, president of the National Assembly—and found him eating a large lunch alone at a great table in a large office, with National Assembly members and hangers-on ranged in chairs along the walls watching as if Herriot were some Bourbon king, waiting to have a word with him when he finished. Munching on lamb chops, he talked boldly about taking a ship to North Africa but refused to depart in Monnet's plane. Georges Mandel, a close associate of Clemenceau's in the

First World War, declined to leave "because I have luggage"—
meaning his lifelong mistress, an actress of the Comédie Française. Cafes and restaurants were jammed, so Monnet and Pleven bought sandwiches and retired to a park bench to eat and
reflect.

Not one front-rank political leader of the Third Republic was
prepared to depart to keep up the fight. But Henri Bonnet, an experienced French diplomat, later Ambassador to Washington, and
his wife, were ready to go. Pleven, by a great stroke of luck, found
his wife and two children. Lord Lloyd rejoined them from an
equally sterile quest and contacts with the remaining British. They
all then boarded the seaplane, and by Wednesday evening were
back in Britain.

As Monnet made his way from the seaplane base back to London, de Gaulle went on the BBC to deliver his first appeal to
France. But in discussions between the two men next day, Monnet
immediately raised fundamental objections to de Gaulle's idea of
forming a Free French Committee. He objected to de Gaulle's automatically placing himself at the head of a movement without any
visible following, and he thought that it was wrong to take action
that would freeze a political situation he felt was still fluid. But of
course de Gaulle sailed straight ahead, with British backing. Monnet then wrote him a formal letter, before his next major broadcast to France on June 23:

"I believe that it would be a great mistake to try to set up in
Britain an organization which might appear in France as an authority established abroad under British protection. I fully share
your desire to prevent France abandoning the struggle. . . . But
this task of resurrection cannot at present be undertaken from
London. If it were, then it would appear to be a French movement
inspired by British interests and therefore condemned to a failure
which would make further efforts at recovery all the more
difficult."

Monnet was correctly foreshadowing a schism that was to divide Frenchmen for years, still even today. He told de Gaulle that
a committee to mobilize "Frenchmen who wish to continue the
struggle alongside Britain" would be useful, but he was against de
Gaulle's seeking to establish himself as a supreme authority and

the embodiment of France. This was an issue of grave political
and juridical importance. But it was also a reflection of the fundamental differences of personality and philosophy of power between these two strong-minded and intelligent Frenchmen—each
great in his own way. Monnet above all valued his own independence. He worked with men of power to achieve certain ends,
but he distrusted the corrupting effects of power. And he saw the
ruthless side of de Gaulle, who was demanding absolute personal
loyalty and was a profligate user of men.

So Monnet and de Gaulle, at this climactic time of French history, came to a parting of the ways, each to continue the fight for
France in his own way.

"If I was able later to play a useful role in Algiers, it was because I had maintained a position of independence, in which I
could give de Gaulle advice and assistance which he knew were
disinterested," Monnet wrote in his *Memoirs*. "Now, in London,
he respected my choice as I admired his determination."

Punctiliously, Monnet sent a formal letter to Marshal Pétain on
July 2, 1940 (through what channels is not clear), in which he
formally resigned as head of the Anglo-French Coordinating
Committee. He sent a similar letter to Churchill on the same date,
and then added in a personal message that his services were available to the British Government if it was thought that he could be
useful. Two weeks later, Churchill responded by asking him to
serve on the British Purchasing Commission in Washington, which
had replaced the Anglo-French organization—and personally endorsed Monnet's French passport for travel.

At the end of August, Monnet and his wife left for the United
States on the Clipper flying-boat service via Bermuda, and arrived
in Washington as President Roosevelt was about to begin his
third-term election campaign. Monnet had no trouble fitting into
the work of the British Purchasing Commission, where he was initially engaged in sorting out the takeover of military equipment
orders that the French had placed and that were now suspended.
He was no stranger to Washington, of course, and with his ability
to make friends and his unerring instinct for establishing himself
in circles of power, he quickly became close to the two key men

who had Roosevelt's trust and confidence: Harry Hopkins and Felix Frankfurter.

No doubt his credentials as a completely independent Frenchman—certainly not a man of Vichy, and with no ties to General de Gaulle—were an advantage in Washington in those days of 1940. The United States Government had continued to maintain diplomatic relations with Vichy after the fall of France, and President Roosevelt and the Department of State had already conceived their almost visceral dislike of de Gaulle. Monnet had nothing to do with either faction, but he was dedicated to winning the war and he was dedicated to the unity of Frenchmen. He therefore was somebody to whom the administration leaders could talk and confide about French affairs, knowing that he was disinterested and thoroughly trustworthy. His gadfly role as a Frenchman working for the British, who could write directly to both Roosevelt and Churchill and dine with Harry Hopkins and Felix Frankfurter was not, by any means, very popular with many of his associates. But Monnet was never a man to allow protocol or bureaucracy or "usual channels" to impede him.

The immediate problem late in 1940 was not the French, but finding the means to sustain and support the British war effort. In mid-November, immediately after Roosevelt's election victory, Monnet wrote Salter in London urging him that the moment had come for the British to state their war needs from America "clearly and in big terms" as a challenge to Roosevelt, and then leave it to the President to work out the means and method of fulfillment. Three weeks after that, Churchill sent just such a letter to Roosevelt, with an impassioned appeal for arms, and some way around the "cash-and-carry" policy that would soon practically wipe out British overseas resources. The result was Roosevelt's most decisive prewar move to place America in the fight: lend-lease.

About this time, Monnet was expounding on the military supply problem at dinner one evening with friends including Frankfurter. He was not a great phrasemaker or public speaker, but as he talked he remarked that "the United States must become a great arsenal—the arsenal of democracy."

Frankfurter interrupted and said: "Very good, but promise me not to use that phrase again!" Monnet asked why not, and Frank-furter said that he thought he could soon find a good use for it. Ten days or so later, Roosevelt delivered his end-of-the-year fire-side chat in 1940 to rally public support behind his new lend-lease proposal, and the phrase "arsenal of democracy" slipped into the Roosevelt annals.

Through 1941, as the British battled on alone in the skies over London, in the menacing seas of the North Atlantic, and in the Middle East, Monnet pleaded and preached with the Americans his old themes of 1914–17 and 1939–40: the need for unity and the need to establish intergovernmental mechanisms to accomplish the obvious. By the time of Pearl Harbor, when Churchill came to Washington for the first great Allied conference, which took so many basic decisions on shaping the transformed war effort, Mon-net's patient lobbying with the Americans had helped to pave the way for the organization of joint supply and production boards that emerged.

In November 1942, the Americans and the British landed in Morocco and Algeria. Not only was the military tide now at last turning against Nazi Germany. The French political snarl involv-ing de Gaulle's Free French, Vichy Admiral Jean Darlan and his cohorts in North Africa, and the American-backed General Henri Giraud, who had been brought out of France to Algiers, was com-ing to a head. Roosevelt and Churchill met at Casablanca in Janu-ary 1943 and managed to get de Gaulle and Giraud together for a stiff handshake for the benefit of photographers—with distaste written all over the faces of the two men. De Gaulle returned im-mediately to London to sulk in his tent like Achilles, and Giraud went back to Algiers, where he was sadly inadequate, hopelessly out of his depth in internecine French politics. The time had come for Monnet to return to the French scene.

In Washington, Secretary of State Cordell Hull, whose dedication to keeping General de Gaulle out of power was practically a major war aim, was against allowing Monnet to leave. He cer-tainly sensed that although Monnet was no card-carrying Gaullist, this independent-minded Frenchman, full of ideas, could not be "controlled" and would shape his own policy on French affairs.

Nevertheless, Harry Hopkins overruled Hull's objections, and
Monnet arrived in Algiers at the end of February 1943. He found
General Giraud "tall, with a clear, blank gaze, conscious of his
own prestige, inflexible on military matters, hesitant on everything
else." Here was the key. "Where he was obstinate, he had to be
respected, and where he was hesitant he could be steered."
Giraud, for his part, had never even heard of Monnet until they
were introduced. Within two weeks, Monnet had made up his
mind that French unity was the overriding priority, and began
steering Giraud toward a necessary and inevitable coalition with
de Gaulle.

These maneuverings, in which Monnet played the key role
in the messages that went from Giraud to de Gaulle, the tor-
turously negotiated organizational arrangements and protocol
agreements between these two strange prima donnas, ran their
intricate and time-wasting course in a mixture of French farce
and Greek tragedy. At long last, General de Gaulle agreed to
move from London to Algiers on June 1, 1943—and by November, as practically everybody who knew anything about French
affairs was certain would happen, he had shoved Giraud to one
side and become sole president of the French Committee of National Liberation. Monnet then returned to Washington as the
Committee's representative to negotiate lend-lease supply arrangements and handle other financial and political matters. He had
correctly foreseen the disunity for France of de Gaulle's course in
1940, and he negotiated the way back to unity in 1943, but de
Gaulle was no man to waste time in gratitude to others.

Monnet returned briefly to France in September 1944, after the
liberation, for a visit to Cognac to see his mother and sisters after
four years, but he continued to handle French aid and economic
matters in Washington until late in 1945. Then, at last, he was
back, with the overriding problem of organizing postwar French
recovery. In talks with de Gaulle, he struck the note that he knew
would focus the General's attention: "You speak of greatness, but
today the French are small. There will only be greatness when the
French are of a stature to warrant it. For this purpose, they must
modernize—because at the moment they are not modern. They

need more production and greater productivity. Materially the country needs to be transformed."

De Gaulle told Monnet to draw up proposals before the end of the year for overhauling the French economy. Monnet saw it first of all as a human problem—of creating willpower for the effort, and the full involvement of the trade unions, farm leaders, industrialists, the financial community, the civil servants and bureaucracy, and after that the men with political power. In December he sent de Gaulle a five-page memorandum of priority economic targets and the outlines of an entirely new state planning machinery to direct the effort. De Gaulle acted swiftly, translated the Monnet memorandum into an official decree, and signed it on January 3, 1946, establishing the Commissariat-General of the French Modernization and Investment Plan, with Monnet at its head.

It was virtually de Gaulle's last act as head of the postliberation French Provisional Government. On January 20, he assembled his ministers at a special Cabinet meeting, and before they even sat down he abruptly announced that he was fed up with the return to party politics in France and was resigning. He said good-bye and walked out.

For the next five years, Jean Monnet and his small, brilliant planning commission practically ran the economy of France, as governments came and went. His mind and his energies were concentrated on modernization of his country—but his vision was on the future of Europe.

6
The Schuman Plan

THE RECOVERY OF EUROPE AFTER WORLD WAR II WAS FOUNDED on the Marshall Plan. The security of Europe continues to rest on the North Atlantic Treaty. The unity of Europe springs from the Schuman Plan.

There are unusual diplomatic, political and historic similarities in the birth of the Marshall Plan and the genesis of the Schuman Plan. Both were essentially simple proposals or concepts to break out of European situations of crisis or impasse. In the case of the Marshall Plan, it was of course the parlous postwar economic condition of the continent. In the case of the Schuman Plan, it was the growing danger of a historic repetition of Franco-German enmity, which had brought such disaster to both nations and to Europe and the world. Both plans therefore went to root problems of European stability. They dealt with fundamental questions that had become the desperate worry of large numbers of diplomats, politicians, economists, commentators, historians and government leaders looking bleakly at what seemed to be a dead end. But in each case only about a dozen people were secretly involved behind the scenes in elaborating and launching the proposals that emerged. Moreover, both the Marshall Plan and the Schuman Plan were conceived and decided upon in the amazingly short time of only about three weeks. Both were sprung with maximum surprise, without any advance warning or public buildup. But there was some secret diplomatic preparation in each case to ensure a positive response where it would be most needed. Dean Acheson sent advance signals on the Marshall Plan to the British. On the Schuman Plan, the French consulted secretly in advance with the Americans, and more important, with Chancellor Konrad Adenauer, in Bonn. Both plans then triggered far-reaching, positive changes in the diplomatic and political outlook in Europe, and both altered the course of history.

By the spring of 1950, the postwar outlook for Western Europe had been transformed in two basic respects. On the economic side, the Marshall Plan was succeeding beyond expectations in stimulating recovery and strengthening the ability of governments to cope with internal problems. On the political-security side, the Berlin airlift had successfully contained the Soviet challenge in Germany, and the North Atlantic Treaty had come into force. Democratic government was functioning in West Germany, and the Communists had been progressively ejected from all the governments in Western Europe where they had been taken into power after the war.

But the very positive effect of these changes was again rousing all the old French apprehensions and animosities and fears about the resurgence of German power. On the one hand it was clear and logical that there could be no European economic recovery without German recovery. But all that France could see in German recovery was a renewed threat to France. The French had dragged their feet as long as they could from 1946 to 1948 in merging their occupation zone in Germany with the British and American zones in order to delay or mitigate German resurgence. Then they had fought endless skirmishes over the drafting of the Bonn constitution with the same aim in mind. They had insisted on the establishment of an international Ruhr authority to control the level of German coal and steel production after the Bonn government was formed and occupation controls were dismantled.

Most important of all, they had unilaterally "detached" the Saar Valley from Germany, simply by moving the French frontier posts and customs controls forward one midnight in 1946 to the eastern boundary between the Saar and the German state of Rhine-Palatinate. As in 1919 in the Rhineland, they were avidly pursuing a separatist policy all over again. They had imported a puppet leader, Dr. Johannes Hoffman, who had fled the Nazis and spent the war years in Brazil, to head a Saar government under a tough, no-nonsense Gaullist high commissioner, Gilbert Grandval.

To all intents and purposes, the ultimate French aim was annexation of the Saar. French currency had been introduced and a customs union with France proclaimed. The press was strictly censored, no pro-German political parties were allowed to exist, telephones were tapped and the French gendarmes controlled the Saar police and ensured that there was neither private nor public challenge to French rule. To be sure, in the days of postwar occupation it was not necessary to throw people in jail to maintain Allied rule anywhere. But the French occupation of the Saar was scarcely a model of democratic behavior, and everybody knew it. The French had been able up to 1950 at least to ensure that the Saar kept marginally ahead of West Germany in recovery and living standards, but with the establishment of the Bonn Republic the sands were running out for French policy. Still, in Paris they continued to produce endless statistics, charts and graphs to prove that France plus the Saar would about balance the heavy industry of West Germany minus East Germany, and therefore a permanent link between the Saar and France was essential to European peace and security. The teaching of French was compulsory in the Saar schools, and a bizarre effort was made to graft some kind of French patriotism onto the German-speaking coal miners and steelworkers of the valley.

On one of my visits to Saarbrucken in those days—a city that definitely lacks charm—I recall going to see a native Saarlander who worked in the press office of the Saar government under Hoffman, where I listened to a long briefing on the virtues and enjoyments and advantages of French rule. We left his office together and walked to his car. It was a little French Renault, and he patted it affectionately, looked at me with a conspiratorial grin, and said, *"Das ist die Saarlanders Volkswagen."*

It was a situation that was both absurd and tragic. Was there no end of a lesson? Was this post-World War One or post-World War Two? Was history doomed to repeat itself?

The Bonn government was not yet six months old in 1950, and an almost glacial quality had taken hold in Franco-German relations—to the deep dismay of the United States and Britain and the somber discouragement of Konrad Adenauer, who was the best hope France ever had in a German statesman. Yet German recovery, both economic and political, seemed to be bedeviled and challenged every step of the way by revanchist attitudes and the old fears and antagonisms of France repeating themselves all over again. As a simple example, in the first big negotiation between the Western Allies and the newly established Bonn government, in November 1949, which finally settled the problem of dismantlement of German factories, Adenauer was also granted the right to seek membership for West Germany in the Council of Europe in Strasbourg. But then the French came along right after to vitiate the whole atmosphere of the agreements by announcing that a seat in Strasbourg would have to be found for the Saar government at the same time Bonn joined. This put Adenauer in an impossible political position with the Bonn Socialist opposition, and he had no choice but to withhold any application to Strasbourg. As for the International Ruhr Authority, Adenauer had agreed to West German membership only under heavy Allied pressure. His position was clear: "I should agree to an authority that supervised the mining and industrial areas of Germany, France, Belgium and Luxembourg," but the Ruhr Authority was discriminatory and Germany sought equality. In endless matters great and small in relations between the Bonn regime and the Allied high commissioners, the French held an effective veto power and knew how to use it. Even though Germany, in 1950, was still more or less flat on its back and only beginning to produce again in meaningful terms, French fears were rising a lot faster than German steel production.

Jean Monnet, watching this deteriorating political atmosphere and rising economic challenge to France from his vantage place as commissioner of French economic planning, went off on a vacation in the Swiss Alps in April 1950, to walk endlessly on the mountain trails as was his lifetime habit, and ponder and distill his thoughts and ideas. He returned to Paris and drafted a lengthy memorandum on the drifting state of affairs, giving his view in almost frantic terms:

"France's continued recovery will come to a halt unless we rapidly solve the problem of German industrial production and its competitive capacity. The basis of the superiority which French industrialists traditionally recognize in Germany is her ability to produce steel at a price that the French cannot match. From this they conclude that the whole of French production is similarly handicapped. Already Germany is seeking to increase her production from eleven to fourteen million metric tons. We shall refuse, but the Americans will insist. Finally we shall state our reservations, but we shall give in. At the same time, French production is leveling off or even falling. Merely to state these facts makes it unnecessary to describe what the results will be: Germany expanding; Germans dumping on export markets; a call for protection of French industry; the re-establishment of prewar cartels; perhaps eastwards outlets for German expansion, a prelude to political agreements, and France back in the old rut of limited, protected production."

The French, British and American foreign ministers were scheduled to meet in London on May 10, and at the top of the agenda was the festering problem that was troubling Monnet: a German request for Allied authorization to increase steel production. In September 1949, when the three had last met to discuss German policy at the time the first Bonn government was formed, Acheson and Bevin had tossed the ball firmly into the French court by formally declaring to Robert Schuman: "We fully concur in entrusting our French colleague with formulating our common policy on Germany." But what was France now to do?

Robert Schuman was one of the few genuinely historic figures of the ramshackle, revolving-door French Fourth Republic, which in fact managed to do more good works in spite of itself than it ever got credit for. Of its proliferation of leaders—twenty-three governments headed by nineteen premiers in twelve years and eight months of its life, from October 1945 to May 1958—only Schuman and Pierre Mendès-France left any personal imprint on history. A member of the predominantly Catholic Popular Republican Movement, which was the French equivalent of the Christian Democrats of Adenauer in Germany and the Christian Socialists of Alcide de Gasperi in Italy, Schuman was premier for a spell in 1947–48 and then became Foreign Minister in July 1948. He remained at the Quai d'Orsay for a remarkable run of four and a half years, by far the longest that any man served in any ministry in those days. Thus, while Monnet's Commissariat Général du

Plan managed to give continuity and direction to French economic management as governments were formed and fell, Schuman gave continuity to foreign policy throughout this decisive postwar period. He was an unlikely political leader, ascetic and a loner, with very few intimates, and an elliptical lawyer's style in speaking which generally made even simple problems seem complicated and obtuse. He had a long, lean, rather lugubrious face and a look of baffled solemnity, peering out over the top of spectacles perched on the bridge of a long nose. But he attracted sympathy, and he had keen intelligence, a somewhat furtive sly sense of humor, and deep moral fiber and political toughness. He was a spiritual and cultivated man. Above all, he had lived his life immersed in the Franco-German tragedy. He was born in Luxembourg in 1886 and grew up and was educated under German rule in the Lorraine, which had been annexed to the Reich by Bismarck after the Franco-Prussian War, of 1870. He studied law and went into practice in the city of Metz. German was his first language, and in the First World War he was drafted into the German forces and served as an officer in the Kaiser's army.

With the Armistice, in 1918, Alsace-Lorraine was restored to France after nearly half a century, and Schuman was promptly elected to the French National Assembly in 1919 as a deputy from the Department of the Moselle. He was a man of the border country, and like Adenauer, on the other side, in the Rhineland, he had lived through war and occupation, suppression and liberation, and he knew as a simple conviction that reconciliation had to be the great work of politics. It took a second war before that time came. It was all the more unfortunate, therefore, that on Schuman's first visit to Bonn as Foreign Minister for a bilateral meeting with Adenauer in January 1950, he had to spend his time and potential goodwill on a futile justification of French policy toward the Saar. But the harsh fact of political life in Paris at that time was that no French government could survive for one week if there was the slightest hint of a change in the Saar policy. So Schuman traveled from Bonn back to Paris—across the blood-soaked heights around Verdun, the war-scarred Argonne Woods and Ardennes Forest, the rows and rows of white crosses at Château-Thierry, the banks of the Marne restored to vineyards and farms—knowing that all the old animosities and tragedies of Franco-German relations were again staring Europe in the face, wondering, like Jean Monnet, what could be done.

Monnet had clarified the problem in his memorandum of early April, but he had still not clarified a possible solution. France, he had concluded, "must not try to solve the German problem in its present context—we must change the context by transforming the basic facts." Past history gave ample demonstration of the fact that neither dismemberment nor occupation nor restrictions aimed at the containment of Germany would work, let alone be a basis of Franco-German collaboration. But there was no instant solution of unity, no ready common interest to be exploited or common danger to fight. Monnet knew instinctively what he wanted to achieve, but he groped for the form, the institution, the structure.

During the second week of April, after his return from his vacation in the Swiss Alps, Monnet by chance had a conference scheduled with a lawyer named Paul Reuter, who was frequently called in by the Foreign Ministry and other government departments to handle difficult political-legal problems. Like Schuman, he came from eastern France. He was quick and brilliant, but he preferred life as a professor of law to a government career. He was seeing Monnet about some antitrust problem that was troubling the economic planners, but as usual with Monnet when he had something on his mind he would try it out on everybody he saw. Reuter responded immediately to the concerns about Franco-German relations and the need to "change the context by transforming the facts." Both were agreed that to propose a political institution would be pointless and would not work, since it would simply reflect the political weakness or attitudes they were trying to overcome. Both agreed that at the core of Franco-German relations lay the problem of heavy industry, for this was the basis of war potential and economic superiority. What, therefore, was the way to eliminate the fears a few million extra tons of German steel production automatically raised for the French? Adenauer had signaled his views about some kind of international authority for more than just the Ruhr. So Monnet posed the question to Reuter in legal, structural terms: Could international law be devised to establish a coal and steel pool in the heart of Europe that would abolish the old conflicts and fears? The idea was clear, but Monnet wanted to give it substance by devising the actual structure that would make the idea work. Reuter's quick imagination and practical turn of mind were stimulated, and he fell in step at once with Monnet's vision. Monnet asked him to sketch some concrete proposals on paper and meet again a few days later, on Saturday, April 15. Reuter returned with a paper that—like George Kennan's State Department Policy Planning Staff memorandum on economic aid for Europe, which became the basis of the Marshall Plan—succinctly clarified what was to become the Schuman Plan.

Following Monnet's ideas, Reuter's paper first declared a federal Europe to be the aim of French policy. But it noted the "obstacles accumulated from the past" which would make such a large political leap impossible, and therefore it laid down that as the first stage "The French Government proposes to place the whole of Franco-German coal and steel production under an international authority open to participation of other countries of Europe." Reuter sketched the outlines and the scope of an entirely new international institution with powers to equalize in France and Germany such things as taxes imposed on steel and coal, transport charges, social security and other labor costs, production quotas, financial compensation for price differentials, a re-employment fund for displaced workers, authority to borrow money to finance the rationalization of uneconomic capacity, an end to customs barriers and a uniform basing price for steel among all the participants. It would not be a cartel, but it would be supervised free competition. The institution would be established by international treaty, directed by a High Authority, and "the whole enterprise will be based on equal Franco-German representation, and its president will be chosen by agreement between the two parties."

At Monnet's country home that weekend, he and Reuter were joined by two men from the planning commission, Étienne Hirsch and Pierre Uri, for more drafting and refining. Uri wrote in a key sentence: "The High Authority's decisions shall be immediately binding in France, Germany and other member countries." This was an absolute, basic key to the success of the whole enterprise, but of course when the plan was unveiled it was also the key element that the British were then unable to swallow. But that was for the future. Monnet now had in his hands—as in London in 1940 with the Anglo-French Unity proposal and his 1946 outline for French economic planning machinery—an idea, a concept, and an instrument. The next problem was to find the man or the means to put it into effect.

Monnet knew, of course, that the Big Three Foreign Ministers were to meet in London on May 10. Therefore, he contacted Schuman's personal *chef du cabinet* at the Quai d'Orsay, a discreet and intelligent *inspecteur des finances* named Bernard Clappier, who rose to become president of the Banque de France twenty-five years later. He told Clappier of the coal-and-steel-pool proposal which was being put into final form, and Clappier said that "the minister is looking for an initiative that he can propose in London" and he would talk it over and be in touch later. But a week went by, and when Monnet had heard no more from Clappier he decided to send the draft of his plan to the then Premier, Georges Bidault, to whom the Planning Commissariat was directly responsible. No sooner had the dossier gone off to the Premier's office, at the Hôtel Matignon than Clappier was on the phone, apologetic for not getting in touch earlier, and asking for the papers to pass on to Schuman.

Time was running short. It was Friday, April 28, and Schuman made it his habit to spend the weekend at his home in Metz whenever he could get away from the little official apartment where he lived at the Quai d'Orsay. Clappier went straight from Monnet's office with the plan to the Gare de l'Est, handed it to Schuman in his compartment with other official papers before the train pulled out, and urged him to read it during the weekend, while he had time to reflect. On Monday, Clappier was back at the Gare de l'Est to meet Schuman, who descended from the train and said briefly: "I've read Monnet's proposal. I'll use it."

Bidault, meanwhile, had shuffled Monnet's dossier to one side and failed to read it. At a Cabinet meeting on Wednesday, May 3, Schuman made some rather general allusion to what he was considering and where it had originated. Bidault perked up and sent for Monnet after the meeting, in something of a temper. He had a plan of his own for setting up some kind of Atlantic high council, and he accused Monnet of going behind his back. But when Monnet said he had sent him a copy, Bidault reshuffled his papers and found it.

By this fortunate slipup on the part of Bidault, the great enterprise became the "Schuman Plan" instead of the "Bidault Plan," with far greater chances of political success. Only Robert Schuman, of all the Fourth Republic leaders, had the persistence, the low-key political and intellectual skill, as well as staying power at the Quai d'Orsay as governments changed, to steer the Coal and Steel Community through the diplomatic and political process to success. Monnet knew this, and that is why he first approached Schuman through Clappier. Bidault had neither the temperament nor the political will to bring it off as Schuman did.

Up to this point, the plan was a closely held secret shared by fewer than a dozen people. Such was the conspiratorial nature of the Quai d'Orsay, still emerging from the traumas of Vichy and the divided loyalties of the war, that Schuman had long made it his habit to consult with its career diplomats as little as possible, and then usually only in the execution of decisions rather than development of policy. But after broaching the plan to the Cabinet, Schuman and Clappier now decided to bring the secretary-general of the Foreign Ministry, Alexandre Parodi, in on the secret.

The next essential step for Schuman was secretly to solicit outside support, in advance, which could then be used to present the French Cabinet with a *fait accompli* when it would next meet to approve positions to be taken at the London meeting. Purely by chance, Secretary of State Dean Acheson had decided to stop off in Paris on the weekend before going on to London, primarily to discuss Marshall Plan business and clean up some bilateral problems with the French, in advance of the three-power meeting. He arrived at Orly Airport on Sunday, May 7, and was somewhat surprised to be met by Ambassador David K. E. Bruce with word that Schuman wanted to see him urgently that afternoon—and in reverse of normal protocol he would be coming to the American embassy residence, bringing only an interpreter.

The four men settled into the library of the residence in midafternoon, and Schuman launched at once into an explanation of what he planned to propose at the London meeting. Acheson wrote subsequently that "it was so breathtaking a step toward the unification of Western Europe that at first I did not grasp it." Indeed, Acheson's initial reaction was one of some skepticism, summed up in one word: cartel. As a lawyer, he of course knew that the Sherman Anti-Trust Act is practically as much the lifeblood of American democracy as the Bill of Rights. Moreover, World War II had been fought not only against Nazi Germany but, in the minds of many Americans, against the I. G. Farben cartel as well. Decartelization of German heavy industry, chemicals, banking, etc., was a cardinal principle of U.S. occupation policy. Would not the French plan to pool all of Europe's coal and steel industries under one central high authority simply amount to the creation of another new cartel on an unimagined scale? Schuman simply looked pained at Acheson's lack of understanding.

"The question surprised rather than offended him," Acheson wrote of the meeting. "Of course a cartel in coal and steel could be created, he answered. But his purpose which he tried to make clear was very different. It was basically a political conception: To move toward the unification of Western Europe by economic means. Surely provisions would be made against cartel abuses and for a court to enforce them. He treated my fear almost as an irrelevance, as back he went to the central theme, the unity of Europe, the end of national rivalries in a new, spacious and vastly productive Europe. As he talked, we caught his enthusiasm and the breadth of his thought, the rebirth of Europe which, as an entity, had been in eclipse since the Reformation."

Schuman arranged that Monnet would come to the embassy residence on Monday morning for a longer discussion of the technical aspects of the plan and how the French intended to proceed. Meanwhile, he asked Acheson to observe strictest secrecy on the whole project, since it would take careful maneuvering to line up the French Cabinet before the London meeting, only three days away, and any premature leak might scuttle it before it could be unveiled.* At the same time, he told Acheson that strong support from the American Government would be invaluable in moving the French Government. Acheson gave him assurances on both counts and said he would recommend to President Truman prompt endorsement whenever the announcement came.

Next morning, when Monnet arrived at the embassy residence, John J. McCloy, the American high commissioner in Germany, was also present. The four men were all old friends from wartime days in Washington as well as abroad. Again Acheson laid out his prime worry that the coal and steel pool must not be seen in American eyes as nothing more than a bigger cartel than ever, and that in presenting the plan something must be done to ensure that this kind of instinctive first reaction would not overshadow its vast political importance, which they all clearly grasped and accepted and were anxious to support.

Monnet, like Schuman, was surprised at the American reaction, which he had simply not anticipated. He returned to his office and immediately asked Pierre Uri to insert a passage in the documents to meet the cartel question head on, realizing that it was indeed an oversight to be rectified. Uri wrote out a simple declaration: "The proposed organization is in every respect the very opposite of a cartel—in its aims, its methods and its leadership." He then went on to set out how the high authority would promulgate strict legal rules to ensure full free-enterprise competition, which in effect would amount to a European anti-trust law. Meanwhile, on Monday afternoon Acheson sent off a first "eyes only" cable to President Truman, who was then traveling on the presidential

---

* The plan nearly did leak. In Bonn, where I was then living, at a diplomatic dinner party that Sunday evening I fell into an intensive conversation about the Franco-German situation alone with a friend who held a key job in the French High Commission. To my surprise, he told me flatly that France was about to make a sensational proposal to pool the coal and steel industries of the two countries under an international high authority. Much later I learned that he was one of the few to be cut in secretly in order to make the arrangements to sound out the Germans in advance. It was impossible to write the story from Bonn without compromising a good friend and valued source, so on Monday morning I telephoned the tip to the Paris correspondent of the New York *Herald Tribune*, Russell Hill. But he was unable to get any confirmation or uncover anything. A great scoop was missed, but I continue to enjoy the confidence of my French friend.

train in the Far West. He informed the President that an important announcement was being prepared in Paris and that he hoped
to provide additional details soon, but in the meantime if any rumors began floating he hoped that all Washington comment would
be withheld. He was concerned that if there was a leak either
the Department of Justice or the Department of Commerce might
"start shooting from the hip" on the cartel issue.

While Monnet was conferring at the American embassy, Schuman set in motion the next vital step in his secret diplomacy. He
chose a man of total obscurity for a private mission to Bonn—a
personal friend who was a lawyer and magistrate in his home town
of Metz named Michlich. To him he entrusted the draft text of the
proposals of what was shortly to become the Schuman Plan, together with a personal letter to Chancellor Konrad Adenauer,
written in German, explaining the overriding political importance
of the proposals and inviting German support. Michlich made his
way from Metz to Bonn, unknown and unnoticed, on Monday,
and an urgent appointment with Chancellor Adenauer was then
requested by the French High Commission on Tuesday morning,
May 9.

"That morning I was still unaware that the day would bring
about a decisive change in the development of Europe," Adenauer
recorded in his memoirs. "While the Federal Cabinet was in session, news came that an envoy from French Foreign Minister
Schuman had an important message for me. Ministry-Director
Herbert Blankenhorn received the gentleman, who gave him two
letters from Schuman to myself. Their content, he said, was exceptionally urgent; they must be put before me right away. The
French gentleman, whose name I do not know, told Blankenhorn
that the French Cabinet was at that very moment meeting to discuss the content of the letters. . . . Blankenhorn brought the letters to me in the Cabinet meeting."

From Schuman, Adenauer read a handwritten note which—
wherever it now reposes—must be one of the most poignant and
important documents of European history.

"In his personal letter to me, Schuman wrote that the aim of his
proposals was not economic but highly political. There was still a
fear in France that when Germany had recovered she would at-

tack France. It could also be imagined that in Germany, on the other hand, there was a corresponding desire for greater security. Rearmament would have to begin by increasing coal, iron and steel production. If an organization such as Schuman envisaged were set up, enabling both countries to discern the first signs of any such rearmament, this new possibility would bring great relief to France. . . . I immediately informed Robert Schuman that I agreed to his proposal with all my heart."

In Paris, the French Cabinet had gathered on Tuesday, rather than Wednesday, its regular meeting day, in order to hear Schuman before he was due to depart for the London Foreign Ministers meeting. The faithful Clappier was stationed by the telephone in an outer office of the Élysée Palace while the meeting droned through its routine business, Schuman delaying pending word from Bonn.

In aching suspension, the Frenchmen in the know waited as the Cabinet spun out its discussions while Schuman held back from intervening—eleven o'clock, twelve o'clock, one o'clock. At long last, as everybody began to gather up papers for an adjournment, Michlich left the Chancellery in Bonn with Adenauer's answer and reached a secure telephone in the French High Commission offices to pass the word to Clappier, who then entered the Cabinet meeting and whispered briefly in Schuman's ear. Impassively, Schuman then asked to bring one more matter before his colleagues.

"Exactly what he said is a Cabinet secret," Monnet wrote, "but I have reason to believe that it was even more elliptical and less audible than usual. No one cast doubt on the desirability of the proposal he was taking to London, even if most members of the Cabinet learned its precise terms only from the next day's press."

When the Cabinet meeting broke up, a press conference was hastily convened at the Quai d'Orsay for six that evening, with only the briefest advance notice to French and foreign journalists. In fact, the Quai d'Orsay press officials forgot to invite photographers, so the historic moment was never even recorded on film. But Monnet was there in the Salon de l'Horloge with his wife and Pierre Uri and Étienne Hirsch, who had been instrumental in the drafting. No man to create political drama, Schuman's press-conference style scarcely conveyed the historic importance of his an-

nouncement—but he knew what he was doing and was concerned
with ultimate results, not personal publicity. It was time, he said,
for a bold, constructive act, and this France was proposing. "The
consequences of her action may be immense. We hope they will.
She has acted essentially in the cause of peace. For peace to have
a real chance, there first must be a Europe." This said, Schuman
hastened to catch the overnight cross-Channel sleeping-car train to
London.

In Bonn, Adenauer responded immediately as promised with a
formal statement welcoming "a decisive step forward in Franco-
German relations—not a matter of vague generalizations, but of
concrete suggestions based on equal rights." And he went to the
political heart of the matter for the Germans by adding: "Since
production of the Saar will be pooled, one cause of tension between France and Germany will be removed." In fact, it was to
take five more years before the Saar quietly voted its way back
into Germany in another plebescite, but the process had begun,
and Adenauer, Schuman and Monnet all knew it and intended it.

But, in London, quite a different reaction was unfolding. Acheson flew over from Paris on Tuesday morning, bearing the French
secret, and went to the Foreign Office first for a meeting with
Ernest Bevin and then on to lunch at the Foreign Secretary's
official residence, in Carlton House Terrace. During lunch, word
arrived from the Foreign Office that French Ambassador René
Massigli wished to see the Foreign Secretary urgently right after
he got back to his office, and would also like to see the American
Secretary of State an hour later. Bevin wondered what was up;
Acheson's pain and unease at what was coming grew, but he
maintained his silence. They agreed that they should continue
their conversation at the Foreign Office at 4 P.M.

Acheson knew, of course, that France was now officially and
urgently informing all the European governments of the invitation
to join in the Schuman Plan. He returned to the Foreign Office, he
wrote, "with dragging feet" to find Bevin "in a towering rage." In
his meeting with Massigli, Bevin had held his temper and merely
said, "I think something has changed between our two countries,"
but to Acheson he blew up, charging Franco-American conspiracy
and bad faith for having known of the French plan and never

revealing a word. It all struck at the elemental sense of loyalty which was the core of Bevin's character.

Declining health was not much help to Bevin's normal short temper (he had barely a year to live), and Acheson knew him well enough to know that he would have to let the storm blow itself out. He of course acknowledged that he had been made privy to the French move and sworn to secrecy, but he stoutly denied that he had been part of any conspiracy. He tried to mollify Bevin by agreeing that the British had a legitimate complaint about the short advance notice, barely three hours before the press conference in Paris, and then he turned the conversation toward how each would react officially. If the British were going to be less enthusiastic, then the United States would have to be more enthusiastic, he told Bevin. The effect of this was to put a little more warmth into British official reaction than might otherwise have happened. But it wasn't over yet as far as Ernie Bevin was concerned.

On Wednesday morning, May 10, the three-power talks opened at Lancaster House, near Buckingham Palace. Bevin first asked for a meeting alone with Acheson and Schuman and an interpreter, and launched at once into the way he had been treated—a *fait accompli* which he didn't like at all, what were the rules? He had to know where he stood, what was happening to frank and open dealings among Allies? Acheson, better braced for the second assault, quickly spoke up ahead of Schuman in as soothing a manner as he could muster. Of course there had to be frank and full disclosures and consultations among Allies, he said, but there were also necessities growing out of domestic politics which sometimes warped the ideal. Then he played his trump card. He reminded Bevin that, the September before, he had come to Washington with Sir Stafford Cripps to inform the United States of Britain's intention to devalue the pound sterling, and even though Schuman was there also for a Big Three conference, the British had sworn the United States to secrecy, which it had strictly observed—and Schuman had never complained.

Bevin by now had had enough, and he simply shrugged and said, "Oh, hell! Let's join the others, we're keepin' them waitin'." As they moved to the conference hall, Schuman gripped Acheson's arm and murmured in his heavily accented and somewhat uncertain English: "My friend, you have a large deposit in my bank. You may draw on it whenever you please."

Monnet arrived in London the following day to get down to diplomatic cases with the British in explaining what the French were proposing and how they intended to proceed. Not unexpectedly, he encountered immediately the fundamental resistance to joining Europe which was to plague constructive foreign policy in Britain for the next quarter of a century. Cripps was among the people he saw, and his first question was whether France would go ahead with Germany and without Britain. Monnet responded:

"My dear friend, you know how I have felt about Britain for more than thirty years—there is no question about that. I hope with all my heart that you will join in this from the start. But if you don't, we shall go ahead without you. And I'm sure that, because you are realists, you will adjust to the facts when you see that we have succeeded."

The French were determined to strike fast while the iron was hot, and get a negotiating conference underway on a Schuman Plan treaty not in a matter of weeks but in a matter of days. There then followed ten days of trans-Channel diplomatic exchanges between Paris and London—eleven notes in all, back and forth, totaling some four thousand words—the British in effect trying to negotiate about the negotiations while the French resolutely insisted on acceptance of the principles of the plan in advance—including the supranational concept of the high authority. Monnet, supervising the diplomatic responses on the French end, was utterly resolved that there could be no compromise on being either in the coal and steel pool or out. By June 2 the arguments were exhausted and Britain stayed out.

On June 3, the three Benelux nations joined Italy and Germany in accepting the French invitation to open negotiations on the Schuman Plan. Monnet, who would conduct the negotiations, made a preliminary round of the capitals to brief all the other governments in advance as to how he wanted to proceed. He gave them all much the same advice he gave in his first meeting with Adenauer in Bonn: "It would be a mistake to worry too much about expertise. What counts is a sense of the general interest. I should advise you to choose a delegate who is directly responsible to you. The last word is always political." Adenauer chose Walter Hallstein, a professor of law at the University of Frankfurt, who later became the first president of the Common Market Commission when it was formed in Brussels in 1958. The treaty negotiations opened in Paris on June 20, 1950. It was not easy going, for it quickly became apparent that it had to be an educational process as well as a diplomatic negotiation—the education of national governments in thinking and acting in supranational, European terms, negotiating to give up sovereignty and authority over such elemental matters as taxes and border restrictions to an international body that could not be vetoed or controlled.

This intensive intellectual and technical debate of the highest order at the negotiating table was abruptly jolted from the outside within a week after it opened. On June 25, 1950, the North Korean Army crossed the 38th parallel and invaded South Korea. This open Communist aggression on the other side of the globe instantly transformed the military-security picture in Europe, barely a year after the fragile success of the Berlin airlift. In particular it meant that the issue of German rearmament could not be avoided or ignored. This in turn meant that France, struggling to break out of the old impasse of fears and animosities about Germany through the Schuman Plan, would shortly be confronted with the worst political specter of all: a demand that she consent to the rebuilding of German military power.

The most immediate concern to Monnet was that a precipitous rush to rearm Germany on the part of the United States backed by Britain would backfire in France and lead to a political scuttling of all the careful and intricate work to begin the building of a unified Europe which had gone into launching the Schuman Plan. But the Americans were adamant that there could be no effective defense of Europe—and no essential American reinforcements or Supreme Allied Commander—without Germany again taking up arms. The French stalled for time. By now Monnet's old friend and long-time associate René Pleven was taking his turn as French Premier. He and Monnet conferred at length, and together with Schuman they concluded that the only way out of the corner into which they were being pushed was a military version of the Schuman Plan. Monnet again moved rapidly to produce a draft proposal to meet a diplomatic timetable. Another three-power meeting was scheduled for the end of October. The result was the Pleven Plan, to create a European army of small national contingents that would be integrated side by side into larger multinational units under European command and supranational political control. Pleven unveiled the proposal on October 24, 1950, and the United States bought it immediately, fervently and with relief.

Once the plan was launched, Monnet had little more to do with moving it forward, for his own preoccupation and priority continued to be the Schuman Plan. The same five continental nations again lined up to join the Pleven Plan, and again the British opted out—this time with instant happiness not to be entangled in European affairs. Negotiations for the creation of a European Defense Community opened in Paris in February 1951—while in another part of the city Monnet was bringing the European Coal and Steel Community treaty to a successful conclusion. It was signed in Paris on April 18, 1951.

On April 1, 1952, the Coal and Steel Community treaty passed the French National Assembly by a large majority, under Schuman's skillful handling. On May 27, the Defense Community treaty was signed in Paris in the presence of Acheson and Anthony Eden, who was back at the Foreign Office. Europe, it seemed, was poised for a great political leap forward toward federation—Monnet's dream. But it was too big a jump.

Schuman was in no hurry to present the EDC treaty to the National Assembly, for it was already under heavy attack from General Charles de Gaulle, and it was clear that it was more than the Assembly was ready to swallow so soon after approving the merger of French heavy industry in a pool with Germany. The immediate task was to get the Coal and Steel Community off to a strong start. Tiny Luxembourg was chosen as its headquarters, after a long stalemated argument among the six governments—and Monnet by acclamation became the first president of the High Authority. In August 1952, he arrived in the picturesque little capital of the duchy to put European unity into practical business at last. The Luxembourg Government turned over a railroad administration building in the center of the town for the arriving Eurocrats, and a remarkable spirit of energy and enthusiasm infused the place as they worked under Monnet's dynamic guidance to chart an entirely new course and build the solid foundations of a new Europe. To the Parliamentary Assembly of the new Community, Monnet quoted a Swiss philosopher, Henri-Frédéric Amiel: "Each man's experience starts again from the beginning. Only institutions grow wiser; they accumulate collective experience; and owing to this experience and this wisdom, men subject to the same rules will not see their own nature changing, but their behavior gradually is transformed." So it was with Europe.

In August 1954, with Pierre Mendès-France in power in Paris, the French National Assembly killed the European Defense Community treaty. It was a major setback for the Monnet federalists, but if the European army was dead, the European coal-and-steel pool was alive and flourishing. Monnet gave up the presidency after three years in Luxembourg, in the summer of 1955, and returned to Paris to form his Action Committee for the United States of Europe. He had been in governmental activity continuously for sixteen years, since the outbreak of the war in 1939, and now he wanted to work without any national responsibilities or loyalties as a private citizen of Europe.

For the next twenty years, his headquarters on the Avenue Foch was a kind of intellectual capital of Europe. Throughout his long public life, Monnet had an unquenchable capacity for seizing times of setback or defeat as moments of opportunity. Sometimes it would work; sometimes it wouldn't. But he had proved to himself time and again, often with spectacular success, that the darkest moments of defeat are the times when men's minds are most likely to be open to flashes of inspiration. Setbacks for Monnet were times of progress.

In the ruins of the European Defense Community treaty, the Europeans now pressed ahead with the Euratom treaty and the European Economic Community—the crowning Common Market. In each, from the independent distance and perspective of the Avenue Foch, Monnet played an active but discreet role in negotiating difficulties and then in parliamentary approval. When the British at last came down out of their own clouds and decided to accept the inevitable and join Europe, Monnet, who had been so tough with them in London in 1950, was out in front every step of the way to assist and guide in their new conversion. When General de Gaulle jolted Europe and the Western world with his first veto of British entry, in January 1963, for Monnet it was not the end of the road but a rough detour along the way. It took another decade, but Rome wasn't built in a day either.

On the twenty-fifth anniversary of the press conference launching the Schuman Plan—May 9, 1975—Monnet formally wound up the work of his Action Committee and retired to his country home outside Paris. He was then eighty-seven. There was simply nobody to succeed him, and the quiet end of the Action Committee was a tribute to his uniqueness and success. By that time, Great Britain had entered the Common Market and was at long last fully entwined in Europe, even if its Little Englanders still writhed and resisted the coils. A Britisher, Roy Jenkins, would soon be taking over the presidency of the Common Market Commission. At Monnet's urging, a new French President, Valéry Giscard d'Estaing, had taken the lead in institutionalizing regular summit meetings of the heads of government of the enlarged Community, three times a year, in a kind of embryo European cabinet. All governments were committed to holding a European general election in June of 1979 to choose by popular mandate the members of the European parliament—another Monnet dream. At the end of 1978, in the difficulties of the economic recession, Germany's Helmut Schmidt took the lead with Giscard d'Estaing in creating a new European monetary system—another Monnet goal. He lived to his ninety-first year, to see all of the potential basic institutions of a federated Europe in place: a cabinet of heads of government, an elected parliament, an executive administrative arm in Brussels, and a unified monetary system.

No other man played as continuous and decisive a role in the building of Europe today as Jean Monnet. Government heads and political leaders came and went, each in turn making his vital contribution and impact. Monnet was there through it all. Often he was criticized for misjudging political realities; often his persistence irritated. Often his reach exceeded his grasp—but what are statesmen for?

7
Harold Macmillan

HAROLD MACMILLAN, A MAN OF MANY AMBIGUITIES, MANAGED among his varied and considerable successes to turn the role of the gifted amateur into a high professional political art. It was a role for which he was naturally suited, for he was a consummate politician with an irrepressible streak of the actor in his complex and enigmatic makeup. The British love striving amateurs, and Macmillan gave a national audience his best. He had the longest unbroken run as Prime Minister of any man in this century except Asquith during the First World War: six years and nine months from 1957 to 1963. It was the Indian summer of British imperial history, and Macmillan was the ideal Edwardian to preside over it with aplomb, style and success.

Through it all, achievement was made to look offhanded, haphazard, the luck of the gifted amateur, usually accompanied by apologetic self-deprecation and surprise on the part of the Prime Minister, no vulgar trumpets or champagne corks, please. Setbacks and difficulties were the hard luck of the amateur, who could only persevere and try harder next time. Moments of crisis were the time to take solace in a Trollope novel—not for Macmillan the frenetic worry of professional success seekers. He walked across the English public stage varyingly costumed in Ascot topper and gray morning coat; in Oxford University robes with the mortarboard on backwards; in floppy hat, baggy tweeds and gum boots; in a dinner jacket with the black-tie ends tucked under the collar; or in a cardigan with darned repair work at the elbows—always with the air of a chap rather lucky to be enjoying racing society, the company of top shots on the grouse moors, of distinguished academics, good clubmen and entertaining dinner companions. There was a whiff of mothballs and old lavender, port wine and good cigars about Macmillan.

He was "Unflappable Mac," working diligently at being effortless. With his hats and costumes, his hooded eyes and droopy mustache and toothy grin, his look of somewhat haggard nobility, he was a godsend to cartoonists and parodists. He was the living epitome of the caricature Englishman—a Colonel Blimp, Major Thompson, Mr. Micawber, Mr. Pickwick, Professor Higgins and the Vicar of Wakefield all rolled into one. His banal and elusive House of Commons speaking style was parodied constantly in cabaret acts and music halls ("You may well ask why our Secret Service is still being called 'secret'—but that, I am afraid, is a secret"). One cartoonist did a classic of Macmillan with antlers sprouting out of his head poised alert as the noble stag on a mountain crag in Landseer's famous Victorian painting "The Stag at Bay." The most brilliant caricaturist of that period, Vicky, created "Supermac," the Superman of Politics, swooping around the globe to put things right in Washington, Moscow, Paris, New Delhi, Johannesburg, Melbourne. He remained unflappable about the news media, as he did about everything else—unlike his worrying predecessor, Anthony Eden, and too many other men of power. He realized, it seemed, that it did the country no harm to have a good laugh and it certainly did Macmillan no harm politically.

He adopted his own cliché for his times: "You never had it so good." What is remarkable is not how true this might have been, but how well the label stuck to the Macmillan era, and how many Britons look back two decades later and agree. It was a great act, a maddening act, which would have been a resounding flop if it had not been supported by a scholarly mind, keen intelligence, genuine human compassion, the experience of war, pain, suffering, setbacks and long waiting in the wings watching other big actors, all melded finally into a zest for power and the skill to use it ruthlessly. Laugh the country did, while Macmillan went on unflappably being a very successful Prime Minister.

"You never had it so good" was the voice of Macmillan, the political actor. But there was also Macmillan the statesman. As he lulled Britain domestically with economic soporifics and Edwardian social imagery, he was also effecting a profound reorientation of Britain's imperial past. Almost unnoticed, Macmillan turned out to be the Prime Minister who presided over liquidation of the British Empire. But it was accomplished with such nonchalance and political skill—billed, of course, not as any bitter demise but as an exciting, revitalizing transformation of empire into commonwealth—that even diehard Tories were ready to stand up and applaud Macmillan every time the Union Jack came down. The list of British colonies that either became independent or were set firmly on a timetable to self-government under Macmillan is almost staggering: Ghana in 1957, followed in rapid order by Malaysia, Cyprus, Nigeria, Tanganyika, Zanzibar, Western Samoa, Trinidad, Tobago, Singapore, Sierra Leone, Jamaica, Uganda, Kenya and then, immediately after Macmillan left office, by Malawi, Malta, Gambia and Zambia. Of course the long process began when the Labour government launched independence for India, Pakistan, Burma and Ceylon in 1947. But the clock more or less stopped for colonial independence when Winston Churchill returned to Downing Street, in 1951. After the Suez War, when Macmillan took over from Anthony Eden, the real problem was how to complete a graceful retreat. Under Macmillan, Britain gave up the greatest empire in history with a maximum of goodwill and a minimum of violence and disruption. True, there had been the anti-Communist campaign in Malaysia, the Mau-Mau troubles in Kenya and the EOKA operation in Cyprus, but these all preceded Macmillan's premiership. Nowhere was there anything in the British Empire to compare to the French war in Indochina or Algeria, or the aftermath of the Belgian departure from the Congo or the Dutch departure from Indonesia, or Portugal's exit from Mozambique and Angola. Nothing in the history of the Empire became the British like the leaving of it.

Having finally altered course for Britain as the fading center of a world empire, Macmillan set sail for Europe. After a decade of postwar misjudgments and lost opportunities when Britain could have joined in the formative stages of European unity, Macmillan in 1961 at last took up the challenge for his country of entering the European Common Market more or less on Europe's terms. Again he was skillfully reversing the policies of his Conservative predecessors, Churchill and Eden—indeed reversing a couple of centuries of British history. He then wound up beached on the inhospitable coast of de Gaulle's France. The veto of British entry into Europe by de Gaulle at the height of his power in January 1963, was a bitter and unfair end to Macmillan's efforts of statesmanship. All the more so since the two men had known each other since the wartime days in London and Algeria, and de Gaulle owed much to Macmillan and even more to Britain. But de Gaulle was a man devoid of sentiment, who resented debt and vindictively sought to wipe the slate clean of either whenever the opportunity offered. He could have been magnanimous about Macmillan's political problems in taking Britain into Europe. He could have shown compromise, smoothed the path and still extracted a fair price of admission for himself and France. But, for his own reasons, he chose to keep Britain out. "One day the British will enter Europe, but I will not be around," he said not long after his veto. At least Macmillan had the satisfaction of still being around when Britain did join the Common Market a decade later. De Gaulle, in one of his self-fulfilling predictions, was not.

Maurice Harold Macmillan was born in 1894 of Scottish antecedents on his father's side. He was a grandson of the founder of the Macmillan publishing house, which remains primarily a family firm, of which he was a director to the end of his life. His mother, like Churchill's, was an American—a fact that he often cited as a prerequisite for success in British politics.

Macmillan's mother was indeed a formidable and energetic woman, who dominated the family—so much so that when Macmillan was badly wounded in a wartime air crash in Algiers in 1943, his first words when he came out of shock were "Tell my mother I'm alive and well." She had then been dead for six years. Helen Belles was the daughter of a country doctor in Indiana, brought up a staunch Methodist and educated at a finishing school in Indianapolis. She married a young painter before she was eighteen, but he died shortly after and she was a widow at nineteen. She boldly took her sorrows to Paris, and there, like a heroine in a Henry James novel, she met and married Maurice Macmillan, a rather shy, scholarly man ten years her senior who nevertheless had the hardheaded business sense of his Scottish father. He was in charge of the educational side of the publishing house. Nellie, as she was known, was no drawing-room social ornament. From the start she took a close interest in the business, helped start its textbook side, bore two sons, ran an active household, purchased in 1906 a spacious country house at Birch Grove, in Sussex, where Macmillan lived to the end of his days, and insisted on buying the rights to an enormous first novel by an unknown American southern woman, Margaret Mitchell's *Gone with the Wind*. Macmillan made much of his antecedents, and took with him from government office to government office as he advanced to No. 10 Downing Street a picture of the cottage where his grandfather was born, on the island of Arran, at the mouth of the River Clyde. His mother lived with him and his family much of the time until she died, in 1937.

Young Macmillan was somewhat bookish and introverted, eclipsed in scholarship and youthful personality by his older brother, Daniel, who was to become the head of the publishing firm. In 1908 he entered Eton but then dropped out with a weak heart and was tutored privately at home. But in 1912 he went to Balliol College, Oxford, graduating in 1914 with first-class honors, retaining a permanent nostalgia for its life and stimulation.

From the intellectual cloisters of Oxford, Macmillan, along with the cream of his generation, was hurled straight into the trenches of the First World War. He joined the Kings Royal Rifle Corps, one of the distinguished British regiments, but it was not good enough for his mother, who arranged a transfer to the Grenadier Guards, where he was commissioned and rose to the rank of captain. He had a rigorous, grueling war, wounded first in the head at the Battle of Loos, a body wound a second time, and finally was put out of action for the rest of the war with a third wound at the murderous Battle of the Somme, in 1916. This was an appalling mass slaughter of seventy thousand Englishmen in *one day,* and Grenadier Guards officers habitually led their men over the top in cloth caps with swagger sticks and revolvers. Macmillan suffered a shattered pelvis, and lay for a whole day in no-man's-land reading a pocket copy of Aeschylus. It was the Byronic tradition, the time of Rupert Brooke, Siegfried Sassoon and Robert Graves, and a perfectly natural thing for a Balliol man to do on the battlefield. He was finally rescued and shipped back to England and did not leave the hospital until after the Armistice. He was not fully recovered until 1920, and the old wound gave him pain and a shuffling walk all his life. The war had also given him a sense of his own courage and stamina, and a certain contempt—not always justified —for "gentlemen of England now abed." And it had brought him down out of the rarefied social atmosphere of his upbringing to raw responsibility for men's lives, and contact with a stratum of his countrymen he had scarcely known existed. He stayed on in the Guards and, again through the influence of his mother, was offered the post of aide-de-camp to the Governor-General of Canada, the Duke of Devonshire. He loved his time in Ottawa, for there he met the Duke's daughter, Lady Dorothy. They became engaged and were married in April 1920, in one of the great weddings of London social history.

Out of uniform and working in the family firm, Macmillan was spurred by his arch-Tory father-in-law and an urge to accomplish something on his own to turn to politics and try for a House of Commons seat. The Conservative Party Central Office offered him rather bleak territory: Stockton-on-Tees, a wretched industrial town on the northeast coast of England, full of misery and unemployment in the postwar depression of the 1920s. For the twenty-nine-year-old son-in-law of a Duke, it was rather like going from Balliol to the trenches all over again. All the same, from the security of his own social status, he did manage to convey genuine concern and compassion for his working-class constituents, and it was one of those situations in which they were still ready to vote Tory in the hope that the Tories would reward the loyalty of the masses. Macmillan entered Parliament in the general election of October 1924, and represented Stockton for the next twenty-one years. He promptly aligned himself with the liberal wing of the Conservatives, gaining a certain cachet as a progressive and convert to the economic ideas of John Maynard Keynes. All the same, there was a smugness about him that even his fellow Tories noticed, and he was generally regarded as an independent lightweight. But he gravitated naturally to the Churchill-Eden grouping of the party, and by the time the war broke out, in September 1939, he, like dozens of other Tories, was fed up with the complacency and ineffectiveness of Neville Chamberlain.

After Russia attacked Finland, in November 1939, in the Winter War, he joined a public committee to organize independent aid for the Finns, and then went off in the worst of the winter to see for himself at the front how the Finns were doing. He came back to deliver a speech of major impact in the House, castigating the Chamberlain government for misjudgments and above all misleading claims about its help for the Finns. His was one of the Tory votes that finally brought Chamberlain down, in May 1940.

After sixteen years on the back benches of Parliament, at the age of forty-six, Harold Macmillan at last got a foot inside the door of power. When Churchill formed the wartime coalition government, he offered Macmillan the very modest job of parliamentary secretary to the Ministry of Supply, under Herbert Morrison, a Labourite, as Minister. Macmillan went at it with alacrity, and from then on seldom looked back. It was a key department in the war effort, and an ideal department in which to gain experience of government direction of industry. After two years at Supply, Churchill moved Macmillan on to the Colonial Office, up the political ladder, as Under-Secretary in June 1942. Here he dealt directly with problems of the empire that he would one day quietly dismantle.

In November 1942, United States and British forces went over to the offensive and landed in North Africa to clear the Axis from the southern coast of the Mediterranean. Instantly they were embroiled in the internecine political complications of the French. There were de Gaulle's Free French and Pétain's Vichy French and Frenchmen who would have nothing to do with either but were ready to cooperate with the Allies. There were pseudo allies and pseudo collaborators who turned faster than a weather vane in a cyclone. There were Pétainists, Gaullists, Giraudists, Darlanists, Monarchists and Fascists. Algiers abounded in supporting intriguers and plotters on every side. General Dwight D. Eisenhower, as Supreme Allied Commander, and his Anglo-American headquarters staff and subordinate military commanders were singularly unprepared and naïvely equipped to cope with French politics while trying to fight a war. Just before Christmas 1942, Churchill sent for Macmillan and in a rambling and vivid review of the North African scene, offered him the post of Minister of State with cabinet rank as British political representative at Eisenhower's headquarters. Macmillan could scarcely wait for Churchill to finish his monologue so he could accept.

The job that Churchill wanted Macmillan to do had not existed before and was on no organizational chart—and therefore was ideal for the talents of the gifted amateur. There was an American political adviser at Eisenhower's headquarters, Robert Murphy, a career State Department man. Assisting him was a British Foreign Office official who was highly competent but was a subordinate who could not carry much weight. Churchill wanted a direct pipeline into Eisenhower's headquarters, and he wanted to make British influence felt on political decisions, which perforce were an inevitable problem of war whether generals were prepared for it or liked it or not.

With two secretaries, a personal assistant and a couple of typewriters purloined from the Colonial Office, Macmillan turned up in Algiers on January 2, 1943. General Eisenhower had only heard via a radio news broadcast that he was coming. It had all been worked out between Downing Street and the White House and nobody thought to tell Ike. It was not a very auspicious beginning: "What sort of a Minister are you?" "I am not a diplomatic minister—I am something worse." "There is nothing worse." "Maybe you will think that a politician is even more troublesome." "Well, I don't know about that, but anyway what are you going to do?" After that, Macmillan quickly introduced his American Hoosier mother into the conversation to ease things, and in fact it was the start of a warm friendship and twenty-year working relationship between the two men—totally unalike in background, outlook, intellect and career.

Vichy Admiral Jean Darlan had been assassinated on Christmas Eve, further complicating the French political snafu, in which the Americans were vainly trying to make an effective political-military leader out of General Henri Giraud while General Charles de Gaulle, who was the real power outside France, treated the whole mess with haughty disdain from his headquarters in London. Macmillan saw the first political priority as ridding the Giraud administration of its civilian and military Vichy collaborators, of whom there were plenty, and then working for unity between de Gaulle and Giraud.

As an ex-Grenadier Guards officer, Macmillan was thoroughly at home in a military atmosphere, and he was experienced enough as a politician and shrewd enough as an operator to play himself in with Eisenhower and his staff as a low-key loyal subordinate member of the team. In mid-January 1943, Churchill and President Roosevelt arrived in North Africa for the Casablanca Conference to decide the next moves in Allied military strategy and to attempt at the same time to impose some workable order on the French situation. Macmillan and Murphy were summoned to meet the two leaders, and an incident occurred that cemented things between Macmillan and Eisenhower after their uneasy opening. Macmillan recounts in his memoirs:

"I got a message asking if I could call on the President at 6 o'clock. I found him in a great bed, the splendid head and torso full of vigour and vitality. At the head of his bed was sitting Churchill, and standing to attention like a Roman centurion on the other side, our Commander-in-Chief, General Eisenhower. As I came in through the door, the President threw up his hand in friendly greeting. 'Hallo, Harold,' he called out. 'It is fine to see you—fine.' Murphy joined us and a short discussion followed. When I left, General Eisenhower came out with me. He seemed somewhat surprised. 'You never told me you were a friend of the President,' he said. 'Well,' I replied, 'I don't think I am a particular friend, but I have seen him several times in the United States and we have some friends in common.' 'How strange you English are,' reflected the General. 'If you had been an American you would have told me that you were on Christian-name terms with the President of the United States.' I replied, 'Well, I'm not sure that I am—not mutual; but that's just his way of being friendly.' The General seemed still more perplexed. But this little incident served me well with him."

A few weeks later, the British sent a new director of psychological warfare from London to Algiers: Richard H. S. Crossman, a left-wing Labourite, later a cabinet minister, who was an erratically brilliant, dynamic German specialist. By now Macmillan was thoroughly settled in with the Americans and on top of his job, and he sent for Crossman immediately and delivered to him a speech that Crossman says was probably made to every other British arrival "but impressed itself indelibly on my memory."

"Remember," he said, "when you go to the Hotel St. George you will regularly enter a room and see an American colonel, his cigar in his mouth and his feet on the table. When your eyes get used to the darkness, you will see in a corner an English captain, his feet down, his shoulders hunched, writing like mad, with a full in-tray and a full out-tray and no cigar.

"Mr. Crossman, you will never call attention to this discrepancy. When you install a similar arrangement in your own office, you will always permit your American colleague not only to have a superior rank to yourself and much higher pay, but also the feeling that he is running the show. This will enable you to run it yourself.

"We, my dear Crossman, are Greeks in this American empire. You will find the Americans much as the Greeks found the Romans—great big vulgar, bustling people, more vigorous than we are and also more idle, with more unspoiled virtues but also more corrupt. We must run Allied Force Headquarters as the Greek slaves ran the operations of the Emperor Claudius."

The remarkable thing about Macmillan was that while he fully believed in this insufferable condescension, he never allowed it to surface in his personal dealings with Americans. While thinking this way, he nevertheless managed to act openly toward Americans and straightforwardly, and use his undoubted intellectual training and superiority in a way that usually impressed, often amused, without giving offense. The ploy of the gifted amateur.

In the essential political business at hand in North Africa—getting the French to purge their Vichyites and then unifying the two prima donnas, Giraud and de Gaulle, in order to get on with fighting the war—Macmillan readily and almost automatically gained ascendancy over his American counterpart, Robert Murphy. Macmillan was a weightier character and personality than Murphy, backed as he was with Cabinet status and direct access to Churchill. But beyond that, Murphy came to North Africa from the American embassy at Vichy, where he was assigned by the State Department after the fall of France. He had played an instrumental role before the North Africa landings, seeking out military men who were prepared to help the American and British forces when they came ashore, and then in arranging the cease-fire deal with Admiral Darlan. Along with this, Murphy was of course saddled with the virulently anti-de Gaulle attitude and policies of Roosevelt and Secretary of State Cordell Hull—so it was not very surprising that he was unable to command the confidence and intimacy and disinterested influence with the fractious French that Macmillan could manage. Macmillan and Murphy got on well together, but Macmillan subsequently wrote:

"It would have been far better if at the beginning of January, 1943, when the invasion of North Africa had been successfully launched and Darlan's assassination had allowed Giraud's natural succession to power, Murphy had been withdrawn. It was clear that a new phase was about to begin in the relations between the Anglo-Saxon allies on the one hand and France and the different French groups on the other. Murphy had been primarily employed as the protagonist in a large-scale and ambitious Fifth Column operation. This experience was bound to prove a great handicap to him and his work in the next period. He was inexorably caught in the meshes of a past which everybody now wished to forget. It would have been wiser if they had replaced him with a man as uncommitted as myself. But it would have deprived me of a friendship which I deeply value."

The arrival of Jean Monnet in Algiers at the end of February did much to transform the situation, since there was now inside the Giraud administration a Frenchman of integrity, skill and influence, with whom the Allies could work—a Frenchman, moreover, who could reach out to influence de Gaulle as well. Macmillan and Monnet had worked together on supply problems in London, and as Macmillan wrote, "His work at Algiers was absolutely vital to any solution—he was the lubricant, or even the catalyst, between the two bitterly opposing factions." Monnet, for his part, recorded dryly that "Macmillan plunged with great assurance into these exotic intrigues, which appealed to his cultivated tastes," and then added: "He and I were friends; he and Murphy were accomplices."

Meanwhile, in the midst of the imbroglio of French affairs, Churchill instructed Macmillan to fly to Egypt and make a new attempt to persuade French Admiral René Godfroy, a Pétain-Vichy loyalist, to agree at last, now that the tide had turned in the Mediterranean, to bring his naval forces, which were immobilized under British guns in Alexandria Harbor, over to the Allied side. The force consisted of a battleship, four cruisers and a number of smaller ships. An RAF Transport was assigned for the trip, but a mechanic neglected to remove a covering from an air intake on the fuselage which operated the speedometer. Speeding down the runway, the pilot saw his speedometer wasn't working, braked suddenly, ground-looped and crashed. Macmillan barely managed to scramble out through an emergency exit in the cockpit before it burst into flames, and wound up in shock in hospital with leg injuries and a badly burned face. But a week later, still bandaged, he determinedly set out for Cairo again, and this time made it. Getting the French admiral to cooperate took longer.

Macmillan returned briefly to London at the end of May 1943, to join on the spot in persuading de Gaulle at long last to accept the terms of joining forces with General Giraud, carefully negotiated and drafted by Monnet. De Gaulle stiffly agreed with little good grace. When he arrived in Algiers shortly after, it was mainly to create one political crisis after another inside the French Committee of National Liberation until eventually Giraud was shunted to one side and de Gaulle had full control. Macmillan spent endless hours with the General across this period and probably came to know him as well as any Englishman ever could or did. But it was to little avail twenty years later, when Macmillan was Prime Minister and de Gaulle was President of France.

As the war moved on from North Africa, Macmillan moved with it as political adviser for the Mediterranean Theater—the negotiations for the Italian surrender, in September 1943, during the battle for Sicily; the political problems in Italy that followed; Yugoslavia, Tito and the Balkans; Greece and the installation of a regency and British military intervention against Communist-led partisans in a civil war that very nearly took the country into

Stalin's orbit; the surrender of the German forces in the North of Italy; and finally the Allied confrontation with Tito and the Yugoslavs in the vital Adriatic port of Trieste at the very end. Macmillan had a "good war" and enjoyed every minute of it—even, in a way, the plane crash.

He returned home immediately after Germany's unconditional surrender and the collapse of Hitler's Reich. A few weeks later, at the end of May, 1945, Churchill disbanded the coalition and formed a new Conservative "caretaker government" prior to the general election, in July. Macmillan was rewarded with the Air Ministry. With the election coming up, he was offered a safe Conservative seat in London, but he loyally decided to try once more to woo the electorate of Stockton-on-Tees. Times had changed vastly since 1924, and like so many other Tories, he was swamped in the Labour landslide.

But, luckily for Macmillan, within weeks of the massive Labour victory a safe Conservative seat became vacant when one of the old Tories who had survived the landslide suddenly died. Macmillan sailed back into Parliament in a by-election in mid-November. But he was no longer the "gifted amateur" exercising his political skills among the great captains of the war. Without the stimulation of power, he came on like a hot-air balloon. The pompous actor in Macmillan took over from the incisive politician-diplomat, and he became boringly and predictably right wing in his rhetoric (although not actually in his thinking). His polished barbs and House of Commons witticisms, as a Labour member put it, "reeked of midnight oil." His oratory, which was never memorable anyway, was studded with phrases like "let sleeping dogmas lie" or "they preach planning and practice confusion," cracks about "clever men who in every age were always wrong." Prime Minister Attlee, scarcely noted for repartee, referred to Macmillan during this period as "an elephant who thinks he's a flea."

The real problem was that it was tough to be effective in opposition against an exceptionally strong Labour government with a very powerful team of ministers who could readily dominate the House of Commons. It was a government that was giving Britain what it needed, and most of the Tories knew it, with its mild socialistic program of nationalization of coal, electricity, gas, the railways, the health services, etc. Moreover, although Macmillan was on the Tory front bench, he was not really in the Tory inner circle of power. The key men alongside Churchill were Anthony Eden and R. A. Butler, and among the younger men working on Tory policy were Iain Macleod and Reginald Maudling. Macmillan's role was that of a political performer but not a Tory prime mover. All the same, in this role he managed the essential trick of talking like a right-winger for the benefit of the Tory faithful, while keeping slightly to the left on policy issues, such as India, coal nationalization, and many economic questions.

It was a long wait for the Tories, but Attlee finally felt forced to go to the country in a general election in October 1951, after an intensive, draining six years in office with all the postwar economic, political and diplomatic turbulence. Churchill returned to Downing Street in his seventy-sixth year. But it was an index of Macmillan's secondary status in Tory ranks that he was offered only the Ministry of Housing. Eden, three years his junior, of course returned to the Foreign Office, and Butler, nine years his junior, became Chancellor of the Exchequer. Macmillan swallowed hard, and then told Churchill he would take Housing if he could run it like the wartime Ministry of Supply. In fact he turned a backwater job into one of the great successes of the Churchill government. In the period of postwar shortages, the Labour government had little choice but to ration house building and construction materials along with everything else. When Macmillan took over he boldly set a target out of the blue to build three hundred thousand new houses a year—borrowing, he said, from Lord Beaverbrook, at the old Ministry of Aircraft Production, who said that "it is the duty of a production minister to create a vacuum and then fill it, to make bottlenecks and then break them." When the housing target was reached, and over three hundred thousand more were built in 1953, Macmillan overnight became a Tory hero.

In 1954, Churchill reshuffled his Cabinet and Macmillan went to the Ministry of Defence. He was there only six months and was no great success—in part because Churchill, although aging and edging on senility, still regarded defense as part of his own authority. In any case, the old warrior finally stepped down in April 1955, just past his eightieth birthday. Eden at last became Prime Minister, after twenty years in Churchill's shadow, and he shifted Macmillan to the Foreign Office. But again Macmillan was working in the shadow of a Prime Minister who regarded foreign policy as his own show, and there was not much opportunity for personal success.

He spent barely eight months at the Foreign Office when Eden moved him again. Butler wanted out of the Treasury after five years, and in January 1956, Macmillan became Chancellor of the Exchequer. He had now occupied office in more government departments than any man except Churchill himself: Supply, Colonies, Housing, Defence, the Foreign Office, the Treasury, and of course his war years in the Mediterranean. But there was something dispiriting about the fashion in which he had been shunted around, with a lack of real success anywhere except at Housing, and at this point he seemed tired and defeated and on his way out. In fact his best years were just ahead.

In July 1956, Egypt's Gamal Abdel Nasser nationalized the Suez Canal, and Eden started down the road to the Suez War. Macmillan was fortunate to be out of the Foreign Office and ensconced in the relative independence and political importance of the Treasury, and he knew it. His role throughout the Suez affair constitutes one of the more ambiguous phases of his long political life. He was for it, then he quickly turned against it, and he was the only one to reap political success out of the disaster. At the outset, where Butler wavered over Suez, Macmillan was Eden's loyal supporter in the determination ultimately to use military force. Macmillan knew the overriding political importance of "Tory loyalty," and if he had any doubts about the wisdom of what Eden was doing he never showed them. In fact, the war almost certainly could never have been launched without the consistent support of the Chancellor of the Exchequer. But Macmillan made a monumental error of judgment when he calculated that the operation would cost the Treasury only around £100 million, and he largely ignored the political and economic impact that launching a war would have on sterling. When the predictable run on the pound began with the landing of British troops in the

canal zone, he abruptly took an agitated lead in Eden's demoralized Cabinet in insisting that Britain had to call a halt and declare
a cease-fire. But loyal he had been, and loyalty paid off.

Sir Anthony Eden, broken by Suez in spirit, political authority
and health, gave up the prime ministership after less than two years
in office on January 9, 1957. So abrupt was his departure and such
was the state of his physical and nervous condition that he failed
even in the final traditional duty of a Prime Minister to advise the
Queen on who should form a new government. Maybe he couldn't
or didn't want to make the choice. Maybe he didn't want to reward Butler, his long-time No. 2, after his equivocal attitude in
the Cabinet over Suez. In any case, those who were left behind,
when Eden walked out of Downing Street fighting back the tears,
rapidly agreed that the only way out of the dilemma would be to
have the two senior men not in the running to head a government
—Lord Salisbury and Lord Kilmuir, the Lord Chancellor—conduct a poll of the other ministers individually and alone on their
choice for the succession. Salisbury and Kilmuir accordingly retired to a suitable office of the Privy Council, and received the
Cabinet members one by one—Salisbury, with his lisp, asking each
in turn: "Well, now, is it Hawold or Wab?" (Butler's nickname,
Rab). The vote was never revealed but it was reported in later
years to have been something like nineteen to four in favor of
Macmillan. Apart from Butler's attitude over Suez, there is little
doubt that other Cabinet members also felt instinctively that Macmillan would be easier to work under and more effective a political leader in the House of Commons—as indeed he was.

Salisbury conveyed the Cabinet's sentiments to Buckingham
Palace, and the Queen then sent for Churchill to discuss the selection with him. He promptly gave Macmillan his blessing also.
Shortly after 2 P.M. on January 10, Macmillan walked into a bedroom of the Chancellor of the Exchequer's residence, at No. 11
Downing Street, where his wife was looking after a sick grand-
child. "I've been called to the Palace," he said. "What on earth do
they want?" the Duke's daughter asked. He explained that he was
about to become Prime Minister.

Of all the political performances of his life, there was nothing to
compare with the fashion in which Macmillan, a man of Suez,

now put Suez behind him and disengaged from a disaster for which he bore considerable responsibility. At once he went on the air to rally Tory spirits and scorn defeatist talk about Britain being finished and a second-rate power: "What nonsense! This is a great country and do not let us be ashamed to say so. There is no reason to quiver before temporary difficulties."

He moved from No. 11 to No. 10 Downing Street as if he had belonged there all his life. On his new official stationery, he wrote out in longhand a quotation from Gilbert and Sullivan's *The Gondoliers:* "Motto for Private Secretaries and Cabinet Officers: Quiet Calm Deliberation Disentangles Every Knot."* The frenetic atmosphere of Eden's neurotic worrying, which had infected the whole government and indeed the country gave way quickly to Unflappable Mac. On the evening he formed his first Cabinet, Macmillan went off to the Turf Club for oysters and champagne with Edward Heath, the government chief whip in the House of Commons. Throughout his years in office he was always turning up casually, often alone, for lunch or dinner at the member's table at one of the five clubs to which he belonged, where he loved to perform and could be sure of receptive audiences.

At the peak of power, in the prime of life, relaxed, urbane and secure with a wealth of political and diplomatic experience on which to draw, Macmillan quite naturally set out again to play to the hilt his old, self-conceived role of the Algerian days of Greek guide to the American Romans. Almost immediately, he received a friendly note from Ike at the White House, and he promptly set in motion arrangements for a meeting at Bermuda in March, the first of an endless stream of international summits which were his diplomatic stock-in-trade over the next seven years.

Macmillan's approach to Anglo-American relations was the antithesis of Eden's somewhat resentful, competitive relationship with the United States in general and John Foster Dulles in particular. It was probably not unnatural that Eden, having served as prewar and wartime Foreign Secretary at the apex of British

---

* Three years later, I was writing a magazine article on No. 10 Downing Street, Home of Prime Ministers, and saw Macmillan's motto still taped on the inside door into the Cabinet Room. Macmillan's private secretary took it down and made a photocopy for me.

power and influence in the world, did not take readily to the shifting balance that had put Britain in America's shadow. Added to this was Eden's vanity and his search for personal diplomatic achievement and success—a key psychological factor that led him to Suez. But Macmillan was shrewd enough and skillful enough to derive genuine pleasure and satisfaction out of the role of mentor and guide—a kind of wily second fiddler winking at the audience, and by his gestures and performance conveying that he is really directing the orchestra.

A good example of Macmillan at work in this fashion was the convening of the first summit meeting of heads of government of the North Atlantic Treaty Organization, in Paris in the spring of 1958. In 1957 the Russians sent their first sputnik into outer space, beating the United States by more than a year. American leadership and the American response under Eisenhower were at best somewhat soggy as far as the Europeans were concerned, and Macmillan conceived the idea of bringing all the NATO heads of government together for the first time since the treaty had been signed, in 1949, as a show of solidarity and purpose. Off he went to Washington to sell the idea to Ike. As it happened, the NATO Secretary-General, Belgium's Paul-Henri Spaak, was in town at the same time. At the White House, Eisenhower readily agreed, and then they decided that it would be better if the proposal to other government heads came from Spaak. Macmillan went off to see Spaak, and when he returned he told Eisenhower rather jauntily: "He didn't like the idea very much at first because it wasn't his, but when I explained to him that it *was* his he liked it fine."

Macmillan benefited also from the fact that at this point there was little substantial leadership coming from anybody else in Europe. France was mired in the Algerian War and the last political contortions of the Fourth Republic before General de Gaulle returned to power. In Germany, Chancellor Adenauer was in no position to take much of an international lead and was becalmed in midstream between the launching of the Coal and Steel Community and that of the European Common Market. Moreover, United States foreign policy under Dulles was not all that imaginative or innovative—frozen as it was in cold-war postulations. Macmillan had virtually a clear field, however much the British had messed things up for themselves in the Middle East, and he rapidly sensed and seized the opportunity for diplomatic initiative. But with the chief lesson of Suez in mind, the cornerstone of his policy was never to stray too far away from the Americans, concentrate first on relations with Washington.

Whatever the advantages this held for Britain back in the 1950s, in the long run there was something debilitating and limiting for British foreign policy in Macmillan's overweening pursuit of the "special relationship." He made it politically successful, almost too successful, and as a result it then became too much of a substitute for clear, hard thinking out of British positions on foreign policy, of Britain's own status and problems and opportunities in the world, too much of a crutch and too much of a pretense of power as a substitute for the reality. In Dean Acheson's wounding but precisely targeted phrase: "Britain has lost an Empire and not yet found a role." For Macmillan, and far too long after him, the "role" mainly consisted in trying to influence the Americans and then lining up with them. But in Washington, British advice came to mean less and less as British influence and economic strength in Europe and the rest of the world steadily declined. The Greeks lost influence with the Romans, too.

Macmillan rode the "special relationship" for all it was worth, and for a time—particularly in the Eisenhower years after Dulles left the scene—he reaped considerable political and diplomatic harvest from it both for himself and for Britain. As the Suez debacle faded into history, there was a particular moment of satisfaction, even a sense of British vindication, when Eisenhower ordered United States Marines to land at Beirut in 1958 to cool an incipient Lebanese civil war, and Macmillan ordered British Paratroops in alongside the Americans at the same time to the Jordanian capital of Amman. This was the last time, incidentally, that the Western powers resorted to direct use of their own military power in the Middle East.

Macmillan's most dramatic diplomatic foray was his decision, out of the blue, to visit the Soviet Union in February 1959 to seek to defuse the mounting Berlin crisis and set machinery moving for a four-power summit conference. Eisenhower did not much like the idea, but he wished his old comrade the best of British luck.

Adenauer was upset and worried that Macmillan would misplay things and give something away. De Gaulle was skeptical and indifferent. Off Macmillan went to Moscow in the white fur hat he had worn on his visit to the Finnish front in 1939. For the next eighteen months, East-West relations were dominated by the long climb to the summit.

At last, in May 1960, Macmillan approached the peak of his diplomacy when he and Eisenhower joined de Gaulle in Paris to meet Nikita Khrushchev. But as they gathered, an American U-2 spy plane was shot down seventy thousand feet above the Soviet city of Sverdlovsk—and the summit conference was shot down with it. Khrushchev refused even to sit down with the Western heads of state without a groveling apology from Eisenhower. He stormed out of Paris threatening to sign a separate peace with East Germany and liquidate all Allied rights in West Berlin. Tension was high, and Macmillan paced the British embassy garden in Paris in a state of total anguish. But when it was all over, what little difference it all made!

The crisis simmered on, but instead of signing the threatened separate peace, the Communists erected their infamous Berlin Wall, in August 1961. Meanwhile John F. Kennedy had been elected President of the United States, and Macmillan set out with renewed confidence and aplomb to keep the "special relationship" in good order with a man of a new generation, twenty years his junior. The two indeed got on well together. Macmillan appreciated Kennedy's intelligence and dynamism and the fashion in which he ran his own show after the Eisenhower days. As for the new President, Arthur M. Schlesinger, Jr., subsequently wrote in his book on the Kennedy years: "Kennedy, with his own fondness for British political style, liked Macmillan's patrician approach to politics, his impatience with official ritual, his insouciance about the professionals and his pose of nonchalance even when most deeply committed. They soon discovered that they could match each other's transitions from gravity to mischief and communicate as if in shorthand. It was as if they had known each other all their lives."

In mid-1961, Macmillan at long last set in motion Britain's first bid to join the European Common Market—giving assurances in his public declarations that he had "cleared it with Kennedy." This may have been a clever ploy from the standpoint of British politics but it scarcely commended itself to General de Gaulle, who regarded it as incompatible with proper European spirit to ask Washington first if it was all right to join. De Gaulle expected British entry into Europe to involve a kind of symbolic severance of any pretense to other special relationships—to the Commonwealth, and especially to the United States. But it was thoroughly in Macmillan's political style to want to back into Europe instead of marching in—to attempt this great historic change for Britain as if it were something evolutionary and not revolutionary. All this, of course, played straight into de Gaulle's hands in the famous veto.

Macmillan and de Gaulle conferred four times over the eighteen months of the Brussels negotiations for British entry. The last time was in December of 1962 at the Château de Rambouillet—a stiff and difficult conversation between the old comrades of Algiers. From that meeting, Macmillan flew almost immediately to Nassau, in the Bahamas, to meet Kennedy and talk about acquiring American Polaris missiles for British nuclear submarines. For de Gaulle, this was the final piece in the picture he sought to construct, of a Britain that would always put its relations with the United States above its relations with Europe, and therefore a Britain unready for, if not unworthy of, membership in the Common Market. De Gaulle magisterially lowered the boom on Britain's application to join at a press conference on January 14, 1963.

Two major efforts at international diplomacy had now collapsed on Macmillan in Paris. Moreover, by 1963, after six years in office, he was beset at home by a host of domestic mishaps and scandals—none of them inherently disastrous or of major significance, but all of them cumulatively debilitating to the government and to the image of Unflappable Mac. Spies and sex were the chief problems. The most celebrated case was that of John Profumo—the War Minister who lied to the House of Commons about an affair with a London call girl who was also sleeping at the same time with a Soviet naval attaché. The Soviet officer had decamped for Moscow, and Profumo resigned from the government and the House of Commons in disgrace. In this same period, Kim Philby bolted to Moscow from the Middle East, where he had been under close watch by British Intelligence, and Macmillan had to disclose that for five years during and after World War II,

Philby had been a Soviet agent in the heart of MI-5. In the British Admiralty, a homosexual civil servant blackmailed by the KGB was arrested and tried for spying. Next came a case of a heavy-drinking, love-making ex-Royal Navy petty officer working in a secret submarine warfare research center who was also working for a Soviet master spy in London, Gilbert Lonsdale.

In fact, the record of the British Secret Service over this period under Macmillan's prime ministership was by no means all bad, but effective counterespionage and undercover work could scarcely be publicized, and the negative side made all the head-lines. In the Lonsdale case, the British effectively rolled up a major Soviet spy net, and at the same time British agents were playing the leading role in the Penkovsky case—perhaps the most important penetration of Soviet intelligence services that the West has ever managed.

Unflappable Mac could take the political heat and was no man to rush out of the kitchen. But in September of 1963, illness struck him down. A prostate condition was diagnosed and an operation and a long recuperative period became necessary. He informed the Queen that he must give up office, and she did him the unusual honor of visiting him at his hospital bed. In a last burst of political activity, he maneuvered once again to block Rab Butler from getting the premiership, and Sir Alec Douglas-Home became his successor.

Macmillan, the actor, knew the importance of a quick final curtain. He retired completely to his country home, refusing any title or royal honors. When his health was restored, he resumed the chairmanship of Macmillan publishing, and wrote five volumes of memoirs. All in all, he was perhaps the most enlivening and intriguing political character to perform on the British national stage since Disraeli, whom he indeed most closely resembled of all his predecessors. The warrior Churchill is of course in a historic category all by himself.

It is the ultimate ambiguity that Macmillan's greatest success was in quietly giving up the empire. Otherwise he is remembered for efforts at history-making that failed because of others. But, like the Cheshire Cat in *Alice in Wonderland,* which disappeared except for its smile, Unflappable Mac will always be hovering over No. 10 Downing Street.

8
The Suez War

THE SUEZ WAR OF 1956 WAS AN ABERRATION OF HISTORY THAT
swept the international scene like some political typhoon pulling
everything in its path into a destructive vortex. When it had blown
itself out, it left a trail of diplomatic double-dealing, destroyed careers, damaged reputations, muddled and indecisive leadership,
trans-Atlantic mistrust and misunderstandings that were either real
or deliberately invented, and a residue of personal bitterness in almost everybody who had anything to do with the whole complex,
emotional and ultimately botched affair. Nobody came out of the
Suez War with any glory or honor, and the only people who
gained anything at all from it were the Israelis.

The French were the most single-minded and determined in
plotting and pushing the use of military force at Suez. But the British nevertheless bore the heaviest ultimate onus and suffered the
greatest diplomatic, political and moral damage. The Suez War
was the last death rattle of British imperialism, and with it the climax and near tragic end of the long political life of one of the nation's most distinguished public men, Sir Anthony Eden. With all
its cast of characters and political complexities, the Suez War was
Eden's war. He went into it with a certain exhilaration, came out
of it miserably and bitterly, accepted and embraced full responsibility and defended what he had done to the end of his days. His
life's drama was something of a Greek tragedy. All his years of
diplomatic and political experience, along with his intellectual and
emotional makeup, propelled him inexorably toward a climactic
moment of action, which then left him snuffed out on the stage of
history.

Anthony Eden was the golden boy of prewar British politics—a
young, handsome and gallant army officer in the First World War,

a student of Persian and Arabic at Oxford, a diplomatic appointee
before embarking on a political career. In 1931 he was elected to
the House of Commons and promptly entered Ramsay Mac-
Donald's national government as undersecretary of state at the
Foreign Office. In 1936, not yet forty years old, he moved up to
become the youngest Foreign Secretary in British history, under
Prime Minister Neville Chamberlain. But he rapidly found himself in deep fundamental policy conflict with Chamberlain over
appeasement of Mussolini and Hitler, and in February of 1938
he abruptly resigned from the government in one of the political dramas of prewar history. It was an act of considerable
courage, which won Eden great plaudits and established him
firmly in the public image. It also imbued him with the principle
that appeasement of dictatorship never pays—in itself admirable
but not necessarily applicable to every strong-man regime or diplomatic impasse.

At the outbreak of war, in 1939, Eden rejoined the Chamberlain government as Dominions Secretary. When Churchill took
over, in 1940, he first put Eden at the War Office and then returned him to the Foreign Office six months later. Eden was by
now firmly established as Churchill's faithful *dauphin,* but waiting
in the wings was long and not always easy for a man of his intellect and ability. After the war came the six-year postwar period in
opposition as Churchill's deputy during the 1945–51 Labour government. Then at last he was back at the Foreign Office for the
most effective and productive period in his long career. He played
a key role in the negotiations in Geneva to end France's long involvement in Indochina in 1954. He promptly followed this success with the diplomatic initiative to bring West Germany into full
membership in the North Atlantic Treaty Organization after the
French voted down the European Defense Community treaty later
that same year.

Eden was at the pinnacle of his national and international prestige when Churchill at last stepped down, in April 1955. But he
was not in robust health or a fully well man when he finally arrived at No. 10 Downing Street. More than two years earlier, he
had undergone a complex operation at the Leahy Clinic, in Boston, Massachusetts, that involved a plastic replacement for a bile

duct. Although his general recovery had been satisfactory, the
bile-duct condition left him subject to odd bouts of fever, which
would recur at times of stress or high tension. Complete rest was
then necessary. Eden at best was not a very relaxed or easy man.
Despite his urbane exterior and the public image of a completely
controlled diplomat, he was short-tempered, edgy, vain and given
to violent outbursts against subordinates when things did not go
his way. He was a constant worrier, and as a result his temperament and his physical condition constantly interacted on each
other.

For a worrier, there was plenty to worry about. From the time
he returned to the Foreign Office, he had to cope with steady attacks on British power in the Middle East—an area of traditional
British paramountcy and also a part of the world with which Eden
felt a strong personal and scholarly involvement.

First in 1951 came the abrupt nationalization of the British oil
fields in Iran by Prime Minister Mohammed Mossadeq. Then
came the coup by Gamal Abdel Nasser deposing King Farouk, of
Egypt, and a new wave of Arab nationalism began sweeping the
Middle East. In this atmosphere Eden had to direct the long and
difficult negotiation for withdrawal of British troops from the Suez
Canal base and try to obtain in return a treaty that would preserve
some British strategic advantage in the area. Almost as difficult
with the Egyptians was the winding up of the old Anglo-Egyptian
Condominium Treaty over the Sudan, to give independence to
Khartoum without Egypt taking over the country.

To try to stabilize the security problems and contain these mul-
tiplying political pressures, Eden conceived the idea of forming a
Middle East defense organization as a kind of NATO for the Arab
world. But most of the Arab states promptly took their lead from
Nasser, who rejected the proposal as nothing but British imperialism in a new guise. Eden could get little more than lip-service
support from Washington, and in the end all that emerged was the
ill-fated Baghdad Pact, with only three Middle East adherents:
Turkey, Iraq and Iran. Even King Hussein, of Jordan, under pressure from Nasser, declined to sign and subsequently poured more
salt into British wounds by summarily dismissing from his service
the legendary British commander of the efficient little Arab Le-

gion, Major General John Bagot Glubb, the "Glubb Pasha" of
Jordan.

Nasser meanwhile had been pressing the West for arms to modernize his forces while embarking on the next objective of his
Arab leadership: stepped-up guerrilla warfare against Israel. But
the British were in no mood to be accommodating, given the way
they found their interests under constant attack by Nasser. The
United States could have moved in, but with an election year coming up, the Eisenhower administration was not about to run the
political gauntlet of the Jewish lobby in order to do Nasser a
favor. It should not, therefore, have come as any great surprise
that Nasser would turn to a ready and willing Soviet Union for
military help. But it was a surprise, even a profound shock, when
London and Washington found out, in 1955, what was happening.
Gleefully, the Russians stepped through Nasser's open door. As
the arms began to flow, Egyptian guerrilla action against Israel
began moving up in scale in 1956 from mere sabotage operations
to small, hit-and-run, set-piece battles. Soviet arms were posing an
entirely new balance-of-power situation in the Middle East, and
Nasser's Arab Revolution increasingly appeared to threaten the
vital security of the West.

Such were the mounting tensions and deteriorating diplomatic
and military atmosphere in the Middle East when the Union Jack
came down at the last British outpost on the Suez Canal. On June
15, 1956, without a band or ceremony, a company of Grenadier
Guards marched briskly aboard a troop transport at Port Said, at
the northern end of the Canal, to complete the British withdrawal
and sail for home. The Grenadiers had been the first into Egypt,
at the Battle of Tel-el-Kebir, in 1896, and they were the last out
sixty years later. With British forces gone from Egyptian soil and
arms from Russia pouring in, Nasser was next to the Prophet
Mohammed in Middle East popularity. And the stage was set for
a major crisis.

Hovering over this gathering storm like some brooding archangel
was that enigmatic, devious, moralizing Calvinist lawyer and cold-
war Secretary of State John Foster Dulles. As the decisive six
months unfolded in the Middle East from July to December of

1956, it did not help very much that Dulles and Eden had a mutual antipathy if not downright mistrust of each other. Of course superficial civilities were always observed, and they called each other "Foster" and "Anthony." But there was little more to their relationship than surface cordialities, and before the Suez drama ran its course, Eden was giving as much vent to anger and frustration over Dulles's legalistic maneuverings as he was against Nasser's supposed aggression.

Dulles, for his part, when he took office, in 1953, had given Nasser his support and blessing and made Cairo a stop on his first trip abroad. One of his first objectives was to move American foreign policy away from the total identity with the Jewish cause of the Truman days and onto a more even-handed balance with the Arab world. Every American Secretary of State since Dean Acheson has wrestled with the same problem. Support for Nasser was a ready means of redressment, and at the same time, Dulles, the Calvinist moralizer, found it a convenient way of taking American distance from British colonialism.

But by 1956 the situation in the Middle East had gotten somewhat muddled for Dulles. The Nasser revolution was not turning out to be quite as rational or accommodating to Western interests as Dulles expected it to be. When Nasser turned to the Soviet Union for arms, all the early Dulles goodwill went up in Red smoke. Nasser was now down in the American political black book on two counts: consorting with the Communist cold-war enemy and threatening the security of the State of Israel. Against this background, Dulles took the action that triggered the Suez crisis and led to the botched Suez War.

Along with independence and arms, Nasser's other great dream for his nation was to build the Aswan High Dam—to bring the life-giving waters of the Nile under control, create the most enormous man-made lake in the world, boost Egypt's hydroelectric power supply and industrial capacity, enable agricultural irrigation to push back the desert, and open the way for modest and desperately needed national economic growth. The High Dam became for Egypt what the conquest of the West had been for the United States.

During 1955, a consortium of British, French and German

firms had been formed to handle the enormous construction, and a financing plan of $1.3 billion had taken shape in which these governments would participate, along with the United States and the World Bank. The Soviet Union then intervened with an offer to build the dam at a cheaper price on better terms. Nasser still preferred to deal with the West, and a period of bargaining, if not haggling, began as he sought to drive down the Western terms. Britain and the United States became increasingly disenchanted with Nasser's tactics, and increasingly concerned in any case about Egypt's capacity to cover such heavy financing while spending so much on Soviet arms. By June of 1956, as the last British troops prepared to quit the Canal, the two governments had decided in secret talks to bow out quietly and let the whole deal simply fade away.

Possibly Nasser sensed a change in the Anglo-American attitude. In any case, he brought things to a head by instructing the Egyptian ambassador to Washington, Dr. Ahmed Hussein, to seek a clear answer from Dulles. The two men met at the State Department on July 19, 1956. Dulles at first evaded and temporized as to American intentions. When the Egyptian then brought up the Russian offer to finance and build the dam, Dulles's cold irritation was aroused. He dropped the temporizing tactics and practically waved Hussein out of his office, telling him that if Egypt already had the money from Russia there was no need to go on talking about it to the United States. The American offer of help, he brusquely declared, was hereby withdrawn.

Nasser was on the Yugoslav island of Brioni holding one of his nonaligned meetings with Marshal Tito and India's Pandit Nehru when he received a call from Cairo about Dulles's action. He returned to his capital in a grim and determined mood. One week later, on July 26, 1956, he announced to a wildly cheering throng gathered for a revolutionary rally in Alexandria that he had just nationalized the Suez Canal. That morning, the Egyptian Army moved into all the offices and installations of the French-run Suez Canal Company. An Egyptian canal administrator had been appointed, and all foreigners running the Canal except the pilots had been ordered out of Egypt.

"With the revenues which will now belong to Egypt from our Canal, we will build the Aswan High Dam," Nasser exulted.

"This, O Citizens, is the battle in which we are now involved—a battle against imperialism and the methods and tactics of imperialism and a battle against Israel, the vanguard of imperialism. Arab nationalism has been set on fire from the Atlantic Ocean to the Persian Gulf. Arab Nationalism feels its existence, its structure and its strength."

Nobody in Washington, London or Paris seems to have dreamed it possible that Nasser would nationalize the Suez Canal. Dulles had left Washington on an official visit to Peru when Nasser struck. Eden was presiding at a formal dinner at No. 10 Downing Street for young King Feisal, of Iraq, and his longtime strong-man premier, Nuri es-Said, almost the last of Britain's loyal friends in the Middle East. News of the canal seizure was handed to Eden at the dinner table. He told his guests at once, and the party broke up early—"its social purpose now out of joint," as Eden later put it. He summoned the military chiefs of staff immediately to Downing Street to assess the situation after dinner, and asked the French ambassador and the United States chargé d'affaires to sit in on the discussion as well. Next day, Eden sent off a lengthy personal cable to President Eisenhower in which he outlined an attitude and approach that he followed to the bitter end:

"We are all agreed here that we cannot afford to allow Nasser to seize control of the Canal in this way, in defiance of international agreements. If we take a firm stand over this now we shall have the support of all the maritime powers. If we do not, our influence and yours throughout the Middle East will, we are convinced, be finally destroyed. . . .

"We should not allow ourselves to become involved in legal quibbles about the rights of the Egyptian Government to nationalize what is technically an Egyptian company, or in financial arguments about their capacity to pay the compensation which they have offered. I feel sure that we should take issue with Nasser on the broader international grounds. . . .

"As we see it, we are unlikely to attain our objective by economic pressures alone. . . . My colleagues and I are convinced that we must be ready, in the last resort, to use force to bring Nasser to his senses. For our part we are prepared to do so. I have this morning instructed our Chiefs of Staff to prepare a military plan accordingly. . . ."

French reaction to Nasser's seizure of the Canal was simpler than that of the British, less inhibited and at the same time more implacable. Not for the French any worries about lining up the maritime powers and consulting Washington, any rationalizations about global strategy and imperial lifelines. French reaction was conditioned by two simple facts. First, the Suez Canal was a French achievement—French-built and French-operated, with thousands of small French stockholders going back to the original nineteenth-century company of Ferdinand de Lesseps, even though the British Government had long held a controlling block of 40 percent of the shares, bought by Disraeli from the bankrupt Khedive of Egypt. While the British saw Nasser's seizure of the Canal as an attack on British power and strategic interests, for the French it was a simple case of blatant Arab thievery which had to be punished. The second basic factor for the French was the Algerian War, in which the French Army had already been locked for two years of increasingly savage fighting against the Arab FLN rebels. Cairo was the headquarters of the FLN, with Nasser giving the rebellion all the political and military support he could muster. The French, therefore, saw two simple, clear and compelling reasons to react against Nasser with military force. There was never the slightest French doubt or hesitation of the kind with which the British wrestled. For the French it was simply a question of when and how to attack.

The French Government of the day was headed by a Socialist, Guy Mollet, and in the nature of the politics of the Fourth Republic, a left-of-center government almost had to be ultranationalistic in fighting the Algerian War and defending French interests. As the next weeks unfolded, the French, not for the first time, pursued their policy with total cynicism, while the British, not for the first time, perforce became enmeshed in a policy of dismal hypocrisy.

When Eisenhower received Eden's first telegram, with its declaration of readiness to use force to "bring Nasser to his senses," he

decided to send Undersecretary of State Robert Murphy hotfoot-
ing it to London, in the absence of Dulles, to see his old British
friends and report on what they seemed to have in mind. "Hold
the fort" was the President's only instruction. Murphy arrived on a
Saturday evening. Eden was resting at his country home for the
weekend, but Harold Macmillan at once arranged an "Algiers old
comrades" dinner on Sunday at the Chancellor of the Exchequer's
official residence, No. 11 Downing Street. Field Marshal Lord Alexander, who had been ground-force commander under Eisenhower in North Africa, was the only other guest. They made clear
their belief that the test of Suez could be met only by force. Alexander indicated that military moves would probably start in August and that it would take "only a division or two" and perhaps
ten days of action to "chase Nasser out of Egypt" and restore the
Canal to international control. They left Murphy with "the impression of men who have made a great decision, and are serene in the
belief that they have decided wisely." He went to the American
embassy after dinner to send an immediate report to Eisenhower.

But it is not very clear what impression Murphy left on the
British. He says that he thought that what he heard "made good
sense" and that he shared British indignation over Nasser's action,
which indicates that he must have been a sympathetic listener. But
he adds in his memoirs that "I knew United States policy opposed
the type of 18th century strategy which was in the minds of our
friends." Yet he does not seem to have attempted to make this
point crystal clear to Macmillan and Alexander. All in all, a communications gap opened up from the very first, in which American
sympathy was assumed by the British to imply American support.
The Americans never unequivocally ruled out support for the use
of force, and the British, as the old diplomatic saying goes, "heard
what they wanted to hear."

Next day, Murphy met with French Foreign Minister Christian
Pineau, who had arrived in London, and found him "far more aggressive" than the British. Of their conversation, Murphy wrote:
"Nobody can be more ruthless in playing power politics or more
intellectually insolent than French Socialists, once they believe
their ox has been gored. Pineau did not conceal his contempt for
what he called American naiveté. He acted as if he had received a

blank check from the United States, but he did not take me into
his confidence and I was never privy to French secret plans."

Meanwhile, Eden returned to London, but at a luncheon meeting Murphy found him less open or forthcoming about British intentions than Macmillan and Alexander had been. Eden avoided
any suggestion of immediate military activity, although at the
same time he dropped the offhanded remark that "we do hope you
will take care of the Bear." In other words, Britain and France
could readily handle Nasser on their own, but if things got rough
they would expect the United States to handle Russia.

This was a prospect that had no appeal to Eisenhower whatsoever. He was heading into his second-term election campaign. He
had ended the Korean War and kept the United States out of any
Indochina involvement. His policy was simplistic. He did not like
surprises and he did not like Allies rocking his boat. He was for
peace, rule of law, and application of the United Nations Charter
for great powers as well as small. Although allied with Britain and
France in Europe under the NATO treaty, he felt nowhere near
the same identity of interest with Britain and France over the Suez
Canal. Nor did he much like hints that he would be expected to
pull their chestnuts out of the fire if they went to war and things
got out of hand. As all this evidence of Anglo-French thinking
poured in from Murphy, Eisenhower decided that Dulles, now
back from Peru, had to get to London immediately.

Dulles arrived in London on August 1 and launched at once on a
complex series of legalistic diplomatic maneuverings that dominated the crisis, on the surface at least, for the next two and a half
months. Carrying out Eisenhower's overriding objective of peace,
he simply devised a series of delaying tactics to keep the problem
tied up in diplomatic activity, to head off any Anglo-French military intervention. The longer negotiations could be prolonged in
one form or another, the Americans reasoned, the more the heat
would be likely to go out of the situation so that some kind of
nonviolent settlement in the end would emerge. But the tactic became counterproductive. As the British and French followed
Dulles up the garden path from one maneuver to another, their

bitterness and frustration grew to a point where military action seemed to be increasingly justified, for them the only way out.

Dulles compounded the frustration of his allies, moreover, by playing a kind of brinkmanship game with himself. "The art of going to the brink without going to war," he had called it, and repeatedly over those months he would make statements that appeared to condone use of force, which his diplomacy at the same time was trying to frustrate. At his first meeting with Eden in London he declared that "a way has to be found to make Nasser disgorge what he is attempting to swallow," and Eden warmly recorded that "these forthright words rang in my ears for months." For Eden this was an endorsement of the use of force, but Murphy says that it was only sympathy for the allies, a type of Dulles statement "to be taken with a warehouse full of salt." Dulles almost breathed ambiguities, and the British persisted in hearing what they wanted to hear. Of a speech that Dulles made six weeks later at one of the many Suez meetings, Foreign Secretary Selwyn Lloyd commented: "I do not think that anyone who listened to him could have felt that if Nasser rejected our plans and the Security Council failed to obtain a solution, Dulles would do other than accept the use of force even if the United States itself did not take part." How wrong the British were!

Eden from the first was obsessed with a parallel that he had formed between Nasser and Hitler. For him, seizure of the Suez Canal was simply a replay of Hitler's occupation of the Rhineland all over again. Britain and France had failed to stand up to dictatorship at that crucial point in prewar history, and paid the price of World War II—and Eden was determined it would not happen again. This theme emerged at the outset of the crisis in Eden's House of Commons statements and speeches, and was elaborated to the end in his memoirs. But it was an exaggeration of historic parallel, to say the least, to equate Egyptian power with Nazi power, or Nasser's threat to British security with Hitler's threat. Seizure of the Canal, serious as it was for Western strategic interests, was scarcely a start down the path to World War III. Yet, for Eden, with his experience of appeasement in the prewar years, this became an utter fixation.

In the summer of 1956, there was little chance for cooler

heads to prevail—if indeed there were many cooler heads around in London or Paris. Dulles, who had so precipitously canceled participation in the High Dam project, now of course arrived on the scene to urge prudence and caution. An international conference had to be the first step, and he wanted a delay of one month. But the British and French insisted on a meeting within two weeks. Finally it was agreed to invite to London the nations that had signed the 1888 convention, that guaranteed the international character of the Canal, plus the United States and other major maritime powers that had not signed, twenty-two powers in all. Dulles worried in particular about moves in dealing with the Suez Canal that might in future be taken up by the Panamanians as legal or diplomatic precedent against the United States over the Panama Canal. The conference convened at Lancaster House, in London, on August 16, with the Russians present as a Montreux signatory power but the Egyptians declining to take part.

Meanwhile in early August Eden called up about twenty thousand army reservists, and British reinforcements moved to the Mediterranean, to Cyprus, Malta, Libya and Gibraltar.

On August 10, before the London conference convened, Eden presided at a Cabinet committee meeting to approve plans for a military attack on Egypt prepared by the British Chiefs of Staff. It turned out to be a ponderous recommendation to land troops at Alexandria, seize the port, and then advance up the Nile, capture Cairo, and after that head for the Canal. What on earth the British Chiefs of Staff expected Egypt and the rest of the world to be doing all this time was fortunately never put to the test. If seizure of the Canal and its restoration to international control was the first objective of the exercise, then the British military were preparing to go about it in a most leisurely, indirect fashion, to say the least. In fact, when it came down to cases, the British were not all that well equipped or prepared for an operation such as Suez. They were short on trained paratroopers and short of transports to fly them. They were short on landing craft, and the closest point at which they could load tanks and heavy equipment in the Mediterranean for an assault against Egypt was Malta, five days' slow sailing away. Moreover, at the mouth of the Canal itself, although defenses were light, the beaches were long and shallow, making an assault landing pretty awkward. All in all, these factors seemed to dictate landing at Alexandria, a day closer to Malta than Suez. The French sent General Maurice Challe to London to review the planning, and he was impressed by the lack of aggressive élan in what the British proposed. With an active French Army already fighting a war in Algeria, the French wanted to go hard, straight for the Canal, and they had plenty of battle-hardened paratroopers ready for the job. But at this point the British held sway. A joint Anglo-French operational staff was formed to prepare for action. September 15 was fixed as the earliest feasible date for the operation.

The London conference completed its work on August 22, adopting by a vote of eighteen to four a plan to restore the Suez Canal to international control under a board of maritime powers, while recognizing Egyptian sovereignty and sharing out canal revenues more equitably. Russia, India, Indonesia and Ceylon were the four dissenters, proposing instead that a purely advisory board be established to monitor canal operations with no powers of control. Australia's Prime Minister Robert Menzies, who had been a leading figure in the conference, accepted the task of trying to sell the plan to Nasser on behalf of the eighteen. He arrived in Cairo on September 3.

As the London conference ended, the British ordered the first of several postponements in the target date for military action. They first put the date back from September 15 to September 19, and then, at the end of August, they decided on yet a further delay, to September 26. They cited that time had to be allowed for the Menzies mission, but this didn't wear well with the French, who began to feel not only that the British plan for attacking Alexandria instead of the Canal itself wasn't sound but that the British were weakening in their resolve to use force come what may.

Accordingly, around September 1, in total secrecy from the British, the French threw out first hints to the Israelis about joining in an attack on Egypt. It will probably never be known exactly how the Franco-Israeli collaboration really originated. The French were already selling Mirage jet fighters and other military equipment to Israel, as well as cooperating in the nuclear field, so there was plenty of scope for secret contact. Major General Moshe Dayan, at that time the Israeli Chief of Staff, says that an approach came from the naval officer who was to command French forces in the Anglo-French operation, Admiral Barjot, who simply passed word that the French felt the Israelis should be invited to take part in any attack on Egypt, and inquired how the Israelis might feel about it.

But it is not clear whether Admiral Barjot was taking a flier on his own, or whether he was acting on specific instructions from the French Cabinet or Premier, or whether it was a move that was thought up by the French High Command to see what the response would be—leaving it then to the French Government to accept or reject as it saw fit. In the conditions of the Fourth Republic and the Algerian War, it could well have been another case of the French military seeking to lead the French Government. In any case, Prime Minister David Ben-Gurion quickly gave Dayan full backing to explore the French overture carefully, and Dayan flew to Paris on September 7 for a first discussion with the French military authorities. When he returned to Tel Aviv, the director-general of the Israeli Defense Ministry, Shimon Peres, took things a step further and left for Paris to talk nuts-and-bolts supply and equipment problems with French Defense Minister Maurice Bourgès-Maunoury. Thus, by mid-September the French had laid the groundwork with the Israelis secretly but had taken no actual governmental decision to arrange a joint attack. Nor had the slightest hint yet been dropped to the British.

Meanwhile, in Cairo the Menzies mission, after six days of talks, ended in failure on September 9, with Nasser's complete rejection of the eighteen-power proposals and any arrangements that would in any way supersede Egypt's sole sovereign control and operation of the Canal. Both Menzies and Eden were convinced that the fate of the eighteen-power plan was sealed by a press-conference statement in Washington from President Eisenhower. Menzies had strongly warned Nasser not to take lightly the Anglo-French preparations to use force if some agreement on international supervision of the Canal could not be reached, and he thought that the warning had taken. But at this point in the Cairo talks, Eisenhower, in Washington, was questioned about force and said: "We are determined to exhaust every possible, every feasible method of a peaceful settlement. I am still hopeful that the London proposals will be accepted, but the position of the United States is not to give up, even if we do run into obstacles." After that, Nasser said no.

As Menzies talked in Cairo, Dulles took off for the remote, unspoiled wilds of Duck Island, in Lake Ontario, where he had a cabin without even a telephone, to which he would periodically retreat. Here he thought up his next move in the crisis: a proposal to form a Suez Canal Users' Association (SCUA) to operate the Canal. When he returned to Washington, a cable went off to Selwyn Lloyd in London outlining the idea. On September 11, two days after failure of the Menzies mission, the French ministers, Mollet and Pineau, flew to London to talk over the situation. Very reluctantly the British and French agreed to give Dulles's latest idea a diplomatic try—on the assumption that SCUA would not only manage and operate the Canal but collect all the transit fees as well, as the sole means of putting a real squeeze on Nasser short of use of force.

But the British then ordered a third postponement of the target date for military action—this time to October 9. Field Marshal Viscount Montgomery had gotten a look at the plan to land at Alexandria and had brusquely told Eden that it was foolish and unworkable. Agreeing with the French, Monty insisted that the only effective way to act would be a series of airborne drops on the Canal, backed up by seaborne landings, whatever the difficulties and risks. Thus spurred, the British planners had been sent back to work. But, with this third postponement, the French were increasingly convinced that British readiness to use force was petering out.

A second London conference, to adopt the Dulles SCUA plan, convened at Lancaster House on September 19, attended by the eighteen powers that had supported the proposals put to Nasser by Menzies. But the more the diplomats thrashed around with the plan, the less of a solution it offered. It was agreed that SCUA would, or could, collect canal fees, but there was no way to compel shipowners to pay SCUA instead of Nasser's nationalized Canal Authority for a Suez transit. The conference completed its work, such as it was, in three days.

Robert Murphy subsequently wrote that Dulles never really saw SCUA operating the Canal, and that the idea was no more than "a useful negotiating device to work for time in the hope that public opinion in Western Europe would harden against a military adventure." Dulles himself effectively pulled the rug out from under his own plan less than two weeks after the London meeting when he told a news conference in Washington on October 2: "The United States cannot be expected to identify herself 100 percent either with the colonial powers or powers uniquely concerned with the problem of getting independence as rapidly and as fully as possible." Of the SCUA plan he then added with fatal candor: "There is talk about teeth being pulled out of the plan, but I know of no teeth. There were no teeth in it so far as I am aware." Just as Eisenhower's remarks had seemed to the British and French to undercut all pressure on Nasser to accept the eighteen-power proposals, so Dulles's remarks effectively ended what little diplomatic usefulness the SCUA plan might have had.

After the London SCUA conference, Pineau returned to Paris thoroughly fed up with Dulles's diplomacy, American tactics to thwart military action, and British postponements and seeming hesitations. This was the point at which the French Cabinet decided firmly and unambiguously to "play the Israeli card." A highly secret message was sent to Tel Aviv formally inviting the Israeli Government to send representatives to Paris to discuss joint military action against Egypt. Dayan arrived on September 29. The Israelis needed no excuse or urging. Ample provocation for a major Israeli blow at Egypt had long been building up. Throughout 1956, Nasser had been running an almost nonstop series of fedayeen sabotage attacks deep into Israel, climaxed by frequent small set-piece battles at police stations or outpost settlements. The Israelis had struck back repeatedly in the Gaza Strip and the Sinai Desert, and they well knew the massive buildup of heavy Soviet equipment that Nasser was acquiring. Now they were being handed the opportunity they wanted to move decisively in all-out open war.

Dayan concentrated first of all on what Israel would need from the French in the way of military equipment and air support to launch an effective surprise assault against Egypt deep into the Sinai Desert, close to the Canal. French Defense Ministry representatives then returned with Dayan to Tel Aviv on October 1 and quickly cabled back to Paris what amounted to an open-ended endorsement of an Israeli order list for AMX-13 tanks with 75-mm guns, fast and light for desert operations, which the French had developed, plus Bren-gun carriers, front-wheel-drive trucks for sand conditions, tank trailers for moving fuel to advancing army units, light antiaircraft guns, ground radar, ammunition. The Israelis, with long experience in clandestine arms purchases on the world market, and the French, with long experience in arms sales in which concealment is usually automatic, worked hand in glove to speed secret deliveries across the Mediterranean. In fact, it was only a few days before the Israeli attack kicked off, that American intelligence in the country began to get wind of unusually heavy crates and cargoes unloading at Haifa Harbor.

The French had lit the fuse and it was sputtering, but they still were keeping the British completely in the dark about what they were up to—except for an indirect remark by Pineau to Eden during the London meetings on the SCUA plan. Showing his ready irritation with Anglo-Saxons, the French Foreign Minister told the British Prime Minister that if Britain wasn't going to use force against Nasser, then maybe in the end the French might act alone and even be aided by Israel. But as to the active collaboration to this end that was already in progress, Pineau said nothing.

Meanwhile, to keep up the diplomatic cover for what they were doing, the French agreed with the British as soon as the SCUA meetings were over that the time had finally come to take the Suez Canal dispute to the United Nations Security Council. Dulles added to their joint irritation by urging further delay. No doubt he realized that it would move things closer to military action if this last resort did not produce an agreed diplomatic solution with Egypt.

But Lloyd and Pineau insisted, and a letter went off to the President of the Security Council on September 23. An Anglo-French complaint against the "unilateral action of the Egyptian Government in bringing to an end the system of international operation of the Suez Canal which was confirmed and completed by the Suez Canal Convention of 1888" was placed on the agenda for debate in New York beginning October 5. In advance of the debate, Eden and Lloyd journeyed to Paris to coordinate tactics with Mollet and Pineau on September 26. They held a somewhat acrimonious discussion, and Eden found Pineau "in a mood to blame everyone including us if military action is not taken before the end of October; I doubt whether he wants a settlement at all." But still there was no revelation from the French to the British about what was afoot with the Israelis. In fact, Pineau kept the secret from Lloyd during the entire time they were working closely in New York on the Security Council debate and resolution during the ensuing two weeks.

When the two foreign ministers arrived in New York, they had another confrontation with Dulles, still sulking because they had gone to the Security Council without his blessing. First he told them strongly how much Eisenhower, in the middle of the election campaign, was against war or the use of force because if a war started it would be very difficult to end. But then he told them that it was nevertheless right to keep the "potential" use of force in being. It was another frustrating example for Lloyd and Pineau of Dulles playing brinkmanship with himself and his allies. Little did he realize, and not in the least did Pineau even hint to him, what was already taking place.

By October 10, the Israelis had completed their war plans for an attack on Egypt to be launched before the end of the month, and Colonel Yehashafat Harkabi, chief of Israeli Intelligence, arrived clandestinely in Paris to coordinate the planning with the French High Command.

On Saturday, October 13, the Security Council wound to the end of its complex Suez debate and voted approval of a set of principles concerning the status and operation of the Canal as an international waterway. This, in fact, was a considerable diplomatic success for the British and French as far as lining up wide support for their case was concerned. But the Soviet Union then lowered its veto on the second and operative part of the resolution, which called on Egypt to propose new arrangements with the users for running the Canal in conformity with international principles. In summary, the United Nations had expressed a point of view about the future of the waterway but did nothing to prod Egypt into accepting or acting upon its findings. The situation was close to a diplomatic dead end.

With the Security Council proceedings over, Premier Guy Mollet decided that the time had come to confront Prime Minister Sir Anthony Eden and the British with the "moment of truth." He telephoned Eden from Paris to say that he was sending General Maurice Challe and a deputy Foreign Minister for urgent and important discussions of the military situation. Eden arranged to see them in the discreet setting of Chequers, the official country residence of prime ministers, on Sunday afternoon, October 14. Challe got down to cases at once. The French, he informed Eden, now had firm knowledge that Israel was preparing to attack Egypt —which in turn would give France and Britain the excuse to join in military action to seize the Canal. As soon as the Israelis launched hostilities, Challe propounded, the planned Anglo-French operation could then be launched in coordination to "defend" the waterway.

How much Challe actually disclosed to Eden of Franco-Israeli collaboration is not known, but he probably revealed no more than he felt the British needed to know. In any case, on that Sunday afternoon at Chequers, the French altered the military picture completely for the British from one of theory to one of reality. After all the talk about use of force, the preparations for use of force and the planning for use of force, there was no escaping a decision. It was now put up or shut up. Yet, for Eden, and for wider long-term British interests in the Middle East, the decision was being forced in a form awkward, almost abhorrent, in which Britain would wind up an ally of Israel in the eyes of the Arab world. The French had no such qualms, since they already had the entire Arab world against them as a result of their savage war in Algeria. But the British, despite all the polemics about Nasser, still maintained some pretense to friendships and influence elsewhere in the Middle East. To attack Egypt out of the blue over the Suez Canal would be serious enough, but to attack Egypt in concert with Israel risked a political and diplomatic disaster for British long-term interests and concerns. Eden was trapped. After all of his breast-beating about standing up to dictatorships and not allowing 1936 or 1938 to happen all over again, how could he possibly wobble or retreat from the decision that confronted him now? The French had played their cards beautifully, skillfully, cynically. They wanted a war against Nasser and they were damned well going to have one. But the British would command it, take responsibility for it, and practically all of the international political outcry and onus would fall on Britain. Yet Eden could not walk away from it now.

He sent word to Lloyd to return from New York immediately. After a long final review of the diplomatic situation following the Security Council vote with UN Secretary-General Dag Hammarskjöld, Lloyd flew back Monday night and went straight to Downing Street when he landed, Tuesday morning. Eden disclosed the full truth (as far as he knew) that Pineau had been hinting about. They decided to fly immediately to Paris for a thorough examination of the "new situation" with the French.

On Tuesday afternoon, October 16, Mollet and Pineau, meeting alone with Eden and Lloyd, put the question straight to the British: The Israelis are going to attack Egypt—what will you do? The nub of the argument now lay in the fact that the French wanted direct, coordinated, Anglo-French military action with the Israelis. But Eden and the British found this impossible and therefore sought some hypocritical fig-leaf premise or excuse for taking military action without appearing to be acting in collusion with Israel. Eden later made much of the fact that he urged the French on October 16 "to ensure that if the Israelis do attack it should be against Egypt and not Jordan," with which Britain had a defense arrangement. But there was never any question of the Israelis going for anybody but the Egyptians, and Eden's remonstrations on this point were little more than an additional cover for his own conscience about what he was sliding into. Juggling all the elements around, Eden told the French, in a discussion that stretched into the evening, that there could be no question of Britain either supporting an Israeli attack or going to Nasser's defense in the face of such an attack. But going in with the noble purpose of stopping hostilities from spreading, to protect the Canal from damage by military action and safeguard it in the international interest—this would be a postulation on which Britain could probably act. But he needed Cabinet approval. The French appear to have been more bored than impressed by this display of British logic, but anything to get the British on the hook. Eden and Lloyd returned to London on Wednesday morning.

About this time, the State Department in Washington began to notice a "drying up" of the usual flow of cable traffic with London and Paris. Both the British and the French ambassadors had left Washington and after the feverish activity of the preceding three months, an odd quiet had taken hold. Logically something had to happen following the Security Council voting. What did the French and British have in mind? Nobody was talking very much. It was an uncanny calm.

The British Cabinet met on Thursday, a restricted and ultrasecret session, and after a lengthy discussion gave Eden the backing he anticipated to join the French in military action to "safeguard" the Canal if Israel attacked Egypt. This was communicated to Paris, but the French continued to be uneasy and not fully confident of British determination to see things through to the bitter end. Accordingly on Sunday, October 21, they sent word to Eden that Prime Minister David Ben-Gurion himself, and several other top Israeli leaders, were arriving in Paris next day for final talks on the military plans. The French wanted Britain to take part. Lloyd was delegated by Eden to travel to Paris incognito, in secrecy from most of the rest of the British Government. Monday engagements were canceled on the excuse of a cold, and he and his Foreign Office private secretary drove in the latter's car to the RAF station at Northolt, on the edge of London, to fly in atrocious weather to a French military airfield outside Paris. They were then whisked to a French state villa at Sèvres, not far from the airfield, narrowly missing a collision on the way.

The Israelis, who had already gathered at Sèvres, had been through a worse journey—seventeen hours en route from Tel Aviv. They had been diverted to Marseilles to refuel after long circling in the weather, and then flew back from Marseilles finally to find a hole in the clouds to get into Villacoublay. The arrival of the British did not exactly warm things up.

Dayan later wrote that Lloyd's "whole demeanour expressed distaste—for the place, the company and the topic." Lloyd, for his part, says that everybody was on the point of exhaustion, and that Dayan assumed that the British knew far more of the extent of Franco-Israeli collaboration than they actually did. He found Ben-Gurion "in a rather aggressive mood, indicating or implying that the Israelis had no reason to believe in anything that a British Minister might say." All in all, it was not a very jolly evening.

Ben-Gurion at once asked for a three-power agreement on a co-ordinated attack on Egypt—in particular that the RAF and the French Air Force should eliminate the Egyptian Air Force before Israeli ground troops moved into the Sinai. Lloyd stuck to the position that he and Eden had taken on October 16 with the French: that Britain was not prepared to fight alongside Israel but was prepared to use force "to protect the Canal." He countered with a long exposition of the diplomatic troubles to be encountered at the United Nations over the use of military force from the Arab states, the neutrals led by India, the Communist bloc, the Scandinavians, the Canadians, who would be opposed, and the attitude of the United States uncertain. But the Israelis had not flown all the way to Paris to discuss United Nations diplomacy with the British. Ben-Gurion sarcastically remarked that he didn't trust the British even to act to protect the Canal. Lloyd repeated British rejection of any three-power plans to coordinate an attack on Egypt. The Israelis declined to discuss with the British any dates, timing or details of their own operational plans—leaving Lloyd with the odd impression that they had not yet made up their own minds. This rather acrimonious discussion finally broke up around midnight without any agreement on anything. In a suitably heavy fog, Lloyd and his private secretary drove back to Villacoublay, where there was barely enough clearance to take off for London.

On Tuesday morning, October 23, Lloyd reported to Eden and a small inner circle of key ministers that Eden had formed to take the Suez decision, that he doubted whether Israel would attack in the near future! But in Paris, Mollet and Pineau were so upset and irritated by Lloyd's handling of the Sèvres meeting, and what they took to be continuing British irresolution, that Pineau sent word he was coming to London immediately to sort things out all over again.

Pineau arrived early Tuesday evening, had supper with Lloyd, and then Eden joined them. Again they chased around and around about the degree and form of coordination or collaboration or whatever it might be termed with an Israeli attack on Egypt. Pineau asked for another three-way discussion with the Israelis in Paris next day, and the British agreed. But at the end of the evening's talk, Lloyd wrote a letter to Pineau, who was spending the night at the French embassy, "to make it clear that we had not asked Israel to take action; we had merely stated what would be our reactions if certain things happened."

That same October 23, as Eden and Lloyd, Pineau and Mollet, Ben-Gurion and Dayan argued out the tortuous terms of their "collaboration by any other name," the people of Budapest took to the streets in the beginning of what rapidly swelled into the Hungarian uprising against Communist rule. When this hit the headlines, practically all attention shifted to Hungary, and all thought or speculation about what was happening in the Suez crisis disappeared, in particular from the preoccupations of Dulles and Eisenhower in Washington in the final stages of the presidential election campaign. The Israelis could scarcely have asked for a better cover or diversion for what was about to happen.

For the final step in the Suez collaboration at the second Paris meeting with the Israelis on Wednesday, October 24, the British sent a senior official rather than a Cabinet minister: Sir Patrick Dean, assistant undersecretary at the Foreign Office, later ambassador to Washington. Dean was one of the superior intellects of the British diplomatic service, but it was an odd ducking of ultimate political responsibility on the part of Eden and Lloyd to assign a civil servant to handle the final details of an agreement to go to war. Their excuse was that Lloyd had to answer questions in the House of Commons, and his absence might have tipped off that something was afoot. It was a somewhat limp excuse.

Eden and Lloyd, in sending Dean to Paris, again seemed to be wanting to put as much distance as they could between themselves and the distasteful business of joining the Israeli-French collaboration. This time the Israelis disclosed to the British that they expected to attack by October 29 or soon after, five days hence. Beyond adding that they proposed to capture the position of Sharm el-Sheikh, at the Straits of Tiran, the mouth of the Gulf of Aqaba, on the Red Sea, they gave no further details of their operational plans. Franco-British contingencies were then discussed, including the terms of an appeal that the two governments would make to both Israel and Egypt to stop the fighting after Israel started it! The ultimate hypocrisy of working out an appeal to stop a war while going over the military plans to start one must be unique in the annals of history. In any case, as the discussions progressed, somebody from the French side went into an adjoining room and dictated a memorandum of the outline of the contingency plan and the "stop hostilities" appeal that was to be the excuse or basis on which Britain and France would then move into action. This was typed up, and Dean was asked to sign on behalf of Britain. Up to that point, there had been only verbal understandings about what to do. But the French and the Israelis apparently had decided to take no further chances on British evasion or prevarication. Dean was surprised, but since the paper was nothing more than a record of the discussions of the three delegations for submission to the Cabinet, he signed. Still, it was a record of an understanding on going to war. Eden had placed Dean in a position of political responsibility that was totally contrary to British traditions of the role of civil servants. Moreover, when Labour returned to power, eight years later, his signature on that document almost certainly cost Dean an appointment to the highest post in the British diplomatic service, permanent undersecretary of the Foreign Office.

Dean got back to London at eleven on the evening of October 24 and reported to Eden and Lloyd immediately at No. 10 Downing Street. Next morning, the Cabinet held its regular Thursday session, once again in restricted attendance. Only Macmillan, Butler and Anthony Head, who had become Minister of Defense, knew of the written contingency-plan memorandum that Dean had signed. But the Cabinet then approved the tactic of issuing an ultimatum that Nasser was sure to reject and using that as justification for launching the Anglo-French force at the Canal. The die was now finally cast.

The United States of course had been kept totally in the dark by its European allies as to what was going on. As Lloyd brusquely summarized: "They had let us down on every occasion, even when silence from them would have helped. In addition, it would be easier for them if we did not tell them beforehand." And Pineau subsequently told the French National Assembly: "For three months the Americans knew perfectly our feelings, our disillusionment, our military preparedness and our efforts to secure a pacific settlement of the problem. Everything, therefore, allowed our reaction to be foreseen. As regards our methods, it is perfectly accurate that we did not tell our friends, but we never had the impression that we acted *against* our friends, although we now and then resented the bitterness of certain speeches and certain votes in the UN." Mollet told the same assembly debate that the Americans were not informed "lest they impose additional hindrances to action, delays during which Israel would have taken the risk of being destroyed."

All the same, there was no reason for the total surprise and shock that hit Washington on October 29. Ample evidence plus some direct foreknowledge of what was underway had indeed reached Washington, but as so often happens with American intelligence in a crunch, it had not been put together and fully evaluated.

Parallel to the drying up of the Washington diplomatic traffic with London and Paris, the American code breakers of the National Security Agency began picking up an increase in Paris-Tel Aviv and London-Cyprus traffic on their monitors, which apparently they failed to break. Moreover, there had been a deliberate leak from the French to the Americans, presumably the CIA, although the information was more in terms that covered the French rather than alerted the United States. It was apparently misleading or uncertain as to when an Israeli attack might take place, indicating that it would not be until *after* the American election. All the same, nobody in Washington sat down to pull the potential picture together—riveted as the intelligence people were in those final days on Hungary and Soviet military movements and activity.

On Friday, October 26, the United States Military Attaché in Tel Aviv reported that what appeared to be total mobilization was getting underway. On Saturday, the peripatetic Dulles took off for Texas, where he delivered a speech to the Dallas Council on World Affairs, exulting over the Hungarian uprising and the brutal Soviet display of tanks against civilians to maintain Communist power. Eisenhower was in Walter Reed Hospital for a ritual pre-election checkup. Things were quiet on the Israeli Sabbath, but on Sunday came an urgent cable that full mobilization had indeed been ordered. When Dulles got back to Washington, Eisenhower, at the hospital, had prepared an urgent appeal to Ben-Gurion for restraint, in "the hope that you do nothing to endanger the peace."

At 4 P.M. Monday, October 29, Israeli paratroops took off in transport aircraft provided by the French for an evening drop on the Mitla Pass, deep in the Sinai, only twenty-five miles from the Canal. Egyptian reinforcements would have to come through this pass, and by this deep strategic strike the Israelis went to war.

Night operations had long been a specialty of the Israelis, going all the way back to the 1930s, when the legendary British officer Brigadier Orde Wingate had been in Palestine and helped train the Haganah Jewish paramilitary defense forces. Launching a major war at night, moreover, threw maximum confusion into the Egyptian defenses as the Israelis struck overland into the Sinai to link up with the paratroops at Mitla Pass and also to seize Sharm el-Sheikh. It was not until four hours after the Israeli drop that a first communiqué that fighting had begun was issued in Tel Aviv. This was midafternoon Monday in Washington when the news broke. Dulles was stunned and outraged. All the terrible Soviet misdeeds in Budapest were now to be surmounted by Israeli aggression in the Middle East. Worse was yet to come.

On Tuesday morning, October 30, Mollet and Pineau flew to London to make absolutely certain of the agreed action with the British. They returned to Paris immediately after lunch, as Eden made his way to an excited House of Commons to deliver the final ultimatum to Egypt and Israel. Meanwhile, the Egyptian, Israeli and United States ambassadors had been summoned to the Foreign Office at fifteen-minute intervals to be handed the ultimatum beginning at four-fifteen, when Eden would be speaking. When the American ambassador, Winthrop Aldrich, was handed a copy, for information, of the formal demand that Israel and Egypt pull back ten miles from *each side* of the Suez Canal, he exclaimed to Sir Ivone Kirkpatrick, the permanent undersecretary: "But there is something absurd about what I am reading!" Egypt, fighting the Israelis in the Sinai, was being told by the British and French to withdraw from her own territory to allow Anglo-French forces to land? It was indeed absurd, but that's how Britain and France went to war at Suez.

Eden was in a mood of exhilaration, matched by a short-lived euphoria in the House of Commons, Labour and Tory alike. At last England was going to have a bash at the Wogs after the long summer of tortuous diplomacy. The Egyptians and Israelis had twelve hours to reply, and the absurdity of the terms of the ultimatum made Egyptian rejection a foregone conclusion.

At Malta, the ponderous military loading of tanks and trucks into landing craft for the five-day voyage to Suez had been ordered. On Cyprus, British and French paratroops were waiting for action. England was about to go to war, and for the moment there was a mood of jingo excitement. Bitterness and disillusionment came later.

Soon after Eden returned to Downing Street after addressing the House, an urgent cable arrived from Eisenhower, in Washington. In anger and disbelief at what his allies were doing, the President appealed for withdrawal of the ultimatum. Late in the evening, Eden returned to the House to conclude an urgent debate on Suez and announced firmly that British-French military action to protect the Canal and separate the protagonists would go forward despite the White House appeal. While Eden was on the floor of the House, a White House call was put through to his office in the Commons, and his press secretary, William Clark, answered to hear President Eisenhower say, "Anthony, have you gone out of your mind!"

I had been reporting this tangled crisis since its beginning from London for the New York *Herald Tribune,* and after filing a final story in the early hours Wednesday on Eden's late appearance in the House of Commons, I sped to Heathrow Airport, having gotten the last seat on an El Al flight to Tel Aviv. But the flight was halted in Rome on Wednesday afternoon, and after a long wait at the airport, word came that we would be held there overnight. I fell into a conversation with the Israeli pilot, wearing RAF wings and a row of wartime ribbons, about when I might get to the war. He told me with open nonchalance: "Well, the British and French are starting to bomb the Egyptian airfields, and from here on we will be flying under military control from British headquarters on Cyprus. We probably won't be permitted to enter Israeli air space until Thursday evening."

Deepest secrecy, of course, surrounded all the advance collusion with the Israelis. The ultimatum issued in London by Eden, absurd as its terms were, still provided a certain political cover for what was really going on. To have a corner turned up on the real facts of military cooperation, if not collaboration, in that conversation at the Rome Airport was a startling revelation. Thursday morning we flew on to Athens, where we were held until late afternoon, finally taking off to land at Tel Aviv just after dusk. I almost missed the war completely.

I grabbed a taxi and went straight to the Israeli Government Information Center in Tel Aviv, which I knew from previous reporting trips. From an information officer I got a quick briefing, and a further fill-in from a British correspondent fortuitously just back from the fighting. A few hours before, an artillery barrage and night attack had been launched at the Gaza Strip—which had been bypassed by the Israeli forces when they had first struck into the Sinai Desert three nights before. I got a story off to New York and then checked into the Dan Hotel. Early next morning, I joined other correspondents with a military escort to enter Gaza town as the Israelis were cleaning out a few little pockets of resistance in the dense Palestinian population.

With the overrunning of Gaza, the Suez War was effectively over for the Israelis. The Franco-British parachute drops at Port Fuad and Port Said, and the subsequent seaborne landings at the mouth of the Canal were still to come, but that was not my story. The Israelis had been overwhelmingly successful, with a speed of attack and coordination of forces, command and control on a par with any army in the world. In fact, they made the Anglo-French part of the Suez War look like something out of the nineteenth century—Kitchener, Napier, Roberts and all that.

Despite all the secrecy, the evidence of collaboration and outside help and preparation for the Israelis was pervasive. At the fronts in Gaza and the Sinai, at key defensive positions close to the Syrian and Jordanian borders where there had been no fighting, there were AMX-13 tanks all over the place, in new-paint condition, some barely scratched. That weekend of victory, there were French Air Force pilots in uniform drinking at the bar of the Dan Hotel. None of this of course could be reported, under strict Israeli censorship. But by the osmosis process of reporting, we soon knew that the French had provided the planes for the Israeli parachute drops and had flown supply sorties into the Sinai Desert to drop ammunition and stores to the advancing ground forces. More important, French Air Force squadrons were transferred to Israel before the attack to fly high-level defense cover with their Mirages over Tel Aviv and Jerusalem against possible Egyptian air strikes, thereby enabling the Israeli Air Force to concentrate on forward ground-support missions in the Sinai with the advancing troops. The French had given the Israelis what the British refused at the Sèvres meeting: direct military support in their attack on Egypt. By the weekend, Tel Aviv was something of a dead center in a swirling typhoon.

At first light on Monday, November 5, six days after Eden's ultimatum, British and French paratroops at last dropped on the two port towns at the mouth of the Suez Canal. The seaborne forces at last arrived from Malta to land tanks and infantry on Tuesday morning—election day in the United States for Eisenhower. There was not much to the fighting, Nasser having withdrawn the bulk of his forces from the Canal Zone bases back to cover Cairo. By Tuesday afternoon, the British paratroops had managed a twenty-three-mile advance up the Canal. But at 5 P.M. Eden signaled the British commander on Cyprus to order a cease-fire and halt at midnight, Tuesday, November 6.

Why did Eden throw in the towel at the next-to-the-last moment—why did he not at least keep going, as the French pleaded with him to do, until the entire length of the Canal was in the hands of British and French forces? The short answer is that for a full week he had been holding out against the entire Republican administration in Washington, its anger turning into implacable fury. He might conceivably have been able to resist the purely political condemnation from Washington and in the United Nations and elsewhere for another twenty-four hours, but the economic pressure was the last straw. On election-day morning, Harold Macmillan telephoned Washington to seek an immediate call on Britain's drawing rights in the International Monetary Fund for something like $1 billion to halt a massive run on sterling. But drawings must be approved by the IMF Board of Governors, and back came the blunt retort on behalf of the United States from Treasury Secretary George M. Humphrey: No help for sterling from the IMF until there is a cease-fire in Suez. Macmillan, after his staunch support for Suez, had already been talking cease-fire, and when this message was handed to him at Downing Street on Tuesday while the Cabinet was in session, according to others present at the meeting he became almost hysterical in insisting that the fighting stop immediately. At that same meeting, Selwyn Lloyd had advised Eden that holding twenty-three miles of the Canal would probably accomplish the political objective of the operation without going on to capture the entire length. Thus, the two key cabinet supporters of Suez had reached the end of the road.

There is simply no parallel, in history, to match the international atmosphere of total emotional outrage and bitterness among traditional friends and allies on all sides in all directions, that marked the end of the Suez War. Everybody was furious with everybody else—and heaven knows there were enough botching and blame to go around.

Denunciations of the devious Dulles by the British and French were matched by the denunciations of the egregious Eden and British colonialism and imperialism by Vice-President Richard M. Nixon and Ambassador Henry Cabot Lodge at the United Nations, who was enjoying an election-eve chance to perform in the spotlight in the tradition of his illustrious isolationist grandfather. All the Eisenhower administration joined in the anti-British chorus, keyed to a last-minute election slogan: "One law for all—friends as well as enemies." In that tumultuous week at the United Nations, there was little differentiation between the situations in Hungary and Suez, except that nations showed more alacrity in condemning Britain and France than they did in voting censure on the Russians.

The British at home were bitterly divided between those who condemned Eden for botching the whole affair and those who denounced him for knuckling under to Dulles and American pressure at the last moment and failing to see things through to the end of the Canal. The French were totally scornful of both the United States and the British—but they had no worries of sterling balances. When Eisenhower forced the Israelis to evacuate the Sinai after the fighting ended and return what they had overrun to the Egyptians, Israeli anger against the United States was like the wrath of the Old Testament God.

From Moscow, at the height of the crisis, the day before the election and the cease-fire, President Nikolai Bulganin sent an angry warning to London and Washington threatening nuclear war unless peace was instantly restored in Egypt. Although neither Eisenhower nor Eden treated this as more than a propaganda effort to shift the focus away from Budapest, there were others in high places—in particular Herbert Hoover, Jr., who was Assistant Secretary of State under Dulles—who were reduced to abject fright that Britain and France were plunging the world into nuclear war, on election eve!

Dulles, at the height of the crisis, on Saturday, November 3, collapsed in his office with severe abdominal pains and was rushed to Walter Reed Hospital. He was operated on at once, and cancer was discovered, from which he died three years later. Paradoxically, Dulles later told the British that he would have moderated things for Britain and France had he been in charge in the ensuing crucial days. But as it was, his collapse only added to the tensions, the emotions and the hysterical anger that erupted against Britain on all sides.

Three junior ministers resigned from Eden's demoralized government, and two weeks after the cease-fire the Prime Minister's health broke. In the long Suez summer he had been forced three times to break away for complete rest to allow eruptions of fever from his bile duct to subside. On November 23, despite remonstrations from several of his cabinet ministers about his leaving the country after having taken it into war, Eden and his wife flew off to Jamaica for recuperation in the sun at the home of Ian Fleming, creator of James Bond. Eden had lost his political ascendancy over his own government, and final retirement was only a matter of time. He returned from Jamaica in mid-December, and on doctor's advice gave up completely on January 9, 1957.

Eden went into Suez to keep the waterway open and preserve it from damage by fighting—but well before the ponderous Anglo-French expeditionary force ever got there, the Egyptians had sunk some forty ships to close the Canal completely. It was five months before it was back in use.

Eden went into Suez to restore the Canal to international control—but when it reopened, in mid-1957, Nasser's Canal Administration was in sole charge and it operated peacefully and normally with freedom of passage for everybody except the Israelis.

Eden went into Suez to "chase Nasser out of Egypt"—but Nasser emerged from the debacle with a stronger hold on power and greater popularity and influence in the Arab world than before.

Eden went into Suez to preserve an international agreement—but the use of force broke the more fundamental laws of sound political judgment, statesmanship and common sense in resolving an international problem.

Eden went into Suez, as he wrote Eisenhower at the outset, because "if we do not, our influence and yours throughout the Middle East will, we are convinced, be finally destroyed"—but the Suez War instead virtually destroyed British influence in the region and was a godsend to the Soviet Union. It was five years before the British even got an ambassador back into Cairo again.

Everything that propelled Eden into the Suez War is clear, recognizable, even understandable: the historic background, the political challenge, his own temperament and the emotions that grated against the frustrations of dealing with Dulles, the psychological determination to be a Prime Minister of action. But the results and the damage to British interests could have been foreseen —had Eden once paused to ponder or consider or attempt to analyze all the negatives, and perceive and accept what the outcome of the use of force at Suez might realistically turn out to be.

As Fouché said of Napoleon's execution of the Duc d'Enghien: "It was worse than a crime—it was a blunder."

9
Charles de Gaulle

CHARLES ANDRÉ JOSEPH MARIE DE GAULLE IN HIS LIFETIME dominated his nation with a personal ascendancy unknown to the French since the age of Napoleon a century and a half before.

"The history of the world is but the biography of great men," wrote Thomas Carlyle, and certainly the history of France over a third of this century can be read as the biography of Charles de Gaulle. He was not merely a great Frenchman—he was an era of French history. From the depth of the French defeat at the hands of Nazi Germany in 1940 to his abrupt retirement as President of France in 1969, de Gaulle was the embodiment of his nation. Even during the period of his self-exile from French political life (1946–1958), he was shaping France's future with his bitter warnings and prophecies, with his implacable and scornful opposition to the Fourth Republic and its weak institutions and revolving-door governments, and with his preparations behind the scenes for the possible day of return to power.

Like Napoleon, General de Gaulle left both lasting achievements for France and lasting controversy. In the French spectrum, his greatness and place in history will be secure. But on the wider scale of Europe and his role in world affairs, de Gaulle's true stature will long be debated. The sweep of his vision of France, his mastery of the art of power, the force of his actions, his intelligence, style and grandeur in the supreme direction of French affairs for so many years, must inevitably be balanced against his narrow nationalism, his roughshod selfish disregard of any but his own interests, his vindictiveness, his diplomatic tactics of deviousness and surprise, his ruthless and stubborn exercise of power, and the bitter prejudices that he harbored and that governed so much in his policies.

Generosity and accommodation or compromise were not in his imperious, despotic, arrogant nature. Compassion, sentimentality, warmth, regard for human frailty, were beneath him. Magnanimity had no part in his makeup. Often it seemed that he was born to oppose rather than create. He thrived on battering at obstructions and surmounting opposition, which he would often invent for himself. For de Gaulle, the Atlantic Alliance was not a guaranty of French security but a threat to French independence. The European Common Market was a roadblock. The United Nations was an obstruction. He adopted for France policies and attitudes of nationalism and self-interest, of opportunism and independence, of boycott and denunciation that were deliberately at odds with the European spirit of the postwar world and that he would have been the first to condemn with outrage had such blatancy been aimed against French interests by others. He was great and he was petty. He inspired absolute dedication and absolute disdain, and he was indifferent to both. A decade after his death, French politics still revolves around the mystique of Gaullism—a faith which in France seems to have more apostles and theologians than Christianity. He restored France as a dynamic and stable European power, and that was his great, undying achievement. But he weakened the Atlantic Alliance, played games with European security, and kept Europe divided and uncertain of its future. Only history will balance out how right General de Gaulle was and how wrong he was.

There was nothing in Charles de Gaulle's origins to point any finger of destiny at the man—any more than in Napoleon's Corsican heritage. He was born in the dull industrial city of Lille, in northeastern France, in 1890, son of an intensely Catholic, conservative, monarchist school professor, Henri de Gaulle. He was one of five children, reared in a strict French bourgeois atmosphere enlivened primarily by the intellectual quality and passion for history and literature of his strong-minded and dynamic father.

It was the France of the Belle Époque, of the Impressionist painters and Rodin, of the new Eiffel Tower, of Sarah Bernhardt, Anatole France, Guy de Maupassant and Marcel Proust—but, for the young and eternally serious de Gaulle, it was a France of humiliation, degradation, lack of moral fiber, of which he later wrote in his *War Memoirs:* "Nothing saddened me more profoundly in my youth than our weakness and our mistakes . . . the surrender at Fashoda, the Dreyfus case, social conflict and religious strife." He held a melancholy view of his nation all his life. He grew up when the Franco-Prussian War, the siege of Paris and the slaughter of the Paris Commune were living memories. At the Place de la Concorde, the statue representing the city of Strasbourg was permanently swathed in black crepe as a reminder, if any were needed, of the German occupation of Alsace and Lorraine. World power was wielded by England and Germany. France was even a bystander in her own possession of Morocco when the Kaiser provoked the crisis of 1911 by sending a German cruiser into Agadir Harbor. It was the British who stepped in, threatened war, and forced a momentary retreat by Germany—the same British who had cleverly bought a controlling interest in the French-built Suez Canal from Egypt.

De Gaulle watched the Agadir crisis unfold from the cloisters of the Military College of St. Cyr, where he was by then an officer cadet. Steeped in French history, encouraged by his father to view the weaknesses of France as a result of the downfall of the monarchy and the advent of republican government, it was inevitable that de Gaulle would turn to the Army as a career. The Army and the Church—for Conservatives these were the stable elements of society, the true France. Moreover, at the turn of the century it was as inevitable as the tides that France and Germany would again go to war. So in 1909 de Gaulle joined the 33rd Infantry Regiment, stationed at Arras, to serve the required year in the ranks before St. Cyr. He returned to the same regiment with his commission in 1912. His new commanding officer was Colonel Philippe Pétain.

For the next thirty years the lives and careers of these two men, and ultimately the fate of France, were to be remarkably intertwined. In 1912 Colonel Pétain was already fifty-six years old. He had been old as a captain and as a major, and it looked as if the 33rd Regiment would be his last command before early retirement. Promotion had been slow in his career because he was then something of a maverick, holding strong views of his own on strategy and tactics which differed from the orthodox doctrines imposed by the French General Staff. He was a strict disciplinarian and an able commanding officer in the French style and tradition of those times—distant, aloof, calm and unapproachable. But he inspired confidence and loyalty.

Pétain's great argument with the French General Staff in the end was fought out at terrible cost in the slaughter of the First World War. There was but one official doctrine for the French Army in 1914: Attack, attack, attack. But Pétain for more than a decade had been preaching: Firepower, firepower, firepower. It was not, finally, until the awful slaughter of the Nivelle offensive in the spring of 1917, when the French once more attacked into superior German firepower, that the High Command finally accepted that it would not work.

Of his two years at Arras before the outbreak of war in August 1914, de Gaulle later wrote succinctly: "My first colonel—Pétain—taught the art and meaning of command." De Gaulle was certainly struck too by Pétain's unorthodoxy and his readiness to assert his own views to his superiors, which he regularly displayed before his officers in summing up lessons of maneuvers and lecturing on tactics. Pétain, for his part, signed a comment on de Gaulle at Arras in October 1913: "Very intelligent, passionately devoted to his profession. Handled his section perfectly on maneuvers. Worthy of all praise. Promoted to lieutenant."

At the outbreak of war, Pétain's regiment moved at once to the Meuse River, where it went into action on August 15, 1914, on the flank of the massive German advance wheeling through Sedan and Belgium. De Gaulle was wounded in that very first action. By the time he returned to the regiment, three months later, Colonel Pétain had left and shot up rapidly to higher command—first to brigadier and only two months later to a corps command. De Gaulle became regimental adjutant and was promoted to captain. Ever conspicuous with his great height of six feet four and ever disdainful of gunfire and danger, he was wounded again, in March 1915. This time he took five months to recover. He was back with the 33rd Regiment when it was thrown into the murderous Battle of Verdun, in February of 1916, where Pétain had now arrived at the pinnacle of his military career as Army Commander. In combat of extraordinary and sustained intensity for six days, de Gaulle led his company at the key position of Douaumont until it was practically wiped out and he himself had again fallen wounded. When he regained consciousness this time, he found that he was a German prisoner of war. Meanwhile Pétain had signed another order, unknown to him, bestowing on him the Croix de Chevalier of the Legion of Honor with a citation of lavish praise: "Renowned for his high intellectual and moral qualities . . . led his men in furious hand-to-hand fight . . . the only solution which he felt compatible with his view of military honor . . . fell in battle . . . an officer without equal in every respect."

Shuttled from one German prison camp to another, de Gaulle made five escape attempts, until he was finally lodged in a high-security fortress at Ingolstadt, where he remained until the Armistice, in 1918. Nevertheless, he learned German, and from books and periodicals that were available, he made notes on politics, philosophy and history for future writings, a suitcaseful that he brought back to France when the war ended. But, at once, to make up for lost time in his military career, he volunteered for service in Poland, where the French were helping the Poles hold back the Red Army from Russia.

The division to which de Gaulle was assigned fought in a crucial battle outside Warsaw in August 1920, when Pilsudski's apparently defeated Poles suddenly exploded an attack on the southern flank of the Red Army, which had advanced into Poland from the Ukraine. In four days the Poles took seventy thousand prisoners, virtually destroyed the invading force, turned defeat into victory and saved Poland—at least until 1939. When the fighting was over, de Gaulle was asked by the Poles to stay on in Warsaw as a lecturer at their military staff college. There he used all that material he had prepared and pondered while a prisoner at Ingolstadt. But in Paris his old commander, Pétain, had become Inspector General of the French Army and the key figure in all career military assignments. De Gaulle was recalled to France in October 1921 and appointed lecturer in history at St. Cyr. He was now headed for the higher echelons.

Meanwhile, during a leave from Poland earlier that same year, he had married Yvonne Vendroux, daughter of a wealthy biscuit manufacturer, after proposing to her, romantically, in the middle of a waltz at the ball of the École Polytechnique at Versailles. They settled in a little Left Bank apartment, and he commuted to St. Cyr, outside Paris. De Gaulle was an impressive, indeed formidable lecturer—his commanding height, his presence even as a junior officer, always immaculately uniformed with white gloves laundered and pressed every night by Mme. de Gaulle. Above all, it was his intellectual thoroughness, his capacious memory and his beautiful command of language and expression that made him outstanding at St. Cyr.*

While lecturing at St. Cyr, de Gaulle also took a competitive examination for the École Supérieure de Guerre, the road upward to the General Staff. He was accepted, and entered one of the strongest classes in the school's history, drawn from the cream of young officers who had emerged in the First World War and taught by old officers who had survived. But, just as there had been the prewar split over attack versus firepower between the General Staff doctrine and Pétain, now in postwar lectures and tactical arguments a new split quickly emerged over tanks versus defense. The General Staff, from its overweening belief in attack, had swung 180 degrees to total dedication to defense. De Gaulle was no great theoretician of war, and in the 1920s and 1930s the most important writings on the subject were British—Fuller and Liddell-Hart. But de Gaulle was in no doubt about where the future lay, and he plunged down on the tank side of the debate with that sardonic, ironic, wounding brilliance and arrogance that was his hallmark. It almost cost him his career.

He did not suffer fools gladly even if they were his superior officers, as this comment on his record at the end of his second

---

*More than forty years later I heard a unique de Gaulle military lecture, possibly his last. I was with the press party on his visit to the Soviet Union in June 1965 and watched as he stood at the vast Stalingrad War Memorial, on the heights above the Volga, before an audience of Soviet officers. Without a note, de Gaulle launched into a twenty-minute lecture of impassioned language and flowing detail on the Battle of Stalingrad and its place in history. It seemed as if the open-mouthed officers were hearing about their battle for the first time.

year rather prophetically noted: "A very intelligent officer, cultivated and serious; has brilliance and facility, greatly gifted, much
stuff in him. Unfortunately spoils his incontestable qualities by his
excessive assurance, his severity towards the opinions of others
and his attitude of being a king in exile. Moreover, he appears to
have more aptitude for general studies and for the synthesis of a
problem than for its detailed examination and the practicalities of
its execution."

The crunch came at the end of the course, when there were
only three grades given: "Very good," "good," and simply "pass-
able." On intellectual and scholarly performance de Gaulle clearly
rated a "very good," but on the critical aspect of personality and
his relations with fellow officers he had gone too far. His professors were determined to cut him down by giving him only a "pass-
able" rating.

At this point, Marshal Pétain personally intervened. He reviewed de Gaulle's records, interviewed his professors, and then
went over a crucial controversy which de Gaulle had caused by his
handling of tanks on a particular field maneuver, against prescribed doctrine and with an effectiveness that had proved the maneuver concept wrong. Magisterially, Pétain pronounced de
Gaulle to have been correct. But the professors would not relent
entirely. They bowed grudgingly to Pétain's pressure and passed de
Gaulle out of the École de Guerre as merely "good" instead of
"very good." In a fury, de Gaulle declared that he would never
enter the school again except as its commandant, when he would
show people how things had changed. He came pretty close to
achieving just this.

For the moment, with his secondary grading, he was shunted to
one side with inferior postings and slow promotion instead of
shooting ahead to the General Staff, as would have been the case
with a "very good" passing. He was given a logistics staff job in
northern France and then assigned to the headquarters of the
French occupation army in the Rhineland, at Mainz. But Pétain
was still watching over him.

He recalled de Gaulle from Germany in 1925 and made him a
member of his personal staff—primarily as a ghostwriter and
deep thinker to take the marshal's simple ideas about French mili-

tary policy and flesh them out with intellectual content and decoration. Next, at Pétain's insistence de Gaulle was given the exceptional honor of an invitation to lecture at the École Supérieure. Pétain attended the lectures, on Leadership, Character, Discipline and Prestige—which were largely regarded at the time as an elaborate tribute by de Gaulle to Pétain, and a critical attack on those who had given him an inferior grade when he left the school, three years before. But in fact, the lectures, later published in a slim volume entitled *The Edge of the Sword,* were very much a personal creed.

"Is there not a connection between a man's inner strength and his outward appearance?" he said. "Every page of Caesar's commentaries shows how carefully he measured the public gestures. And we also know how careful Napoleon was to produce his greatest effects with his public appearances. . . . Prestige arises from an elementary gift, from a certain natural aptitude which cannot be analyzed. The truth is that certain men carry with them almost from childhood a certain aura of authority. . . . Yet such a natural gift must like any other natural talent, be developed. And in the first place prestige cannot go without mystery, for people feel no reverence for anything with which they are too familiar. . . ."

Clearly de Gaulle had no doubt of his gifts and was hard at work developing them. But despite Pétain's patronage, the wheels of the French military machine ground slowly. De Gaulle remained a captain for twelve years before he finally was promoted to major. In 1928 he again returned to Germany, with the occupation forces—a Germany rapidly plunging into political and economic chaos. His next assignment was on the General Staff of the French Army of the Levant, in Beirut in 1930–31. But his stay there only convinced him that policing an empire was a waste of time for the French Army and the French nation—a drain and a diversion from the central mission of the security of France itself.

In 1931, almost as a last act before finally retiring from military duties at the age of seventy-five, Pétain transferred de Gaulle from the Levant to the secretariat of the Conseil Supérieur de Guerre, at that time the French equivalent of the Joint Chiefs of Staff. He was thus at the policy-making center in Paris during the days of the Popular Front government and the crucial decisions involving the Maginot Line and the future of the French Army as Nazi Germany began rearming with a new formation: the *Panzer* divisions.

In 1934, de Gaulle produced a book titled *Toward the Army of the Future,* in which he refined the writings of the British and others on the subject of tank warfare and called for the "urgent creation" in the French Army of "a mechanized, armored and maneuverable army for shock warfare . . . a specially picked body of men making maximum use of their powerful and diverse weapons with an aweome superiority over massed troops who will be more or less in disorder." At the same time, he was introduced by a mutual friend to Paul Reynaud, one of the most talented and lively of the French political leaders of the 1930s. After a number of talks and exchange of correspondence with de Gaulle, Reynaud agreed to take the fight for creation of an armored corps into the National Assembly. Pétain, meanwhile, had taken off his marshal's uniform but had been appointed Minister of Defense at this time. Not only was there now a split between de Gaulle and Pétain over tank doctrine. Pétain was also incensed at de Gaulle's going to politicians to get his ideas adopted. Finally, after three years in Paris arguing his case for tanks inside and outside the military machine and government, de Gaulle was posted to command a tank regiment at Metz in 1937. The parting words from his political superiors at the War Ministry were: "You have given us enough trouble with your paper tanks—let's see what you can make of the metal sort."

At Metz, de Gaulle came under another superior officer with whom he was to cross paths in history: General Henri Giraud, corps commander in the Lorraine. At a military maneuver in 1939, with war only months away, de Gaulle thrust his tanks far out beyond the prescribed doctrinal limit, and at a critique after the maneuver was over, Giraud turned on him in front of the assembled officers to declare: "As for you, *mon petit* de Gaulle, so long as I am commanding this army corps . . ." and proceeded to defend the view that tanks were solely for support of infantry, not to be wasted dashing around the countryside. De Gaulle sat in furious silence.

But he was writing letters. To Reynaud at the time of the Munich conference with Hitler at which Britain and France acceded to the dismemberment of Czechoslovakia in March 1938 he wrote from Metz: "My regiment is ready. As for myself, I see coming, without surprise, the greatest events in France's history, and I am confident that you are marked out to play a leading part in them. Let me assure you that in any case, should I survive, I shall be resolute in your service if you feel you can use me."

In September 1939, World War II, the predictable, the inevitable, the "greatest events in France's history," began—not with a bang but a whimper: The Phony War. De Gaulle, restless and frustrated in the Lorraine behind the Maginot Line, went on writing letters—so many, in fact, that the postal censors noted with surprise the volume of the colonel's correspondence with political personalities in Paris. In March of 1940, Reynaud succeeded Édouard Daladier as Premier. In early May, only days before the Nazi *Panzer* divisions struck and the battle for France began, Reynaud received another letter from de Gaulle:

"The French Army is conceived, organized, armed and commanded in opposition on principle to the law of modern war. Radical reform of the whole system is the most vital and immediate necessity, on which victory depends. . . . The military establishment will not reform of its own accord. . . . Due to your post, your personality and the position you have taken in the matter—taken for six years without any support from others—you are the only man who can carry out this task. I might add that by making it your government's most urgent business, you will change the atmosphere at home and abroad, gaining many immediate advantages. . . . I would aspire to no greater honor than that of serving you in this vital work, as soon as you decide to undertake it. . . ."

In a matter of days, de Gaulle was to be proved painfully right about the condition of France's army. But is there any other instance in history of a colonel in command of a front-line regiment in the midst of a war writing such an unctuous letter directly to a Premier, soliciting a post in the government? De Gaulle never doubted that he was destiny's chosen, and throughout his life he was always ready to use any means, any man, to serve his—and destiny's—end. In May of 1940 he did not have long to wait.

On May 10 the Germans struck through Holland, Belgium and France. On May 15, before his tank regiment had seen action (the Germans had bypassed the Lorraine area), de Gaulle was promoted to brigadier general and ordered to take command of a scratch armored division being assembled at Laon, in the North, in the path of the advance of the top German *Panzer* commanders, Guderian and Rommel. When de Gaulle arrived at his new divisional headquarters, he did not even have a radio set, and some of his tank crews had spent only three hours inside a tank before being ordered into battle. But de Gaulle flung himself into the fray, and the French 4th Armored Division knew that it had a commander, if nothing else. In fact, he staged a successful counterattack with the division against the German advance at Abbéville at the end of May, briefly checking the thrust toward Paris.

After only three weeks in command, de Gaulle received the telegram he had hoped for from Reynaud. On June 6, he was summoned to Paris to become undersecretary of state in the War Ministry. But Reynaud had also recalled Marshal Pétain from Madrid, where he had been sent as French ambassador in March of 1939, to join the new Cabinet as Minister of State without Portfolio. Pétain and de Gaulle were serving together again, but in the cataclysmic events of the next two weeks, they seldom spoke and barely acknowledged each other.

Reynaud dispatched de Gaulle immediately to London on June 7. The evacuation of Dunkirk had been completed—338,000 officers and men, of whom 139,000 were French. De Gaulle was instructed to see Winston Churchill to ask that the French troops be reequipped and sent back to France via the Brittany ports as quickly as possible. And he was to ask for additional British air squadrons for France. Churchill agreed to the first request, more as a gesture to bolster the Reynaud government than for any practical military reasons. But he turned the French down on sending more air squadrons in a historic decision to husband resources for the coming Battle of Britain. It was de Gaulle's first meeting with Churchill, whom he found "equal to the rudest task, provided it had also grandeur. . . . Fitted by character to act, take risks, play the part out and out and without scruple." In short, whatever their considerable differences later on in the war, Churchill was a man after de Gaulle's own heart.

When de Gaulle got back to Paris, on June 9, the panic and the crumbling had rapidly accelerated. The military commander-in-chief, General Maxime Weygand, was already demanding that the politicians ask for an armistice. On June 10 Reynaud and the government left Paris, declaring it to be an open city. On June 11, Churchill caught up with the government at the town of Briare on the Loire, and for a few brief hours he stiffened things by his presence and his bulldog determination face to face with Weygand and Pétain. De Gaulle was present at the meetings, and then the government moved on to Tours. Churchill was back on June 13, his last visit to France for four years, to plead with Reynaud at Tours to move the government to North Africa and above all keep the French fleet out of German hands. On June 15, Reynaud reached the end of the road in Bordeaux. That same day, he again dispatched de Gaulle to London—this time to ask the British for ships or planes if he decided to evacuate the French Government to Algiers or Morocco.

De Gaulle reached London that Saturday evening after a destroyer dash across the Channel from the Brittany port of Lorient to Plymouth. He went immediately to the apartment of Jean Monnet, on Mount Street, near Grosvenor Square. He was greeted by Monnet's wife, but he then sat in silence, waiting for Monnet to return for dinner. Finally Mme. Monnet asked politely how long his mission to London would take, and de Gaulle replied: "I am not here on a mission, Madame. I am here to save the honor of France."

Monnet arrived, and de Gaulle announced at once that he had decided to stay in London—that it was too late and nothing more could be done in France. Monnet then unveiled his plan for a declaration of British-French union, on which he had made considerable headway behind the scenes with the British. De Gaulle was skeptical, but as a representative of the French Government in London, he agreed to give it his support. Sunday, June 16. In the morning, a final draft of the proposed declaration was completed. Churchill took de Gaulle to lunch at the Carlton Club while the draft was being polished in two languages and typed. Together they then telephoned Reynaud in Bordeaux to read him the text. Reynaud's reaction was one of short-lived jubilation. De Gaulle left No. 10 Downing Street at 5 P.M. to fly to Bordeaux with the text in a Royal Air Force plane that Churchill had made available. When he landed in Bordeaux, it was all over. The Cabinet had overturned Reynaud, and Pétain had become Premier to seek an armistice.†

It was nine-thirty in the evening when de Gaulle landed, and he immediately sought out Reynaud to urge him to return with him to London on the RAF plane in the morning. Reynaud refused but gave de Gaulle what little he had in secret funds in his office, barely five hundred dollars. As de Gaulle left, the British ambassador, Sir Ronald Campbell, arrived with Major General Sir Edward Spears, military liaison officer to the French Government.

In a brief exchange in the darkened hallway outside Reynaud's office, de Gaulle arranged to see the British later at the Hotel Montré, where the ambassador was staying. From there, late that night, Campbell got through by phone to Churchill (how did the phones work in all that chaos?) to get permission for Spears to return with de Gaulle on the RAF plane in the morning. Spears meanwhile warned de Gaulle that he might be arrested at any moment by the Pétain government. De Gaulle left, and nobody knows where he spent that last night in Bordeaux, but he was back at the hotel next morning accompanied by his faithful aide, Lieutenant Geoffroy de Courcel (in the 1960s de Gaulle's ambassador to the Court of St. James's). Shortly after seven o'clock the three men left for the airport. Twice on the way the limousine stopped outside temporary government offices and de Gaulle went calmly inside to ask that appointments be arranged for later in the day. Ostensibly he was simply going to the airport to see General Spears off for London. They drove to the parked aircraft and stood chatting while luggage was loaded. The engine on the little plane was revved up, and the two generals and the lieutenant exchanged salutes. Spears climbed aboard. Then, at the last min-

† See also Chapter Five, "Jean Monnet."

ute, as the plane was ready to taxi to the runway, de Gaulle and de Courcel scrambled in behind.

The plane climbed, banked and headed across Brittany and the Channel Islands for England. De Gaulle wrote: "I seemed to myself, alone as I was and deprived of everything, like a man on the shore of an ocean proposing to swim across."‡

The little plane reached London before midday on Monday, June 17, in superb weather that in fact continued all through the Battle of Britain that historic summer of 1940. Spears, bilingual in French, took de Gaulle to lunch at the Royal Automobile Club, where the General's long travail with English cooking promptly began. Word came that they should go to Downing Street to see Churchill, and when de Gaulle arrived he found the Prime Minister in the garden. Neither man left any record of the conversation, but Churchill agreed that de Gaulle should broadcast to France over the BBC when, as was fully expected, Pétain asked for an Armistice. After leaving Downing Street, de Gaulle sent off a number of important personal telegrams. One went to the Ministry of War, at Bordeaux, proposing that he be authorized by the new government to complete the negotiation he had been sent to London by Paul Reynaud to conduct, for British ships to evacuate the government to North Africa. Another went to the French commandant in Morocco, General Noguès, offering to serve under him if he opted to continue the fight from the French Empire. Whether any of these and other messages ever reached those to whom they were addressed is not clear, but if they did they got no response. Shortly after midday on June 18, Pétain, eighty-four years old, was heard over the radio from Bordeaux: "I bestow on France the gift of my person to alleviate its misfortune." The French Army was ordered to cease fire (the Germans paid no attention; the Nazi advance continued), and an Armistice was requested from

‡ Both de Gaulle and de Courcel later avowed that this account of the departure from Bordeaux, given by Major General Spears in his book *Assignment to Catastrophe,* was exaggerated and overdramatized, but Spears was writing on the basis of notes he made at the time. De Gaulle later clashed with Spears during the war, in Syria, and probably did not regard this version of his escape to Britain as being in keeping with proper Gaullist legend.

the Nazi government. Meanwhile, a telegram arrived in London for de Gaulle ordering him to return to France and surrender at Saint Michel Prison, in Toulouse.

That evening, de Gaulle made his famous broadcast to France—a great deal more famous in history than it was at the time. Few heard it, and it was not even recorded by the harassed BBC studio technicians. But it was a message and a call repeated and reechoed in French legend, debated and argued among Frenchmen with a vehemence and passion rivaling the war itself.

"The cause of France is not lost. . . . France does not stand alone. . . . I, General de Gaulle, now in London, call on all French officers and men who are at present on British soil, or may be in the future, with or without their arms; I call on all engineers and skilled workers from the armament factories who are at present on British soil, or may be in the future, to get in touch with me. Whatever happens, the flames of French resistance must not and shall not die."

In that first broadcast, de Gaulle, contrary to legend, did not use the famous phrase "France has lost a battle, but not lost the war." This he wrote out a few days later for a poster with a tricolor border which was printed and displayed all over Britain at the instigation of General Spears. Nor, in that first broadcast, did de Gaulle proclaim himself the leader of France. That decisive and divisive move came the following evening, on June 19, when he went on the air a second time, this time to declare: "I realize that I now speak for France. In the name of France, I make the following solemn declaration: It is the bounden duty of all Frenchmen who still bear arms to continue the struggle."

Meanwhile, Jean Monnet had made his last-ditch flight to Bordeaux in a British seaplane to try to bring out somebody—anybody—from the government or political leadership of the dying Third Republic. But nobody—not one—would leave France. When Monnet returned to London to find that de Gaulle was now claiming to "speak for France," he objected strongly, and a basic argument of principle ensued. "You must stop sending off telegrams," he told de Gaulle. "Those to whom they are addressed cannot help but think that with the help of the British Prime Minister you, a young French general, are arrogating to yourself the right to represent

France—they, your seniors in age and service, are to take orders
from you, issued in London, from foreign soil?"

Monnet's argument echoed throughout the French embassy in
London, where not one *fonctionnaire* joined de Gaulle, although
an honorable number quit to find tasks in the war effort with the
British. It was an argument that split the French civil service and
the military establishment and divided France itself—not two ways
but three or four ways in that tragic hour. There were those who
blindly, even enthusiastically, followed Pétain not only as the legal
head of state but in the full belief that France had no other course
but collaboration with the New Order of Nazi Germany. Moreover, there was plenty of Anglophobia in defeated France, which
continues even now. Then there were the vast majority of Frenchmen, who simply bowed inertly to what seemed inevitable, who
detested the occupation and its humiliation but remained docile
and loyal to Pétain until they felt the tide turn. Then there were
those like Monnet, inside and outside France, who believed as
much as de Gaulle in Allied victory and the ultimate liberation
and rejuvenation of France and were prepared to fight on with the
British or anybody else but who declined to accept that de Gaulle
was the sole voice of France or had the right to "speak for France
in the name of France." Monnet, at the end of the argument,
wrote a firm letter to de Gaulle outlining his stand on this principle and departed for Washington to work for the British on supply
problems.*

Then there were the Gaullists, at the outset only a handful who
rallied to the General in London, most of them imbued with an ill-
concealed contempt for the rest of their countrymen. Over the
next four years this split among Frenchmen was, for France,
bigger than the war itself.

It did indeed take a supreme ego for a fifty-year-old brigadier
general who had commanded a division for only three weeks and

---

* De Gaulle never forgave Monnet, and showed his vindictiveness in an odd
way. When Robert Schuman, of the Schuman Plan, died, in Metz in 1963,
political leaders came from all over Europe for the funeral, and Monnet of
course was among them. But de Gaulle gave specific orders to the local Prefect in Metz that only foreigners were to be invited to the official French
Government reception following the funeral—thus excluding Monnet from
attending.

been a junior minister in the government for only two weeks, whose name was virtually unknown to the French at large outside military and official circles, now suddenly out of the blue over the BBC from London to be proclaiming that it was he—not Marshal Pétain—who spoke for France. But de Gaulle's ego was up to the historic opportunity. France had descended to that depth of degradation that he had been anticipating with melancholy certitude since the days of his youth. At this moment, de Gaulle might again have been just another prisoner of war, but the political accidents of the past two weeks had landed him in London. He was alone, free to act, uninhibited by anyone any longer giving him orders. All his life he had studied, lectured and brooded with fascination on the subject of power and its exercise. Now power lay at his feet, and there was no man to challenge him. No politician arrived in London to speak for France, and none could from Bordeaux except Pétain. The only challenge to de Gaulle was the intellectual argument raised by Jean Monnet, and this the General rather haughtily dismissed and ignored as nothing more than buzzing noises when action and an exercise of power was required, not debate.

As for legitimacy, by what legitimacy did Napoleon take the crown of laurel leaves from the hands of the Pope, lower it on his own brow, and proclaim himself Emperor of France? By what legitimacy did Marshal Pétain elect to use the defeat of the nation to "bestow on France the gift of my person to alleviate its misfortune"? For de Gaulle, simply to proclaim at that moment that France had not been defeated, that the struggle was continuing, was legitimacy enough. And if it was not enough, legitimacy was soon bestowed upon him and the Free French Movement by his indomitable champion, Winston Churchill.

On June 26, a week after his decisive BBC broadcast, de Gaulle submitted a memorandum to Churchill that became the basis for recognition of the General "as chief of all the Free French, wherever they may be, who rally to him for the defense of the Allied cause." But there was great argument and much misgiving behind the scenes. Anthony Eden and the Foreign Office, as well as the British Chiefs of Staff, were opposed to such a sweeping grant of power and authority to an unknown brigadier general and foresaw many of the difficulties that later dogged the arrangement. But Churchill wanted, needed and was determined to have a fighting French ally, and de Gaulle was the only one at hand. The British agreement with the Free French was published on August 8, 1940.

Meanwhile, two developments—one military and the other diplomatic—sharply influenced the course of events for de Gaulle. On July 3, Churchill, in one of his most implacable and dramatic decisions of the war, personally ordered the British Fleet to open fire and destroy the French warships that had retreated after the Armistice to the Algerian port of Mers el-Kébir. The French admiral commanding had refused either to immobilize his vessels or move under British escort to distant ports away from the Mediterranean. In a ten-minute action, three French battleships were destroyed or put out of action, along with smaller vessels, but more than two thousand French seamen were killed by British guns. The excuse for the British action was, of course, to ensure that the French Fleet would not go over to the Nazis and alter the vital naval balance in the war, but the real reason was political and psychological, as Churchill said in his war memoirs: "Here was Britain which so many had counted down and out, supposed to be quivering on the brink of surrender, striking ruthlessly at her dearest friends of yesterday and securing for herself the undisputed command of the sea. It was made plain that the British War Cabinet feared nothing and would stop at nothing."

While Churchill was showing such indomitable determination to stop at nothing and fight on, the United States, under President Franklin D. Roosevelt, was taking a very different tack with prostrate France. First of all, Ambassador William C. Bullitt had decided on his own to remain in Paris instead of following the Reynaud government to Tours and then to Bordeaux. A vain man, he was obsessed with the example of his World War I predecessor, Myron Herrick, who also stayed in Paris, during the Battle of the Marne, when the French Government removed to Bordeaux, in 1914. But it was a very different war and a very different France. Thus, there was no strong American representation to try to stiffen or influence events in Bordeaux at the decisive moment when Britain offered the declaration of union with France. Perhaps it would have made no difference, but history is full of accidents, and Bullitt was certainly in the wrong place at the wrong time.

In any case, after the Armistice the United States—or, rather, Roosevelt, Bullitt and Secretary of State Cordell Hull—decided not only to continue unbroken recognition and diplomatic relations with the defeated government set up in Vichy by Marshal Pétain, but almost to embrace it by sending a very prestigious if narrow-minded new American ambassador, Admiral William D. Leahy. The battle for France had at last roused the United States out of its isolationist hang-ups over World War II, and Roosevelt was really seeking a role of involvement without yet going to war. Somewhat naïvely, he figured that by sending an American four-star Admiral to Vichy, he could help stiffen French Admiral François Darlan to keep the French Fleet out of Nazi hands. Churchill, of course, preferred the more certain course of simply sinking the French ships that did not come over to General de Gaulle. To complicate this mess of maneuver and intrigue, Admiral Leahy and Admiral Darlan shared a mutual anti-British, professional resentment of the Royal Navy for its admitted snobbery and smug superiority toward lesser breeds of navies in the world.

Thus at the outset, while de Gaulle had an important and vital piece of paper from Churchill granting him recognition, two large cards had also been dealt against him face up on the table. In defeated France, natural Anglophobia, stoked by Nazi propaganda, swelled to livid outrage over the sinking of French ships and the killing of French sailors by the Royal Navy. In London, de Gaulle, the military realist, understood what was behind Churchill's action even if he did not agree with it. But the affair was of little help in rallying Frenchmen to his side, with the United States meanwhile giving full aid and comfort to Marshal Pétain. Small wonder, therefore, that only a derisory few hundred turned up in the first month at Olympia Stadium, in London, which the British had turned over to de Gaulle as a processing center for the Free French. Out of two thousand French soldiers wounded and evacuated from Dunkirk and still in Britain, barely two hundred said they were ready to join the Free French. Still, forty Breton fishermen sailed in their boats with their village

priest when they heard the call, and did vital work from Cornwall
smuggling agents back into France.†

Then Admiral Muselier, a swarthy, swashbuckling fighter, arrived in London and brought over the nucleus of the Free French
Navy. Yet he was so outraged over the Mers el-Kébir affair that
he nearly abandoned the fight to return to France. Sympathetic
support from high-ranking British naval officers overcame the crisis. By the end of July, de Gaulle's numerical strength had crept
up to seven thousand, most of them under Muselier, in the Navy.
The first piece of French overseas territory to respond to his call
was the New Hebrides Islands, in the far Pacific—not exactly a
basing point for a political-military campaign to liberate France itself.

In late August the first real break for de Gaulle came in Africa
when the black governor of Chad, Félix Éboué, switched allegiance from Vichy to the Free French. French Congo followed,
and then the French Cameroons, Ubangi and Gabon. It was a beginning, but it was still pretty small pickings, and de Gaulle badly
needed a military victory, some show of strength. Instead, in the
first action attempted under the banner of the Cross of Lorraine,
he suffered a humiliating defeat.

In mid-September 1940, emboldened by political successes in
Africa and urged on by Churchill, de Gaulle sailed with a small
contingent of Free French soldiers in a Royal Navy task force to
seize the strategic African port of Dakar. Almost everything went
wrong. Security had been lax, so the attack was no surprise. With
memories of Mers el-Kébir still fresh, there was real and effective
resistance from Vichy loyalists, particularly from the French battleship *Richelieu,* which was in the harbor. Pro-Gaullists in Dakar
were quickly locked up. In the end, an unusual morning fog ham-
pered supporting fire from the Royal Navy, which finally had to
break off and head out to sea to avoid possible German submarines. De Gaulle and the Free French soldiers retreated to the Af-

---

† De Gaulle's wife and two children, Philippe and Élisabeth, were living in
Brittany when France fell, but he had arranged passports for them in the
final hours in Bordeaux and they were spirited out of France on a Polish destroyer from the port of Brest. Otherwise they would have been major hostages for the Nazis.

rican port of Freetown. In Vichy there was jubilation. It was probably the low point of de Gaulle's life—he even contemplated suicide. But then the tide turned.

He decided to stay on in Africa and visit the colonies that had come over to his side, and it was like a royal procession. At the end of the tour, in Brazzaville, in the French Congo, he issued a Charter of the Free French movement and formed an Empire Defense Council. That same week, at the end of October, Pétain had his first meeting with Adolf Hitler, at Montoire-sur-le-Loir, and formally committed France to a policy of collaboration. Thus, by the time de Gaulle returned to London, the Battle of Britain had been won and the choice for Frenchmen was unequivocally clear.

Nevertheless, the next four years for de Gaulle were years of unrelenting conflict—not with Nazi Germany but with Britain and the United States. From de Gaulle's own, self-centered point of view, everything revolved around consolidation of his own power to speak for France. He treated any challenge to that power and authority, to his self-legitimized role as leader of France, as if it were a challenge to France itself. Indeed, from this time on to the end of his days, de Gaulle wrapped himself in the tricolor and never ceased to regard himself as one with his country, the custodian, guardian and voice of France.

But his was not the sole voice, and Churchill and Roosevelt had other problems in the war. In a formal sense, the British had only recognized de Gaulle as the head of a fighting movement—not as a government-in-exile such as the Dutch, the Poles, the Czechs and the Norwegians had established in London. And in France the great mass of Frenchmen indubitably if regrettably were still behind Pétain, with whom Roosevelt had diplomatic relations. Churchill also took up very secret contacts with Pétain before the end of 1940 through a French professor of history who visited London and returned circuitously to Vichy with a personal communication for the Marshal in which Churchill hinted that food would be allowed through the British naval blockade as long as the French Fleet and colonies did not fall under Nazi control. De Gaulle was informed privately by the British of this move, but it only aroused his suspicion that they were ready to dump him if somebody in Vichy would show signs of rejoining the fight against

Hitler. Accordingly, as a means of demonstrating that he was France and not a British tool, of forcing the British to increase his power by making concessions to him, he adopted tactics of intransigence, stubbornness and relentless independence, which produced Churchill's famous remark: "The heaviest cross I bear is the cross of Lorraine."

In Washington, the attitude of Roosevelt and Hull toward de Gaulle was not even one of sufferance, but of downright hostility. During this period I was a correspondent in Washington, frequently covering both the White House and the State Department, and I well recall the personal animosity and disdain for de Gaulle that both men would display at press conferences. On one occasion, Hull caused consternation by referring icily on the record to "the so-called Free French." In those good old days there were no prying television cameras to flash a presidential expression around the world, and Roosevelt was a past master at nuance, conveying dislike even with the tilt of his cigarette holder. Their Vichy policy was of course becoming less and less palatable to American public opinion, and de Gaulle was daily proving it bankrupt and wrong. But the stubborn Dutch in Roosevelt and the stubborn Gaul in de Gaulle acted against each other. Instead of making some obeisance or conciliation to Roosevelt—as Churchill and Eden pleaded with him constantly to do—de Gaulle seemed positively to revel in an attitude of haughty disdain toward the Americans for their dealings with Vichy. He was not interested in making concessions to win Roosevelt's approval—it was the Americans who would have to come to him. In the end they did, and what time was wasted, what arguments and squabbles there were, what a way to have to fight a war!

All this culminated in the North African landings in November of 1942. It was primarily an American show. Reflecting in particular the advice of the American career-diplomat intelligence man in Vichy, Robert Murphy, Roosevelt argued that anti-British and anti-de Gaulle feelings were so strong among the French in Morocco and Algiers that resistance would be much less if the invasion was American-led and dominated. So it was, except in eastern Algeria, where British forces landed to push immediately for Tunisia. And at Roosevelt's insistence, de Gaulle was not even told of the plans until the troops were about to go ashore. No Free French took part in the operation at all.

To compound this affront to the leader of French resistance, on Murphy's advice the Americans smuggled out of France de Gaulle's old corps commander, General Henri Giraud, to take over command of all French forces in North Africa after the landing. Not only was Giraud a poor choice politically and as a military man, with virtually no clout or authority; by an accident of history, Admiral François Darlan was in Algiers when the American and British forces came ashore. Like it or not, he had far more authority and power than any Frenchman, but when General Dwight D. Eisenhower then made his famous cease-fire deal with the Vichy admiral, there was an instant uproar of public opinion in the United States and Great Britain. A French assassin fortunately relieved Roosevelt of all these embarrassments by shooting Darlan on Christmas Eve of 1942. Giraud was then elevated by the Americans to run North Africa for them, but he was painfully inadequate.

De Gaulle sat out these events in haughty outrage in London. As the North African political mess worsened for the Americans and British it was overwhelmingly clear that Roosevelt and Churchill were going to have to turn to him to sort out their mistakes. In January 1943, the two leaders met in Casablanca. De Gaulle was asked to come, but he replied with hauteur that the leader of France did not accept invitations from others to visit French soil. In other words he would only come on his own terms. In London, Anthony Eden practically had to force de Gaulle onto an airplane for Casablanca. There he and General Giraud met with Roosevelt and Churchill in an atmosphere of stony hostility on all sides. About all that came out of it was the famous photo of a stiff and disdainful handshake between the two prima-donna generals. But, all the same, de Gaulle was now on the way to a final consolidation of his power and authority for France.‡

De Gaulle returned to London to sulk like Achilles in his tent, and the indefatigable Jean Monnet arrived in Algiers at the end of

‡ For other aspects of these events, see also Chapter 5, "Jean Monnet," and Chapter 7, "Harold Macmillan."

February 1943, to assume the role of mediator and negotiator between the two hostile French camps. But it was not until May that de Gaulle finally agreed to terms for joining Giraud in Algiers in a unified French Committee of National Liberation. By November, de Gaulle had ruthlessly maneuvered the hapless Giraud out of the committee entirely. There was now nobody inside or outside France who was a challenge to his leadership. But Roosevelt implacably withheld recognition.

By the beginning of 1944, no fewer than twenty-six governments, including the Soviet Union, had recognized de Gaulle's committee as having virtually the status of a government in exile. Even crusty old Admiral Leahy, who had returned from Vichy to become Roosevelt's personal chief of staff, recommended recognition, but Roosevelt would not be moved. De Gaulle was scarcely making it easier, with a series of high-handed and often petty assertions of his own authority over French troops, vetoing orders from General Eisenhower or any other Allied officer or political official whom he found in his path. Larger interests of the common war effort never stopped de Gaulle in his determination to demonstrate and consolidate his own power. Churchill pressured Roosevelt almost to the breaking point for a change in the American attitude, but Roosevelt's response was a direct order to Eisenhower, as Supreme Allied Commander, to sign no agreement with de Gaulle and surrender none of his authority as commander-in-chief over occupied territory when France was invaded. Eisenhower was thus placed in the absurd position of having territory that he was about to liberate administered by a provisional government that he was not allowed to recognize, run by civilians with whom he could not negotiate. Again, de Gaulle was cut out of all advance military planning and brought to London from Algiers only on the eve of D day. There was then a towering argument between de Gaulle and Churchill as the troops were loading to sail. De Gaulle refused to accept the arrangements that had been made for him to broadcast to France after the Allies landed.

But if Roosevelt would not recognize his authority over France, then he would return to France and establish that authority regardless. In the French destroyer *La Combattante* (with a trunk containing 25 million French francs) de Gaulle crossed the Eng-

lish Channel on June 13, 1944, one week after D day. He headed
for the town of Bayeux, with its famous medieval tapestry of
William the Conqueror's invasion of England in 1066. British
troops had liberated Bayeux, and Field Marshal Sir Bernard Montgomery had an honor guard at the beach to salute de Gaulle on his
return to France. De Gaulle then met Monty in his operations
trailer, and after a discussion of the battle situation, de Gaulle
remarked almost casually that when he entered Bayeux he would
be appointing a new prefect to take over the local administration.

Monty may not have been aware of the significance of this, for
Eisenhower was under Roosevelt's orders that it was he, as Allied
Commander, and not de Gaulle, who should exercise authority
over the civil administration. Instead, Monty acknowledged what
de Gaulle was about to do as a routine matter. De Gaulle then set
off for Bayeux, where word of his coming had been circulated in
advance. The entire town was gathered before the Hôtel de Ville
to give him a rapturous welcome. Pétain's picture came down and
the Vichy prefect departed. François Coulet, a career administrator who had joined de Gaulle in London, became the first
Gaullist prefect in liberated France. The General had thus as-
serted his legal authority over his nation in a scene that was to be
repeated at one prefecture after another up to the climactic liberation of Paris, on August 24.

When de Gaulle entered Paris in those tense and tumultuous
days in which Nazis, Communists and Gaullist *résistants* maneuvered and battled for control of the city, he headed first for the
Ministry of War, while Leclerc's Free French Division spread out
to secure the city. De Gaulle wished to establish both symbolically
and factually that France had its own government in Paris again.
In his *War Memoirs* he wrote:

"I was immediately struck by the impression that nothing had
changed inside these venerable halls. Gigantic events had overturned the world. Our army was annihilated. France had virtually
collapsed. But at the Ministry of War the look of things remained
immutable. In the courtyard, a unit of the *Garde Républicaine*
presented arms as in the past. The vestibule, the staircase, the
arms hanging on the walls—all as they had been. Here in person
were the same stewards and ushers. I entered the Minister's office

which Monsieur Paul Reynaud and I had left together on the night
of June 10, 1940. Not a piece of furniture, not a rug, not a curtain
had been disturbed. On the desk, the telephone was in the same
place, and exactly the same names on the call buttons. Soon I was
to learn that this was the case in all the other buildings in which
the Republic housed itself. Nothing was missing except the State.
It was my duty to restore it: I installed my staff at once and got
down to work."

Between landing at Bayeux and arriving in liberated Paris, de
Gaulle finally accepted an invitation to visit Washington, arriving
in an aircraft flown specially on Roosevelt's orders to Algiers to
pick him up on July 6. It was an anticlimactic and inconclusive
two-day meeting. De Gaulle was restrained and courteous—but he
also made it clear that he had nothing to ask and nothing to negotiate about. The two men sparred fairly gently. Roosevelt
preached his anticolonial, anti-imperialist sermon and made it
clear that he did not expect to see France become a great power
again. De Gaulle said there could not be a strong Europe without
a strong France. Apart from Casablanca, it was the only meeting
of the two men, and it did nothing to close the gap of understanding. But Roosevelt did grudgingly, ambiguously recognize the
French Committee of National Liberation as "qualified to exercise
the administration of France." De Gaulle then made his first visit
to French-speaking Canada, and hurried back to face the urgent
problems of the liberation of France.

It was one thing for de Gaulle to establish his authority by installing new prefects in the wake of the Allied armies moving
across France, but it was another thing to restore order. The country, in fact, was in a state of suppressed civil war, as resistance
groups rose to settle scores with the Vichy collaborationists, and
then with each other. The Communists, by their underground
training and discipline and ideology, were of course the most adept
and ruthless of all. The situation, roughly from August to November of 1944, was so confused and chaotic, so turbulent and out of
control, that there are only guesses and estimates of the scale of
what happened—but de Gaulle's Minister of the Interior at the
time, Adrien Tixier, put the number of murders, summary execu-

tions and other politically inspired killings at a staggering 105,000. Whatever the figure, it is certain that more Frenchmen were killed by Frenchmen than at any other time in history since the Hundred Years' War. Had it not been for de Gaulle's exercise of authority, the country might well have plunged into anarchy and open civil war, which was what the Communists appeared to be aiming for. De Gaulle sped from one trouble area to another, and with the backing of his own tough and loyal lieutenants, cracked down ruthlessly to disarm the disparate resistance groups and then incorporate them into regular French Army units. De Gaulle never got from the Allies anything like the arms and equipment he asked for, but by the end of the war there were fifteen French divisions in the line.

In September of 1944, de Gaulle formed his first provisional government. But it was clear from the outset that not even de Gaulle could conjure political unity out of the ashes of the war. For four years, in London and Algiers, his authority and discipline over his movement and its adherents had been total. His style was to make decisions and leave them to subordinates to carry out. But, in order to unify postliberation France, he needed to bring in political leaders from the resistance, who had been used to giving orders, not taking them, and who had their own ideas about how things should be run. Even though de Gaulle was supreme, factionalism began at the outset.

Moreover, his own great preoccupation was not with the mundane tasks of economic reconstruction but with the political restoration and recognition of France as an equal power with Britain, the Soviet Union and the United States in the treatment of Nazi Germany and the organization of the postwar world. Being de Gaulle, he of course went about asserting France's rights in the most challenging, arrogant and irritating manner possible. All of this climaxed with the arrangements for the Big Three conference at Yalta in February 1945. Before the conference, Roosevelt sent Harry Hopkins to Paris to see de Gaulle. There were even tentative plans to invite the General to take part in the Yalta political (but not military) discussions, but the invitation was never passed along, because it was clear that it would be refused. In the meantime, de Gaulle, in his memoirs, records:

"I said this to the special envoy of the President. In the mortal dangers which we French have been passing through since the beginning of this century, the United States has not given us the impression that it considers its fate linked to that of France, that it wants a great and strong France, that it is doing what it could to help France remain so or to become so again. Perhaps indeed we are not worth the trouble. In that case, you are right. But perhaps we will rise again. Then you will have been wrong. In any case your behavior tends to estrange us from you."

When Hopkins asked how the two nations might act in agreement and confidence in the future, de Gaulle rolled on:

"If such is the intention of the United States, I cannot understand how they can undertake to settle the fate of Europe in the absence of France. I understand this all the less since after having appeared to ignore France in the forthcoming discussions at Yalta of the Three they will have to turn to Paris to ask its agreement on what will have been decided.

"You have come on behalf of the President of the United States in order to clarify the crux of the matter with respect to our relations. I think that we have done this. The French have the impression that you no longer consider the greatness of France as necessary for the world and for yourselves. Hence the cold wind which you feel on our approach, even in this office. If you want the relations of America and France to be established on a different basis, it is up to you to do what is necessary. Pending your choice, I send President Roosevelt greetings of friendship on the eve of the conference for which he is coming to Europe."

But de Gaulle then pulled one of his vindictive tricks. He received a message from Roosevelt proposing that they meet following the Yalta conference at a French port on the Mediterranean. Roosevelt was traveling aboard the U. S. Navy cruiser *Augusta*. De Gaulle at first accepted, and arrangements were made for the *Augusta* to put in at Algiers. But then, when the President reached the Egyptian port of Alexandria, a message arrived from de Gaulle abruptly refusing a meeting—on the pretext that it might imply French ratification of decisions taken at Yalta in France's absence. Roosevelt was furious at the snub (so, indeed, were the French press and public opinion), and it was only the persuasion of his interpreter and adviser, Charles E. Bohlen, that prevented his issuing a terse and insulting retort to de Gaulle.

De Gaulle was certainly not without gall. Having deliberately affronted Roosevelt, he now cabled Washington asking the United States to supply equipment for fifty French army divisions! The dying President minuted on the request rather curtly that to fulfill the French requirement would interfere with prosecution of the war. It was Roosevelt's last decision on French affairs. He died three weeks later, on April 12, 1945.

De Gaulle pressed remorselessly, relentlessly on. He instructed French army commanders in the closing stages of the war that they were to cross the Rhine and advance on his orders as rapidly and as deeply as possible into southern Germany and Austria in order to enlarge France's claims to an occupation zone—regardless of any other orders they received from General Eisenhower or Allied command. As a result, the French seized the city of Stuttgart and then refused to withdraw to let the Americans take over. At this point, President Harry S Truman stepped in. The old World War I artillery commander simply barked out to de Gaulle that all supplies for French forces would be cut off forthwith unless he complied with Eisenhower's plans. The French then withdrew from Stuttgart. But, almost at once, de Gaulle repeated the maneuver by ordering a French invasion of northern Italy, all the way to Turin, in revenge against the dead Mussolini. Again Truman threatened to cut off supplies unless the French pulled back. After that, de Gaulle got into a near shooting war with the British in the Middle East when he tried to send French forces into Syria and then Lebanon, which the British were then holding. And in the Far East, he ordered a murderous naval bombardment of the port of Hanoi in order to reestablish French colonial rule—an action that set Indochina on the course of conflict that is still going on today.

Yet with all of this posturing and gesturing to reassert French power outside its boundaries, de Gaulle's political authority inside the country was steadily eroding during 1945. He presided over some solid advances and achievements in the life of the nation in the immediate postwar period: nationalization of the gas and electricity industries, of the major banks, of the Renault automobile works, new social legislation, and perhaps most decisively the establishment of economic planning machinery under Jean Monnet. But he had to share power with an increasingly recalcitrant National Assembly, and there was political deadlock over a new constitution. He was never a man to play by any rules except his own.

His very style of leadership—the remoteness which was supposed to inspire a power mix of mystery and fear—began to backfire not only with the resentful politicians but with the French people. He was not merely remote. He was out of touch, while other politicians were showing concern, building constituencies, debating, arguing and attracting power. In the end, de Gaulle was faced with a defeat from the National Assembly over a budget vote, and although he in fact won on the immediate issue, he saw that his unchallenged sway was about at an end. He detested going down to the National Assembly to speak in debates and fight for votes, and as the new year began in 1946, he realized that he faced one such battle after another, with majorities growing smaller and smaller. He could neither impose a Fourth Republic constitution embodying his ideas of authoritarian democracy nor persuade the politicians to adopt one, and he could not or would not share power.

He summoned an unusual cabinet meeting for a Sunday morning, January 20, 1946. He entered the room and shook hands with his ministers all around, French style, and then, before anybody could sit down, he said: "The exclusive regime of parties has reappeared. I disapprove of it. But aside from establishing by force a dictatorship, I have no means of preventing this experiment. I must therefore withdraw. I sincerely thank each of you for the support you have given me, and urge you to remain at your posts in order to assure the conduct of business until your successors are appointed."

With that, de Gaulle walked out into retirement.

But he was still France's greatest figure, and he was only fifty-five years old. He set up an office in Paris and commuted to the capital a few days each week from his country home, 120 miles east of the city, at Colombey-les-Deux-Églises. He began work on three volumes of memoirs, while receiving a steady stream of visitors, old cohorts and devoted supporters.

For the politicians of the National Assembly, de Gaulle's departure was like a stone rolled away, but the activity was akin to that of maggots suddenly exposed to light. A new constitution was cobbled together, but power was again as diffuse as it had been under the Third Republic. Governments came and went—twenty-three governments headed by nineteen men in thirteen years of its life. De Gaulle watched all that was happening with the same melancholy despair, and contempt for national weakness, with which he had viewed the Dreyfus affair, Fashoda and the Agadir crisis in his youth, and the Popular Front, the Stavisky riots and the Munich crisis in his manhood. Periodically he would sally forth and call a press conference, always well attended, and always with the same litany of scorn for the political leadership and the party games that were again bringing degradation to France.

In the spring of 1947, he decided to reenter the political arena himself, and proclaimed the birth not of a party but of a movement: the Rally of the French People. There was the Cross of Lorraine, of course, and the faithful hard core from the early days in London: Jacques Soustelle, André Malraux, Olivier Gichard, Jacques Foccard, Michel Debré, Gaston Palewski, René Capitant, Jacques Chaban-Delmas, and a new adherent who had turned up out of nowhere after the liberation of Paris, Georges Pompidou. For a time, the Gaullist movement prospered, but then it began to take on a somewhat fascist tinge of dissatisfied militarists who wanted a virtual dictatorship. De Gaulle, as was his style, gave his name to the movement but then remained aloof and distant from its actual management or operations. At first, in municipal elections in 1947, the RPF swept 40 percent of the vote, but then it began to slip, and by the spring of 1953 it was a spent political force. It would remain in being not as a political movement, de Gaulle announced, but against the day when "restless dissatisfaction could lead the French people to unite to transform itself."

Meanwhile, the Fourth Republic, first under Robert Schuman as Premier and then Foreign Minister for four years, followed by the brief but brilliant tenure of Pierre Mendès-France, managed to steady itself politically and economically in the first half of the 1950s. De Gaulle seemed increasingly an anachronism, politically irrelevant to the mood of the times. He himself, bitter and profane about all that was happening, finally called a press conference in July of 1955 and announced in haughty majesty: "It is my intention not to intervene again in what are conventionally called the public affairs of this country. I say farewell to you, and perhaps for a long time to come. . . ."

He settled now almost permanently behind the walls of Colombey-les-Deux-Églises, making the journey to Paris less and less often, watching with bitter scorn the decline of the Fourth Republic as he had watched the decline of the Third Republic. When history turned to him the next time, he would settle all the old scores, wipe the old slate clean, and remake the nation in his own image.

10

The Fifth Republic

IN GAULLIST LEGEND, THE FOURTH REPUBLIC OF FRANCE WAS little more than a disastrous interregnum between General de Gaulle's abrupt departure from office in January of 1946 and his sweeping and dramatic return to power with the country on the edge of civil war in June of 1958. In fact, the Fourth Republic was remarkable not for how disastrous it all was but for how effective its successive governments still managed to be with all the built-in constitutional weaknesses and political stresses under which they had to operate. Its floundering demise became inevitable, but its achievements were not inconsiderable.

Under the Fourth Republic, France had one of the best records of postwar economic recovery in Europe. Gross national product rose by about 50 percent in the eight years from 1949, when the Marshall Plan got rolling, to 1957. Over this period, living standards improved by about 22 percent. Governments came and went, but economic planning and policy direction under the machinery that had been established by Jean Monnet in 1946 gave continuity and stability to the postwar recovery effort.

In foreign relations, France rapidly regained her voice and essential role in shaping postwar occupation policies in Germany and Austria, in the formation of the Bonn republic, in the United Nations with a permanent seat with the major powers on the Security Council, in negotiations for the North Atlantic Treaty, and above all by taking the lead through the Schuman Plan and creation of the Coal and Steel Community. For all the scorn and opprobrium heaped on the Fourth Republic by General de Gaulle, there was no lack of French independence or defense of French interests by its governments or dearth of French ideas and proposals in the world in those days. But in General de Gaulle's book, everything the Fourth Republic did was mush and muddle.

The leaders of France who succeeded General de Gaulle after 1946 were certainly "Gaullist" in their efforts to see France restored as a great power and the center of a world empire. With the General watching their every move from Colombey-les-Deux-Églises and regularly pouncing on them at press conferences filled with rhetorical scorn, they could scarcely be anything but nationalistic and chauvinistic, no matter what their party politics. The trouble was, of course, that France was vastly overextended in strength as well as ambition, and the men of the Fourth Republic were attempting to pursue Gaullist aims without Gaullist power. This got the Fourth Republic mired in the war in Vietnam—which General de Gaulle helped to launch by reimposing nineteenth-century French colonial rule on Indochina in 1945 and refusing to countenance any change or any negotiations with leaders of the new nationalist forces, among them the young Ho Chi Minh. By 1954, the war was in its eighth year, had cost France nearly $5 billion, had tied down a French expeditionary force of some two hundred thousand army regulars and Foreign Legion mercenaries, and had produced a casualty list approaching 150,000 killed, wounded and missing. The Fourth Republic was beginning to bleed to death, economically and politically as well as militarily. At this point, Pierre Mendès-France stepped into the premiership. With single-minded drive and brilliant political skill, plus a large assist from Britain's Foreign Secretary Anthony Eden, Mendès-France went to Geneva in June of 1954, sat down with the Vietminh Communists and the Red Chinese and the Russians, and negotiated a cease-fire. Vietnam was partitioned into North and South, and France was extracted from a draining commitment and an unwinnable war—which the United States then drifted into a decade later. Mendès-France held office only a little over seven months, but in that brief time he gave the Fourth Republic new vigor and a new lease on life.

But, four months after the Indochina cease-fire, fighting broke out against the French in the Khabil Mountains of Algeria, on November 1, 1954. Another seven-year colonial war had begun for France, and this time the Fourth Republic did not survive.

From the outset, the very fact that France had successfully disengaged from Indochina made it politically impossible for the leaders of the Fourth Republic to retreat from Algeria. Moreover, there was the fiction that Algeria was "French"—because it had been constitutionally incorporated into the French Republic and was governed as a department of France, not a colony or an overseas possession. Of course the whole thing was a sham, and it was only the French *pied noir* colonists and a handful of wealthy Algerians who enjoyed the benefits of French citizenship. There was not even much fictional pretense that the Algerian masses had any voice in running their country or how they were governed. Thus, not only was a military retreat from the Algerian War made impossible for the weak governments of the Fourth Republic; it was even impossible for any government to attempt any meaningful political changes or reforms in the administration of Algeria that even hinted at giving the Algerians the real benefits of French citizenship and a real voice in their own affairs.

Standing in mounting intimidation over successive governments in Paris was the French Army. It had been defeated in France in' 1940 and defeated in Indochina in 1954, and it was not going to be defeated on French territory in Algeria. Backed by the militant *pieds noirs* in Algeria and vociferous right-wing politicians in the National Assembly, the Army demanded but one policy from governments in Paris: ruthless prosecution of the war, a military victory over the FLN rebellion against France. Governments that failed to deliver, or attempted briefly to turn away from military repression and look for some political way out, were quickly toppled. Meanwhile, as the war grew more and more unpopular with liberals, intellectuals and moderates in France (it was of course opposed by the Communists from the outset), governments came under fire from both the Left and the Right and were increasingly frozen in immobility—condemned to defeat in the National Assembly whether they attempted to step up the fighting or tried to disengage through policies of reform.

But the greatest danger to French democracy was the fashion in which the French military with its *pied noir* supporters began increasingly to exploit the *immobilisme* that it was deliberately creating in Paris in order to take matters into its own hands. In fact,

the political leaders really lost control over the Algerian policy
and thus their own destiny, on a precise date, February 6, 1956,
more than two years before the end of the Fourth Republic finally
came. On that date, the leader of the Socialist Party, Guy Mollet,
had just taken over the premiership (he was number 19) and had
announced that he was naming one of France's most respected
soldiers, General Georges Catroux, to the post of Minister-
Resident in Algiers. Catroux, who had been closely associated
with de Gaulle during the war, had an excellent reputation and
record with the Arabs in long service in the French Empire, and
the appointment signaled just what Mollet intended: a more liberal and understanding and conciliatory attitude by a Socialist-led
government toward the Moslem community of Algeria. But instantly the *pieds noirs* took to the streets in Algiers in protest, with
the tacit blessing of the military. Mollet bravely announced that he
was flying to the scene, but when he landed the mob attacked his
official limousine with violent, savage hatred all the way from the
airport to the city. It was pelted with stones, eggs, tomatoes and
even manure, and Mollet emerged at the government residence
white and shaken. From Paris, Catroux then telephoned to offer
his resignation from a post that he had not yet assumed. Mollet
accepted with relief, and in his place he named a fellow Socialist,
Robert Lacoste, who promptly put Socialist principles on the shelf
in order to pursue a policy of Algerian pacification with a vengeance. The Algerian mob had dictated to Paris, and from that moment the Fourth Republic was doomed. A spiral of decline began,
and at the end the government couldn't even control the Paris
police. It was the salvation of France that the Algerian mob could
not dictate to General de Gaulle—but it certainly tried.

Of the plotting by his old adherents in politics and in the military
that preceded his return to power, General de Gaulle remarked
loftily in the last volume of his memoirs that he completed before
his death: "I was not mixed up in any way. They acted without
me and without consulting me." But de Gaulle was a very subjec-
tive historian, and this statement is disingenuous to say the least.
He was constantly aware of what was happening, informed all
along the way by key figures in the plotting—in particular Jacques

Soustelle, who had been his official spokesman and one of his intelligence operatives in London from the earliest days in 1940; Jacques Chaban-Delmas, who had been in command of the resistance forces in the Bordeaux area; and Michel Debré, who had been a principal Gaullist agent inside the Vichy government and who drew up for de Gaulle the list of Gaullist loyalists in the civil service who were then installed as prefects all over France during the liberation. Of course de Gaulle kept his distance from any direct involvement in the plotting. It was incompatible with his intellectual qualities, his style and personality, his philosophy of power, to get mixed up in the sordid details of a revolt to overthrow a French government. That was the business of others—if they wanted to plot it was their affair. He would offer no advice, no leadership, but he would not refuse the consequences. He would wait for power to be offered him, when he could then dictate his own terms with complete freedom of action, and commitments to no one, and take charge of the whole *bouillabaisse*. So if he was not "mixed up" in the plotting, he certainly knew what was going on, and if he was not "consulted" he certainly used his knowledge of the plotting to maneuver and control the final outcome in those dramatic last days of May 1958. As the year began, the visitors and secret communications to Colombey-les-Deux-Églises increased, while the military in Algeria, operating beyond the control of Paris, began to prepare the last blows to bring down the tottering Fourth Republic with the aid of Gaullist supporters inside and outside the government.

On February 8, 1958, the High Command in Algiers, without any permission or even prior notification to the government in Paris, launched a full-scale bombing attack by French Air Force planes across the Algerian border on the Tunisian town of Sakiet-Sidi-Youssef—on a market day, when the town was crowded and also, as it happened, was being visited by a representative of the International Red Cross. More than sixty people were killed. The military excuse was that the Tunisian border area was a haven of supply bases and training camps supporting the FLN rebellion (a forerunner of the American bombing of Cambodia twelve years later). There was an international outcry at the blatancy of the action and the impotence of the French Government to control its own military. The Premier of that day, Félix Gaillard, managed to hang on for another two months, but when he presented the National Assembly with proposed terms for a settlement of the affair with the Tunisian Government, he was promptly voted out of office for allowing foreign interference in French internal affairs! Thus, on April 15, 1958, President René Coty began the search for the twenty-third and last premier of the Fourth Republic.

But first, municipal elections were scheduled throughout France on April 20, and Coty and the other politicians all wanted to await the outcome before resuming their political minuet. In the meantime the Socialist Party insisted that its man, Robert Lacoste, be recalled from Algeria after two years in charge there—and as a result there was no government in Paris and no responsible administrator in Algiers for nearly four weeks. It was an interregnum that was a godsend to the plotters.

Jacques Chaban-Delmas had served as Minister of Defense in the Gaillard government, and out of the shadows of the old Gaullist political movement, the Rally of the French People (RPF), he had drawn a man named Léon Delbecque, a businessman and ex-reserve officer, into the ministry early in 1958 with a secret and specific assignment to organize Gaullist cells throughout the Army in France and Algeria under the cover of courses in psychological warfare.

At the same time, on the civilian front Michel Debré had begun working assiduously to reactivate the political apparatus of the RPF, which General de Gaulle founded in 1947 and then put to sleep after a series of election losses in 1953 against the day when "restless dissatisfaction could lead the French people to unite to transform itself." Meanwhile, Jacques Soustelle, the arch-plotter of them all by nature, personality and habit, was all over the place —Paris, the provinces, Algeria, Corsica, political cells, military posts—agitating and organizing those on whom he could count on a future day of uprising to bring back de Gaulle.

But among the senior military commanders, in particular the high officers in Algeria, the attitude toward de Gaulle was suspicious and hostile. He had never been a popular figure in the French Army, and the fashion in which he propelled himself in 1940 from the obscure rank of brigadier general to the "voice of

France" did not endear him to the military conservatives. He was disliked and resented. Moreover, it was well known in the French Army that he was ambivalent in his attitude toward France's overseas possessions. In the first half of this century the French Army divided into those who made their careers and sought advancement in colonial service in the French Empire, and those who focused on the security of France itself. De Gaulle, like Pétain before him, was resolutely in the home camp, and regarded the policing of overseas possessions to be a drain and a diversion from the primary mission of the French Army. He developed a devotion for the French Empire only after the African colonies were the first to rally to his support in 1940. After the war, he then saw all these scattered and impoverished possessions as a *raison d'etre* of France's role as a world power. But in fact, everything that had happened in Indochina and was now transpiring in Algeria reinforced de Gaulle's original conviction that policing an empire was the wrong strategic mission for the French forces and was weakening to France itself.

But he had resolutely kept this conviction to himself. He had not held a press conference for three years, and accordingly had made no public pronouncement on the Algerian War. In 1957 his staff even issued a public warning against anything attributed to the General from private conversations. "When General de Gaulle thinks it useful to make known the opinion he holds, he will do it himself and do it publicly," the statement said. In fact, he was saying one thing to one visitor and another to the next—sometimes expounding on the nobility of France's role "to ensure a genuine association of the two principal elements"; other times heaping scorn on the "miserable Algerians" and asserting that "it is in the nature of things that Algeria will become independent," and always blaming the Fourth Republic for the Algerian mess. Never once, despite pleading and pressuring from Soustelle and others, would he agree to "go public" with a declaration on the Algerian question. When Delbecque went to him in the final days before his return to power and asked point-blank what he would do, he simply raised himself and propounded: "I would know how to assume my responsibilities."

This studied and oracular silence on the Algerian question of course only reinforced the suspicions of the senior commanders in Algiers: General Raoul Salan, General Maurice Challe, General Edmond Jouhaud, and in Morocco the most senior, Marshal Alphonse Juin. But silence preserved for de Gaulle his complete freedom of action when he regained power, and for him that was the essential. Moreover, he did have one strong supporter and ally in a key role in the armed forces, and that was General Paul Ély, Chief of the Defense Staff, in Paris.

As Coty and the politicians stalled in Paris to await the municipal elections, Delbecque made the first move by the Gaullist plotters. He announced in Algiers the formation of a "Committee of Vigilance" and called for a great public demonstration in the city on April 26. By this maneuver, he hoped to get members of his committee to declare publicly, after the demonstration, for de Gaulle.

But the military commanders in Algiers and the *pieds noirs* had other ideas, and they had been plotting too. They did not want to be controlled by General de Gaulle—they wanted to control the French Government. By late April they were ready, moreover, with a comprehensive plan for a military takeover and the installation in Paris of a "Government of Public Safety" under military auspices. The first to revolt was to have been the commander of the Southwest District, at Toulouse, and four of the other nine regional commanders were committed to join in the action, including a senior aide-de-camp to General Ély, who was to lead the operation to seize the government buildings in Paris. Most probably it was he who leaked word of the plot to Ély, who in turn informed President Coty—for on May 5, in the midst of a search for a new Premier, Coty made a secret approach to de Gaulle to ask on what conditions he would be prepared to take office. De Gaulle's first response was to demand emergency powers for eighteen months and a reform of the constitution. Coty then made a second secret approach on May 8, and this time de Gaulle moderated his demands to the extent of saying that he would be agreeable to submitting his candidature to the National Assembly but would not go there in person to seek power. Coty then abandoned these first efforts to negotiate with de Gaulle and turned to an austere Alsatian, a Catholic centrist, Pierre Pflimlin. Meanwhile, from

Algiers, General Salan, the military Commander-in-Chief, sent a less-than-veiled warning to Coty that there would be a "reaction of despair" if he was unable to produce "a government firmly committed to defend our flag in Algeria."

On May 13, 1958, the final power struggle began. In Paris, Pflimlin was due to go before the National Assembly for a vote of investiture. In Algiers, Delbecque called for another massive demonstration for his Committee of Vigilance. And that same day, the French Air Force put into operation the first phase of the military *Putsch,* Operation Resurrection, sending transport to Algeria to embark paratroops for France.

The French people of course knew nothing of the secret plotting, but there was drama enough out in the open to establish that this was the gravest crisis in French peacetime history, with democracy at the brink. For General de Gaulle the suspense was acute, but he never lost his sense of timing or feel for the control of events. It was but one aspect of his greatness. Delbecque had gone into action, and de Gaulle knew from General Ély of the military plot also launched in secret—but he did not yet know whether if he moved openly to take power he would have the backing of the military and the Algerian *ultras*. Moreover, he did not want to make a move that would result in the onus falling on him if Pflimlin failed to get an investiture vote in the National Assembly and thus aligned the politicians against his return. So on May 13, de Gaulle waited in silence at Colombey-les-Deux-Églises.

In Algiers, things were not going well for Delbecque. Jacques Soustelle was to have flown to the city to join him to give Gaullist weight to the Committee of Vigilance. As a former governor-general of Algeria, dedicated to *Algérie française,* Soustelle was wildly popular with the *colones*. But de Gaulle had instructed him to remain in Paris in the expectation that Pflimlin would lose in the National Assembly—in which case the next vital political moves would be in the capital. Delbecque's massive demonstration in Algiers ended with the mob breaking into the Government-General building and sacking offices and files while the Army looked on. But the Committee of Vigilance did not produce any ringing call from the highest military and political personalities in

Algiers in a unified front for de Gaulle. In particular, General Salan kept his distance.

On the night of May 13, spurred by demonstrations in Algiers and the rapid political deterioration, the National Assembly in near panic gave Pflimlin one of the biggest investiture votes in the history of the Fourth Republic. The Cabinet put Soustelle under house arrest, declared a blockade of Algeria and closed all French airports—but these moves added up to Canute battling the tides.

Nevertheless, France did now have a legally constituted government again. There was a pause in events on May 14, while frantic messages passed between Paris and Algeria—between de Gaulle and Delbecque, Salan and Pflimlin, and endless others. Salan, who had served in the Orient and was known as the "Chinese General," could not or did not want to make up his mind which way to jump, and therefore was performing a remarkable act of a snake crawling along a fence. If he declared openly his support for Pflimlin and the new government, he might face mutiny in his own command, but if he declared for de Gaulle, which he did not want to do, and Pflimlin managed to reassert power, then he ran the risk of court-martial. Meanwhile, however, some of his subordinate commanders, including the popular paratrooper General Jacques Massu, had come out publicly for de Gaulle. But again it was a day of silence at Colombey-les-Deux-Églises.

On May 16, Delbecque's Committee of Vigilance again called out a vast throng to the Forum in front of the Government-General building in Algiers—this time for a "unity appearance" with the military commanders. Salan addressed the tens of thousands with an adroit declaration that he had assumed full military and civil powers, without any clarification as to where he stood or on whose behalf he would be exercising authority. He ended with the traditional *"Vive l'Algérie française, vive la France!"* and stepped back. At his elbow, Delbecque hissed: *"Et vive de Gaulle."* Salan hesitated visibly but then stepped forward to the microphone. *"Vive de Gaulle!"* he cried, and a roar went up from the crowd.

It was the call de Gaulle had been waiting for. As Salan went home to be upbraided by his wife for what he had done, de Gaulle prepared a statement that was issued in Paris at five o'clock that afternoon: "Once before, from the depths of the abyss, the country gave me its confidence to lead it back to salvation. Today, with new trials crowding in upon it, it is right that it should know that I am ready to assume the power of the Republic."

But the drama still had another excruciating two weeks to run. Pflimlin was an upright and honorable man, not about to be pushed out of power by a military insurrection. Moreover, the initial reaction to de Gaulle's statement from political leaders and the trade unions and even the Communists, which probably did not help, was to rally to the support of the constituted government. In particular, de Gaulle had said nothing to condemn the insurrection growing in the Army, from which it was deduced that he was in cahoots with the revolt. In Algiers, his statement produced almost hysterical rejoicing.

De Gaulle's next move was to announce that he would hold a press conference on May 19. In the meantime, Soustelle escaped from house arrest by hiding under the rear seat of a car. He got across the border to Switzerland and flew to Algeria. Then the Communists called for a general strike to pressure for the formation of a popular-front government with the Socialists to "save the Republic." Finally, and most important, Delbecque passed word to de Gaulle that four separate military missions had departed from Algiers for mainland France to make final preparations for the military coup, Operation Resurrection, with the aim of installing a right-wing Government of Public Safety, not with de Gaulle but under Georges Bidault. It was a race between a military coup and de Gaulle awaiting a legitimate political call to return to power.

The de Gaulle press conference, before some twelve hundred newsmen in the ballroom of the Hôtel Palais d'Orsay, was a masterpiece. He began with affable irony by remarking that it had been three years since he had last "had the pleasure" of seeing the press, and by the time he finished there was something in it for everybody. He was majestic, aloof, soothing, reassuring, good-humored and grandfatherly. He was out to smooth his way back to power, not batter his way. In particular he surprised everybody with generous words of praise for the Socialist leader Guy Mollet, whose support would be crucial in the political maneuvering that lay ahead.

On the crucial question of the Algerian War, his responses were a masterpiece of evasive understanding. There was sympathy for the Algerian population (French and Moslem) "that has seen that the present system established in Paris cannot solve its problems." Then there was praise for the Algerians who had cried, *Vive de Gaulle,* which he saw as "the best proof that they do not want to break away from Metropolitan France, for one does not shout, *Vive de Gaulle,* if one is not on the side of the nation!" So at one and the same time he was saying that he sympathized, and would solve their problems, but it was also noted that he never used the words *"Algérie française."* When he was asked what he would do about Algeria, the reply came magisterially: "It would be necessary to hear the parties involved. What would a judge be who gave his judgment before the hearing?" What about fears of people that he would attack public liberties? Magisterially again: "Have I ever done so? On the contrary, I restored them when they had disappeared. Is it credible that I am going to begin a career as a dictator at the age of sixty-seven?" And then the finale: "If the task should fall on me to lead the state and the nation out of the crisis, I would approach it without presumptuousness, for it would be hard and fearsome. I have said what I have to say. I shall now return to my village, and I shall remain there at the disposal of the country."

As the military advanced and the politicians resisted, the public response to the de Gaulle press conference was overwhelming. General de Gaulle was the only way out of France's troubles. Pflimlin still did not budge, but one of his key Cabinet members, former Premier Antoine Pinay, headed secretly for Colombey-les-Deux-Églises. The military plotters, who had held off acting when de Gaulle announced his press conference, also moved to the brink by dispatching a key leader among the Algerian *ultras,* Paratroop Lieutenant Philippe LaGaillarde, to France to take final charge and push the button. He arrived secretly on May 21, but General Ély was aware, and he kept both de Gaulle and President Coty informed.

Frantic at this point that the military coup might still supersede de Gaulle's bid for power, Delbecque, Soustelle and General Massu all put heavy pressure on General Salan in Algiers to hold off final orders to strike in Metropolitan France and simply seize power on the island of Corsica as a first step. The logic of not getting overcommitted appealed to the Chinese General, and on Sunday, May 25, a handful of paratroopers landed at Ajaccio and took over, to establish a "Committee of Public Safety" rule, without firing a shot. Even a company of elite Ministry of the Interior troops, the Republican Security Companies (CRS) anti-riot police, went over to the insurrection as final proof of the impotence in Paris. Meeting that night, Pflimlin and the Cabinet had to face the fact that whatever their outrage and fears, they were powerless to act.

Through Pinay, de Gaulle had sent word that he was ready for a meeting with Pflimlin at any time. Long after midnight on the night of May 26–27, the two men arrived in total secrecy from different directions in darkened cars at one of the old royal residences, the Château de Saint-Cloud, outside Paris. They talked for two hours, and although nothing was decided, de Gaulle drove back to Colombey-les-Deux-Églises, 120 miles east of Paris, knowing that Pflimlin and Mollet were at least ready for him to assume power.

When he got home, de Gaulle decided to force Pflimlin's hand. At noon that day he issued a statement through his office in Paris: "I began yesterday the regular process necessary to establish a Republican Government capable of restoring the unity and independence of the country." Then, still wary that the military plotters would decide to follow up their success on Corsica, de Gaulle called on "land, sea and air forces to maintain exemplary discipline under the orders of their commanders." Notice was thus served on Salan and the others that they would risk court-martial at the hands of General de Gaulle if they triggered a coup and failed.

On the night of May 28, de Gaulle again journeyed to the Château de Saint-Cloud—this time for an acrimonious argument about constitutional procedures with the president of the National Assembly, André Le Troquer, and the president of the Senate, Gaston Monneville. After more than an hour of discussion, de

Gaulle rose, walked out, slammed the door and drove back to Colombey-les-Deux-Églises to bed. Next morning, President Coty made up his mind to use his ultimate powers to resolve the crisis. He rose at 7 A.M. and wrote out in longhand a message to the National Assembly that the country was on the verge of civil war and that he had asked "the most illustrious of Frenchmen" to form a Government of National Assembly. As his own ultimatum, Coty announced that if this failed he would resign. Before sending the message across to the Palais Bourboun, where the Assembly meets, he telephoned de Gaulle at Colombey at 9:30 A.M. Informed that the General was still asleep, the President of the Republic sighed politely that he envied him, but would his aide please inform him when he woke.

That afternoon, with the National Assembly in a turmoil at Coty's ultimatum and pressure mounting among the military plotters to go into action to seize power, de Gaulle journeyed back to Paris to call formally on the President of the Republic at the Élysée Palace. His terms were simple: Unlimited emergency powers for a period during which the National Assembly would be recessed, and a referendum later on an entirely new constitution for a Fifth Republic.

Knowing that he had won, de Gaulle now made a concession of form that he had earlier refused in his meetings with Pflimlin, Le Troquer and others. He agreed to go to the National Assembly in person to obtain a vote of investiture. On Sunday, June 1, a Paris day of dazzling beauty, he entered the Chamber, and with courtly *politesse* faced the deputies on whom he had heaped so much scorn. He spoke briefly of the conditions on which he had accepted office, and departed to the applause of all but the Communists. That evening, he was invested with power by a vote of 329–224.

At last General de Gaulle had achieved power on his own terms. But it was power that had to be consolidated and refined before it could be used to the fullest. Everything still revolved around the Algerian War. It had brought down the Fourth Republic, and until de Gaulle could get a grip on the situation and exercise his control over events, instead of being controlled by Algiers as the

Premiers who had preceded him had allowed themselves to be, his power would be threatened, diluted and uncertain. He began his new reign with moves that were designed to calm the scene after all the political and emotional turbulence of the preceding weeks. He needed time to reinforce his power base.

Two days after taking office, he flew to Algiers. On arrival, he pointedly snubbed the Committee of Public Safety of Delbecque and company, which had spearheaded the uprising that brought him back to power. He would be in debt to nobody. Instead, he set out to reassure the Army and those who had opposed his return. He elevated General Salan to the title of Delegate-General for Algeria, in addition to Commander-in-Chief, and declared him responsible for "the workings of regular authority." He appeared before yet another vast throng in front of the Government-General building at the end of his first day, and to the chants of *Algérie française,* de Gaulle stretched out his arms and responded with the marvelously misleading phrase: *"Je vous ai compris!"* (I have understood you). Next day, in one of the Algerian provincial towns, Mostaganem, he did use the words *Algérie française* for the first and only time in a public utterance. Later he closely questioned those who had been with him about this, and when he was assured that he had indeed been heard to say it, he retorted impatiently that he must have been carried away by the crowd but that the words were superficial anyway. If so, they must have been the only superficial words that this master of words ever uttered.

Thus, General de Gaulle left behind in Algiers misgivings among the *ultras* over his treatment of the Committee of Public Safety and how things might now be heading on the fundamental question of those superficial words *Algérie française.* But he had mollified the Army with what seemed to be assurances that it could now get on with the job of suppressing the rebellion. He had in fact set a tactical pattern that he was to follow for the next four years: Two steps forward toward Algerian independence, then one step backward in order to stay in control.

His own first priority had to be France itself. Constitutionally, he was still a Premier of the Fourth Republic and President Coty was still at the Élysée Palace. All of this was soon to be swept away, but his first Cabinet that summer of 1958 was a genuine po-

litical coalition. It included his immediate predecessor, Pierre
Pflimlin; the Socialist leader, Guy Mollet; and elder statesman Antoine Pinay at the Finance Ministry. De Gaulle even made a polite
reappearance before the National Assembly, before taking off for
Algiers, to intervene briefly in its last debate on a vote of his
emergency powers and wish its members a *bonne adieu* before
they adjourned forever. But these pretenses of a national political
coalition were alien to everything de Gaulle wanted to do and the
way he intended to run things. It was a holding operation until he
was ready.

After all the draining drama, therefore, the transition to de
Gaulle's rule was almost anticlimactic. The French Civil Service,
for better or worse, is almost totally inured to changes in government, and even republics, across two centuries. It stays in place,
does its job and awaits orders. If new orders do not arrive, then it
runs on inertia. It ran for Napoleon III before the Franco-Prussian War, and Gambetta after. It ran for Clemenceau, Léon Blum
and the Popular Front, Paul Reynaud, Marshal Pétain, and Pierre
Mendès-France, and now it would run again for General de
Gaulle.

When he took power, it was like turning on the bellows of an
ill-used pipe organ and starting to play. Dossiers of the Fourth
Republic that had never gotten attention were dusted off and
brought forward, and fresh ones were rapidly inspired. Ministers,
secure in their jobs, could command action and get results. Taxes,
fiscal policy, the national budget, public-spending and social-
security programs, and even an ordinance for the cleanup of the
buildings of Paris were all rapidly formulated in the confines of
the ministries and swept through cabinet proceedings and into the
Journal Officiel, to be put into effect without any tiresome problems of Assembly debate or precarious voting combinations.
France is a bountiful nation (in everything but coal and oil), and
despite the economic drain and political unrest of the Algerian
War, the country rapidly regained its equilibrium and resumed
steady growth and progress.

De Gaulle placed the faithful, mordant Michel Debré at the
Ministry of Justice and charged him with chairmanship of a committee to draft a constitution for the Fifth Republic. It was rushed

to completion in barely three months ("the worst-drafted text in our constitutional history," declared René Capitant, an ardent Gaullist and professor of constitutional law). Approved by a 4–1 referendum majority on September 28, 1958, the constitution did not go quite as far as de Gaulle would have liked in the way of powers, but some compromises with tradition and political reality had to be made for the sake of wide popular support. It achieved the essential for de Gaulle of establishing a presidential system, with the chief of state empowered to appoint or dismiss Prime Ministers, preside over cabinet meetings, dissolve the National Assembly, direct and control the entire running of the government. He is also Commander of the Armed Forces. The National Assembly can overthrow a Prime Minister and his government (although after more than twenty years it has yet to do so), but it cannot overthrow or change the powers of the President.

De Gaulle was no great respecter of constitutionality. On one occasion when the Constitutional Council handed down an advisory opinion against some act he wished to promulgate, the General simply informed his Cabinet that "events are more important than constitutional texts—after all, France has had seventeen in 150 years." Probably the most important element in the constitution of the Fifth Republic, which de Gaulle personally insisted upon, was the power of the President to go directly to the people for approval by referendum of just about anything he wished to do —from changing the constitution itself to granting independence to Algeria. Not only was this procedure used by de Gaulle to bypass the National Assembly and the normal legislative processes completely; each referendum also was treated as an endorsement of his personal power, a kind of plebescite renewal of his increasingly authoritarian rule. There were five in all in de Gaulle's time —down to the last referendum, on April 27, 1969, which he lost. He took this as dismissal by the French people and instantly withdrew from office. Those that live by the sword die by the sword.

Less than three months after his return to power, de Gaulle made his first major basic diplomatic-political move in the realm of foreign policy. Practically every public declaration or press conference of his life included some passionate reference to the independence of France—as though it were a country writhing in the tentacles of sinister forces ensnaring its freedom and personality, forces that had to be hacked and chopped and fought with eternal vigilance. Everywhere, de Gaulle pictured his nation as hemmed in by strangling extraneous evils—of which the greatest was Anglo-Saxon hegemony, exemplified by the North Atlantic Treaty Organization. He had fought the Anglo-Saxons throughout the war for recognition. It was the Anglo-Saxons who had sold out Europe at Yalta. France must either be recognized as an equal by the Anglo-Saxons—or be free of Anglo-Saxon domination.

No matter that NATO was the very guaranty of French security, of the United States presence in Europe and a United States commitment to do for France what de Gaulle had ceaselessly rebuked Americans for failing to do twice before in the century, in 1914 and 1940. It was an organization whose strategy, command, weapons and above all decision-making were essentially in American hands. Others might relish the comfort of this American security guaranty—but not France! In any case, could the Americans be trusted? France must be her own guarantor and must make her own decisions, must control her own forces and her own destiny. Above all, she must possess her own nuclear weapons and the means to deliver them. As the great Italian journalist-writer Luigi Barzini once wrote with an Italianate sigh of resignation: "The French are always looking for victories—the Italians are always forgetting defeats."

For de Gaulle, the shackles of NATO must be struck from French wrists so that France could emerge from the Anglo-Saxon shadow strong, independent, standing alone, making her own voice heard in the world. On September 17, 1958, he addressed parallel letters to President Eisenhower and Prime Minister Macmillan on the subject of the future of the Alliance.

NATO, he declaimed, no longer met the needs of French security. France would soon have its own nuclear bomb and had global responsibilities in the North Atlantic, Africa, the Indian Ocean and the Pacific, as did the United States and Great Britain. Therefore, de Gaulle continued, the world situation no longer justified the United States making the decisions of world defense. It was time to organize tripartite machinery for global strategy and policy, above and outside NATO, to take joint decisions and formulate strategic plans of action—in particular the use of nuclear weapons. With the involuted grace of the French language, de Gaulle concluded that France "would henceforth subordinate any development of French participation in NATO to this achievement, and would if necessary propose a revision of the North Atlantic Treaty."

President Eisenhower sent a considered reply a month later, pointing out the difficulty of "adopting any system which would give to our allies or the free world countries the impression that basic decisions affecting their own vital interests are being made without their participation." Eisenhower did offer to explore the matter further. Macmillan responded less formally, but in the same vein. But de Gaulle got exactly the responses he had anticipated and wanted.

"As I had expected, the two recipients of my memorandum replied evasively," he wrote in his final volume of memoirs. "Now there was nothing to prevent us from taking action. Even so, circumstances forced me to act without causing too much shock. We did not yet possess the nuclear bomb. Algeria still monopolized the attention of our Army, our Air Force and our Navy. We did not know in which direction the Kremlin would go in its relations with the West."

With that letter of 1958, de Gaulle's long-term course against NATO was set. His first practical move followed in March of 1959, when he withdrew the French Mediterranean Fleet from command assignment to NATO on the excuse that its operations had to be directed primarily by the requirements of the Algerian conflict. At about this same time he also decreed that French forces, earmarked for NATO, that had been shifted temporarily to Algeria were now permanently withdrawn. The French air defense system was withdrawn from the integrated NATO system for all of Western Europe, which was being developed, and French controls were imposed on NATO overflights of French territory. Then he decreed that no nuclear weapons were to be stationed on French soil unless they were placed under French command and control—after which all United States Air Force tactical air squadrons had to be pulled out of France and transferred to fields in

Great Britain. It was the beginning of a clear and consistent step-by-step course which climaxed when de Gaulle booted out NATO headquarters and the Americans entirely, and tore up five Franco-American defense agreements, in 1966. The surprise was how little the United States and the NATO Allies perceived what was coming.

In part, these early anti-NATO pinpricks did not seem to draw much blood, because de Gaulle at the same time was playing such a strong and determined role against Nikita Khrushchev and the Soviet Union over Berlin, in what proved to be the final stages of Cold War diplomacy. To be sure, he contrived to play a lone hand and assert an independent role as much as possible. He was against Harold Macmillan's foray to Moscow in February of 1959, which led to the long and futile Geneva Foreign Ministers Conference on Berlin in the summer of that same year. He was contemptuous of Khrushchev's threats to sign a separate peace treaty with East Germany and "liquidate" the presence of Western forces in Berlin. He was icily calm at Khrushchev's walkout from the ill-fated Paris "Big Four" Summit Conference, which Macmillan engineered in 1960. He was dead against the "Berlin probe" of Soviet intentions launched by President Kennedy and Secretary of State Dean Rusk in 1961–62, refusing to have anything to do with it, insisting that there was only one policy: firmness, a refusal to countenance any negotiation that must inevitably imply Western concessions or change. Moreover, he used all these diplomatic episodes to address oblique warnings to Chancellor Konrad Adenauer, in Bonn, on the need for France and Germany to stand firm against possible Anglo-Saxon weakness. In the grand finale of the Cold War—the Cuban missile crisis—de Gaulle stood at Kennedy's side with instant resolution. Former Secretary of State Dean Acheson flew to Paris secretly on Kennedy's behalf, bringing with him the photoreconnaissance evidence of the installation of Soviet missiles in Cuba. Acheson outlined what Kennedy proposed to do, and de Gaulle, after peering with fascination at the photos through his thick lenses, straightened up and responded: "You may tell the President that he has the full support of France. I would do exactly the same if I were in his position." He paused, and then added: "I must note that I have been advised, but not consulted." Measured against this forthrightness with the Western camp, the maneuverings against NATO by de Gaulle seemed small, even insignificant.

Indeed, the benefits to the rest of the world of a strong and stable France were clear for all to see, whatever the difficulties of dealing with its prickly, imperious leader. De Gaulle moved with exceptional speed to transform France's outdated colonial empire into a new association of independent African states, the French Community. In a whirlwind tour of every French African capital from Chad to Madagascar that summer of 1958, reminiscent of October 1940, he offered independence to all, within or outside the French Community, as part of the constitution of the Fifth Republic. If independence within the Community was something less than total (currency tied to the French franc, a large dose of French "advice" and assistance), it was nevertheless better than straight colonial rule. Out of fifteen colonies, only one—Guinea—opted to stay outside the Community, and got independence with a vengeance. When the French colonial administrators departed from the capital of Conakry, even the telephones were ripped out and taken back to France. Still, de Gaulle had achieved at a stroke what the British were already doing step by step in the transformation of their empire into the Commonwealth. Potential liabilities had been converted into potential long-term political assets that France continues to realize today. Only Algeria remained.

On the first anniversary of his return to power, in May 1959, de Gaulle recalled General Salan from Algiers, honored him with a regal official luncheon at the Élysée Palace, presented him with another medal and ceremoniously installed him as Military Governor of Paris—where his most important function would be to lead the Bastille Day parade every July 14. General Maurice Challe, perhaps the most intelligent professional soldier in the French Army at that time, took over in Algeria with a mandate to press for a rapid victory. In fact, under Challe, the French Army's strategy and tactics both improved. Vast areas were "pacified," but Challe's best was still not good enough for victory. In any case, while Challe fought, de Gaulle had begun to negotiate to get out.

On September 16, 1959, de Gaulle made his first major public move. He went on the air to announce "in the name of France and the Republic" that he was offering Algeria the right of self-determination—independence if that was what the Algerians wanted. The offer was hedged with conditions about the rights of the European population, retaining Sahara oil under French control, etc., but it was a 180-degree turn away from *Algérie française* and it was the start of the peace process. In Algiers there was consternation, and in January of 1960 the *ultras* erupted by building barricades in the city to take things into their own hands. It looked like the start of the 1958 rebellion all over again. For a full week the barricades were defiantly manned while the Army remained passive. De Gaulle fumed in Paris in a rage, but held back ordering the Army to fire on the barricades, knowing that this might explode into civil war. Challe prudently moved his headquarters out of Algiers. In the end, de Gaulle put on his brigadier general's uniform and went on television with an emotional broadside appealing for "return to law and order," which worked. It was more urgent than ever that he rid himself and France of the Algerian problem.

Over the summer of 1960, the first genuine negotiating moves with the FLN rebel leaders began. In November, de Gaulle sprang his next surprise. He announced a political referendum: a vote by the French people, bypassing the National Assembly, on extraconstitutional powers for the government to end Algerian attachment to France and allow the Algerians "to choose their own destiny." It had long seemed to most foreign correspondents reporting from Paris at the time that the people of Metropolitan France were increasingly indifferent to the cause of *Algérie française* and growingly fed up with the spill-over of violence, bombings, demonstrations and disorders with which they were having to live in Paris for the sake of the *pied noir* colonists on the other side of the Mediterranean. On January 8, 1961, they voted overwhelmingly for de Gaulle's policy to let Algeria go.

The General now had a clear mandate, but negotiating with the FLN proved more difficult than selling the French people. He still had to jockey two steps forward and then one step backward. He still had to retain control over the Army and the city of Algiers. But as he pressed implacably toward his goal, relieving such senior generals as Salan, Challe and Massu who disagreed with his policy, tensions built up as in a pressure cooker. It blew suddenly again in the "Revolt of the Generals," when the Fifth Republic seemed to be teetering on the brink as the Fourth Republic had done only three years before.

Salan, after finally being retired from the post of Military Governor of Paris, slipped off to Madrid early in 1961, there to take up contact with the *ultras* who had staged the affair of the barricades. Challe resigned from a senior NATO command that he had been given when he was brought home from Algeria. Both secretly made their way to Algiers, where they joined two other seniors, General Marie-André Zeller and General Edmond Jouhaud. Together, on Friday, April 21, 1961, they proclaimed that they had taken over the city, established military government, and placed under arrest a member of de Gaulle's Cabinet who happened to be visiting Algeria. Military uprisings in Oran, Constantine and other cities followed later in the day. Radio intercepts indicated that a parachute assault on Paris was being prepared. Shaken but outwardly calm, de Gaulle remained silent to await events, while the government declared a complete blockade of Algeria, placed trucks on French airfield runways, reduced gasoline allocations at all army units that might be tempted to join the revolt, and prepared to resist. On Monday de Gaulle appeared on television in bull-like anger, ordering French soldiers to use "all means" against their officers to subjugate the revolt. By Tuesday it was clear that the revolt had been checked, and on Wednesday it collapsed. Challe surrendered, Zeller was arrested. Jouhaud hid out until September, while Salan kept on the run for a full year. All four were eventually jailed by a special security court. Jouhaud barely escaped execution, through a legal technicality.

The last great challenge to de Gaulle's rule had been broken, but peace in Algeria was still nearly a year away. Units that had joined the rebellion were summarily disbanded—notably the Foreign Legion Parachute Brigade. Officers who participated were rooted out, court-martialed, cashiered, demoted, transferred, executed. The first withdrawals of the French Army from Algeria began. But, in the city itself, a new and vicious period of guerrilla warfare opened up between the *ultras,* who had gone under-

254   TEN MEN AND HISTORY

ground, and the French Army backed by the gendarmerie, the police and *barbooze* counterintelligence killer squads. Salan, in hiding, took charge of the Secret Army Organization (OAS), dedicated to frustrate by terrorist operations any peace with the FLN. The OAS mounted at least nine different plots or attempts on de Gaulle's life, two of them miraculous near-misses. In this hellish atmosphere, peace negotiations were tortuously pursued, first in secret and finally out in the open around a conference table at the town of Évian, on the Lake of Geneva. But the OAS murdered the Mayor of Évian as the talks were about to open, for his role in organizing the physical arrangements. At long last the peace was signed there, on March 18, 1962. A cease-fire was proclaimed by both sides next day, and the agreements were then endorsed in France by national referendum in April. On July 3, 1962, Algerian independence was declared after 132 years of French rule. The victorious leaders of the FLN arrived in their capital, still echoing to bombs and gunfire from the last, mad *pied noir* diehards of the OAS.

Only General de Gaulle could have brought France through the nightmare of the Algerian War, and only an end to the Algerian War could have saved France itself. With the nation no longer encumbered and weakened by this political-military millstone, de Gaulle turned his attention at once to realizing his vision of France at last independent, restored to a great-power role, a voice to be heard and listened to throughout the world.

At the time of the Cuban missile crisis, that voice had been resolute and reassuring to President Kennedy. But the two Presidents drew diametrically opposite lessons and conclusions. For Kennedy, the crisis had been a supreme, almost orgastic victory of power, after his stormy meeting with Khrushchev in Vienna in May 1961 and all the testing of nerves and will and maneuverings over Berlin. He had won in Cuba due to his total control over all the conventional sea power and nuclear arms that were needed to obliterate either those missile bases or the Soviet Union itself. The lesson for Kennedy therefore was that world peace and security were best preserved by retaining undiluted concentration of power and decision in the hands of the leader of the Atlantic Alliance.

But General de Gaulle drew the opposite conclusion. For him, the building of the Berlin Wall, in 1961, followed by the Cuban crisis in 1962 marked the effective end of the Cold War. He had gone along in the missile crisis with little enthusiasm ("I must note that I have been advised but not consulted") because he knew that he had to, but he did not relish the thought that France might one day again be caught up in another superpower confrontation in some obscure part of the world where she had no national interest but was told that war or peace hung in the balance. Therefore, as he saw it, past strength in Berlin and Cuba had paid off by opening up a new era of détente and diplomatic maneuver, in which he could now take France safely out from under the NATO security umbrella and assert his own role and a role for Europe between the superpowers. So while Kennedy moved to consolidate Alliance solidarity, de Gaulle moved to break farther away from NATO entanglements and above all to speed the development of France's nuclear *force de frappe* so he would have his own finger on his own button.

Events began to play into de Gaulle's hands from three directions toward the end of 1962. First, the Kennedy administration, in order to allay unease over control of nuclear weapons in the Alliance, came up with a proposal to create a NATO mixed-manned multilateral nuclear force of submarines and surface vessels. The theory was that this would give other nations some kind of say-so in firing off American seaborne nuclear missiles. But it was a cumbersome gimmick to try to peddle to any of the Allies, let alone General de Gaulle.

Meanwhile, Great Britain had been inching forward in negotiations of great complexity in Brussels to join the European Common Market. De Gaulle had little enthusiasm for British entry, but there was no certainty that the negotiations were going to succeed. He had contented himself for more than a year with watching and waiting.*

Throughout this period of 1961–62, de Gaulle had worked assiduously to cultivate his relations with Chancellor Konrad Adenauer, in Bonn. By his own example of continuous resolution in

* See also Chapter 16, "Britain into Europe."

the running saga of Berlin for four years, de Gaulle had reinforced Adenauer's fears of supposed Anglo-Saxon weakness. It was natural, moreover, that these two aging statesmen would be drawn to some great common act of Franco-German reconciliation, to turn a page on the past forever. Late in 1962, de Gaulle suggested that they draw up an agreement for permanent Franco-German political cooperation. Adenauer responded enthusiastically by proposing that it not be merely an agreement, but a full-fledged treaty. De Gaulle agreed.

That December, Macmillan arrived to visit de Gaulle for a weekend at Rambouillet Château to talk about the negotiations to enter Europe. It was a notably cool discussion. Macmillan then flew almost immediately to Nassau, in the Bahamas, to negotiate a deal with President Kennedy to obtain Polaris missiles for British submarines. In return, Britain gave tacit, unenthusiastic support to the multilateral-nuclear-force idea. Kennedy then made the same missile offer formally to de Gaulle.

The stage was set for the most famous, dramatic and decisive press conference of General de Gaulle's long career. On January 14, 1963, he settled himself regally in an enormous armchair on a dais before correspondents gathered in the Salon de Fête of the Élysée Palace and set out to do no less than alter the course of history. It was his first news conference since May 1962, and much had happened on which his comments were awaited. Nobody anticipated the force or weight with which his blows would be struck.

First, he magisterially lowered the boom on Britain's effort to join the European Common Market: "Sentiments, as favorable as they might be and as they are, cannot be put forward in opposition to the real factors of the problem," he began. Britain was an island with Commonwealth commitments, and must "transform itself" to be truly European in outlook. Until then, it had no place in the Europe that France envisaged. Otherwise "in the end there would appear a colossal Atlantic Community under American dependence and leadership which would soon completely swallow up the European Community, which is not at all what France wants to do and is doing." While de Gaulle lived, Britain would remain outside the Common Market.

Next, he turned almost scornfully on Kennedy's offer of nuclear weapons for France in return for participation in the multilateral nuclear force: "It is completely understandable that the French undertaking to equip herself with an atomic force of her own does not appear to be highly satisfactory to certain American circles. In politics and in strategy, as in the economy, monopoly quite naturally appears to the person who holds it to be the best possible system. It is quite true that the number of nuclear weapons with which we can equip ourselves will not equal—far from it—the mass of those of the two giants of today. But since when has it been proved that a people should remain deprived of the most effective weapons for the reason that its chief possible adversary and its chief friend have means far superior to its own?"

Macmillan and Kennedy had jointly handed de Gaulle a rare historic opportunity to strike a double blow at the great hobgoblin of Anglo-Saxon hegemony, and he struck with the deep satisfaction of twenty years of waiting, all those past arguments and affronts—real, imagined, self-induced—at the hands of Churchill and Roosevelt. On the diplomatic chessboard, the United States and Great Britain had been checked by de Gaulle (but not checkmated). France's voice had been heard. On the heels of the press conference came the announcement that Chancellor Adenauer would be arriving in Paris a week later to sign a bilateral treaty of Franco-German cooperation.

Until that de Gaulle press conference, postwar Europe had been evolving along fairly consistent lines: Monnet's Europe, joined for security to the United States, the whole an ensemble loosely called the Atlantic Community, more united by common outlook and common political principles and democratic systems than any formal bonds of treaties or obligations. Above all, this Euramerican system was the essential strategic and geopolitical balance against the great military power and outward thrust and pressures of the Soviet Union. But in place of this postwar structure it now seemed that General de Gaulle had a new Grand Design: a return to the previous century, a purely continental system to be led by France, as the continent had not been led since the days of Napoleon, when, also, Britain had been outside, until, of course, the Battle of Waterloo.

But would it work? The answer for de Gaulle came rather quickly. When the Franco-German treaty of 1963 was laid before the West German Parliament, the political parties voted overwhelmingly to add a preamble to the effect that nothing it contained was to be construed as superseding the commitments of the Federal Republic to the NATO Alliance. Closer ties with France could be no substitute in West Germany for the security guarantees of the United States and the North Atlantic Treaty.

De Gaulle was incensed. Here he was, declaring independence of American domination, pointing the way to a truly European Western Europe emerging between the superpowers, and West Germany, on whom the design depended, was suddenly vitiating the whole enterprise. In short order, Gaullist amity toward Bonn began to give way to Gaullist asperity. The defender of Berlin threw out hints that France might recognize the Communist East German Democratic Republic. The phrase "Europe from the Atlantic to the Urals" took its place in the litany of Gaullist foreign policy, along with "disappearance of the power blocs." If Germany and the European Community declined to follow his lead, then he would leap over and renew France's friendship of Czarist days with the new Russia. De Gaulle's great friend Adenauer faded from the scene, prodded into retirement at last in October 1963, remarking sadly toward the end that Franco-German reconciliation was like cultivating roses, which he had done all his life: the most beautiful usually have the heaviest thorns.

From 1963 until his retirement, General de Gaulle's foreign policy was primarily a series of declamatory lunges in one direction after another, a selection of "targets of opportunity" at which to hurl verbal volleys of thunder and lightning, a kind of *son et lumière* foreign policy. The sole consistency or common denominator was that the voice of France be heard—but, more often than not, the fact that France was heard seemed to be more important to de Gaulle than what was said. There was surprisingly little follow-through in de Gaulle's foreign policy. As in the case of the Franco-German treaty, if his lead was not followed he would turn to something else. To his unending frustration, de Gaulle was confronted over and over again with the simple fundamental fact that the Euramerican system was really working to everybody's satisfaction but his. He could rant and rail about domination and independence and Europe standing on its own, but when the *son et lumière* faded, what was he really offering in its place?

Europe was secure. Europe was prosperous. Europe was more stable with Germany divided than it might be with Germany reunited. Europe had no reason to want to encourage the Americans to draw back across the Atlantic. Would France be happy to see the revived German Army operating outside an integrated NATO European Command? European unity was evolving. What was de Gaulle really seeking to accomplish? Why was de Gaulle trying to throw things off course? Would Gaullist leadership of Europe or Gaullist foreign policy enhance either the security or the unity or the economic well-being of the continent or the world?

For six years, de Gaulle bludgeoned on, but his very style and tactics were self-defeating. Repeatedly he alienated those on whom he would have to count for support if he were really to lead Europe. The voice of France declaimed at everybody but spoke for very few. Of course, de Gaulle drew the requisite applause in the world at large with his running bilious anti-Americanism. But it was not much of a base for world leadership. In the end, few were ready to align with de Gaulle or follow de Gaulle for the simple reason that there was no trust in de Gaulle. Trust was the last thing he inspired. He had built his power, his very image, in a Machiavellian combination of surprise and fear of what he might do next, of secrecy, capriciousness, deviousness, vindictiveness and total self-interest. It was completely alien to de Gaulle's personality and philosophy of power to cooperate, compromise, negotiate. Jean Monnet once remarked to me in one of our conversations: "You cannot negotiate with de Gaulle. But he is a realist. So what you have to do is confront him with conditions to which he must adjust. Then he can be very flexible." In the final analysis, General de Gaulle was born to command, but not to lead.

But the French loved it. In 1964, de Gaulle headed for South America to carry the voice of France in person. On a month-long tour, he visited twenty capitals of the southern hemisphere—something no American President has ever done—preaching all the way the virtues of independence from Yankee domination. In 1965 he turned on the Common Market. He didn't like integration in Europe any more than integration in NATO. So he brusquely withdrew France from all Common Market meetings and decision-making in Brussels for nearly six months. He demanded that the Treaty of Rome be revised and shorn of its supranational trappings. But the other five signers of the Treaty sat him out, refusing to budge. In the end, he had to retreat. A fuzzy, face-saving compromise was worked out. Walter Hallstein, head of the Common Market Commission, a German integrationist who had worked with Monnet on the original Schuman Plan negotiation, was sacrificed on the altar of de Gaulle. France then returned to the Common Market, but the Rome Treaty was intact, unchanged.

In 1966, reelected and reinstalled at the Élysée Palace for another seven-year term, de Gaulle at last felt ready to deal with NATO, his ultimate *bête noire*. Since 1958, he had pursued his policy of "being in NATO less and less," but nothing very dramatic had resulted. He had been locked in the diplomacy of the Cold War, but Khrushchev had departed and the Soviet Union had remained quiescent since the Cuban crisis. After his setback with the Franco-German treaty, de Gaulle had avidly pursued closer contacts with Moscow. "Détente" was replacing "peaceful coexistence" as the new catchword of East-West relations. A journey to the Soviet Union was being arranged. De Gaulle could not very well wait to make his break with NATO *after* visiting Moscow. But it would be spectacular preparation to do it *before*. In his style of surprise, he had kept quiet about NATO for some months, and the lull certainly heightened the impact when he finally moved.

He retired to Colombey-les-Deux-Églises on the weekend of March 7, 1966, and there, at his desk, in the regal style of Louis XIV, he wrote out in longhand personal letters to President Lyndon Johnson and four other NATO chiefs of state. On Monday they were delivered to the respective ambassadors at the Quai d'Orsay, not in envelopes but in special green leather folders. France, he informed Johnson, "proposes to recover the entire exercise of her sovereignty over her territory, presently impaired by the permanent presence of Allied military elements or by the constant use which is made of her airspace." All French officers were immediately withdrawn from Supreme Allied Headquarters and other subordinate NATO commands. All French forces in Germany, all French air and naval units, ceased to be under NATO integrated commands. SHAPE headquarters was given one year to vacate its buildings in suburban Paris. The United States was asked to withdraw all its forces and close down all its supply lines and bases in France within the same time. Five Franco-American bilateral defense agreements were abrogated by de Gaulle. But, dining *à la carte,* France would continue to adhere to the North Atlantic Treaty and remain a member of the Alliance.

De Gaulle went off to the Soviet Union three months later in something of euphoria. The Russians responded by flying him to their hitherto ultrasecure missile-launching base at Bikanour, beyond the Urals, to witness a rocket launch. They cordially agreed that France and the Soviet Union should begin cooperation in the exploration of outer space.

The other fourteen NATO nations, bruised but more united than ever and unbowed, took stock and embarked on a crash program to build a new SHAPE military headquarters, in Belgium, near the city of Mons. Although de Gaulle did not kick out the political headquarters of the Alliance, it was clear that he was less than a cordial landlord. So NATO followed to new buildings outside Brussels in 1968.

Rid of NATO, welcomed in Moscow, de Gaulle next proclaimed France's affection for and natural leadership of the Third World. With the United States mired in the Vietnam War, he had a new pulpit from which to preach against America. He flew to the Cambodian capital of Pnom-Penh to declare France's respect for independence and neutralism where it once exercised colonial rule. He went to Canada and cried out to the French Canadians *"Vive le Québec libre!"* He recognized Red China. He had withdrawn French representation from the Geneva disarmament talks early on, and he refused to sign the nuclear test ban treaty, refused to sign the nuclear nonproliferation treaty, refused to sign any of the agreements that Geneva was producing. He launched his attack on the American dollar and on American investments in Europe. He pulled France out of the international gold pool and called for a return to the gold standard and an end to dollar hegemony. He blocked a second attempt by Britain, under Prime

Minister Harold Wilson, to join the Common Market, in 1966, this time refusing even to allow negotiations in Brussels to begin. His Finance Minister, Michel Debré, fought tooth and nail to block the adoption of the special-drawing-rights plan by the International Monetary Fund. In 1967, when Israel went to war against Egypt and the Arab states, he found the chance at last to reverse, overnight, completely, the role France had played under the Fourth Republic in the Suez War of 1956. This time, an instant total embargo was lowered on all French arms sales to the Israelis, in particular any parts or replacements for Mirage aircraft.

And so, as the fateful year 1968 began, General de Gaulle had ascended the heights and stood at the peak of his power—alone at last. He did not see, he was unable to see, the abrupt *chute* on the other side.

11
Paris, May 1968

FROM THE ÉLYSÉE PALACE IN THE SPRING OF 1968, PRESIDENT Charles de Gaulle looked out serenely upon foreign lands awash in seas of troubles, in the midst of which France seemed secure and sure of herself as the tenth anniversary of his return to power approached.

The United States was mired in the hopelessness, uselessness and futility of the Vietnam War, which de Gaulle had long been preaching. Like France during the Algerian War, the draining conflict was tearing at the fabric of American economic and political stability. The dollar was plunging in value, and violence swept back and forth across the continent. The antiwar movement, the civil rights movement and the growing cult of student unrest all fed each other, with violence escalating like some chain reaction inside society. Martin Luther King was assassinated on April 4, 1968, and Robert F. Kennedy was struck down two months later. From Berkeley to Columbia, universities were in turmoil: "Student power" was proclaimed to be a new political and social force. Such impenetrable pedagogues as Herbert Marcuse and Jean-Paul Sartre gave their cachet and intellectual blessing to violence as a justifiable means of forcing changes on unresponsive bourgeois society.

As the unrest spread to Europe, there was one common denominator, and that was the population explosion in the universities. In the decade from 1958 to 1968, American university enrollment jumped from 2.6 million students to 7 million. In Britain it went up from 216,000 to 418,000, in West Germany from 115,000 to 250,000, and in France from 200,000 to 515,000. Within the European universities, little was keeping pace with the growth. Teaching, administration, courses, regulations, ideas, politics, contemporary awareness, relation to economic and social needs, above all the buildings and equipment and physical environment were lagging ten years, fifty years, a hundred years behind the times.

The famous Free University of West Berlin had been reduced to an educational shambles by left-wing agitators, and troubles erupted across West Germany on the old campuses of Heidelberg, Frankfurt, Freiburg, Göttingen, Munich, Tübingen. In Italy, in early April, students suddenly occupied the University of Rome (the country was without a government, as usual), and student uprisings spread to seven other Italian cities. Even the rather staid British staged demonstrations in early 1968 at the universities of Leicester, Sussex, Liverpool and Essex and at the famous London School of Economics. In Spain, Franco's police were fighting running battles against the students at the University of Madrid, who had plenty of political as well as intellectual reason to revolt.

The worst civil violence had been unleashed to the east, in the Communist world, by Mao Tse-tung in the Cultural Revolution in Red China, with the paradoxical aim of renewing and resolidifying his own grip on his country by turning out his Red Guards to smash everything. This was then taken up by Communists outside the control of Moscow as a new revolutionary model for frustrated left-wing activists everywhere: those who were churning for action against society, ready for violence for the sake of violence, fed up with Stalinist discipline and Moscow orthodoxy, tired of the dreary waiting for signals of revolution that never came, determined to storm the barricades of existing order. Students, intellectuals, disaffected workers—now, at last, in the name of Mao, they could act!

In Warsaw it took particular courage and fervor for Polish students to face the brutal, overwhelming police power of the Communist regime, but in the spring of 1968 they were showing themselves to be no less brave, tough and nationalistic than their forefathers as they fought in the streets for a modicum of intellectual freedom.

In Prague, the eclipse of Stalin in the Communist world had resulted in January of 1968 in the most significant internal upheaval to take place in any of the regimes of Eastern Europe since the war. In a palace-guard revolution, the Politbureau of the Czechoslovak Communist Party deposed Moscow's man, Antonín Novotný, as the party leader. His place was taken by an independent-minded Slovak comrade who had come up through the party ranks named Alexander Dubček, and his promise to the Czech people was "communism with a human face."

General de Gaulle could survey this world scene with some self-satisfaction. American dominance, real or imagined, against which he had long declaimed, was certainly in recession, and America had come to recognize the limits of its power and accept his view of the Vietnam War. President Johnson had already bowed to the pressures of the antiwar movement and abandoned any hope or effort to win another term of office. In so doing, he had also finally set in motion the first determined steps to negotiate peace. After protracted and difficult preliminaries, the United States and North Vietnam were about to sit down and at least start talking across a table, face to face. De Gaulle was well pleased that his policies and his public opposition to the Vietnam War had brought the peace talks to Paris, where they would open on May 10, 1968.

In Prague and Warsaw, de Gaulle could readily discern the stirrings of nationalism and independence that he had long preached. His vision of Europe from the Atlantic to the Urals, a Europe in which the power blocs were fading away, no longer seemed a cloudy abstraction. He had set the example by withdrawing France from the NATO Alliance in everything but treaty signature, and in his entourage that spring there was little doubt that he was looking for the moment to renounce the treaty completely. His eyes were averted from minor distractions of the French domestic scene. He was preparing for an official visit to Romania in mid-May, where he would give his backing and blessing to that most independent-minded of the Warsaw Pact states.

It was in the nature of Gaullist rule to ignore or obliterate as far as possible any admission or recognition of blots, blemishes, smears, smirches or troubles on the image of a serene and stable France. For the government, it was a simple matter to anodyze the state-controlled television and radio transmissions, and reduce the reporting of social or economic problems to a minimum, more

generally simply keep them off the air completely. In de Gaulle's
time, no opposition political leader was *ever* seen on television,
not even for a fleeting moment of comment, except during prescribed opposition broadcasting time in election campaigns. Of
course there were angry debates in the National Assembly (never
broadcast), and of course there was plenty of free reporting and
comment in the French press. But at the Élysée Palace, a government minister would have to be both brave and foolhardy to speak
up to General de Gaulle and declare that there was a political
problem getting out of hand, or trouble in the offing that needed
to be defused. De Gaulle did not like to be bothered with mundane problems, and to talk this way would be nothing but an admission of weakness and an inability to cope. In any case, since he
almost relished confrontation, issues and problems could safely be
left to fester and accumulate to allow the General to choose his
moment to step forward, demonstrate who was running the country, and impose his will. After ten years of de Gaulle's rule, there
was virtually no political dialogue in France between government
and the governed.

But all was not well in the spring of 1968. The growth rate had
dropped from 7 percent to less than 4 percent. Unemployment
was at a postwar high of 450,000. Housing starts were down by
nearly 40 percent. De Gaulle's passion for a balanced budget had
pushed the country into increasing stagnation. A stabilization program had been imposed, but the workers of course saw themselves
getting the short end of the wage-price cycle. Above all this, General de Gaulle and his government remained aloof, indifferent and
inaccessible.

The proverbial cloud no bigger than a man's hand already had
formed over this scene in the Paris suburb of Nanterre—had anybody in authority been prepared to perceive it. Nanterre is a
dreary industrial appendage to the city where there was and still is
a heavy concentration of Algerian population and other migrant
workers. Here, in order to take the population pressures off the
Sorbonne University, in the heart of Paris, a bleak and soulless
educational factory of glass-and-concrete prefabrication had been
thrown up in the early 1960s. But, in five years, the Nanterre cam-

pus, administered as a branch of the Sorbonne, had swollen from
two thousand students to ten thousand. Its facilities and its faculty
were a hopeless muddle: four professors of English with two thousand students to lecture, for example, and five professors of Greek
for ninety students. Commuting students started from home at 6
A.M. to get places in lecture halls holding a thousand, as hundreds
more pushed to get in from the corridors.

It was here that the first spark in the French student revolt was
struck—prosaically enough, a male invasion of the female dormitories, surely the oldest protest in the history of education. The
rule at Nanterre was that women could visit the men's dorms, but
men were barred from the female dormitories. Thus, if a girl got
pregnant, it was clearly her responsibility and not the fault of the
university authorities or the Ministry of Education. *C'est logique,
n'est-ce pas?* But when a platoon of men students invaded a
women's dorm at Nanterre and staged a sit-down in the lobby
(not the rooms), there were two things that lit the long fuse that
eventually exploded over the whole of France: The university rector, in a rattled moment, called in the police for the first time to
clear the dormitory lobby. And the students had a leader—Daniel
Cohn-Bendit, a fiery, redheaded leftist revolutionary, disdainful of
anybody's discipline—who became the folk hero of the events of
May 1968.

Danny the Red, as he was known among the students, was
about the most improbable person imaginable to take on Charles
de Gaulle and the might of the Fifth Republic of France. His father was a German Jew who had escaped from the Nazi regime in
the 1930s and settled in France, where he managed to submerge
himself successfully throughout the Vichy period and the wartime
occupation. He married a Frenchwoman, and Danny, the second
son, was born in 1945. Both parents apparently died when he was
quite young. An older brother opted for French citizenship, but
Danny, at some point in the 1950s, left France for Germany,
where he finished secondary school and rather courageously took
his citizenship from his father. He came back to the land of his
birth and got a scholarship to Nanterre to study sociology. He had
a quick, agile mind plus a sharp, sardonic wit, and a crowd-pleas-
ing, comedian's sense of timing. His voice reached to the rafters in

three languages. He was strong-minded and strong-willed, but totally uninhibited by any particular political allegiance or philosophy. He thought that Marcuse was "a joke" and Ché Guevara "only interesting for café talk" and saw "nothing new" in Karl Marx. He was "very anti-Lenin" and laughed off the idea of "making a myth out of Mao." But he did once firmly assert, "There are three permanent themes in which I believe: the fights against repression by the state, against authoritarianism, and against hierarchy." He found plenty to fight in France in May 1968.

After the affair of the women's dormitories, tension escalated steadily at Nanterre between the leftist students and the administration, with ample grievances on which to feed in the condition of the school. Not only did the rector again resort to calling in armed police, but the students were convinced that the campus was also infiltrated by undercover agents and police informers. Danny the Red was constantly at the center of student agitation. Then, on March 22, 1968, five students from Nanterre were arrested and jailed for heaving paving-blocks through the windows of the American Express offices in an anti-Vietnam War demonstration at the Place de l'Opéra, in the heart of Paris.

Fellow students organized a protest meeting at Nanterre, and at some point there was a proposal to occupy the ultimate seat of authority at the university, the Professorial Council Chamber. Cohn-Bendit, on the platform, at first was opposed, because he didn't think it would be effective, but when students demanded action he swept along with them. The sit-in lasted six hours, and by the time it was over, Danny the Red had talked his way back to its leadership. The students left peacefully, but this time Nanterre was shaken to its foundations. The rector closed the school for two days. Then he reopened it under faculty pressure. But discipline had broken down completely among students and teachers alike. The *Mouvement du 22 Mars* burgeoned into a continuous talkfest of dissatisfied youth. The school was in a state of near anarchy. But at least the situation had not turned violent.

In this atmosphere things rocked along to mid-April, when General de Gaulle's Minister of Education, Alain Peyrefitte, issued one of those Gaullist edicts by which France was governed from on high. Peyrefitte was young, arrogant, ambitious, close to de Gaulle, and an ardent disciple anxious to demonstrate to the General that he, too, could command and not be pushed around. He announced that in order to relieve the pressures of university enrollment, admission in the future would be selective by special examination, instead of automatic, as it had been for anybody who could pass the famous *baccalauréat* after the age of eighteen. This meant, inevitably, that it would be harder for working-class sons and daughters to make it on to higher education, and was like waving a red flag at the student population of the country, whatever the logic as educational policy.

By the end of April, Nanterre was close to explosion. Prodded by Peyrefitte, the rector again closed the school, on May 2. At the same time, Cohn-Bendit was ordered to appear before a disciplinary council in Paris at the higher headquarters of the university in the precincts of the Sorbonne.

At this judicious moment, Prime Minister Georges Pompidou, declining to treat very seriously what was happening, took off with Foreign Minister Maurice Couve de Murville on an official visit, long arranged, to Iran and Afghanistan. Nothing was to be allowed to disturb the Gaullist government.

On the morning of Friday, May 3, Daniel Cohn-Bendit headed for his rendezvous with hated authority in revolutionary style: at the head of a procession of some four hundred Nanterre students who walked with him all the way across Paris to the Sorbonne. At the same time, a right-wing student group at the Sorbonne calling itself "Occident" was gathering in the Latin Quarter, augmented by some hard-core anti-Communist veterans of the final stages of the Algerian War and the OAS who were still around the university. They were waiting when the Nanterre marchers reached the Sorbonne. Violence was inevitable. Students began breaking up tables and chairs to arm themselves and take sides.

On Friday afternoon, the rector of the Sorbonne, Jean Roche, acting almost certainly with the blessing if not the urging of the Élysée Palace, went to the fatal extreme of calling in the paramilitary riot squads of the hated Republican Security Companies, the CRS, to cordon off the university, clear out the students and restore order. At the same time, as the CRS poured into the Latin

Quarter, Roche did what only the Nazi occupiers of Paris had ever done before in seven hundred years, and declared the university closed. "The authorities," *Le Monde* commented, "seem to have lost their nerve."

At first an uneasy truce was negotiated for the students to leave the university precincts—and then all hell broke loose. As they passed through the CRS lines, some were grabbed, systematically beaten up, thrown into police vans and driven away. By nightfall the entire Latin Quarter had turned into a running battlefield between the CRS and the students. For the next six weeks, France rocked in a state of near anarchy.

The CRS was created in the early postwar days of the Fourth Republic to give the Ministry of the Interior a powerful special force to deal specifically with civil violence beyond the means of the regular police—in particular the wave of Communist-led strikes and demonstrations that plagued France at the time. Its recruits were all big, powerful men physically, and they were rigorously trained in shock tactics of charging demonstrators with attacks of short, sharp, ruthless brutality, their long truncheons and their heavy boots flailing and kicking anything or anybody in their path. Acting under ministry orders, strictly disciplined until they went into action, they were immune from the law, from prosecution by any accidental victims or disciplinary action by their superiors. The concept of their whole training was to break and physically beat the front-line leaders of any demonstration as a brutal warning against flouting French authority, no questions asked, no pleas heeded.

It was highly provocative of the government to have authorized calling out the CRS against young students in the first place. But presumably somebody somewhere in authority concluded that what the situation needed was one short, sharp, brutal crackdown by these powerful Myrmidons to teach the students a lesson, after which they would get back in line and stop disturbing Gaullist order. It proved to be a terrible miscalculation. The brutality of the CRS in that beautiful May weather, out in the open for everyone to see, simply united the youth of the city and inflamed everybody, not the least the passive residents of the Latin Quarter, and then the trade unions and the entire French labor movement—all joining in a spontaneous uprising against authoritarian order with such intensity and staying power that it brought the regime to its knees. Although General de Gaulle's rule survived, the Gaullist image of France was shattered and his ascendancy gone. After May 1968, the end for de Gaulle was only a matter of time.

That first Friday night of flailing truncheons and tear gas and concussion grenades, there were 596 arrests, just about anybody the CRS and the police could grab and club into the police vans. There was a pause on Sunday as the students gathered to regroup and prepare, and on Monday, May 6, in twelve hours of running clashes another 422 were arrested and at least six hundred wounded. Three excerpts from a collection of student stories of those days, *Le Livre Noir des Journées de Mai,* tell what was happening:

"Suddenly the café was surrounded by the CRS and a civilian knocked at the glass door. The owner hurried to open. The civilian, a long club in his hand, came in, followed by a CRS carrying his helmet. He gave the order to evacuate, banging on the table with his stick—and also on some people who didn't hurry to obey. I found myself behind a relatively young man who, as he went out, kept saying with a strong accent, 'I'm a foreigner. . . .' He was cut off by a CRS, who struck him, yelling 'Yes, and you've come to shit on us in France.' Then I was grabbed and beaten over the head and body with clubs. I fell to my knees and a CRS kicked me in the stomach and as I fell back I was hit in the face. I pulled myself up as well as I could and managed to get away, up a side street. After a dozen yards, bleeding terribly, I stopped and asked people at a doorstep to help me. . . ."

This was how things went at the regular police interrogation centers:

"We were driven into a small room where an officer took our personal effects. About fifteen regular police formed an alley in front of an immense waiting room. On the way there, the prisoners were savagely beaten. I protested, pointing out that most of us were innocent. I was seized and in my turn suffered truncheon blows, fists, knee, foot, all over my body, in particular my head, stomach and testicles. Dazed, I pulled myself up and joined the

terrified group at the other end of the room waiting to be let into
an office.

"From time to time we could see a lieutenant move among his
men and prudently advise them, 'Not on their heads.' As for me,
the violence of the blows was so great that when I was thrown into
a cell my breath was gone and I was trembling so severely that a
physical-education teacher who happened to be in the cell had to
help me to do breathing exercises. That police team, naturally,
bore no matriculation numbers or any identity markings."

And in a private apartment:

"A young couple took us in. We were seven. The CRS beat on
the door—'Open up or we'll break down the door.' Then they went
downstairs to find an officer, and the officer gave the order to
throw paving-stones through the windows, and then gas grenades.
The couple and three comrades went down, and the girl in her
night-dress found herself completely naked as they dragged her
into the street, doing I don't know what to her, but wanting to
make her go across all Paris stripped. They pushed their sticks between her legs 'for a joke.'"

Still, there is one fact about this whole violent scene—and that is
that firearms were never used by either the CRS or the students.
Gun control in France is extremely tight, and if the students had
any guns they were certainly few in number and were not used.
The CRS are all armed with side arms, but some senior Ministry
of the Interior officer at least had the prudent good sense to withdraw all ammunition from the CRS except the side arms of
officers. Each CRS platoon was then backed up by men firing tear-
gas grenades from shotgun launchers. But throughout it all there
was only *one* death from gunfire: a man killed by a ricocheting
shot in a doorway, and it never was established where the shot
came from. There was a theory that somebody was trying to use
the confusion of the street fighting to settle an old score. It was
primitive, elemental violence and fighting: fists, clubs, truncheons,
stones, boots, iron bars, fires and barricades of overturned automobiles and uprooted trees.

On Wednesday, May 8, Peyrefitte appeared before the National
Assembly and loftily proclaimed that the disturbances were "the
work of specialists in agitation and elements foreign to the univer-

sity." The fatuous implication was that all was well in the Gaullist educational system, except for that German student, Daniel Cohn-Bendit. As the CRS went about its brutal work, the Minister of Education said: "If order is restored, everything is possible; if not, nothing is possible."

Next day the students formulated their first demands: those arrested to be freed and charges dropped, the police and the CRS to be withdrawn from the Latin Quarter; otherwise the demonstrations would go on. (So spontaneous and chaotic was the whole affair, so lacking in any central control or direction by the students, that they never did formulate any outline or declaration of what they wanted in the way of university reforms. What they really wanted was attention to the problems and to what they had to say—and this they were now finally getting.) The government response was an offer to withdraw the CRS and reopen the Sorbonne, but no release of those arrested. A brief and dramatic dialogue then took place via the transmitters of Radio Luxembourg between the student leaders at the barricades and the Sorbonne rector in his office, with all of France listening. But no other concessions were offered, and on the night of Friday, May 10, the fighting reached a new pitch. By now more organized, the students seized, overturned or set fire to 188 automobiles, building a series of barricades across the Boulevard St.-Michel and other Latin Quarter avenues. By the next morning, another 460 had been arrested and at least 367 injured before Cohn-Bendit gave a radio order to break up and disperse.

That same Friday, the Vietnam peace talks began on the other side of Paris, between Ambassador W. Averell Harriman for the United States and a North Vietnamese delegation headed by ex-Foreign Minister Xuan Thuy.

In the distant Afghanistan capital of Kabul, Prime Minister Pompidou, in touch with Paris by crackling, fading radiotelephone, decided that he had better get home. The troubles had spread to the universities of Strasbourg, Lille, Lyon, Toulouse, Marseilles, Rennes, Bordeaux, Tours and Clermont-Ferrand. Pompidou's plane reached Paris on Saturday afternoon, and he went almost immediately to confer with a fuming, furious President de Gaulle—who had of course remained silent behind the walls of the Élysée Palace throughout the tumultuous week, preparing his trip to Romania, while his ministers tried to restore order. Pompidou had written out a speech in the airplane on the way home, and to demonstrate that he was back in charge, he went on the air Saturday night, a few hours after landing. He announced that the Sorbonne would reopen on Monday, that the Court of Appeals would speedily decide the fate of the jailed students, and that the CRS would be withdrawn from the Latin Quarter. It was a virtual capitulation by the government—but it was too little and too late.

The leaders of the French Communist Party, with their heads in their own particular clouds, had been caught as much off base, as surprised and unprepared for the student uprising as the Élysée Palace. From its very beginning, the French Party leadership was (and still is) totally controlled by rooted proletarian workers, slavishly Moscow-oriented and disciplined. A little intellectual window dressing has been tolerated in party ranks, but never in the Politbureau or the hierarchy, which remains self-perpetuatingly working-class. The suspicions of hard-fisted workers like Waldeck Rochet, Maurice Thorez, Jacques Duclos and Georges Marchais toward bourgeois intellectualism was ingrained and acute. Moreover, in the two years preceding the student uprising, there had been a running leadership fight going on between these old Stalinist hard-liners and young, new-left Communist intellectuals over control of the party's student front organization, the *Union des Étudiants Communistes de France* (UEC).

By the spring of 1968, the leaders of the Politbureau had finally managed to curb, discipline or expel the "bourgeois activists" in the UEC and reimpose their own full control over the organization. This battle of course had left the Communist Party leadership more suspicious and opposed than ever toward student action that it did not control. But it also meant that the most vocal and effective of the left-wing agitators on the campuses were outside the Communist Party and were full of disgust at party orthodoxy and discipline—"Stalinist scum," in Cohn-Bendit's usual colorful language. Of the principal leaders at the barricades, Cohn-Bendit could probably be loosely classified as an anarcho-

Marxist-Maoist, while Alain Krivine was a Trotskyist and Alain Geismar, of the left-wing University Teachers Union, was an independent Marxist. On the day Cohn-Bendit led his procession from Nanterre to the Sorbonne, the Communist Party paper *L'Humanité* denounced him as a "German anarchist" and screamed that "false revolutionaries must be energetically unmasked because, objectively, they serve the interests of Gaullist power and the great capitalist monopolies." Throughout that first week of street fighting between the students and the CRS, *L'Humanité* kept up its party-line sniping at "rootless bourgeois" leaders who refused to see that they were only playing into the hands of the authorities. Given what was actually happening in the streets, *L'Humanité* and the Communist Party were looking slightly ridiculous, to say the least. By mid-week, as the arrests grew and the stories of CRS brutality multiplied, rank-and-file pressures within the Communist-dominated trade-union federation, the CGT, as well as the Socialist-led unions, the CFDT and the Force Ouvrier, were rising for some show of solidarity with the striking, besieged students. Whereupon the party made one of its typical shifts—and called for a one-day general strike on Monday, May 13, the day the Sorbonne was to reopen and the tenth anniversary of the beginnings of the Algerian coup that brought de Gaulle back to power. But now the popular slogan was "Ten years is enough!"

On Monday, students and workers united in an enormous march of some eight hundred thousand from the Place de la République to Denfert-Rochereau. Danny the Red and the student leaders were in the front line with Rochet, Marchais and company trailing along somewhat glumly in the ranks behind. The general strike, meanwhile, was one of the most effective labor actions in years from one end of the country to the other. On the other side of the Seine, Pompidou was as good as his word, and the CRS had withdrawn from the Latin Quarter. The police were under orders to handle things gingerly, and the vast parade passed off peacefully. But when the Sorbonne reopened, it did not resume its functioning; instead, it was occupied by students in a carnival victory mood, for a round-the-clock permanent sit-in. Nevertheless, some of the heat seemed to be going out of the situation despite the new development of the general strike, and Pompidou confidently urged General de Gaulle that he should not cancel his plans for his official visit to Romania. "The tempest is really over—if you don't leave, the people will think that the whole affair has not yet ended," the Prime Minister told the President. Accordingly, very early on the morning of May 14, the presidential Caravelle jet took off for Bucharest.

But de Gaulle was scarcely airborne when a new development, far away from the Paris epicenter, altered everything. A one-day general strike was not enough to satisfy the pent-up urge for action in the labor movement. At the city of Nantes, near the Atlantic coast, north of Bordeaux, far to the west of Paris, workers at the nationalized Sud Aviation plant, building wings and fuselage sections for the Caravelle jets, spontaneously decided to occupy the whole factory with a sit-in instead of going back to work when the general strike was over. Just as the student protest action had spread like a forest fire to the other universities, so the spontaneous worker occupation of factories now swept the country. And the general strike continued.

On Wednesday, as workers took over the state-owned Renault Automobile Works, first at Cléon, north of Paris, and then at Boulogne-Billancourt, within the city itself, students on the Left Bank extended their sit-in beyond the Sorbonne and occupied the famous Théâtre de l'Odéon. The Odéon director, France's most distinguished actor, Jean-Louis Barrault, rushed to the theater from his Paris apartment when he heard that the students had marched in. But after listening to Cohn-Bendit and others act out a formless, unending "theater of combat" on his stage, he rose and declared himself in agreement with what was happening. "Barrault is no longer the director of this theater, but an actor like all the others," he told the students dramatically. "Barrault is dead." Subsequently, the Gaullist Minister of Culture, André Malraux, took Barrault at his word and fired him as director of the Odéon company, once the events of May were over and the government was back in control.

Violence had ceased with the withdrawal of the CRS to its barracks, but from the standpoint of the government the situation was more out of control than ever. A kind of peaceful anarchy reigned, with no mail, no trains, nobody working, no gasoline,

continuous gas and electricity cuts, no buses or subways, and nobody in charge of anything. At Nantes, workers literally welded
shut the factory gates, and everywhere they were hoisting the Red
Flag over occupied factories in a defiant reminder of the Paris
Commune of 1871. Nobody was in control anywhere—neither the
government nor the union leaders nor the university administrations nor the police.

A Renault worker recounted how spontaneous it all had been:
"Until that Monday, the unions kept telling us the students
were fooling around. Then it was, Up with the students, go demonstrate with them. That made us think. We'd seen how they'd
fought and what they had got. It worked. Burnt cars, things
smashed, it didn't matter. You can't make an omelette without
breaking eggs. We'd still be in the soup if it hadn't been for the
barricades.

"We talked about it all on the shop floor. Next, the union
leaders told us that the student business was blown up, and then
we saw the students demonstrating for us. Then we reckoned
something was wrong with the unions. On Thursday afternoon in
our shop, a boy said: 'I've had enough,' and put down his tools.
His neighbor said, 'You crazy?' 'Come on,' he said, and others followed and the whole shop downed tools. The news spread from
assembly line to assembly line, from stand to stand, from shop to
shop, over there, here, everywhere. The oldies said we should wait
for the union—wait, wait, wait. In half an hour all Boulogne-
Billancourt downed tools. We decided to occupy the place, like
the students. The unions followed along."

In Romania, General de Gaulle, touring the country, receiving
bouquets of flowers from Communist maidens in embroidered
blouses, inspecting spruced-up collective farms and polished Communist factories, finally concluded that he had had enough and cut
short his visit by eighteen hours to return to Paris on Saturday,
May 18. First it was announced that he would address the nation
on May 24. Back in the Élysée Palace, in a fury he ordered that
the Sorbonne be cleared by the CRS. It was only with great argument that both the Minister of Interior and the Prefect of the Paris
Police convinced him that this could not be done without gunfire,
which had so far been avoided in the streets, that students were

certain to be killed, and that the reaction would be overwhelming, a disaster. De Gaulle sulked, venting his wrath on everybody, as Pompidou kept urging him to "leave it to the government, *mon Général*, the Head of State must not become involved." By now there were two million French workers on strike, and all air, rail and road traffic into and around the country had come to a halt—with no break in sight.

As the strikes and sit-ins virtually paralyzed the country, the students again took to the streets to demonstrate, and with de Gaulle back at the Élysée Palace, the CRS was again brought into the city to maintain order. On Thursday night, May 23, a vicious battle was fought at the Pont Neuf as the CRS blocked students from crossing the Seine. The next night, the de Gaulle who appeared before the French people on television screens was an old man of seventy-eight pleading almost pathetically for Frenchmen to remember all he had done for France, to return to work and stop messing up the Fifth Republic. Resorting to his favorite device, he announced that he would soon call a referendum "to give the State, and above all its Chief, a mandate for renovation," and if it did not succeed, then he would step aside.

The address was a disaster. That night, students poured out into the streets, surged across to the Gare de Lyon, and then, when the CRS attacked, one group broke and raced around the police lines to that citadel of capitalism, the Place de la Bourse. A mob of two or three hundred smashed a breach in the iron railings surrounding the old, hexagonal stock-exchange building, shattered heavy plate-glass windows and stormed inside. Piling up chairs and tables, plus packing cases from piles of uncollected trash outside, they sprinkled gasoline over the heap and set the place on fire. Yelling in wild exhilaration, the Bourse burners got away before the CRS arrived, and raced all the way back across the river.

The CRS was now ordered into action with a vengeance, and the night of May 24 was the worst of all, three full weeks after the troubles had begun. By Saturday morning, the Boulevard St.-Michel and the rue Gay-Lussac looked like a scene out of World War II. There were 795 arrests, seventy-two large trees had been toppled, twelve hundred square yards of paving stones had been ripped up, countless automobiles had been overturned and fired, and windows had been shattered for blocks. More than five hundred had been injured, including 212 CRS and police.

This could not go on—or so it seemed. Pompidou, his original efforts to calm things now a shambles, announced Saturday morning that the CRS had orders "to disperse all demonstrations with the greatest energy, to execute orders without weakness or delay." At the same time, he summoned leaders of the three big trade-union federations and the Patronat (manufacturers' association) to a round-table conference, over which he would preside, at the Ministry of Social Affairs, on the rue de Grenelle, to hammer out an overall package wage settlement of the strikes in a nonstop negotiation. From Saturday afternoon, they worked, ate, negotiated, slept in relays and kept talking for thirty-six hours, Pompidou active most of the time. At 7:30 A.M. on Monday, May 27, the Grenelle Agreements were announced—an immediate 7 percent across-the-board wage boost for all French workers plus another 3 percent to follow in October, and fringe benefits in social security from the government, which brought the package up to around 15 percent overall.

The government, the union leaders and the public heaved a sigh of relief—but only briefly. Before the day was out, the Renault workers hooted down the Communist CGT leader, Benoit Frachon, when he arrived at Boulogne-Billancourt to present the settlement and get the plant back to work. At sit-ins in factories throughout France, where young activists had taken over leadership ad hoc from the old unionists, the Grenelle package was rejected out of hand. The strikes continued.

At the Élysée Palace, de Gaulle was now sunk in brooding melancholy at the staggering extent of the physical, economic, political and emotional disaster that had struck his proud tower, France. Pompidou was urging him, emotionally, that all was not lost—to forget about his referendum, and instead to dissolve the National Assembly and elect a new legislature. But de Gaulle talked openly for the first time of giving up, getting out. In fact, he wrote out some kind of final testament or declaration, sealed it and put it in his personal office safe.

On Wednesday morning, May 29, with no break in the strike situation yet in sight, General de Gaulle without a word of warning or explanation to anybody suddenly emerged from his office and ordered a regular Cabinet meeting, which was to start in half an hour, at 11 A.M., to be canceled. He walked out, got into his black Citroën with Mme. de Gaulle, drove out the gates of the Élysée Palace—and literally disappeared. A military aide followed in a security car, but nobody remaining behind knew where he had gone. "We have lost the General," an Élysée official admitted in stupefaction to radio reporters in the courtyard a little while later. Of General de Gaulle's many surprises, this was the most staggering. By midday, Paris seethed with rumors that he had left the capital and would never come back. In fact, he *had* left the keys to his personal office safe with Bernard Tricot, secretary-general of the Élysée, telling him as he departed that he was to open the safe only on his telephoned instructions, and then act in accordance with a letter he would find inside. Without any doubt, when de Gaulle left his office that morning, it was an open question whether he would ever come back.

His military aide, in strict secrecy, had ordered a small plane to be standing by at a French Air Force base east of Paris. De Gaulle arrived and took off immediately for a French Forces airfield near Baden-Baden, in West Germany, the Black Forest country. There a helicopter was waiting to take him to the headquarters of General Jacques Massu, veteran of the Algerian War and French commander in Germany. They spent about three hours alone together, and nobody knows what they discussed, although it is presumed that de Gaulle wished to have a direct opinion from a military commander about the reaction of army conscripts if he went to the extreme of calling out the Army to support him in crushing a civil disturbance. In any case, early Wednesday evening, de Gaulle finally turned up at Colombey-les-Deux-Églises and telephoned Tricot to say he would be back in Paris at noon on Thursday.

Thursday, May 30, 1968. General de Gaulle slipped back into the Élysée by a side entrance to avoid photographers and reporters who had been admitted to the courtyard. Shortly after one o'clock, a press aide came rushing out to announce that the President of the Republic would address the nation by radio—not television this time—at 4:30 P.M. A Cabinet meeting was hastily convened at 3 P.M., and broke up after barely forty minutes. Then, at last, the usual musical ruffles and flourishes over the radio, and de Gaulle's voice—this time not the quavering appeal of the previous Friday night, but vibrant, forceful, strong and clear.

"I have envisaged all eventualities, without exception. In the present circumstances, I shall not resign. I have a mandate from the people. I shall fulfill it. . . . The Republic will not abdicate, the people will regain control. Progress, independence and peace will come, along with liberty. . . . *Vive la République! Vive la France!"*

Half an hour later, across the river at the National Assembly, its president, Jacques Chaban-Delmas, announced that de Gaulle had ordered the legislature dissolved. Elections for a new Assembly were fixed in two rounds of voting on June 23 and June 30. De Gaulle had taken Pompidou's advice. The tension in Paris broke.

When the Assembly adjourned, its Gaullist members flocked across the bridge to the Place de la Concorde, where Michel Debré, André Malraux and others of the so-called Barons of Gaullism formed the head of a procession that had materialized out of nowhere as the General finished speaking. It was the Gaullist bourgeois backlash—a vast spontaneous gathering of well-dressed, middle-class men and women who then headed up the Avenue des Champs-Élysées singing, chanting, shouting, exuberant with pent-up Gaullist patriotism after watching a month of violence and disruption at the hands of students, workers and the Left.

Next day, Prime Minister Pompidou reshuffled his Cabinet (Peyrefitte had already been dropped), and armed police moved into the Central Post Office in the city of Rouen in the first direct effort to break the sit-ins and the general strike. The union leaders, in particular the Communists, seemed almost as anxious as General de Gaulle to reassert control over the situation, and the first big break finally came on June 5, when the state-owned Électricité de France signed a new wage agreement based on the Grenelle formula with some improvements, and its workers began returning to their jobs.

But there was still one more major eruption of violence. The tireless CRS had been sent to seal off a Renault plant near the town of Flin, outside Paris on the banks of the Seine. In the familiar truncheon charge against the strikers, a seventeen-year-old boy named Gilles Tautin either fell or was pushed off a bridge into the river and drowned. Others said they had seen him beaten and clubbed by the CRS and that he was allowed to drown. That night, June 10, and the following night the Left Bank again erupted in protest. Over the two nights another fifteen hundred were arrested, seventy-two policemen injured, several hundred students treated in their own aid stations, seventy-five cars wrecked, ten police trucks damaged, twenty-five more trees cut down for barricades, five district police stations attacked, three hundred fire alarms set off, two dozen traffic lights destroyed, and three Gaullist election campaign headquarters smashed. Pompidou then issued a complete ban on all demonstrations and left little doubt that it would be fully enforced.

Finally, on Sunday, June 16, the CRS surrounded the Sorbonne. Even the students had grown a little weary—and smelly—from the long sit-in. There was a brief effort that afternoon to rally last-gasp resistance, but after more than six weeks of exhausting emotional and physical violence, nobody had much energy left for yet another fight. By 8 P.M. the Sorbonne at last was cleared. Some of the students left singing "Auld Lang Syne." Danny the Red was picked up and expelled from France.

The elections at the end of June produced, quite predictably, an overwhelming Gaullist victory. The General's men captured 350 seats in the National Assembly, against a mere 137 for all other parties and independent members combined. The Communists in particular were routed at the polls. But as Pompidou ruefully remarked at the height of the general strike, "Things will never be the same again."

In particular, this applied to Pompidou himself. After five years as de Gaulle's Prime Minister, he was abruptly fired ten days after the election victory that he himself had done so much to organize. In the General's lofty phrase, he was "placed in the reserve of the Republic." As one of de Gaulle's longtime adherents once remarked, "There is no friendship between the hand that moves the chessmen and the pieces on the board." The reasons for Pompidou's departure were cumulative, complex and scarcely justified. But it boiled down to the fact that de Gaulle did not like the advice he had been given during the events of May, and decided to make Pompidou something of a scapegoat and at the same time demonstrate firmly who was running the country, who held supreme power.

The new Prime Minister was Maurice Couve de Murville, ultra-loyal to de Gaulle, without political ambition, detached, ice-cold, a Protestant and the epitome of a French career diplomat. He was not a man to excite, inspire or warm the electorate. Nor did he particularly relish taking Pompidou's place. France had lost something like one billion dollars' worth of industrial production in the period of the general strike, and another three billion dollars in salaries that normally would have then been injected into consumer spending. The country's big May-June tourist trade of course disappeared completely in 1968, and hundreds of small hotels and restaurants had closed down during the demonstrations with no business, unable to pay employees or overheads. In place of a balance-of-payments surplus, there was now a trade deficit, and the Treasury went out to raise $1.5 billion in short-term credit from other central banks.

After years of technocratic, faceless Gaullist government, a politician was finally brought into the Cabinet to take over the Ministry of Education and promulgate university reforms. He was Edgar Faure, once a Premier of the Fourth Republic. The Faure reforms consisted primarily of decentralization of control over the universities, which had existed since Napoleon's time, breaking up the larger schools such as the Sorbonne into a number of smaller, independent units, and creating elected student councils to participate in planning courses, curricula and administrative policy. But diplomas from French universities for the year 1968 were scarcely worth framing.

The greatest loss of all in the events of May 1968 was of course the intrinsic loss for General de Gaulle—his ascendancy over his nation, his control of its destinies, his hold over the French people, his foundations of power and the image he had sought to create for France in the world. On the heels of this domestic earthquake for de Gaulle, Soviet tanks rolled into the Czechoslovakian capital of Prague in August 1968 and snuffed out the short-lived Dubček experiment in "communism with a human face." The Russians snuffed out at the same time the Gaullist vision of Europe from the Atlantic to the Urals and a disappearance of the power blocs. The NATO Alliance, which de Gaulle so scorned, suddenly became more vital and important than ever to the security of Western Europe, France included.

For de Gaulle, in the face of the new situation in France there was but one course open: another referendum. The victory in the National Assembly elections was not a victory for de Gaulle but a victory for Parliament—and besides, it was more Pompidou's victory, anyway. De Gaulle must go directly to the people of France and renew his mandate of power. Couve de Murville and his ministers could not say no to de Gaulle, but they dillydallied as long as possible, sensing clearly what the outcome might be.

De Gaulle insisted, and at long last the referendum date was fixed: Sunday, April 27, 1969—almost exactly one year after that fateful weekend when the Nanterre students marched behind Daniel Cohn-Bendit to the Sorbonne. De Gaulle asked the French people to approve his proposal to abolish the French Senate in a major constitutional change, and to institute a program of government restructuring and regional reform. He wanted a major renewal of his power and authority—or he wanted out. Most French in retrospect believe that he really wanted out and that he chose to pose questions that would result in his dismissal. He did not have to resign from office if the referendum was voted down, but he made it a personal plebescite as well. In the end, 53 percent voted "No."

De Gaulle had gone to Colombey-les-Deux-Églises that Sunday, and watched the returns alone with Mme. de Gaulle. He never came back to Paris. Shortly before midnight he spoke with Couve de Murville and instructed him to announce his resignation immediately over television. At the Élysée Palace, his staff was already packing up and removing all his personal files, every trace of his presence. Then, during the ensuing presidential election campaign, he went off to spend a month in Ireland. He did not offer one word of support for Georges Pompidou, who was duly elected on June 15, 1969, as his successor.

Back at Colombey, de Gaulle plunged into writing a new set of memoirs, but only one volume was completed. On Monday, November 9, 1970, he had finished his day's writing and was sitting with Mme. de Gaulle before his television set, waiting for the evening news program to begin, when he was stricken with a heart attack, and died.

> *"He was a man, take him for all in all*
> *We shall not look upon his like again."*

12

Georges Pompidou

WHEN GEORGES POMPIDOU, PRESIDENT OF THE FRENCH REpublic, arrived at Colombey-les-Deux-Églises to pay his last respects to General Charles de Gaulle, he was escorted by a military aide into the small drawing room of the de Gaulle family home. There, resting on trestles, was a simple oak coffin that had been completed by the village carpenter only a few hours before. Tall white candles burned at either end. The coffin was closed.

For nearly a quarter of a century, Pompidou had served de Gaulle as an intimate and trusted collaborator, not only in politics and affairs of state but in private, personal, family matters as well. Others who arrived earlier at Colombey—Michel Debré, General Jacques Massu—saw the General dressed in his brigadier's uniform with a single decoration, the Cross of Lorraine, on his tunic and a faded French tricolor that had often flown over his home draped around the still frame. But Pompidou was not permitted to look upon General de Gaulle's face.

From intimacy, confidence and even warmth, the relationship between de Gaulle and Pompidou after the events of May 1968 had fallen into something of a Shakespearean drama—the aging, harassed, embittered King coming to the end of his reign, the vigorous Dauphin no longer admitted to the court but waiting inexorably for the inevitable hour when power would at last drop into his hands. It mattered not at all to de Gaulle that Pompidou was a worthy successor, experienced, intelligent, steady and a man of integrity. He might still be a schoolteacher but for de Gaulle, and he had committed the unforgiveable sin of openly declaring his readiness to succeed to power.

"And lean-look'd prophets whisper fearful change;
Rich men look sad and ruffians dance and leap,
The one in fear to lose what they enjoy,
The other to enjoy by rage and war:
*These signs forerun the death or fall of kings."**

"It's much too difficult—we'll never know," said one of the government ministers of that period when asked about the breach between the two men. "Pompidou was an enigma. And the General resorted to allusions, as if challenging his interlocutor to react. To be realistic, one can only say that the two of them worked side by side, and together lived through fair and foul weather. Then they parted."

Georges Pompidou, like de Gaulle, was the son of a schoolteacher, but after that any similarities in background or upbringing abruptly end. Pompidou was born in 1911, twenty-one years after de Gaulle, in the Auvergne region, the very heart of France. His father's family was entirely of peasant stock, and on his mother's side the family was also either small farmers or tradespeople. From them, Pompidou inherited qualities of the Auvergne which are well known in France: a tough, hard, peasant shrewdness, a mask of great personal reserve, taciturn and secretive. And he also inherited great intelligence and a capacity for efficient hard work, along with a relaxed side to his nature:—a love of poetry, literature and the arts, lively company, good food and good living. Reserved he was, and an enigma, but no stick-in-the-mud.

A village schoolmaster had persuaded his father's parents to allow their son to try for a scholarship, and Léon Pompidou responded handsomely by placing first in an entrance examination for a teachers college. His mother also left the farm to become a teacher, and his parents met when both were appointed to posts in the same district. In 1914, the elder Pompidou was drafted into the French Army as a noncommissioned officer. Seriously wounded in early fighting, he recovered and was sent back to the front lines to take part in the great Battle of the Somme. After that he was transferred to the French Army in the Eastern Medi-

* *Richard II*, Act 2, scene 4.

terranean at Salonika, in northern Greece, and did not return home until 1919.

Under his mother's guidance and tutelage in those early years of childhood, young Pompidou was proving an adept and disciplined student. He was quick to learn, and made things look easy. He finished his secondary schooling by taking a first prize in a nation-wide contest for Greek translation, and then he went on to earn his *baccalauréat* in Latin, Greek and philosophy. His parents naturally encouraged him to aim high: for the famous École Normale Supérieure, in Paris, which is France's top school for the teaching profession and liberal arts. It took two tries for the young man from the Auvergne to make it through the rigorous written and oral entrance examinations, but in 1931 he settled down in Paris on the Left Bank, at the center of the city's burgeoning literary, artistic and intellectual and political life of the interwar years. Among those he met in school at the time were Jacques Soustelle, who joined General de Gaulle in London in 1940 and played a key role in de Gaulle's return to power in 1958, and René Brouillet, who entered the French diplomatic service, also joined de Gaulle, and ended his career as ambassador to the Vatican. For Pompidou, as for every other Frenchman, entrance to one of the Grandes Écoles was more than just an education—it was also an entrance into the whole administration and governing structure of the country.

After graduation, in 1934, Pompidou spent his required year of military service with an Alpine Infantry regiment stationed at Clermont-Ferrand, in central France. He then obtained a teaching post at a secondary school in Marseilles, where he remained for the next three years. But, on a brief visit to Paris, he met a young law student, Claude Cahour, and they married in 1935. In 1939, Pompidou transferred to a new teaching post at the prestigious Henri IV Lycée, in Paris, only a few months before the outbreak of the Second World War.

In August of 1939, Pompidou was recalled to the Army and assigned to the 141st Alpine Infantry Regiment, first in the Army of the Alps and then on the Maginot Line in the Lorraine. When the Nazis invaded Norway, in April of 1940, his regiment was ordered to the port of Brest to prepare to embark for northern Norway, where French and British forces were fighting a forlorn action with the Norwegians around the city of Narvik. But before the Alpine troops could sail, the German *Panzer* divisions crashed into Belgium and northern France. Pompidou's outfit rushed back to face the Germans on the Somme. It was a well-trained regiment, which had been issued with good, new equipment for northern Norway—light tanks and artillery—and in the midst of the debacle it managed to hold together and fight an effective series of retreating actions in good order. At the end, the regiment made a last, speedy withdrawal to avoid being surrounded by the Germans, and wound up in the Limoges region, in unoccupied France, when the armistice was signed. There, instead of going into a prison camp, Pompidou was demobilized, in August 1940.

He made his way back to Paris to rejoin his young wife and quietly resumed his teaching post at the Henri IV Lycée. He settled down to an uneventful war under German occupation. He could scarcely be described as an active resistance fighter, but he was in contact with the resistance, occasionally used as a courier, sometimes hiding those who were on the run. Toward the end, in July 1944, he was warned that he might be picked up for his activities, and he went into partial hiding until just before the liberation of Paris.

Through resistance contacts, Pompidou met Émile Laffon, a key civil servant who was secretary-general at the Ministry of the Interior. Looking for young *resistants* with good educational qualifications to move in over the heads of the *fonctionnaires* who had served the occupation, Laffon made Pompidou the head of the liaison service with de Gaulle's Commissioners of the Republic in various provincial capitals of liberated France.

But very soon after, early in 1945, Pompidou got a call from his old school friend René Brouillet, who was working directly under General de Gaulle at the Ministry of War, on the rue St. Dominique. Thus, Georges Pompidou, out of nowhere, joined the inner circle of power in France at the age of thirty-four, on the staff of de Gaulle.

Although Pompidou's position of course was modest, he quickly made his mark with de Gaulle's *directeur du cabinet,* Gaston Pa-

lewski, who had been with the General since the first London
days. After the prosaic life of a schoolteacher and the numbing
years of the occupation, Pompidou reveled in being active at the
very center of power. He had intelligence, efficiency, swiftness and
a capacity for hard work in a particularly relaxed and unflappable
manner. At the same time, his reserved and somewhat secretive
nature was admirably suited to work on General de Gaulle's staff.
But in January of 1946, de Gaulle abruptly walked out to retire
for the first time to Colombey-les-Deux-Églises. A few weeks before, Pompidou had been nominated to an important and sought-
after civil service post in charge of the disputes section of the
Council of State, the highest review body of the French Government. The appointment was approved by de Gaulle's successors,
and at the same time Pompidou was invited to lecture at the Institute of Political Sciences. Inside the French establishment, he was
on the rise.

About a year after quitting power, de Gaulle decided to resume
active politics, and created the Rally of the French People. He
needed somebody to act as a personal staff assistant, and Palewski
suggested Pompidou. He was somewhat bored with the paperwork
of the disputes section, but in order not to compromise the Council of State, he never officially joined the de Gaulle political movement. It was the kind of political moonlighting that often goes on
in the French civil service.

By 1953, the Rally of the French People was a spent force, and
de Gaulle, partly at Pompidou's urging, bowed to the realities and
put the movement on the shelf in a kind of state of political suspended animation. But in the meantime his reliance on Pompidou
and his regard for his staff chief's intelligence, efficiency and above
all his total discretion had grown considerably. He entrusted Pompidou with two important personal tasks. The first was the negotiation with the Paris publisher Plon for publication of his *War
Memoirs,* which he finally began writing in 1954. The second was
the arrangements for the establishment and administration of the
Anne de Gaulle Foundation, which the General created in memory of his mentally retarded eldest daughter, who had died in his
arms at Colombey soon after the war and who occupied a place in
de Gaulle's heart that no one else ever found. The Foundation,

funded from a part of his book royalties, offers discreet financial grants to needy handicapped children. With these personal responsibilities for de Gaulle, Pompidou continued to be a regular visitor to Colombey and at the General's offices in Paris, on the rue Solferino.

Meanwhile, he had decided to give up his work with the Council of State and look for something more active, where he could make more money. Yet another friend from his days at the École Normale Supérieure now came in handy, René Fillon, who held a key post in the Rothschild group headed by Baron Guy de Rothschild. Anxious to put some new life and vigor into the operation, Rothschild was enlarging his commercial banking house and offered Pompidou a directorship. No doubt it was also shrewd of the Rothschilds to have a close collaborator of General de Gaulle in their inner circle, but this did not detract from Pompidou's abilities. He rose steadily to the role, if not the actual title, of director general of the Rothschild banking operations.

Pompidou stayed completely outside the politics of the Fourth Republic, and for that matter even the politics of Gaullism surrounding General de Gaulle. Accordingly he played no role in any of the plotting or maneuvering that preceded de Gaulle's return to power in 1958, although of course he was fully aware from the inside of what was going on. Despite that, or more probably due to that, as soon as de Gaulle was installed he sent for Pompidou to become his *directeur du cabinet* and chief of staff for the government. In this period, when de Gaulle ruled by emergency powers pending adoption of the constitution of the Fifth Republic, Pompidou was of enormous influence and importance behind the scenes in coordinating government policies, particularly fiscal and economic, as well as in the preparation of the constitution itself. In January of 1959, when the new constitution had been approved by referendum and de Gaulle was formally installed as President of the Republic, it was Georges Pompidou, completely unknown to the French public, who rode at the General's side in the open limousine from the Arc de Triomphe to the Élysée Palace.

But, having served de Gaulle actively for six months, political life still had little attraction for him. Michel Debré became de Gaulle's first Prime Minister, and Pompidou declined to take a proffered Cabinet post. He returned to the Rothschild Bank, where he was officially elevated to the lucrative position of director general.

He remained, of course, in close contact behind the scenes with de Gaulle—somebody with whom the General could talk in complete, open confidence, and a man who also brought much insight and information from the world outside politics and government, where de Gaulle had little contact. The Algerian War was the overriding preoccupation of that period, and in 1961 de Gaulle chose Pompidou for the delicate task of the first secret direct negotiating contacts with the leaders of the FLN rebellion. In a series of meetings along the Swiss border that were like rendezvous with kidnapers, Pompidou laid the groundwork for the formal talks that subsequently produced the cease-fire agreement at Évian in March 1962.

General de Gaulle had already made up his mind that he wanted Georges Pompidou as his Prime Minister—and in any case, Michel Debré was near to exhaustion after three grueling years and wanted out. Debré was a chronic worrier and a fussy administrator. Even though Pompidou was completely untried in the political arena of the National Assembly, there was a certain sense of relief when de Gaulle firmly turned the page on the Algerian War, dropped Debré, and placed Pompidou at the Hôtel Matignon, in April 1962. As far as taking charge of the government was concerned, Pompidou slid into the job like a firm hand in an old glove. He was less successful in his appearances before the National Assembly—but with a Gaullist majority he had no basic worries about the legislature's getting out of hand, and he was a quick learner in the political art of parliamentary debate, as he was in everything else.

At the outset, few thought of Pompidou as a potential successor to General de Gaulle—indeed, in 1962 nobody thought about *any* successor to de Gaulle. If anything, it looked as if the General had deliberately chosen a close personal confidant of no political experience or image so that there neither could nor would be any speculation about a distant successor. But, as the years turned over, Pompidou grew in his own way into a major power in the land.

He never attempted in any way to come out from under de Gaulle's shadow, nor in any way did he ever attempt as Prime Minister to insert his authority into the fields of foreign policy or defense and military affairs, which the General reserved entirely for himself. But de Gaulle's very inaccessibility and aloofness from "political games," from his own fervent supporters, gave Pompidou an enormous field in which to exert his own power and influence. Outwardly urbane and sympathetic, in contrast to the nervous, excitable, emotional Debré, Pompidou was shrewd, tough and hard as nails. Above his half smile and dangling cigarette, his restless, cold gray eyes were always alert—the *visage* of a Monte Carlo *croupier* about to rake in all the chips.

For de Gaulle he was an ideal collaborator. Pompidou, for his part, knew the General more intimately than most, and was well versed in the art of careful handling. Unlike Debré, Pompidou seldom brought dossiers to discuss with de Gaulle, saving such business for the formality of cabinet meetings. Instead, he would arrive at the Élysée Palace empty-handed, simply to talk over problems with the Head of State and ascertain his wishes. This suited de Gaulle admirably—a Prime Minister who never bothered him with tiresome details.

But, in one matter of grave importance very early on, Pompidou showed his mettle and his shrewdness in checking de Gaulle in a manner that the General certainly never forgot and probably never forgave. General Edmond Jouhaud, one of the four involved in the dramatic "revolt of the generals" in Algiers in April 1961, had been sentenced to death by a State Security Court, and de Gaulle was utterly determined that there would be an execution. All legal appeals machinery had been exhausted, and the final order was on his desk to be signed. Not only had the date been fixed—a firing squad had been ordered. But senior officers of the French armed forces were appalled at what de Gaulle was about to do. The Air Force Chief of Staff, General Paul Stehlin, made a personal appeal to Pompidou for Jouhaud, who was an Air Force officer. Meanwhile, the general commanding the fort where the execution was to take place resigned his commission, rather than carry out the impending orders.

The Algerian War was over and it was more than a year since

the generals had staged their abortive revolt, and Pompidou
judged that enough was enough. He found a final loophole. The
fourth man, General Raoul Salan, had been captured and was
awaiting trial. Pompidou went to de Gaulle on the eve of the
scheduled execution and advised him that Jouhaud would be
wanted as a witness at the Salan trial and that the execution therefore must be postponed. De Gaulle was furious, but he could not
ignore the formal advice of his Prime Minister. In the end, Salan
got a prison sentence, Jouhaud was reprieved, and all four men
were let out of jail just before the election of June 1968.

Actions and decisions of this kind by Pompidou, which seldom
reached public knowledge but were quickly known in the corridors
of power, soon established his firm authority and control behind
the scenes over the French Government. He was the man to whom
Gaullist deputies in the National Assembly could turn for a sympathetic hearing about some distant local problem, and his political base grew along with his power base. But he continued to operate unobtrusively and discreetly, quietly gathering the reins of
power into his own hands while General de Gaulle went about his
grand designs of French independence and the projection of
France's image in the world.

It is of course impossible to know when it began to form in
Pompidou's mind that he might, indeed, become the successor to
President de Gaulle. But, whenever it was, he certainly realized
that he had to keep any such ideas completely to himself—that the
legitimacy of his eventual claim would depend entirely on the
confidence that de Gaulle placed in him. The longer he remained
Prime Minister, the more automatic his claim would become. But
it was not to be talked about, and any rumors or suggestions of his
ambition were to be instantly quashed. The prime-ministership of
the Fifth Republic is a dangerous place for an ambitious man. If
he makes too big a mark with the public, if he tries too hard to
demonstrate that he has policies and ideas of his own, then he is
automatically challenging the President of the Republic. Neither
Michel Debré nor Maurice Couve de Murville harbored any such
ambitions or false illusions in serving de Gaulle, and although
Pompidou did his tactical best to keep the image of the loyal
humble servant, there was no way, in the end, to avoid the truth of

what was happening. And so, the Dauphin was banished from the court.

By May of 1968, Pompidou had been Prime Minister for six years, longer than any man in French history, and without any doubt he had also come to reflect that smug self-satisfaction at the top which enveloped the de Gaulle regime on the eve of the student revolt. He led a good life. In his days with the Rothschilds, he had purchased an elegant apartment on the Ile St. Louis, that little gem in the Seine behind the Cathedral of Notre Dame. His apartment windows looked across to the Left Bank and the Latin Quarter, where he and his wife had been students thirty years before. De Gaulle matured in the rigid atmosphere of St. Cyr Military Academy and the Army, but the Pompidous matured in the student world of cafes and flirtations and idle talk about artists and ideas. They entertained unobtrusively but a great deal, and they enjoyed the lively, young company of film directors and actors and actresses, *avant-garde* artists (whose works Pompidou occasionally would purchase with a keen eye). He liked to shake off the Hôtel Matignon when he left his office for the day, and change his environment completely. It was a very different lifestyle from that of General and Mme. de Gaulle, dining in stiff formality, usually alone, at the Élysée Palace.

The longer Pompidou remained in office, the more confident he became in displaying his power and influence—not openly to the public so much as in private, at cabinet meetings, and in his own dealings with departmental heads. He would shrewdly size up how cabinet discussions were going and then interject: "We are taking up the General's time—let us continue our discussions elsewhere to resolve the matter before our next meeting." Often he would propose decisions himself for de Gaulle to endorse, rather than waiting for the General to take the lead. But he was tirelessly efficient, and de Gaulle had no reason, yet, to turn to anyone else or replace him. Still, Pompidou remarked to one minister in an unusual moment of candor: "There was a time when the General liked me, liked me very much. But today I feel that he likes me a good deal less. And that really hurts."

When the events of May 1968 began to engulf France, it was a disaster for Pompidou that he was off touring Iran and Afghanistan. Of course, the trip had been arranged long before, with de Gaulle's full blessing for showing the French flag in places he himself had little interest in visiting. But that scarcely mattered. Nor did it matter that everybody in Paris misjudged the force of what was happening as much as Pompidou, thousands of miles from the scene. The Prime Minister continued his travels, even remarking to one of his entourage rather smugly: "When I get back to Paris, my name will be unsullied." Instead, when he got back to Paris, he found de Gaulle in a rage and the government in a condition of shock.

But Pompidou's very first move on his return from Kabul was contrary to de Gaulle's ideas or wishes. "We will not retreat—we will not capitulate," de Gaulle had remarked, typically, to Christian Fouchet, the Minister of Interior, shortly before Pompidou landed. But then Pompidou walked in and informed the President of the Republic that while airborne he had decided to reopen the Sorbonne, withdraw the CRS from the Latin Quarter, and arrange for release of the jailed students. To de Gaulle, this was capitulation. But the Prime Minister was back in charge. So the Sorbonne was reopened—and promptly occupied by the students in a sit-in that lasted for more than a month. Another blot for Pompidou in de Gaulle's book. That done, Pompidou assured de Gaulle that the worst was over and that he must not cancel the official visit to Romania, long arranged. So de Gaulle went off to Bucharest until, finally, he felt forced to cut short his tour and hotfoot it back to Paris, with the country now totally paralyzed by a general strike, factory sit-ins and the continued street fighting with the students. Another blot for Pompidou. De Gaulle wanted the students thrown out of the Sorbonne even if it meant gunfire and killings by the CRS, but Pompidou and others opposed, and he had to give in.

Pompidou was against de Gaulle's idea of announcing another national referendum as an appeal to everybody to return to work and studies. But de Gaulle went ahead anyway, and the result—his television broadcast of May 24—was a disaster. Then Pompidou went off to negotiate the wage settlement. When the Grenelle Agreement finally emerged, success belonged to the Prime Minister, not the President of the Republic—but de Gaulle and his Finance Minister both moodily agreed that the Prime Minister had given away too much. The situation certainly drove de Gaulle to the brink of resignation, but when he came roaring back, he adopted Pompidou's advice and dissolved the National Assembly. When the outcome was an overwhelming Gaullist victory, de Gaulle could see it only as a victory for Pompidou. The National Assembly was Pompidou's arena and power base; de Gaulle's was the people of France. In this seething atmosphere, it only made things worse for Pompidou that, despite his mistakes, he had been more right than wrong, more right than de Gaulle himself would have been had he imposed his ideas about handling the students unchecked. No one could challenge de Gaulle with impunity.

By the end of May, de Gaulle had made up his mind: Pompidou must go. Secretly, he sent for Maurice Couve de Murville and told him to prepare himself to take over. His decision made, he then proceeded to stroke Pompidou and lull him into total unawareness of the guillotine above his head. Pompidou reshuffled the Cabinet as if preparing for the long haul and threw himself into organizing and stimulating the election campaign. On at least two occasions during the crisis, he had offered his resignation, and both times de Gaulle had refused. De Gaulle went out of his way to heap praises on his Prime Minister during the campaign. When the returns were in, Pompidou once more told de Gaulle that he wished to resign, wanted out, but de Gaulle's reply was: "We have won together. We must continue. Think it over for two days. I still need you."

The end for Pompidou came with brutal ill grace. During those few days when de Gaulle asked him to reflect, rumors that he would be replaced began to spread, but Pompidou paid little attention. He spent the evening of Thursday, July 4, 1968, talking it all over alone with his wife and family, and decided that night to heed what he thought was de Gaulle's sincere urging, and stay on. Saturday morning, he went to his office at the Hôtel Matignon and telephoned Bernard Tricot, secretary-general at the Élysée Palace, to give that message to General de Gaulle. About an hour later, the editor of *France-Soir,* Pierre Lazareff, arrived for a luncheon date. He walked into Pompidou's office and greeted him somewhat tentatively by remarking, "What will you do when you're no

longer here?" Pompidou looked momentarily startled and said,
"Have you heard something?" Taken aback, Lazareff broke the
news that he had been dropped. At that moment, Pompidou's
phone to Tricot's office rang and he picked it up. "I gave the General your message but it was too late. Steps had already been
taken. Couve was appointed Prime Minister yesterday, after
dinner."

De Gaulle had acted with cruel humiliation after six years of intimate collaboration, and the customary exchange of letters between the two men did nothing to conceal the truth of how the execution had taken place. Pompidou, deeply hurt, apparently never
imagining that he might one day be a victim of the monarch's in-
gratitude, nevertheless acted with the great dignity his Auvergne
temperament gave him. He had won a National Assembly seat in
the election as a deputy from the Cantal, which he would have
had to give up had he remained as Prime Minister but which he
now, of course, occupied. He was the most important back-bench
member of the legislature, and Gaullist deputies flocked to him
personally as they never could flock to de Gaulle. Above all, he
was the man of the future. De Gaulle, in firing him, had also
released him from any obligation to hold ambition in check,
and Pompidou knew that the end for de Gaulle himself could not
be long delayed.

Four months after Pompidou's dismissal, one of the sleazier stories of French political life began oozing around Paris. In October
1968, a young Yugoslav immigrant living in France named Stefan
Markovic was found murdered under rather sordid circumstances.
It would have been just another murder but for one fact. Markovic was employed as a bodyguard by the prominent young French
film actor Alain Delon. The police naturally began hauling in and
questioning a gaggle of friends, associates and hangers-on of
Delon and Markovic from the film and night-club world and the
demi-monde of Paris to try to piece together a motive and a possible killer. No arrests were ever made, but as the investigation proceeded, the Paris press blossomed with the kind of half-
documented-innuendo crime reporting in which it specializes.
Markovic had been more than a simple bodyguard. He had been

something of a procurer, mixing freely with criminal types. There were reports of wild, lascivious sex parties at which intricate perversions were practiced. Blackmail was said to be the obvious motive for having Delon's bodyguard bumped off. There were hints that it was most probably a professional killing. Then the rumors and hints followed that the affair was being hushed up by the police because somebody high up in French politics had been involved. Finally the word began to spread: Mme. Georges Pompidou had attended the Markovic-Delon parties, and compromising photographs of her were in existence.

When the innuendos about a "prominent politican" began in the French press, Pompidou was so far removed from the whole affair that he had even kidded some of his associates at a staff meeting about who it could be. When he was finally informed by an old friend inside the government that a dossier did indeed exist on the Markovic case in which Mme. Pompidou was named, he simply paled into a cold inner rage. He concluded at the outset that for political reasons he was deliberately being made the target of false scandal.

Pompidou knew more than enough about the French legal machinery and the power workings of the French Government and its undercover agents to know that there were plenty of ways and means to stop false rumors about a former Prime Minister and his wife if there were instructions to do so. Not only did the rumors not stop; photographs now began to circulate, in the way that filthy-postcard sellers used to operate in the days before wholesale pornography. A French journalist whom I knew well, who was always full of interesting gossip and had a reputation of being something of a "Gaullist agent," not only recounted supposed details of these sex parties to me but assured me that he had seen the photos. Perhaps he had—but when, eventually, they reached Pompidou himself, he had no trouble at all in pointing out immediately how they had been faked. Yet, for several weeks, the rumors and innuendos and stories circulated through Paris without a word or a move from the government or the Élysée Palace to stop them.

The whole truth of the Markovic affair will never be known. No doubt, when Pompidou was elected President of the Republic, all the dossiers on the case were delivered to the Élysée Palace and probably no longer exist. But a few people in the government at the time have since recounted enough to piece together at least the outlines.

To begin with, it is an established fact that *somebody* in the course of the many interrogations into the Markovic murder *did* tell the examining magistrate that Mme. Georges Pompidou had been present at parties given by Markovic and Delon. It was well known in Paris that the Pompidous enjoyed the company of the film world. In a purely circumstantial sense, therefore, they were probably vulnerable, in that they almost certainly had been at a party or a dinner at one time or another and had met Alain Delon. But, given the crudities of the Markovic murder case, it ought to have been self-evident to any examining magistrate that his witness was dragging in the Pompidous in order to try to indirectly blackmail the French authorities to lay off, cool the investigation.

Instead, the salacious dossier was sent to the Élysée Palace, where, on November 1, 1968, Bernard Tricot placed it before General de Gaulle. A few days later, de Gaulle called in Prime Minister Couve de Murville; Minister of the Interior Raymond Marcellin, who was a good friend of Pompidou's; and René Capitant, the Minister of Justice and an old Gaullist. Much later, Capitant told of his advice to de Gaulle: "I said that I thought we were confronted with an ugly case of blackmail. And I added that the Pompidous were perhaps somewhat imprudent in their choice of acquaintances. I said that justice will have to take its course. If there is the slightest doubt about the insinuations regarding the Pompidous, and if the government hushes the matter up, the opposition will not hesitate to use it against the government." De Gaulle's response was, "Well, then, let justice take its course."

And so the rumors spread. It was also an exceptional opportunity to mount a smear campaign against the one man in the nation who could be regarded as a political challenge to General de Gaulle. Who doctored the fake photos that eventually reached Pompidou himself? Why was the investigating magistrate not summarily instructed to "speed up justice" and make a finding on whether or not Mme. Pompidou had or had not attended any wild

parties? Was it beyond the wit of French detectives to run down
the truth, promptly? Were there any corroborating witnesses? Why
did the government not make some statement of disclaimer, a
warning that a thorough investigation was underway? Why, indeed, did nobody in the top circles even lift up the telephone and
call the former Prime Minister personally when the dossier
reached the Élysée Palace? It is little wonder that Pompidou became convinced that he was a deliberate victim of character assassination by the Gaullist entourage, that his mere dismissal by General de Gaulle was evidently not enough. In private, Pompidou did
what he could to counterattack with rigorous denials and denunciations to friends and trusted journalists, and to his staff he said
grimly: "Nothing will be forgotten, nothing will be forgiven."

Twice Pompidou went secretly to the Élysée Palace to see de
Gaulle about the affair—only to come away with the bitter feeling that de Gaulle himself, despite expressions of regret and
confidence and denunciations of the rumor-mongering French
press, had allowed the matter to burgeon instead of acting to have
it quashed. Last ties of personal loyalty disappeared.

For more than four months, the Pompidous lived with the Markovic-Delon rumors, as a new round of interrogations by an examining magistrate brought them back into the headlines in January of 1969. A brother of the murdered Yugoslav was quoted
directly as having told the magistrate that he had been at a party
at Delon's residence with the Pompidous present. At this point,
Pompidou finally broke public silence and issued a brief formal
statement: "General de Gaulle's former Prime Minister and Mme.
Pompidou know nothing about the causes or circumstances connected with this news item." Almost immediately, it was announced that the President of the Republic and Mme. de Gaulle
had invited M. and Mme. Pompidou to dinner at the Élysée Palace. The dinner, on March 12, 1969, was a very strained and
heavy affair. Mme. de Gaulle was distinctly ill-at-ease, while
Mme. Pompidou scarcely uttered a word. Courses were served
rapidly, conversation was stilted, with long silences, and the Pompidous left in the minimum time that politeness allowed, at 9:30
P.M. After that, nothing more was heard of the Markovic case,

nobody was ever arrested, and the rumors stopped. It was the last time Georges Pompidou saw General de Gaulle.†

Nevertheless, Pompidou drew a great deal of sympathetic personal support during this period from Gaullist members of the National Assembly, who realized full well that de Gaulle's time was nearing an end and that Pompidou was by far the strongest man in the country for the succession. By his attitude and actions, Pompidou left little doubt that he, too, felt the same, but he still avoided any public declaration of ambition. However, the Markovic affair almost certainly released him from self-imposed caution. On a visit to Rome early in 1969, he met a small group of French journalists in his hotel suite. This time when the routine question about succession after de Gaulle was posed, Pompidou, instead of turning it aside, replied, "I think it's no secret to anyone that I will be a candidate." When this simple statement hit the headlines in Paris, de Gaulle erupted in a fury that Pompidou "would stoop so low—and in a foreign country." So rattled and indignant was de Gaulle that he issued a formal statement after a Cabinet meeting declaring that it was his "duty and intention of completely discharging" his election mandate of seven years. Pompidou next visited Geneva, and there, before Swiss television cameras, he first said that "the question of the succession has not been raised" but then added: "This being so, it must be said that someday elections for the President of the Republic will have to be held." Back in Paris, de Gaulle's television watchdogs promptly forbade any use of this Swiss film interview on French TV, and at the same time issued a ban on Pompidou's being shown on French screens at all!

In this atmosphere of squalid rumors and political pettiness, the

† Pompidou devised an ironic "penalty" for Alain Delon. After de Gaulle's death, the original handwritten copy of the General's first proclamation to the Free French in London, in which he used the famous phrase "France has lost a battle but has not lost the war," was put up for sale by its owner, a Frenchman who had been with de Gaulle. An Argentine buyer was reported to be prepared to bid seventy-five thousand dollars for the document. Instead, Alain Delon was given the privilege of spending his money to purchase this historic manuscript and present it to the Museum of the Order of the Liberation, where it is on permanent display. Pompidou attended to watch Delon perform this rite of obeisance in a special and much photographed ceremony.

de Gaulle era drew to an end. Pompidou's supposed "treachery" became almost an obsession for de Gaulle, as he raged like some King Lear—"How sharper than a serpent's tooth it is, / To have a thankless child!" At last the referendum of April 27, 1969, brought to an end France's great *son et lumière*.

When General de Gaulle resigned from office and closed the gates at Colombey-les-Deux-Églises, his successor under the Constitution pending the presidential elections was the president of the Senate, Alain Poher. Here lies an intriguing footnote to French history. De Gaulle had long shown his contempt for the French Senate, and it would have been abolished if he had won the referendum of April 27. A new Senate had been elected in 1968 along with the new National Assembly, not by popular vote but under a kind of electoral-college system. Its composition, therefore, was quite different politically from the National Assembly, with no clear Gaullist majority. But de Gaulle, intending to abolish the institution anyway, ignored the politics of selecting a new Senate president. Into this situation stepped the ubiquitous influential figure of Jean Monnet. While the Gaullist members of the Senate stumbled around without any orders from the General, unable to decide on whom they would like to see in the presidency, Monnet quietly went to work to put together a coalition for his old friend and associate—Poher. A modest and unassuming man, Poher had served as a junior minister back in the days of Robert Schuman, when the European Coal and Steel Community was created, and was an ardent Monnet European. While the Gaullists diddled, Monnet lined up the support of the Socialists and other center-left and center-right senators to back Poher. Unable to come up with any candidate of their own, the Gaullists gave up and Poher was elected. So it was that in the vital period of transition after de Gaulle departed, the man who occupied the Élysée Palace was a convinced European of the Monnet school. Monnet, the man of influence, in the end had outmaneuvered de Gaulle, the man of power.

Poher immediately announced his candidacy against Pompidou for a full seven-year presidential term, and he ran with surprising effectiveness, at one point even pulling ahead in public-opinion polls. He forced Pompidou into a second-round, runoff vote. But, above all, he forced Pompidou to shift ground in campaign speeches, away from a rigid Gaullist line on Europe and on British entry into the Common Market.

Georges Pompidou was elected President of the Fifth Republic on June 15, 1969, shortly before his fifty-eighth birthday. In style and personality he was of course the antithesis of de Gaulle. He once remarked to a former Gaullist minister: "I'm not any historic personage. I represent no personal equation. I have my own style, my own manner, my own methods—and there's the difference. But in essential matters I will not deviate an inch. All that counts is the independence of France, her role in Europe and her position in the world. Little by little, day by day, I will see to it that she gets her proper share of things, without fanfare or drama. But I will see to it."

Nobody could question his Gaullist credentials, his Gaullist education and idealism. He was therefore an ideal leader to move away from Gaullist extremes and concentrate on the substance. At the very outset, soon after taking office, he ordered a devaluation of the French franc—a move that de Gaulle had resisted against all economic logic after the events of 1968, really for reasons of personal prestige. Pompidou had no such illusions, and the nation promptly took off on another long period of sustained growth and expansion to become one of the world's leaders in industrial exports.

In his relations with the United States, Pompidou made a genuine and sincere effort to take the de Gaulle heat out of things and get to a more equitable basis of understanding. Even if this was not wholly successful, Pompidou certainly avoided any French acts of deliberate exacerbation—unless his refusal to join Kissinger's creation the International Energy Agency in 1974 counts as an anti-American move. But Pompidou met twice with President Richard Nixon, once in the Azores and once at Reykjavik, in Iceland, and the relationship was straightforward, about the limits of possibility with Nixon. The Azores meeting, in 1971, was of particular importance, coming with American abandonment of the Bretton Woods monetary agreements and the crisis that led to devaluation of the dollar.

But it was in Europe where Pompidou's policies showed the

most results, the most important retuning from the days of General de Gaulle. First, he opened the door that de Gaulle had kept closed for enlargement of the Common Market from six to nine, with the admission of Britain, Ireland and Denmark. Second, he initiated the practice of periodic summit conferences of the heads of government of the Common Market countries, plus coordinating machinery on foreign-policy questions going beyond the economic matters of the Treaty of Rome. De Gaulle always resisted summit conferences. Finally, Pompidou, despite his own ingrained suspicious reserve about the Germans, worked with persistence to expand Franco-German cooperation under the 1963 treaty, which had withered under de Gaulle. In all these endeavors, Pompidou was fortunate in his European collaborators: Chancellor Willy Brandt in Bonn and Prime Minister Edward Heath in London.

Early in 1973, it began to become evident that something was wrong with Pompidou's health. His face became exceedingly puffy, his walk very stiff. Unlike the United States, where a White House spokesman is expected to announce every time a President takes aspirin, in Paris complete silence and secrecy surrounded the question of what was wrong with Pompidou. It was not until close to the very end that it was established that he had contracted a rare, and finally extremely painful, bone cancer, but there never was any official medical statement, even when he died. He continued to carry on with almost incredible fortitude and self-discipline.

In mid-March of 1974, he had a long-scheduled meeting with Soviet leader Leonid Brezhnev that was to take place at Mys Pitsunda, on the Black Sea coast—a kind of Soviet Riviera, where the Communist rulers vacation in a cluster of luxurious modern dachas in a park of eucalyptus trees behind a wide stretch of brilliant white sand beach. I flew there with the French presidential press party.

Pompidou had scheduled a windup press conference on the second afternoon of the meetings, and we were bused through a high wall and ample security guards to wait on the wide stone terrace of the dacha where the French delegation was staying. Word was then passed that the President had earlier left an official luncheon to rest and that his afternoon meetings with Brezhnev had been canceled. We waited, and finally, about forty-five minutes late, Pompidou came shuffling out onto the terrace. In rather balmy weather, he was bundled up in a camel-hair coat, puffy and color-less, but with a forced smile of greeting. It must have taken an ex-traordinary effort of willpower to go through that news conference at all, for much later I learned that he had been through a spell of severe hemorrhaging after he left the luncheon table. All of us were taken aback by his appearance, but his manner, as always, was courteous and friendly. His answers to questions, usually fairly concise, were this time rambling, overelaborate. But finally he rose and shuffled back to a waiting car to take him to his plane to Paris. It was the last time he was seen by anyone outside his own personal entourage. On his return, his condition began to de-teriorate rapidly, and a week later, on April 2, he died in great pain.

Without pretension but with confidence and competence, this solid man from the Auvergne served his country—and Europe—well.

13
Willy Brandt

POSTWAR GERMANY COULD SCARCELY HAVE PRODUCED TWO leaders of stature and vision with greater contrasting personal and political backgrounds than Konrad Adenauer and Willy Brandt. This was fortunate for Germany and for Europe. The essence of democracy is the disparate nature of its leaders and its popular support. *Der Alte,* Adenauer, a nineteenth-century conservative, dominated the German scene for fourteen years, from 1949 to 1963, and to him goes the historic credit for the firm guiding hand in the solid democratic foundations and functioning of the Bonn Republic. Willy Brandt, a Social Democrat born in 1913, and the pre-eminent political figure in his country from 1966 to 1974, brought West Germany to a political maturity, an understanding and awareness, and above all an *acceptance* of Germany's diminished but essential place in Europe and the role it can play in world affairs.

Adenauer was an "insider," a Cologne Rhineland Catholic who lived in German politics and history from Bismarck's time and who scarcely traveled beyond the borders of his country until he became federal Chancellor. Brandt was an "outsider," born in the old Hanseatic port of Lübeck, in the Protestant North, and a Socialist from his earliest political awareness. Forced to flee the Nazi regime in 1933, he spent the next twelve years in Norway and Sweden. When he returned to settle in Berlin, after World War II, and regain the citizenship that the Nazis had taken from him, he had a wider vision of patriotism and a deeper perspective of Germany, its virtues and its weaknesses, along with a combination rare in postwar Germany of outside political experience, intelligence, toughness, articulateness and a knowledge of people.

Rooted in the working class, Brandt had a sense of human compassion and an empathy that was lacking in the remote, aging Adenauer.

Under Brandt's leadership, the pendulum of democratic power in West Germany finally swung to the Social Democrats in 1969, after twenty years of dominance by Adenauer's Christian Democrats. Along with this realignment of domestic politics, Brandt's even greater achievement lay in diplomacy and foreign affairs. With insight, sureness and political skill, he steered the Federal Republic into a major reorientation of foreign policy—away from the rather rigid postures of the 1950s and the Adenauer era, and onto a new plateau of *Ostpolitik*. In essence, *Ostpolitik* (eastern policy) was simply a recognition by West Germany that nothing short of another war was likely to change the geographical, military and political realities growing out of World War II and the Cold War: Germany divided probably irremediably, certainly some German territory irretrievably lost. In practical terms, therefore, *Ostpolitik* meant a de facto acceptance by West Germany of the borders and frontiers that divided Europe into the Communist and non-Communist worlds, and the opening up of diplomatic relations with the states of Eastern Europe, including the Communist regime that uneasily rules East Germany with the support of the Soviet occupation forces. It was one thing to state the bald realities, but quite another to take the political leadership in getting them accepted by an understandably suspicious, sensitive, conservative and reluctant or even hostile nation. Almost certainly, this could have been achieved in West Germany only by an "outsider." The "insiders," such as Adenauer and his immediate successors—Ludwig Erhard and Kurt Georg Kiesinger—were too rooted in the past, too tied up in Christian Democratic inward-looking domestic politics, to reach out for fresh approaches in foreign policy. Brandt took over concerned not with rebuilding Germany, which was going well, but with her place in Europe and the world. He was a statesman. And it took an "outsider" to navigate the political shoals and turn the page in Germany on the results of World War II. Without Brandt's *Ostpolitik,* there could be no true East-West *détente,* no de facto peace in Europe.

To reach the pinnacle of national political power and then turn it into historic achievement for the German nation, Willy Brandt probably had to overcome more virulent prejudices and greater personal and political obstacles than any other leader in postwar Europe. He was not, as he sometimes remarked, "born with a silver spoon in my mouth." He was illegitimate, and he never knew or even tried to find out who his father was. He was born on December 18, 1913, and christened Herbert Ernst Karl Frahm, which remained his name until the 1930s, when he changed it formally to the Socialist Party *nom de guerre* that he had adopted, Willy Brandt. In an autobiographical sketch published in 1960, "My Road to Berlin," Brandt wrote poignantly of his origins and childhood:

"Of the boy Herbert Frahm, I have only a vague recollection. The mother was very young, a salesgirl in a cooperative store. He bore the name of his mother; the father was never mentioned at home. Home was a modest worker's flat—one room and a kitchen —but to him it was not a home. His mother was working. There were practically no playmates. An opaque veil hangs over those years, gray as the fog over the port of Lübeck. It is hard for me to believe that the boy Herbert Frahm was—I, myself."

While his mother worked, he was taken care of six days a week by a neighbor lady. It was not until he was five years old that he had anything like a normal home. His Grandfather Frahm came back from World War I, after the Armistice of 1918, and remarried following the death of his first wife. He took his grandson to live with him. It was a warm family atmosphere, and Brandt called his grandfather "Papa." He was, Brandt wrote, "a simple, honest man" who had been a farm laborer and in Lübeck found a job as a truck driver. He remembers his grandfather telling him how he watched *his* father, a bonded farmhand on a vast estate in Mecklenberg, being publicly whipped on the orders of the aristocratic count who owned the land. Grandfather Frahm, not surprisingly, was a Socialist.

This was one of the most chaotic periods of German history, with the weak but idealistic leaders of the Weimar Republic trying to find roots in stony ground. Although the Social Democratic Party was the largest single party in Germany in the 1920s, it was never a majority party. Its leaders in Berlin had to turn constantly to the embittered generals of the shadowy German General Staff to prop up their democratic power. Brandt remembers a workers' council taking over the municipal buildings in Lübeck, with his grandfather in charge of the police station. It was the Germany of rampant inflation and poverty, along with the political and economic burdens of the Versailles Treaty, which fueled the revanchist feelings that Hitler eventually rode to power.

But with all this swirling around him, Brandt was a first-class student, eager to learn, almost certainly spurred by the social and psychological handicap of illegitimacy. When he was thirteen, he won a scholarship to the Johanneum, which was Lübeck's only *Realgymnasium,* the equivalent of a superior American high school. It was a citadel of privilege in Lübeck, and Brandt was one of the few working-class boys in the student body. If this increased his sense of isolation and class struggle, it did not hamper his ability or work as a student. Of these years he later told an interviewer: "I missed having a father, in different ways, but there were boys who were worse off than I was. I felt it difficult to confide in other people. From my early years I maintained this reserve. I had many friends, but not one who was really close to me. Accustomed to live within myself, I found it not easy to share my sentiments and thoughts with others."

He was fortunate in having a stimulating and liberal-minded history teacher at the Johanneum, and he became a voracious reader. He gravitated automatically to Socialist political activities, and to writing and journalism—getting a few political essays and short features printed in the Social Democratic Party newspaper *Lübecker Volksbote.* Here he gained the attention of the paper's editor and the Lübeck SPD leader, Julius Leber, a strong and fearless man who was eventually executed by the Nazis.

By the age of fifteen, Brandt was leader of the Lübeck branch of the Social Democratic Party's youth movement and had made his first trip abroad: to Denmark in a youth exchange program. When he came out of school, Leber arranged a job on the *Volksbote* and then sponsored Brandt's entry into the SPD as a full party member, in 1930. That year, the Nazi Party made its big breakthrough in national elections, capturing 107 seats in the

Reichstag. The SPD was still the strongest single party, with 143 seats—and for that reason, if no other, it became the principal target of the Nazi Brownshirts in their street-fighting tactics to bring down the Weimar Republic. Brandt, a husky and virile young man with a talent for public speaking and a craving for political action, became so strongly committed in the fight against the Nazis that he broke with his mentor, Leber, and quit the *Volksbote* due to compromises that the SPD leadership was making in Berlin. By the end of 1931, a number of left-wing Socialist groups had broken away from the SPD for similar reasons, and at a gathering in Berlin they formed a new party, the Sozialistische Arbeiter Partei (SAP), with a Trotskyist coloration. Brandt joined, but in the Reichstag election in November of 1932 the SAP polled only a derisory forty-five thousand votes. That election brought the Nazis to power, and within a matter of months all political parties and all trade unions in Germany were banned.

In March of 1933, Brandt went to Berlin for the first time, using also for the first time the name Brandt instead of Frahm, to attend a secret SAP meeting—which at the last minute was then switched to Dresden to avoid Nazi arrest. At the conclave, the party decided to declare itself dissolved, and go underground, with centers outside Germany to be established in Paris, Prague and Oslo. Brandt returned to Lübeck, and in the meantime the SAP party man chosen to go to Oslo was caught by the Nazis on the Baltic island of Fehmarn, trying to reach Denmark. At the end of March, a Lübeck lawyer, Emile Peters, warned Brandt that he was on a Nazi blacklist and liable to be picked up at any time.

Brandt got in touch with an old friend in the trucking company where his grandfather had worked to see about the possibilities of getting out of the country. On April 1, 1933, the friend sent him to a fisherman at the town of Travemünde, fifteen miles beyond Lübeck on the Baltic coast, who worked a boat owned by the trucking firm. The fisherman proposed to sail that night, with Brandt hiding behind cases of stores and fishing equipment in case of a port check when he asked for clearance. Brandt then adjourned to a *Bierstube* until it was time to sail, and had a tense moment when he ran into an acquaintance who had joined the Hitler Youth. But he was scarcely dressed for a rough-weather voyage on the choppy Baltic, and no suspicions were aroused. They sailed at dawn, got a perfunctory port clearance, and saw no patrol boats. It was a miserable journey in blustery weather that took five hours, twice as long as usual, and Brandt finally wobbled ashore in Denmark at the town of Rodbyhavn, on the island of Laaland. He had a briefcase with a few shirts and a copy of *Das Kapital* and about twenty-five dollars in German marks. Fortunately, he had also kept up a valid German passport. He was not yet twenty years old.

He made his way first to an address in Copenhagen that he had kept in his head: that of Oscar Hansen, a Danish poet. But his destination was Oslo, where he had spent a vacation in 1931 and where he wanted to settle to take up the underground work of the SAP. There his contact was Finn Moe, then foreign editor of the Norwegian Labor Party newspaper *Arbeiderbladet*. Moe found him a place to live and work for forty dollars a month—which was all the Labor Party could afford to pay him—helping to look after political refugees. He buckled down at once to mastering the Norwegian language, and with exceptional talent as a linguist, within three months he was writing articles for the *Arbeiderbladet*. He became completely bilingual in Norwegian, and in addition is fluent in English, French, and Swedish and has a working knowledge of Italian and Spanish.

"I never dimly dreamed that the Nazi era would last twelve years," Brandt told a friend in later life. "I even remember—it must have been fairly soon after I came to Norway—walking along a fjord, reciting the speech which I intended to make when I got back to Lübeck."

Fortunately, along with his language ability, he got on well with Norwegians—even their reserve and rather taciturn nature matched the reserve in Brandt himself. He was a good journalist, active and hard-working, young, with a strong personality and attractive, strong features, a good drinker and popular at Oslo University, where he spent a year of study. But in particular he was accepted into the inner circle of the Norwegian Labor Party, where he got to know well such leaders as Halvard Lange, Norway's great post-war Foreign Minister, and Einar Gerhardsen and Trygve Bratteli, each later Prime Minister of Norway. Almost automatically, he became the contact man between the Norwegian Labor Party and the SAP as well as other Socialists or leftists in exile and inside Germany.

From his secure base in Oslo, he began to travel. In February 1934, an International Bureau of Revolutionary Youth Organizations was founded, and Brandt journeyed to the Netherlands for a conference that nearly was the end for him. A pro-Nazi mayor in the Dutch town of Laaren handed over four young German delegates to the Dutch police as "undesirable aliens," who then took them to the border and delivered them to the tender mercies of the Gestapo. Brandt was taken to Amsterdam, questioned and expelled, fortunately in the direction of Norway. Next there was a stay in Paris, where a Free German Youth Organization had been founded. Finally, most dangerously of all, he slipped back into Germany in 1936, during the Olympic Games. On a forged passport, he spent several weeks in Berlin making clandestine contact with the remnants of the SAP, and then got out via Prague. Soon after his return to Oslo, the Spanish Civil War broke out, and in 1937 he arrived in Barcelona as a correspondent for Norwegian and Swedish newspapers.

He spent only four months in Barcelona—enough to be sickened by the behavior of the Stalinist Communists, who were pursuing a fratricidal struggle against the Spanish POUM United Marxists, practically ignoring the war against Franco, with side conflicts going on among Anarchists, Socialists, Trotskyites, Catalán Nationalists, and a bewildered contingent of foreign idealists and left-liberals. The great British writer George Orwell was wounded fighting with the POUM at this time, and immortalized this sad and vicious story in his book *Homage to Catalonia*. Brandt, as a result of his four months in Spain, found himself denounced by the Communists as a Gestapo agent, and by the Germans as a Bolshevik Red.

By the time war broke out in September 1939, Willy Brandt, not yet twenty-six years old, had lived a pretty full life of politics, civil war, underground activities, travel, writing and journalism, had been educated in two languages and could work in five, and had accumulated exceptional experience in dealing with a constantly changing circle of people of varying trustworthiness and temperaments. It was a far different maturing from what his German contemporaries were going through under the Nazis. His citizenship had been taken from him, and all he had, officially, was a League of Nations stateless Nansen travel document—not much protection in Europe as the war approached. He had applied for Norwegian citizenship, but the process was slow. Meanwhile he had met and fallen in love with a Norwegian girl, Carlota Thorkildsen, and in 1939 they had settled down together, intending to get married. Then came the war.

On April 9, 1940, Nazi forces moved simultaneously on Denmark and Norway, calling on both countries to surrender, charging them with violating their own status as neutrals. Denmark, flat, wide open, and defended by not much more than a police force, was a walkover for the Nazi *Panzers* rolling out of Schleswig-Holstein. Norway, despite its military weakness, was different terrain and a different people.

Although the Nazis had the puppet Norwegian politician Vidkun Quisling ready to form a government, 146 out of 150 elected members of the Storting, the Norwegian parliament, left Oslo with King Haakon to retreat north and keep a government and national resistance going. Brandt's position was, to say the least, pretty dicey. He felt it was his duty to do what he could to help the Norwegians, who had helped him, and he made his way to a "People's Aid" headquarters which had been set up in the town of Lillehammer, north of Oslo. With this group, he retreated north until finally any further escape was blocked by German forces cutting the country in two with an advance out of the northern city of Trondheim. At this point, his Norwegian friends decided that he would be safest in a Norwegian Army uniform, to be taken prisoner of war. The uniform didn't fit, but his Norwegian was impeccable. He was put in a prison camp at the town of Dovre, and in June—after King Haakon and members of the government had sailed in a British destroyer from the far northern port of Tromsø for England—Brandt and the other PWs were released. But after a few weeks hiding out in a small cottage on the Oslo fjord, with furtive visits to Carlota, who had become pregnant, his Norwegian

Labor Party friends urged him to escape to Sweden. He was prepared to stay with the Norwegian underground, but its leaders reasoned that he was too exposed for underground work, since he was
already on a Nazi blacklist. He therefore would face greater risks
than they would, and at the same time if he were picked up it might
put others at risk as well. So Brandt took a train to the Swedish
frontier, made his way to the farmhouse of a captain in the Norwegian Army, and there got a guide who steered him through the
forest to Swedish soil. He turned himself in immediately at a Swedish military post, and was lucky enough to be able to call on a
Social Democratic member of the Swedish Parliament whom he
knew to get him through interrogations and see that he was granted
political asylum.

He slipped back into Norway at the end of 1940 to see Carlota
and a baby daughter who had been born and christened Ninja,
and arranged for them to be smuggled out to Sweden, where they
were married, in Stockholm in 1941. But the marriage ended in an
amicable divorce after the war. Brandt's political life was too
intense and dominant, particularly since he was clearly intent on
returning to Germany instead of making his life as a Norwegian.

Stockholm, after London, was the most important wartime
gathering place for political exiles from Nazi conquests—even
though Swedish hospitality was, to say the least, cool and restrained. Although Brandt stuck primarily to Norwegian circles,
there were some thirty-five hundred German exiles in Sweden,
about three hundred of them Socialists or other leftists. They
clubbed together in a kind of "socialist international in exile,"
made up of like-minded political exiles from Denmark, Spain,
Norway, Germany, France, Austria, Hungary, Poland and Czechoslovakia, as well as Sweden and Iceland. One of the prime
movers, with whom Brandt became a close friend, was Bruno
Kreisky, later to become Chancellor of Austria at the same time
Brandt was Chancellor of West Germany. But mainly Brandt concentrated on political writings and underground information
leaflets along with resistance propaganda for the outside world. In
all, he published six books in Sweden during the war—four of
them written in Norwegian and two in German—on war aims and
postwar political problems.

With the liberation of Norway and the end of hostilities, in May of 1945, Brandt returned to Oslo, where he had already been granted Norwegian citizenship. His old newspaper, the Labor Party's *Arbeiderbladet,* together with the Norwegian news agency, NTB, proposed that he take on a major journalistic assignment: the Nuremberg trials of the German war criminals. So in late September he returned to Germany, with a brief stop first in Lübeck to see his mother. Grandfather Frahm had committed suicide during the Nazi period.

Brandt settled down with the foreign press contingent at Nuremberg from October 1945 to February 1946, when sentences were finally pronounced on Göring, Ribbentrop, Hess, Speer, and company. But in between trial sessions, he again took up contact with the few old associates of the Social Democratic Party who had survived the war. The breakaway SAP, which Brandt had joined in 1932, was finished, and in any case Brandt was a socialist of the moderate center, rather than the extreme left. From his contacts, it was clear that he would be welcome back in the SPD, but he took his time, as he did in most things. When the trials were over, he returned to Norway, and in September the Norwegian Foreign Minister, Halvard Lange, who had barely survived a Nazi concentration camp, asked Brandt to join the Norwegian Foreign Ministry—offering him a choice of jobs as head of its press service in Oslo, press attaché in Paris, or press attaché with the Norwegian Military Mission in Berlin. He did not take much time this time to accept the post in Berlin. He arrived at the end of the year, in Norwegian military uniform, as was then required under Allied occupation regulations. He was joined in Berlin soon after by a young Norwegian widow he had met in Stockholm who was to become his second wife, Rut Hansen. His duties with the military mission of a small power were not very demanding or exciting, but he did a lot of political reporting and contact work among trade unionists and Social Democrats for the Norwegians. The pull back to Germany was there, and it was only a question of time. The moment came when the SPD offered Brandt a post as the party's special representative in Berlin, which of course was then still the hub of Germany and the center of four-power occupation administration. On November 7, 1947, he wrote Lange in Oslo of his decision to leave the Norwegian Foreign Ministry and retrieve his German citizenship.

"There is much to be done inside Germany in the interests of Europe, democracy and peace. There are positive forces within the German people which will be able to make their mark on future developments. You know that I have no illusions. But I wish to try to help bring Germany back into Europe. It is fairly certain that I shall suffer disappointment and perhaps more than that. I hope I shall face defeat, if it comes, with the feeling that I have done my duty. I shall carry with me all the good things I have experienced in Norway. No artificial lines of demarcation can prevent me from feeling that I am a part of Norway. You can depend on me for the future."

Brandt took up his new post with the Social Democratic Party in February 1948 just as the last elements of democracy in Czechoslovakia were strangled by Stalin's henchmen and the noose began to tighten around Berlin.

The outsider had come home, but the personal and political sniping and resentments that were to dog Brandt's public and private life for the rest of his career had already begun. "A number of so-called friends are doing their best to give a worm's eye view of me" at the SPD headquarters at Hanover, he wrote to an old associate at the time. It took a long while for Brandt to overcome the prejudices within his own party, and the sniping at his record by his political opponents still goes on. At one point in the 1960s, he was forced finally to go to court in a libel action simply because he could not allow the smears to go unnoticed or unchallenged any longer. The biggest smear attempt was the charge that he had fought in a foreign uniform and bore arms against his fellow countrymen. He had put on a Norwegian Army uniform to escape arrest as a German in 1940, and again after the war as an accredited Norwegian correspondent at Nuremberg and as an accredited Norwegian member of the Military Mission in Berlin. But he never bore arms against his country, and was never more than a political resistant. In any case, the Nazis had stripped him of his citizenship long before the war began.

There was a considerable psychological gulf in post-Nazi Ger-

many between Germans who had been in the country and suffered
the worst in the concentration camps or at the hands of the Gestapo for their democratic principles, and those who had gotten
away and had lived in relative comfort and security outside until it
was all over. Both those who had suffered under the Nazis and the
neo-Nazi right-wing extremist on the fringe of German politics
joined in the taunt: "And what were you doing for twelve years,
Herr Brandt?"—often heard from respected politicians in rhetorical rabble-rousing during elections when Brandt was leading the
SPD. Then there was his illegitimacy. Even the dignified and honorable Chancellor Konrad Adenauer once sank to a malicious low
by referring to Brandt from a campaign platform as "Herr Brandt,
alias Frahm." Added grist to the personal smears and sniping were
his marriage for a second time to a Norwegian woman, the fact
that he habitually spoke Norwegian at home, his capacity for and
enjoyment of drink, in which he combined both German and Norwegian proclivity, and then in the 1960s there was the left-wing
student activist life of his eldest son, Peter. Among old-timers in
the SPD, there were suspicions of Brandt due to his breakaway
membership in the leftist-Trotskyite SAP in the last days before
Hitler came to power, and even his time in Barcelona during the
Spanish Civil War was seized upon for suspicions from both the
Left and the Right. It took integrity and toughness to walk upright
and straight ahead through all of this, and Willy Brandt had
plenty of both.

He was fortunate in this early period of his return to German
political life to have as his mentor and close friend the great Ernst
Reuter—another Social Democratic "outsider" who returned to
Berlin in 1947, after twelve years teaching school in Turkey, to
become the city's mayor and indispensable leader during the days
of the blockade and the airlift. Reuter was twenty-five years older
than Brandt, but they were of the same humane outlook and
toughness, the same moderate Social Democratic philosophy, and
the parallel experience of outsiders returned.

Brandt's immediate assignment for the party in 1948 placed
him between Reuter in the city government and Kurt Schumacher,
the SPD's erratic, fiery, difficult and dictatorial leader in West
Germany. The gaunt victim of twelve years in concentration

camps, missing an arm and a leg, Schumacher's politics were a
strange mix of acute German nationalism wrapped up with Social
Democratic ribbons. At a time when working closely with the
Western Allies was so clearly an overriding necessity, Schumacher
sought to make political capital with unending denunciations of
the Allied occupation. But Brandt wrote him firmly at the outset
of his return to the party: "Let me declare to you unambiguously:
I stand by the principles of democratic socialism in general and
the policies of the German Social Democrats in particular. I reserve the right to work out my own views on any new issue that
may arise. And I shall never agree in advance to every detailed
formulation of policy, even if stamped by the leader of the party
himself."

Meanwhile as the blockade approached, Brandt plunged into the
vital task of strengthening the organization of the Berlin SPD to
spearhead resistance to the Communists, who were attempting to
take over the entire machinery of the city government with the
backing of the Russians. The blockade began in June of 1948, and
the Berlin airlift got underway, somewhat hesitantly at first, a few
days later. In September came the breakup of the city government
for Greater Berlin, when Ernst Reuter and the Social Democrats
walked out of the City Hall in the Soviet sector and set up a separate administration for West Berlin with Reuter as *Oberburgermeister* in the borough Rathaus of Schoeneberg, where it continues
today. The airlift saved Berlin physically, and the Social Democratic Party saved it politically.*

The blockade ended in May 1949, and almost simultaneously
in Bonn the draft of the constitution for the new Federal Republic
was completed by the Parliamentary Council. Elections for the
first Bundestag and formation of the Bonn government were
scheduled for August 14, 1949. By a decision of the Western Allies, West Berlin was denied the status of one of the states of the
Federal Republic even though it was to be governed from Bonn in
virtually all other respects. In that first election, Brandt campaigned arduously for the SPD up and down West Germany, and
the party's defeat by Adenauer's Christian Democrats came hard

---

* See also Chapter 4, "The Bonn Republic."

for Schumacher and the leadership. But Schumacher had badly misjudged public feeling with his campaign tone of rabid anti-Allied oratory and his efforts to outdo even the political parties of the Right in fervent nationalism. When it was over, Brandt took a seat in the Bundestag as a member of the special eight-man Berlin delegation that was chosen by the Berlin Senate (city council), to differentiate its status from the elected Bundestag membership. Along with his growing role in Berlin alongside Reuter and his work as a party liaison man and organizer, he now took on an active role in parliamentary committee work in Bonn, where he rapidly found friends and allies who were as uncomfortable as he was with Schumacher's leadership.

Schumacher died in 1952, worn out by his physical, emotional and political battles. His successor was a rotund, colorless, honorable and indecisive man named Erich Ollenhauer, who had about as much leadership personality as a railway conductor. Moreover, the Social Democrats lost their other big national figure a year later: Ernst Reuter died in Berlin of a heart condition in September 1953. And at the same time, the SPD lost the second Bundestag election in West Germany, under Ollenhauer's leadership. But these transitions combined to open the way to the top for Willy Brandt.

In Bonn, Brandt had moved up to membership in the executive committee of the SPD's Bundestag parliamentary group, and in the meantime he had also been elected to the City Senate in Berlin. In 1954 he ran for chairmanship of the Berlin SPD and lost by only two votes to an old party traditionalist, Franz Neumann, who continued to harbor much prejudice against the rising young outsider. At this same period, Ollenhauer, still hesitating to bring new blood into the party's national leadership, resisted Brandt's candidacy for a place on the SPD executive. But Brandt was a good party man who knew the value of loyalty and could take his time. Meanwhile in the Berlin city election of 1954, with Neumann leading the party, the SPD lost ground with the voters, and a new coalition administration was then put together with the CDU—a forerunner of what was to happen in Bonn after Adenauer's end. Otto Suhr, of the SPD, became Berlin mayor, with Brandt as president of the City Senate. Suhr was a competent if not very imaginative mayor, but he fell ill at the end of 1955. Brandt more and more became the city's leading spokesman, traveling widely, speaking in the Bundestag in Bonn, and representing the city in various European meetings and parliamentary forums.

In 1956, tensions in Eastern Europe began to rise again. The Communist regime in East Germany formally proclaimed East Berlin to be its capital. In July, troubles broke out in Poznań, in Poland, and spread to other cities, and were only barely suppressed by the Polish Communist regime without Soviet intervention. Then the fury broke in November of 1956 with the uprising of the Hungarian people in Budapest. Berliners who had watched in impotent rage when a similar uprising in East Berlin and East Germany had been crushed by Soviet tanks three years before, in June of 1953, flocked to a massive demonstration before the Schoeneberg Rathaus on November 4, 1956. The events of that day put Willy Brandt indisputably at the top in the city.†

More than a hundred thousand Berliners gathered in a restless, agitated mood. The first speaker, Ernst Lemmer, who was a Christian Democrat representing the Bonn government in Berlin, singularly failed to contain the emotions. After that, Franz Neumann spoke as chairman of the SPD—only to be interrupted by whistling and chants and catcalls and a call for a march to the Brandenburger Tor, in the heart of the city at the demarcation line with the Soviet sector. At this point Brandt, who had not even been scheduled to speak, took the microphone and tried to regain control with a ringing denunciation of the Red Army—coupled with a warning of the dangers of a march on East Berlin. But the crowd wanted action. So he climbed into an open police car equipped with a loudspeaker at the head of the spontaneous march and diverted the mob to the Steinplatz, off Kurfürstendamm, well away from the sector border. Here he addressed them again, and then called for them to sing an old German Army song for fallen soldiers: *Ich Hatt Einen Kameraden.* As this crowd began to disperse, Brandt got word over the police radio that another, smaller

† That same day, British and French troops were poised to land at the Suez Canal. See Chapter 8, "The Suez War."

but younger and more volatile group, of a thousand or so, had reached the Brandenburger Tor and were skirmishing with the West Berlin police to try to break through and attack the East German Volkspolizei across the sector line several hundred yards away. Again he sped to the scene, and again he cooled things by warning that nothing could be accomplished by Berliners throwing themselves on Russian guns, and again he got the crowd to sing. The police regrouped, but more Berliners kept arriving. Finally, for a third time, Brandt mounted the roof of a police truck as the November dusk settled over the city, shepherded the crowd back into the Tiergarten, and this time brought the day of tensions to an end by getting them all to sing the German national anthem.

"In political situations it is useful to remember that my countrymen are fond of singing," he remarked later on. In that afternoon he vaulted into leadership of the city. When Otto Suhr died, the following year, Willy Brandt became mayor of Berlin, on October 3, 1957.

In West Germany, a few weeks before Brandt became mayor of Berlin, the Social Democratic Party under Ollenhauer lost another national election for a new Bundestag to Konrad Adenauer and the Christian Democrats, the third time in a row. The SPD managed to gain a little, from 29 to 32 percent of the vote, but the CDU leaped from 44 to 50 percent. It was painfully evident that the SPD needed new ideas and new blood at the top, but Ollenhauer wouldn't be budged and was reelected party chairman. A year later, when the city of Berlin went to the polls in December of 1958, with Brandt leading the SPD from the mayor's office, the SPD vote jumped from 44 to 52 percent, while the CDU, trailing behind, improved from 30 to 37 percent. Brandt was a party winner, in contrast to the dim, bureaucratic image of Ollenhauer.

On the eve of the Berlin city election, Nikita S. Khrushchev fired the opening gun in a new Soviet campaign to strangle West Berlin and snuff out the Allied presence in the city—ten years after Stalin had failed. Without much doubt, Khrushchev gave a big boost to the election fortunes of Brandt and the SPD. On November 10, 1958, he declaimed from the Kremlin that the situation in the city had become intolerable and that he intended to hand over full responsibility to the puppet East German regime. He demanded that within six months the whole of Berlin be transformed into a demilitarized "free city," and if the Western Allies failed to agree with his ultimatum, he said, then they would have to deal with the East German regime on the question of access in and out of West Berlin.

Over the next four years, Berlin was seldom out of the headlines as the confrontation between Khrushchev and the Western Allies surged and receded from one test of strength to another—until it finally subsided and ceased to be an East-West flash point any longer after the Cuban missile crisis of 1962.

The Kremlin's problem was the deplorable weakness of the Communist regime in East Germany, with Berlin then still an open city and an easy escape route for anybody who wanted to leave. Up to 1958, roughly 2.3 million East Germans—a staggering 15 percent of the total population—had fled to the West, most of them coming out through Berlin. This was what was "intolerable" to Khrushchev and the Russians, and their answer to their problem, of course, was to snuff out West Berlin.

John Foster Dulles was still the American Secretary of State when Khrushchev delivered his six-months ultimatum at the end of 1958, and in Paris General de Gaulle had just gotten his new constitution adopted and was about to become the first President of the Fifth Republic. The initial Allied reaction to Khrushchev was simply to restate the old formula that the Soviet Union could not unilaterally alter four-power responsibility for Berlin and could not push the Western Allies out of the city. But in London, Prime Minister Harold Macmillan took the problem more seriously, and in February of 1959, with only minimal advance warning to the other Allies, he scheduled a trip to Moscow to confer with the Soviet leader. His trip helped defuse the immediate crisis, and in place of the ultimatum the Russians agreed to four-power talks on Berlin at the foreign ministers level, which then took place in Geneva in the summer of 1959—three months totally without result.

In the next phase of the crisis, again under Macmillan's prodding, Khrushchev agreed to holding a four-power summit conference to discuss Berlin. But, in advance of this, both President Ei-

senhower and President de Gaulle decided that they should each
see Khrushchev for bilateral talks, like that Macmillan had held in
Moscow. So Khrushchev first met Eisenhower at Camp David in
the autumn of 1959 and then met de Gaulle in Paris in March of
1960. At last everything was set for the four-power summit in Paris
in May. But as the Big Four gathered, an American U-2 spy plane
was shot down over Siberia. The summit collapsed. Khrushchev
stormed out of Paris, hurling dire threats of an immediate separate
peace treaty with East Germany.

But nothing happened. Khrushchev's thunder and lightning
blew itself out, and 1960 was a year of relative calm in Berlin.
Pinprick harassments continued, but the Soviet Union had notably
failed to dent the Allied position or presence in the city—even
though Allied responses to Soviet moves and threats had not always been imaginative or quick or forceful. Still, for the time
being, the Khrushchev offensive seemed to have run out of steam.

But Willy Brandt was on the move, both politically and physically. With Berlin under constant threat, he stepped up his travels,
using his unique position as the city's mayor for ready access to
heads of state: de Gaulle in Paris, Macmillan in London, Eisenhower and later Kennedy in Washington, Jean Monnet, Bruno
Kreisky in Vienna, British Labour Party leaders, Socialist International meetings, the Council of Europe in Strasbourg, NATO par-
liamentarians. He was all over the place, and with his excellent
command of languages, his natural ability with people, his intelligence and firmness and his combination of modesty and authority,
he was a welcome and growing figure, where Konrad Adenauer
had hitherto had things pretty much to himself as Germany's only
recognizable international statesman.

At the same time, as the decade of the 1950s ended, the SPD
was slowly facing up to the fact that it had to do something to get
ready for the next election campaign, coming up in 1961. From a
membership of 875,000 at the time of the first West German
election, in 1949, the party had skidded to a mere 534,000 adherents in 1959. Ollenhauer was still party chairman, but he had
accepted that he should not be the party candidate for the
chancellorship against Adenauer a third time. A special party
commission was established, outside the National Executive, to

overhaul the SPD's basic political doctrine, prepare a new campaign platform, and make changes in the party's organization and tactics.

Brandt automatically took a place on this commission, and its first big step forward was a complete rewriting of the party's basic political objectives: to get rid of outmoded Marxist doctrine on such questions as nationalization of industry, and deliberately move away from the image of a working-class party to that of a middle-class party. It was a vital and decisive political modernization, with the Social Democrats emerging as a pragmatic left-of-center, forward-looking body of wide popular appeal and youthful leadership, in contrast to the Christian Democrats under the octogenarian Adenauer. The new program was adopted at a party congress held in Bad Godesberg, near Bonn, in November of 1959, which was something of a turning point in West German political history. It was this political new look that paved the way for ultimate SPD victory a decade later, and unbroken SPD rule in Germany for the entire decade of the 1970s. Brandt, as the prime mover in drafting the new program, really remolded the party in his own image, even though he was not yet its leader. But with his dominant influence inside the party and his growing stature and image abroad, there was no question that the mayor of Berlin was the strongest man to lead the SPD in the 1961 elections. Still, the old prejudices died hard, and it took time for the party to get used to the prospect. Finally, on August 24, 1960, the SPD executive formally invited Willy Brandt to become the party's candidate for the post of Chancellor of West Germany.

In his acceptance speech, three months later, Germany heard a new leader. Along with a call for firmness and a warning against Soviet "pressure, blackmail and destruction of all normal diplomatic usages," Brandt also called for flexibility in place of the rigid attitudes of the Adenauer foreign policy, in particular flexibility in dealings with East Germany. "We are all one family," he declared. "Because of that our people must at last make peace with itself. I want to contribute to this end to the best of my ability. This, too, belongs to the new style which we want to introduce into German politics."

Across the Atlantic, John F. Kennedy had been elected President of the United States, and soon after taking office, in January 1961, he sent out feelers to Khrushchev in Moscow for an early summit meeting. In the meantime, Brandt traveled to Washington in March for his first meeting with Kennedy and a discussion of the Berlin situation, which was now swinging back to increased tensions after the relative calm following the collapse of the Paris Big Four Summit. As Kennedy prepared for his confrontation with Khrushchev, he received a report on the military aspects of Berlin from Secretary of Defense Robert S. McNamara that disturbed him deeply. In effect it concluded that any military action in defense of Berlin would escalate almost immediately into a nuclear exchange, simply because United States and NATO forces in Western Europe were inadequate for even a brief conventional fight with the Russians. It was an appraisal that had a sobering effect on Kennedy's actions—in the end, he preferred confrontation in Cuba to confrontation in Berlin.

After a glittering state visit to President Charles de Gaulle in Paris, Kennedy traveled to Vienna for two days of talks with Khrushchev on June 3 and 4. The Soviet leader, in his own peculiar Russian mixture of ebullient truculence, was at his worst. Berlin had become more "intolerable" to him than ever. By the end of 1961, he now declaimed, he would sign his peace treaty with the East German regime, terminate any Soviet involvement in quadripartite responsibility for the city, and leave it to the Western Allies to get out or deal with Ulbricht and company. Kennedy repeated the standard litany of Allied positions, to which Khrushchev barely listened. On the steps of the American Embassy residence in Vienna, when they finally parted in brilliant June sunshine, Kennedy turned to Charles E. Bohlen, his chief Soviet adviser, and said grimly: "Well, it looks like a cold winter."

In Moscow, Khrushchev ordered an increase in Soviet military spending and a halt to a planned reduction in Soviet ground forces, at the same time making secret preparations to resume nuclear testing, which had been suspended in a moratorium agreement with President Eisenhower. Kennedy returned to Washington, went on the air on July 25, 1961, and in a sober report to the nation announced a $3.2 billion increase in American defense spending, an increase of 217,000 in the armed forces, and the dispatch of additional supply and combat troops to West Germany and Western Europe. "Our presence in West Berlin and our access thereto cannot be ended by any act of the Soviet Government," Kennedy said. "The immediate threat to free men is in West Berlin. But that isolated outpost is not an isolated problem. The threat is worldwide." As the two superpowers headed inexorably for a showdown in Berlin, with the threats from Moscow becoming more and more hysterical, a near panic began to sweep through East Germany, and the refugees fleeing to West Berlin reached the proportions of a flood. In June, at the time of the Vienna summit, the daily average was around five hundred, but in early July it rapidly swelled to more than a thousand a day. In August, in a frenzy, it hit 2,000 a day, more than five thousand in two days after another fire-breathing speech by Khrushchev on August 7, and then an all-time one-day record of nearly four thousand crossing from East Germany into West Berlin on August 11.

Meanwhile the West German election campaign was in full swing, and Brandt was shuttling in and out of the city on a rigorous eighteen-hour daily schedule of speeches, meetings, rallies and party and city business. On Saturday, August 12, he arrived in Nuremberg, after a stop in Bonn for a meeting at the Foreign Ministry, and he told an SPD rally in the city's Marktplatz: "We all know that our compatriots in the East Zone fear that their escape route may be cut off, that they may be left on their own and locked in." Brandt was being far more prophetic than he realized. He later wrote: "Had I genuinely known what would happen, I would have flown back to Berlin at once. I had discerned only the basic situation, not the timing and course of events."

Instead, after a series of party meetings and dinner, Brandt boarded a special lounge-sleeping car attached to the regular night train from Nuremberg to Kiel, where he was to address a rally on Sunday. In the early morning hours of Sunday, August 13, when the train reached Hanover, he was awakened by the conductor. A message had been telephoned to the train from Berlin. Complete closure of the sector border across the center of the city by East German troops and Volkspolizei had begun shortly after midnight.

The mayor was asked to return to the city as fast as possible. Brandt and several officials traveling with him dressed hurriedly and got off the train at 5 A.M., drove to the Hanover airport and caught an early-morning flight to Tempelhof. From Tempelhof, he drove straight to Potsdamer Platz and then on to the Brandenburger Tor, at the edge of the Tiergarten, to see what was happening. Concertina barbed wire had been unrolled during the brief summer night all the way across the center of the city. East Germans—not Russians—were in charge, supervising the installation of concrete posts to hold the wire. Under clear skies that warm August Sunday morning, East Germans were gathering in despondency, staring vacantly from behind the barbed wire, while West Germans gathered in impotent fury on the other side.

. The sudden traumatic appearance of barbed wire across the center of Berlin, followed a few days later by the first cement blocks in the building of the Berlin Wall, was one of the climactic events of the postwar era, and the Wall remains today the most infamous piece of construction on the continent of Europe, unmatched in any city or any country anywhere else in the world. It is a monument to many things: to Adolf Hitler's war, which brought the Red Army into the heart of Europe, to the Yalta and Potsdam conferences, to the victory of the Berlin airlift and the success of the Marshall Plan, to the recovery of Western Europe and the failure of the Communist system in the East. It is the permanent high-water mark of the advance of Soviet power in Europe. And it is the imposed artificial frontier of Western civilization, of Western values, to the East.

But the Berlin Wall is also a monument to a dismal failure of all the intelligence services and apparatus of the Western powers—a failure on the scale of Pearl Harbor, fortunately without the consequences of war. Nobody—but nobody—was prepared by the slightest inkling or intuition or imagination, let alone by any hard information, for the overnight appearance of the barbed wire across the middle of Berlin. Moreover, despite all the diplomatic-military-political-emotional attention that the Berlin crisis had been getting, the reaction of the Western Allies on that Sunday morning was supine, purblind and shameful.

From the barbed wire at the Brandenburger Tor, Brandt went

first to an emergency meeting of the Berlin Senate and then to a meeting with the American, British and French commandants at the old Allied Kommandatura headquarters. As a realist, Brandt knew full well that it was impossible to expect Allied tanks to advance and rip down the wire and cross into East Berlin. But he asked that at least the Allies immediately send patrols of military police to the sector borders to show the Western presence and back up the harassed West Berlin police. He asked that an immediate protest be delivered to the Soviet commandant in East Berlin, that diplomatic protests be made in Moscow and the capitals of the Warsaw Pact powers which were associated with the operation in a formal declaration of support. But the Allied commandants sat impotent around the table, waiting for instructions, waiting on that Sunday morning for everybody to wake up in Washington and stir themselves in London and Paris. These generals defending the outpost of democracy, when the chips were down, couldn't even order their own military police out of barracks and downtown to the center of Berlin. It was twenty hours before Allied military police appeared at the barbed wire, forty hours before a protest was delivered to the Soviet headquarters, seventy-two hours before a protest went to Moscow.

President Kennedy was at Hyannisport getting ready for a Sunday sail in his yacht. General de Gaulle was at Colombey-les-Deux-Églises, not to be disturbed. Prime Minister Macmillan was at Chequers, and the rest of the British Government was in its traditional weekend deployment all over the English countryside. There was only one NATO ambassador on hand in Paris that mid-August weekend (the Norwegian), and nobody could even call an emergency meeting of the NATO Council. For Brandt and the Berliners, memories welled up of the test of the airlift, the East German uprising of June 17, 1953, the "food parcel war" later that same year, the near explosion at the Brandenburger Tor during the Hungarian uprising in 1956. Now Brandt would have to go out and cope with the emotions of the city in this worst trauma of all, and he left the meeting with the Allied commandants without one decision or action of support. No wonder his bitter comment to the British, French and American major generals as he got up from the table: *"Dann lacht der ganze Osten von Pankow bis*

Wladivostok!" (The entire East will be laughing from Pankow to Vladivostok.)

The truth was, and is, that in Washington, London and Paris the real reaction to the building of the Berlin Wall was one of relief. If somebody had tried to wake French Foreign Minister Maurice Couve de Murville with the news, he would have rolled over and gone back to sleep. "That solves the Berlin problem" was his first comment when he got the news on Sunday morning. Kennedy had told a White House staff conference two weeks before, in early August: "I can set the Alliance in motion if Khrushchev does something against West Berlin, but not if he starts something in East Berlin." In West Germany, old Chancellor Adenauer went blissfully on with his election campaigning, and didn't even bother to visit the city for ten days. It was in one of his speeches in this period that he referred maliciously to "Herr Brandt, alias Frahm," and later on he even went so far as to speculate before an audience that Khrushchev had built the wall to help out the SPD and Brandt in the West German election!

Finally, on August 16, with the Berliners seething over this astounding display of indifference on the part of their Allies, Brandt cabled a forceful personal letter to President Kennedy. Moreover, he then announced what he had done in a speech later that morning at a protest rally of a quarter of a million Berliners gathered in front of the Schoeneberg Rathaus, in the square that was later renamed John F. Kennedy Platz. In Bonn, the West German Foreign Ministry indignantly rebuked the Berlin mayor for a breach of protocol in daring to communicate directly with a foreign head of state and for subjecting the Western Allies to "intense pressure" on the Berlin question. But Kennedy, even though not pleased at being hassled in this fashion, did respond positively. He announced that the United States Berlin garrison would be reinforced at once by an additional combat group, and that Vice-President Lyndon B. Johnson and General Lucius D. Clay would arrive on a visit to the city in a few days.

When the army combat group arrived in its vehicles at the Helmstedt checkpoint to cross Soviet-controlled territory to West Berlin, its commander, Colonel Glovers John, made a disastrous mistake. The Soviet control officer at the checkpoint demanded that the American soldiers dismount from their vehicles to be counted. Contrary to all previous Allied practice, Colonel John acceded—because the Vice-President would be waiting at the other end in Berlin, and the Colonel didn't want to risk being late. So the convoy cleared, but for the next two years there were constant arguments and confrontations with the Russians over this counting procedure. By such insignificant issues, the security of Berlin was constantly tested for twenty-five years and could be tested all over again anytime.

Johnson distinguished himself on his Berlin visit by getting shops to open up on a Sunday so he could buy shoes and electric razors, and a porcelain factory to open up to take an order for a sizable number of small ashtrays which, the Vice-President pridefully said, "Look like a dollar and cost me only 25 cents."

But at least there had been some action by the Americans, and General Clay then returned to Berlin, in September, as President Kennedy's special representative. Symbolically this was a useful gesture, but Clay's authority and powers were far different from those of the halcyon days of the Berlin airlift. The climactic moment of his second tour in the city came when he ordered American tanks to Checkpoint Charlie in October 1961 to face Soviet tanks for a grim eighteen hours in order to establish the right of American officials and American military personnel to enter East Berlin under four-power agreements without any control or check by the East German Volkspolizei or anybody else. But Clay was soon at odds not only with the other Allied commandants, over whom he had no authority, of course; even Washington was not all that prepared to endorse the General's zest and readiness to demonstrate firmness. After eight months, Clay returned to the United States, but his remains a revered and legendary name in Berlin.

Khrushchev had accomplished one major purpose: the sealing off of the big escape route from the wretched East German Democratic Republic. But he still hadn't forced the Western Allies out of the city. The Berlin problem may have been solved, as Couve de Murville saw it, but the testing and economic strangulation and war of nerves went on, ebbing and flowing, for another decade, until completion of the Four Power Berlin Agreement, in 1971. So

also did West Berlin write for itself a new chapter of daily hero-
isms with ingenious escape operations, a reassertion of its great
toughness and vitality, a surge in outside investment to secure its
economic future, a kind of "crisis benzedrine" atmosphere of special fortitude of its 2.2 million people surrounded by barbed wire
and the Wall. "The worst crisis will be when there is no crisis,"
the Berliners used to joke.

Willy Brandt, looking beyond the Wall, came to some hard
basic conclusions about the political realities it embodied.

"I wondered then, not for the first or last time, whether the two
superpowers might not, with adamantine consistency, have been
pursuing the same principle in Europe since 1945: That whatever
happened, they would respect the spheres of influence broadly
agreed at Yalta," he wrote.

"This would have presupposed a division of Germany and the
continent. Nothing since Stalin's offensive policy in Berlin has, in
fact, managed to shake this principle—neither the remilitarization
of both parts of Germany, which stemmed logically from such a
policy, nor attempts to modify internal power structures in the
countries of either Western or Eastern Europe. The Western
powers, with America in the van, stood idly by while various
forms of insurrection in East Germany (1953), Poland and Hungary (1956) and Czechoslovakia (1968) were quelled, crushed
and smothered. The Russians, in their turn, accepted the suppression of the Communists in Greece (1948) and tolerated Tito's
withdrawal from the Soviet camp (1948) although with much
gnashing of teeth because Yugoslavia lay at the intersection of the
two spheres of influence. Finally, they have done little to support
the Communist parties of Italy and even France in their efforts to
gain power.

"Here lies the underlying pattern of a power strategy in Europe
which, for all of its complexity of detail, appears to have survived
almost unaltered since 1945. Events in Germany must likewise be
viewed against this background. The basic principle governing the
tacit arrangement between Moscow and Washington remained in
force during the construction of the Wall and thereafter."

The question that faced the mayor of Berlin and candidate for
federal Chancellor of West Germany was what the foreign policy

of his country should be in the face of this superpower division of his city and the German nation. Was West Germany, with its burgeoning economic dynamism, to remain immobile and indifferent to the East? Could it really content itself to remain frozen in the center of Europe? Could the Federal Republic go on simply subsisting on the foreign policy of the United States? For Willy Brandt, the lesson of the building of the Berlin Wall and the doleful Allied response that followed was that West Germany must have a foreign policy with room for maneuver on its own. The answer he then began to nurture was *Ostpolitik*.

14
Ostpolitik

GREAT ACTS OF HISTORY OFTEN HAVE BEEN SIMPLE INVENTIVE proposals that take time to bring to fruition but have the focus of a single central idea and objective. The Marshall Plan (recovery), the Schuman Plan (unity) and the North Atlantic Treaty (security) are examples. But *Ostpolitik,* which has been Willy Brandt's primary contribution to Europe and to history, falls into a somewhat different category.

Ostpolitik is indeed a simple label for a foreign-policy concept with a fairly concise purpose (the West German diplomatic opening to the East), but in fact it has been a continuing process, the pursuit of a broad political strategy that still goes on, not some concerted political-diplomatic drive focused on a single objective. It is the difference between putting together a jumbo jigsaw puzzle and carving a piece of wood. Ever since the mid-1960s, when *Ostpolitik* became part of the proclaimed foreign policy of the Bonn government, its execution has required a very cautious matching and fitting of diplomatic moves in the capitals of both the Warsaw Pact and the NATO Alliance, along with ever-present considerations of internal German politics. No foreign policy is any better than its domestic political support. There have been pitfalls and dangers every step of the way in *Ostpolitik* for the Bonn government, at home and in every capital, East and West, suspicions, opposition and antagonisms to be overcome along with applause and enthusiasm that often could be just as misleading as hostility. The pieces had to be assembled slowly, prudently, from endless diplomatic conversations, tireless negotiating, exhaustive analysis, patient explanations and courageous leadership. Many in West Germany contributed to the process. But Willy Brandt brought it all together, gave it direction and continuity for seven years, and in particular provided the political momentum and drive. It was Brandt who built *Ostpolitik* into German foreign policy.

When the Berlin Wall went up, in August 1961, both East and West were locked in various fixed positions of foreign policy, icebergs of the Cold War. Berlin of course was the centerpiece, the biggest iceberg or rock of all. To a large degree, the Cold War was fought out around Berlin: the twenty-year effort by the Soviet Union to extinguish the Allied presence in the city and absorb it completely into the East German Communist state, countered by Western determination not to yield, but to stand firm, in the full realization that to surrender West Berlin would be not merely a tactical loss but a strategic defeat. Yet once the Berlin Wall went up, the Soviets had accepted a stalemate, whether they realized it or not. To be sure, they went relentlessly on for most of the decade of the 1960s with a kind of mechanical pursuit of their aim of forcing the Allies out, but it was a mindless, pointless, hopeless effort. The long-term problem facing the three Western Allies and the mayor of Berlin was how to get the Russians to acknowledge the self-evident stalemate and move on to some kind of agreement or arrangement that would openly recognize and accept the realities of the *status quo:* the permanence of the Western Allied presence, the links between West Berlin and the Federal Republic of Germany, and the right of unrestricted access in and out of the city over agreed and defined air corridors, rail connections, canals and waterways, and the autobahns. Put another way around, since a stalemate had clearly been reached in the Cold War in Berlin with the building of the Wall, how could this reality be used as a *dégel* focal point of *détente*. As the Wall grew in physical ugliness and in the psychological, political and morale effect on the Berliners, Brandt brooded unceasingly over what could be done. The Western Allies did nothing when the Wall went up, and although they stood firm inside the Wall in West Berlin like Beau Geste in his desert fort, there was no sign in Washington, Paris or London of any initiative looking beyond the Wall. So, breaching the Wall became the starting point for *Ostpolitik*.

But there were other realities, other fixed positions, other rigid attitudes to be overcome as well. The first of these was the frozen policy of the Federal Republic under Adenauer on recognition of the Communist German Democratic Republic. This had been enshrined almost from the birth of the Bonn government in what was called the Hallstein Doctrine, formulated by the first State Secretary of the reconstituted German Foreign Ministry, Walter Hallstein. With Adenauer's enthusiastic approval, Hallstein decreed that there could be no diplomatic recognition whatsoever by West Germany of the East German puppet regime, and that West Germany would have no diplomatic relations with any government that did recognize East Germany. Behind the Hallstein Doctrine was the aspiration of German reunification, the belief and fervent hope that the Federal Republic, a true democracy risen out of the Nazi ashes, was the only government that could or should speak for a reunited Germany. Any recognition of East Germany would of course be tantamount to recognition of the division of Germany—a political impossibility in Adenauer's time.

All the NATO Allies lined up solidly behind Bonn on the Hallstein Doctrine, and refused any dealings with the East German state. Secretary of State John Foster Dulles, with his dreams of "rolling back" the Communist regimes of Eastern Europe, was in enthusiastic accord. The most extreme application of the Hallstein Doctrine came in the case of Yugoslavia. After Tito's break with Stalin, diplomatic relations were established between Bonn and Belgrade, in the mid-1950s. But in 1958, as a gesture to Moscow in the post-Stalin period, Tito then established diplomatic relations with East Germany as well as Bonn. The West German ambassador was promptly withdrawn from Belgrade under the Hallstein Doctrine, and relations were reduced to a trade mission and consular offices. Similarly, all over the world in the 1950s, West Germany threw its weight everywhere to isolate East Germany from all international diplomatic recognition.

The sole exception to the Hallstein Doctrine had been West Germany's establishment of diplomatic relations with the Soviet Union, agreed to by Adenauer in 1955 after a historic and stormy visit to Moscow at the invitation of the Russians. Adenauer justified the move on three grounds. First, he got the release of some ten thousand German prisoners of war who had spent more than ten years in Soviet labor camps. Next, there was the indisputable fact that Russia was one of the occupying powers of Germany. And finally, Adenauer sought to outflank East Germany by going over its head to establish diplomatic relations in Moscow. Thus, despite his Cold War rigidity, Adenauer, the realist, had already opened up an essential channel for *Ostpolitik* a decade before it became German policy.

In the meantime, throughout the decade of the 1950s and into the 1960s, West Germany found wide support in the world behind the Hallstein Doctrine. It was an easy way for governments also to demonstrate against Soviet aggressive pressures on Berlin, and in any case nobody could pretend that the East German Government was anything but an imposed regime kept in power by Soviet occupation troops with a record of squalid servitude to Moscow, despicable before its own people. It still is. But the Soviet Union fought back in every capital and every United Nations forum on behalf of its puppet. It was essential to Soviet policy to end the pariah isolation of East Germany in order to consolidate the Warsaw Pact system and establish the permanent division of Germany.

At the same time, other claimants pressed against Germany from Eastern Europe—the Poles in particular, who wanted permanent acceptance by West Germany of the Oder-Neisse frontier and the incorporation of what used to be German Silesia and the old Free City of Danzig into Poland. The Czechs wanted West Germany to expunge the Munich agreement from the records of history by some act or declaration. Russia insisted on West German recognition of its annexation of East Prussia.

The Hallstein Doctrine had kept all these problems bottled up, locked in the files, sitting on the shelf of history. But, all in all, there were the elements of a bargain to be struck: abandonment of the Hallstein Doctrine by the Federal Republic and the NATO Allies and diplomatic recognition for East Germany, in return for Soviet recognition of Western rights in West Berlin and the links and access of the city to West Germany. Here was the core of *Ostpolitik,* the nucleus around which West Germany could take the diplomatic initiative. She had something to give the Soviet Union, that was certain, but what would the Soviet Union give in return? That was the question.

"Above and beyond the German question, we felt it impossible to persevere in a simple acceptance of prevailing conditions in Europe," wrote Brandt. "What really mattered was to create a climate in which the *status quo* would be changed—in other words, improved—by peaceful means. I was unjustly accused, both then and later, of 'bowing to realities.' I was, and still am, of the opinion that realities can be influenced for the better only if they are taken into account. An essential ingredient of *Ostpolitik* was that we applied ourselves to our own affairs in a new and more positive manner instead of relying solely on others to speak for us. That meant that, while remaining in touch with our Allies and retaining their confidence, we became the advocate of our own interests *vis-à-vis* Eastern Europe."

But the idea of Germans talking independently to Russians was not all that popular in Washington or other NATO capitals. In historic terms, it raised the specter of the Rapallo Pact, of 1922—not to mention the infamous Nazi agreement between Ribbentrop and Molotov in August of 1939, which triggered World War II. Despite the fact that these past strokes of German diplomacy bore no relation or valid comparison to the conditions and political realities of the 1960s, the parallel was all too easy to recall.

Brandt himself acknowledged that in Washington "it was clear that men like General Clay, John J. McCloy, Dean Acheson and last but not least the veteran trade union leader George Meany, were filled with concern. Acheson referred to 'an insane rush to Moscow.' George Ball had been one of our critics, but was among the first to recant. There were signs that substantial reservations persisted in the Defense and State departments." Brandt was fully aware from the outset that he would be threading his way through a political and diplomatic minefield. This was where his political record, his wide experience inside and outside Germany, his integrity, and the sense of personal trust he inspired became so vital to the success of *Ostpolitik*.

In 1961 and 1962, all Brandt could do was ruminate and wait, while Kennedy and Khrushchev continued to test each other. In the weeks immediately following the building of the Wall, Brandt still had an election campaign to fight against Adenauer for the

chancellorship of West Germany. He altered his campaign schedule to a grueling degree, leaving Berlin most mornings to fly to
election rallies in West Germany, returning to the city late every
night. *Der Alte* realized that Brandt was his first real challenger
since the first election, in 1949, and he pulled out all the stops.
Brandt did not really expect a victory in 1961, his first campaign
as the party's candidate, but he was shocked and bitter at the malicious way the campaign was fought against him personally, even
to his illegitimacy, with Adenauer taking the lead. It was during
this period that he went to the courts in libel actions to keep the
record straight on his wartime activities in Norway and Sweden.
When the votes were counted on September 17, 1961, he had
carried the SPD to a new high, from 31.8 to 36.3 percent of the
vote, and from 169 to 190 Bundestag seats—a very substantial
gain. Adenauer and the CDU had dropped 8 percentage points
and were down from 270 to 241 seats. In order to remain Chancellor, Adenauer was forced to form a coalition with the Free
Democratic Party.

Brandt of course remained mayor of Berlin, to cope with the
considerable economic, physical, political, security and morale
problems facing the city in the aftermath of the Wall. But in Bonn
there was an important change at the Foreign Ministry. It went to
Gerhard Schroeder. Although of Adenauer's party, he was a man
with a mind of his own, prepared to move away from some of the
old Chancellor's rigid positions. He spoke of "a foreign policy of
the possible" and the need to take steps to improve conditions for
the people of East Germany. Although he produced no dramatic
changes or shifts, he did change the atmosphere in which German
foreign policy operated. He opened up subjects and possibilities
that had been closed, and Schroeder's cautious first steps laid the
groundwork for what eventually was proclaimed as *Ostpolitik*.

Little could be done diplomatically by anybody while the superpowers continued on their collision course over Cuba. In West
Berlin there were serious concerns in 1961 and 1962 that the
Soviets might mount a military surprise attack that would snuff out
the city in a matter of hours, before the West could be alerted to
respond. Western aircraft were regularly buzzed in the air corridors
by Soviet fighters—on one occasion General Clay's aircraft with

Brandt on board. One nightmare scenario for which Allied forces tried to prepare was the possibility of Russians and East Germans using the Berlin S-Bahn underground-elevated system, running through both halves of the city but controlled and operated out of East Berlin, to move troops early one morning into the heart of West Berlin and seize key points in an instant takeover. Beneath the general calm, there were very real tensions always.

I had gone to Berlin in August of 1961, when the Wall went up, and was back in the city for three months in the run-up to the Cuban crisis, covering the running harassments and minor confrontations and ingenious escapes which were the daily life of the police, the people and the Allies. Most of the confrontations were utterly frivolous, always artificial but constantly menacing—for example, the appearance of Soviet armored personnel carriers in West Berlin to transport the regular honor guard to the Soviet War Memorial in the Tiergarten, instead of bringing the soldiers through the Wall by bus. McGeorge Bundy, President Kennedy's national security adviser, visited the city at this time to confer with Brandt, and in a public speech made a pointed reference to American readiness to use nuclear weapons. We got into a sharp argument in private during his visit as to why United States Air Force planes were not sent to patrol the Berlin air corridors to confront the Russians decisively with the realities of the game they were playing. I did not know (nor at that point did Bundy or President Kennedy) that the showdown would finally come not in Berlin but in Cuba.

On October 22, 1962, Kennedy's Cuban-crisis address was broadcast over the Voice of America at midnight, Berlin time. Brandt listened at his home, together with Allan Lightner, American Minister in Berlin, and through Lightner sent an immediate message to the White House thanking the President for underscoring the Berlin commitment in the speech and asserting that "we are ready to share the consequences." Both Washington and Berlin braced for the possibility of the Russians' responding to American pressure in Cuba with some decisive counterstroke in Berlin. But it never came. One reason certainly was the fact that the entire NATO Alliance in Europe had gone on a partial military alert along with the United States, so that the response to any sudden attempt to nip off Berlin could have been swift and decisive. Instead, the Russians removed their missiles from Cuba, and the Berlin crisis finally defused and deflated at the same time.

The worst was over, but the Wall remained. Soviet policy toward Berlin, conducted by its East German military puppets, continued in the same menacing momentum even though the fangs had clearly been drawn by the Cuban crisis and the East-West stalemate was more evident than ever. To visitors (of whom I was one), Brandt talked calmly, pragmatically, unemotionally, realistically of trying to do something to ease the lot of the people who had been decimated by the building of the Wall: the separated families, the ending of all intercity commerce, the old people who could not see their children. It was impossible even to make a phone call from West Berlin to East Berlin. He did not yet talk about *Ostpolitik,* which was still in the gestation stage, and there was nothing grandiose in his approach to the realities. But his thrust was clear: maybe the Allies could sit and wait, but as mayor of Berlin he had to think of the people, and he had to try any avenue open to do something about the consequences of the Wall.

For months it was like talking to the Wall itself. But conditions were changing. First of all, there were City Senate elections in West Berlin early in 1963, and whatever bitterness Brandt may have felt over the 1961 campaign was wiped clean when he soared to a massive victory of 62 percent of the popular vote. President Kennedy made his famous visit to the city—his *"Ich bin ein Berliner"* speech to an ecstatic multitude in front of the Schoeneberg Rathaus, the most tumultuous welcome Berlin has given anyone since the war. Then, soon after the Berlin visit, Kennedy took Khrushchev on the rebound from the Cuban crisis to conclude a treaty banning above-ground nuclear testing. The Cold War had begun to melt away into greater diplomatic opportunity for everybody—including the mayor of Berlin. In October of 1963, old Chancellor Adenauer was finally pushed into retirement, as he neared his eighty-eighth birthday. In November, the world was shocked and stunned by the Kennedy assassination. In the grief-stricken aftermath of Kennedy's death came the first break for Brandt over the Wall.

For months, the mayor of Berlin had been bombarding the East German authorities both publicly and in private messages for some opening of the Wall. He used the International Red Cross, church contacts, West German businessmen who traveled through the Wall, and a few key city officials who went over to conduct official business on mundane matters such as water, sewage disposal and fiscal dealings between the two halves of the city. Western journalists of course could also cross into East Berlin and even occasionally see East German officials—and it was a journalist who first brought word back to Brandt that the East German authorities were hinting at willingness at last to talk. Soon after, more detailed and specific information was passed by the East Germans through a West German businessman to the Commercial Department of the West Berlin city administration. Finally, on December 5, 1963, twelve days after the Kennedy assassination, Brandt received a formal letter from a deputy chairman of the Council of Ministers of the German Democratic Republic proposing a temporary arrangement to grant special permits to West Berliners to visit East Berlin for a limited period of time.

It was obvious that the East Germans had a double purpose in their move: to use this humanitarian gesture to maneuver for diplomatic recognition. But Brandt was neither deterred nor afraid of negotiating around this booby trap, and he plunged ahead at once. In fact, he had almost more trouble with the West German Government, in Bonn, behind his back, than with the East Germans. Negotiations opened on December 12, and in five days, seven meetings, thirty hours of talks, an agreement was hammered out to open the Wall on December 18 for three weeks over Christmas. To sidestep the recognition issue, the passes were issued by East German postal workers, who crossed to West Berlin and set up shop at specified post offices in West Berlin! In other words, the passes were made a postal arrangement, not a diplomatic or visa arrangement. More than 1.2 million West Berliners made the crossing, loaded with Christmas gifts and food and drink.

Again I was back in Berlin, for the opening of the Wall, and spent a dreary New Year's Eve in East Berlin, deep snow and bitter cold, being turned away from its handful of restaurants and beer-halls after glimpses of jam-packed morose celebrants, until I finally gave up and drove back through the Wall to the bright lights of Kurfürestendamm. The worst was when the Wall closed at midnight on January 5, 1964, and newsmen and photographers gathered to watch the West Berliners streaming home, sobbing and waving farewells to relatives and friends who had come to the barriers to say good-bye, not knowing if they would ever see each other again. Then the Vopos moved back and the prison gates clanged shut. But this was not a prison of criminals. It was a prison of 17 million people whose only crime was a belief in freedom, for which they were condemned by their Communist overlords to a permanent life in the world's biggest jail.

Nevertheless, the Wall had at last been breached. The pass agreement was renewed in the spring of 1964 for two weeks and again at Christmas; at Easter and Christmas in 1965; and for the same periods in 1966. But in 1967, by which time Willy Brandt had become Foreign Minister in Bonn and was throwing his full weight and energies into *Ostpolitik,* the East Germans paradoxically refused to renew the pass agreement and the Wall remained closed to West Berliners for another five years. The reason, however, was not that hard to figure out. With the advent of a full-blown *Ostpolitik,* the Berlin problem became a major bargaining card, a matter of key negotiating importance not only between Germans but, more important, between East and West. So, not for the first time, the Communist side promptly suppressed any humanitarian considerations in the interests of its bargaining position.

Meanwhile, election time, every four years in West Germany, again rolled around for September 1965. Erich Ollenhauer, the SPD party leader, had died at the end of 1963, and Brandt was now both party leader and party candidate for Chancellor. With Adenauer also gone, he was pitted against Ludwig Erhard, the "economic miracle man" of West Germany.

Brandt campaigned vigorously up and down West Germany, with development of relations to the East a constant theme. There was never any one speech in which *Ostpolitik* was suddenly proclaimed, like the New Deal or the Truman Doctrine or the Marshall Plan. Rather, it grew out of a kind of litany of phrases and references to "doing what we can to normalize relations" or the need to "ease the conditions of life for the East Germans" or, in another formulation: "The problem is to stabilize the *status quo* in the military sense in order to secure the necessary freedom of maneuver for the political conquest of the *status quo*." Brandt of course had the success of the Wall passes to point to as his contribution to the process. By now, in 1965, *détente* was becoming everybody's policy catchword. But, in the case of West Germany, it was clear that *détente* would mean sacrifices of past policies and ideas. Brandt, in both speeches and actions, was really engaged in a patient, persuasive, educative process of politics. He was building *Ostpolitik* slowly into public thinking and acceptance, not by dramatic exhortation or proclaiming a goal that many Germans would have rejected, since it ultimately involved German renunciation of German territory, but by careful explanation and a persuasion to understanding. He clearly captured the high ground of statesmanship and leadership in the 1965 campaign, but it was not high enough to capture the outcome.

Erhard, for all the opprobrium that was being heaped on him by old Adenauer in bitter retirement, and for all the imagery of a *Gummilöwe* (rubber lion) which he bore, ran a campaign of unruffled calm—rather like Harold Macmillan's "You never had it so good" winning tactic in the British election of 1959. Germany was prosperous and doing well, and Erhard, after all, had been Economic Minister ever since 1949—so he couldn't be all that wrong. He almost coasted home, boosting the CDU vote more than a million higher than what Adenauer polled in 1961. Brandt and the SPD in fact gained even more—1.4 million votes—but Brandt was deeply disappointed and depressed at failure to achieve victory. In fact, he was closer to power than he realized.

In Bonn, Erhard formed a new government, again in coalition with the small, liberal Free Democratic Party, and Brandt returned to Berlin to lick his wounds. But the Soviet Union had clearly been monitoring the political trends in the Federal Republic and the speeches of the mayor of Berlin. In the spring of 1966, Brandt received overtures from East Berlin for a meeting with the Soviet ambassador to East Germany, Pyotr Abrasimov. It was a move that could only have come on instructions from the

Kremlin. Brandt was ready, but simply to arrange a first meeting entailed a whole web of diplomatic negotiations and discussions in which the Swedish consul general in West Berlin, Sven Backlund, played a key role. It had to be a closely held secret, and Brandt first consulted privately and personally with the West German Foreign Minister, Gerhard Schroeder, who gave his blessing and left the mayor free to handle it as he saw fit. The British and the French, secretly informed, had no misgivings, but the American reaction was more cautious and suspicious, with various warnings of what might be discussed and what should be avoided. Brandt, for his part, was at pains to assure that it was the Russians who asked for the meeting, not himself, and that he would be received not only as mayor of Berlin but also in his capacity as leader of the West German SPD. At the same time, he insisted that he would meet Abrasimov not as ambassador to East Germany but as the representative of one of the four occupying powers with responsibility for Greater Berlin. These niceties were tedious but absolutely essential. After the Khrushchev bluster, at the time of the building of the Wall, about liquidating four-power responsibilities for Berlin and turning over Soviet powers to East Germany, it was vital to reestablish and reengage the Soviet Union in this fashion. And in fact, the Abrasimov visit to Brandt really marked the end of the Khrushchev campaign, two years after Khrushchev himself had been dethroned in Moscow. The first meeting took place in total secrecy at Backlund's Berlin residence on May 8, 1966—the twenty-first anniversary of Germany's unconditional surrender.

As often happens in such affairs with the Soviet Union, the opening up of the channel was of greater importance than anything that was actually discussed. A second meeting took place a month later, this time quite openly during a reception at Backlund's residence on Sweden's National Day—a "casual contact," prearranged, which lasted more than an hour. They then met three more times during 1966. On one occasion Brandt drove through the Wall during one of the "pass periods" to have dinner at the Soviet embassy. He had flatly refused to cross over by special arrangement when the Wall was closed to West Berliners. On each of these occasions, Abrasimov urged Brandt to visit Moscow. The talk was seldom more than diplomatic sparring, with the Russian seemingly intent on testing and probing Brandt's feelings and basic positions. For his part, Brandt was in no hurry and had nothing to give or propose except to press for continued amelioration of the conditions imposed by the Wall. But it was a contact of key importance in things to come.

Meanwhile, the political swing toward the SPD, which the 1965 elections had shown, was repeated in various elections at state level in 1966, and by late in the year the Erhard coalition was in trouble. In early November, the FDP abruptly pulled out of the government, after which Erhard informed his party executive that he would resign the chancellorship if an alternative government could be formed. Adenauer, still alive, was determined to give Erhard the shove. Interparty consultations went on for two weeks. The outcome, at long last, was a "Grand Coalition" between the two major parties: the CDU and the SPD. Brandt, oddly enough, was at first against the idea and dubious, fearful that the SPD had already swung far enough away from its identity as a working-class party and that going into a coalition with the CDU might dilute its image and appeal still further. But the party leadership in Bonn insisted. Kurt Georg Kiesinger, of the CDU, became Chancellor, with Willy Brandt as Vice-Chancellor and Minister of Foreign Affairs.

By this time in West Germany the consensus support behind a more open, direct and positive policy toward Eastern Europe had widened and grown considerably—thanks to Schroeder's tenure at the Foreign Ministry along with Brandt's activities as Berlin mayor and leader of the SPD. Even Adenauer, in retirement, was talking about how the Russians had been "mishandled" and the need to be more open and realistic. President Charles de Gaulle had perhaps unwittingly contributed to the movement of German opinion by his own foray to Moscow in the spring of 1966. As a result, the new Grand Coalition was probably more united on foreign policy than on any other matter, the aims of its *Ostpolitik* succinctly summarized by Brandt:

"The new government must take steps to normalize our relations with the countries of Eastern Europe and secure a reconciliation with our neighbors in the East. It must define our internal scope for dealings with the rulers of East Berlin and exploit it to the full."

This formulation clearly held back on straight recognition of the East German regime and placed inter-German relations in a different category from relations with other countries of the Warsaw Pact. This was both a political and a tactical necessity, but it was also an approach that roused resentments and suspicions in Moscow. It would be a long and intricate uphill climb to "normalization" of Bonn's relations with Eastern Europe, but at least the goal was clearly set, with both major parties backing it and Brandt in charge of the march.

Schroeder had already laid the groundwork for quietly putting the Hallstein Doctrine to rest. A visit to Bonn by Romanian Foreign Minister Cornelius Manescu and the establishment of diplomatic relations with Bucharest was set for the end of January 1967. A few months later, Czechoslovakia indicated its willingness to exchange trade missions with West Germany as a first step toward diplomatic relations. In early 1968, relations between Bonn and Belgrade were restored to full ambassadorial level after the Hallstein Doctrine break ten years before.

"Not one of our *démarches* in Eastern and Southern Europe took the Soviet authorities by surprise. At no time did we try to conduct an *Ostpolitik* behind the Soviet Union's back. Our sense of priorities prohibited any such lack of realism," Brandt wrote subsequently. Nevertheless, he very quickly encountered a Soviet chill and hard-line response to his first moves, which he attributed entirely to the fact that "we underestimated the influence of East Germany when we persisted in refusing to treat it as a country of equal standing." The initial spurt in *Ostpolitik* in Bucharest, Prague and Belgrade therefore slowed down. Warsaw, Budapest and Sofia would take longer, and diplomatic relations between Bonn and East Berlin longer still. Moreover, the whole question of recognition for East Germany was interlocked with the problem of Berlin—and this in turn was a matter of four-power negotiations between the Western Allies and the Soviet Union, not a matter for the Bonn government. Thus, by 1968, Brandt had gone about as far as he could go in "normalization" of relations with Eastern Europe, and the Warsaw Pact governments in turn had gone

about as far as the Soviet Union would allow them to go in meeting Brandt halfway. The key lay in Berlin—and how to nudge the
United States, Britain and France into a four-power negotiation
with the Soviet Union to resolve the problems of the status of the
city once and for all.

Here Brandt's channel through Abrasimov finally came into
play. In one of their conversations in the spring of 1968, Brandt
again raised, as he always did, the Berlin problem: the refusal of
the East German authorities to renew the Wall pass agreement,
the continued harassment of motorists at the autobahn check-
points, the advantages both humanitarian and economic of finding
some normalization. One idea that Brandt threw out, from his new
vantage point as West German Foreign Minister, was that instead
of charging a toll fee for every individual automobile driving from
West Germany to West Berlin, why not an annual lump-sum fee
for use of the highway, which the federal government would pay to
East Germany? Abrasimov's response this time was open. It could
be discussed.

Brandt took this as a positive sign that the Soviet Union was at
last ready for a serious Berlin negotiation. Shortly after this talk
with the Russian, he journeyed to the semiannual NATO Foreign
Ministers meeting, which, in June of 1968, was held in Iceland, at
the capital, Reykjavík. These meetings are always preceded, the
evening before they open, by a "Four Power Dinner"—American,
British, French and West German ministers—to discuss Berlin and
the specific problems of the Federal Republic. Brandt now reported to the other three the conversation with Abrasimov, and
Soviet readiness to consider a change in the arrangements for pay-
ing the autobahn tolls, which appeared also to indicate a readiness
to negotiate other things as well. He urged the three Western Allies to take the initiative and propose four-power talks on Berlin.
Secretary of State Dean Rusk commented that "if this came off it
would be a major step forward," and they agreed to put experts to
work on a concerted move.

But, a month later, Soviet tanks rolled into the streets of Prague
and extinguished the brave, short-lived rule of Alexander Dubček.
In the immediate aftermath, although there was no response of intervention that the NATO powers could or would make to this So-

viet aggression against one of its own Allies, *Ostpolitik* and the possibilities for a Berlin initiative went back on the shelf. In West Germany, the last thing anybody was ready to talk about now was recognition of East Germany. East-West relations in general simply went into stalemate after the invasion of Czechoslovakia. Other things were happening, of course. The events of May 1968 in Paris had undermined General de Gaulle's dominance of his nation and his power to influence the European scene. Richard Nixon defeated Hubert Humphrey in the American presidential election of 1968, on a campaign slogan of moving from "an era of confrontation to an era of negotiation" with the Soviet Union. When Nixon took office, the Berlin dossier was waiting for attention.

President Nixon made a quick trip to Europe, in February 1969, and included the ritual stop in Berlin on his itinerary, complete with a viewing of the Wall. At Brandt's suggestion, Nixon included in his remarks in Berlin a call for negotiation "to end the tensions of a bygone period." But this was not enough to prod Moscow. In April of 1969, at the regular NATO meeting, on this occasion in Washington for the twentieth anniversary of the Alliance, Brandt finally got the United States, British and French Foreign Ministers to agree firmly on making a proposal to Moscow. It took another two months to work out the details, but on July 6, 1969, the three Allied ambassadors in Moscow formally informed the Soviet Government that they wanted talks on four-power arrangements in Berlin and that the Bonn government, for its part, was prepared to conduct parallel discussions with the East German Government on traffic problems with the city. The joint approach, in short, opened up the prospect of diplomatic recognition of East Germany but linked it firmly to a Berlin settlement. The Soviet Government gave an affirmative response two months later, in September, and after preparatory exchanges on essential matters of agenda and procedure, Berlin talks finally opened on March 26, 1970, in the Allied Control Commission headquarters in West Berlin, where Marshal Sokolovsky had staged his walkout in March 1948 leading to the Berlin blockade.

In the meantime, the most important event of 1969 for Willy Brandt was the national election, on September 27. It was, as

Wellington said of the Battle of Waterloo, "A damn' close-run thing," in which the CDU under Kiesinger came in with 46 percent of the vote. The SPD under Brandt pulled up to nearly 43 percent, and the Free Democrats, whose key figure was Walter Scheel, held the balance with just under 6 percent. On this close result, Nixon, on bad advice in Washington, sent a hasty telegram of congratulations to Kiesinger. But while the message was on its way, Brandt and Scheel were on the telephone agreeing to form a left-of-center coalition. Willy Brandt became federal Chancellor on October 21, 1969.

Brandt moved into the Chancellor's office under a full head of steam, determined to stir things into action in all directions after the near halt of the upheavals and troubles following that violent year of 1968. With Berlin talks at last getting in motion, Brandt in his first major move as Chancellor wisely turned to his *Westpolitik,* rather than his *Ostpolitik.* General de Gaulle had departed and been succeeded by Georges Pompidou, and the time was ripe at last for a major diplomatic effort to overcome the long French veto against British entry into Europe. Moreover, in Brandt's view the enlargement of the European Economic Community was an essential counterpart to his *Ostpolitik*—a necessary reassurance to Bonn's partners in Western Europe that the Federal Republic intended to play a dynamic role, that its commitments were as firm as they were under Adenauer, that Germany was not tilting off into some neutralist posture of trying to play a middle-European balancing act between East and West or flirting with any ideas like Rapallo all over again. Therefore, at a Common Market Summit Conference at The Hague in December 1969, Brandt, in one of the most forceful and eloquent foreign policy statements of his long career, called for negotiations to begin promptly in the new year on enlargement of the Community. The French maneuvered a tactical rear-guard skirmish for the sake of Gaullist opinion in Paris, but the key was turned and the door opened to Britain at last.

Meanwhile, he had made preliminary moves of his own to grasp the most difficult nettles of all in *Ostpolitik*—Poland and East Germany. By various public declarations and private messages, Brandt had declared his readiness to talk to the East Germans, and they had then sought the initiative by forwarding to Bonn their own draft of a treaty between the two Germanies, which they knew would be unacceptable. But Brandt came back with a letter direct to Willi Stoph, head of the East German Government. In mid-February, with the four-power Berlin talks soon to open, Stoph replied, proposing direct negotiations.

Brandt responded almost immediately with a telex message to East Berlin on February 18, asking for a face-to-face meeting without preconditions to get a negotiation moving. After three weeks of back-and-forth, this breakthrough in East-West German relations was finally arranged: A summit meeting between Willy Brandt and Willi Stoph in the East German city of Erfurt on March 19, 1970. In political, diplomatic and emotional impact for the Germans at that time, it was comparable to Egyptian President Anwar el-Sadat's visit to Jerusalem to meet Menachem Begin and address the Israeli Knesset, in 1977.

Brandt traveled by special train direct to Erfurt, which is close to the border between the two Germanies. A high point of his stay of about fifteen hours in the city was his appearance at his hotel window before a spontaneous and cheering East German crowd. The visit had been carefully programed to avoid the public, and apparently the East German authorities thought that since they had not organized or ordered any crowds, there wouldn't be any. Brandt went to the window, but far from waving or grinning in triumph, he gazed down on the East Germans with a look of solemn sympathy and gestured ever so slightly, like some benediction, for them to show restraint, and then retreated back into his room. The police arrived to move the crowd away, and when Brandt came out it had been replaced with a hastily assembled communist rent-a-crowd waving banners calling for diplomatic recognition of their state.

The exchanges between Brandt and Stoph were not much more than a face-to-face restatement of positions with much polemic thrown in, along with an intricate argument, which Brandt led, on the nature and need for a special relationship between two halves of one nation, one people with differing social and economic systems. But it was a turning point simply because the meeting took place at all. They had agreed in advance that a second round of talks would take place in West Germany, at the city of Kassel, three months later.

At Kassel, the polemics from Stoph were harsher than ever. Brandt clearly had the East Germans on the defensive after his appearance at Erfurt. So they pounded the table, demanding that a treaty be concluded at once which would accord them full diplomatic recognition as a sovereign state. In the end, Brandt replied with blunt finality: "Do you under present circumstances believe that any treaty between our two states is practicable, and can be approved and accepted by the alliances in Europe and the countries outside those alliances, which does not declare and affirm that the existing four-power agreements on Germany and Berlin will be respected? Where in your treaty is there any discernible readiness for practical cooperation and the development of relations to the common benefit of the citizens of our states—of the Germans, on whose behalf it is our duty to act? If it is possible to answer these questions, it would also be possible in the course of time to solve the question which you refer to as the legal recognition of the German Democratic Republic."

One small incident took place during the Kassel meeting, Brandt later recounted to a friend, that was highly revealing and almost humorous. Brandt had listened with grim dismay to Stoph deliver, for the record, his long, prepared, polemic denunciation of the Bonn government and its policies. When it was over, Brandt simply proposed that they take a short break. At this point Stoph responded: "Yes, let's take a walk in the garden," and then waved the other members of his delegation aside, took Brandt by the arm and almost shouted: "We don't need interpreters—we both speak German." Out into the garden they went, and when they were alone and out of earshot of the others, Stoph muttered to Brandt in an agitated manner: "Please, no matter what we say, keep the trade going." The West Germans knew full well that their credits and trade were a major prop to the East German economy. Brandt did keep the trade going, but the polemics at the Kassel meeting were too much to plaster over, and there was not even any agreement on a final communiqué after the meeting. In fact, for the rest of the decade of the 1970s the heads of the two Germanies never met again.

The Erfurt and Kassel meetings had at least made it clear to the East German regime that there was no shortcut—no Berlin agreement, no recognition. Meanwhile Brandt had gotten a favorable response from the Poles to his overtures for a treaty negotiation, and a senior official of the Foreign Ministry had been to Warsaw to exchange preliminary positions and demands. In a significant move at the outset, the Poles dropped a previous insistence that Bonn must also accord recognition to East Germany in the process of establishing relations with Poland. But although a Polish negotiation was now underway, the Foreign Ministry at this point strongly urged on Brandt that he had gone as far as he should go in dealings with the Eastern European states, that suspicions might be rising in Moscow, and he should therefore go to the heart of the matter and first conclude a treaty with the Soviet Union. He took the advice. By now, the four-power Berlin talks were underway, and in June of 1970, Brandt dispatched his closest adviser, Egon Bahr, to Moscow to undertake the preliminaries on a treaty negotiation.

The Soviet Union was more than ready to come to a rapid agreement with Brandt and West Germany—a haste which, in fact, upset the Western Allies, who were having a hard slog over a Berlin agreement with the Russians and were concerned and not a little irritated that Brandt was moving too far out in front, going too fast, getting out of step with what should be a carefully coordinated-across-the-board diplomatic process. Not only were the Russians playing tough in the Berlin talks; it was also very slow going between the United States and the Soviet Union in negotiations for the first Strategic Arms Limitation Treaty, which had begun in Helsinki in November of 1969. Dr. Henry A. Kissinger in Washington was irritated at Brandt, feeling that he was unwittingly being used by the Russians, for which his Allies would have to pay a price.

The Russians, for their part, by now were maneuvering and campaigning to push the *détente* process forward once again with a primary objective of expunging the Prague invasion in a whitewash of improved East-West relations. Therefore, their opposition to Brandt's *Ostpolitik* of the early period in 1967 and 1968 had turned to enthusiasm and welcome. Moreover, by 1970 they had also begun to push determinedly all over Europe to convene a European Security Conference to negotiate a broad pan-European agreement which would in effect constitute acceptance and endorsement of the *status quo* in Europe—its borders and its political division. German support for such a conference was clearly crucial. The United States was highly skeptical but the Europeans in general were much less so. At any rate, Brandt was welcome in Moscow.

In remarkably short order, after so many years of virulent polemic hostility, the Soviet Union and the Federal Republic of Germany almost rushed to agreement on a treaty renouncing the use of force against each other, pledging respect for the territorial integrity of all European states and an acceptance of the map of Europe as it stood. The treaty language thus circumvented the issue of recognition of East Germany but constituted an acceptance by West Germany of all the borders that had been drawn as a result of World War II. Brandt went to Moscow for a signing ceremony on August 12, 1970.

His assurance to his Western Allies—whose irritations and concerns had been communicated to Bonn—took a very simple form. The Soviet-German Friendship Treaty could not be ratified, he told Leonid I. Brezhnev, until the conclusion of a four-power agreement on the status of Berlin and a parallel agreement between Bonn and East Germany on access arrangements for German traffic to the city.

This done, Brandt again turned to Poland. Somewhat outmaneuvered, the Poles would have liked more explicit language on the Oder-Neisse frontier, but they could not very well insist on something that the Russians had conceded. Brandt traveled to Warsaw to sign the treaty on December 7, 1970. The event was most remembered for the famous photo of Willy Brandt on his knees before the Jewish Memorial in the Warsaw Ghetto.

It had been a year of almost dazzling diplomatic achievement for Willy Brandt—and even those whose suspicions had been aroused by what seemed at times to be throwing caution to the winds could not, in the end, fail to accept and applaud the fashion in which he had skillfully altered the diplomatic posture and political image of the West German state *vis-à-vis* Eastern Europe

while at the same time enhancing and enlarging its relations with
its Western partners. By the end of 1970, Brandt had put into
place about all of the jigsaw pieces of *Ostpolitik* that were in his
power to sort out, and there remained only Berlin.

The negotiations were being conducted by the Big Four ambassadors in Germany—Pyotr Abrasimov, Kenneth Rush, Sir Roger
Jackling and Jean Sauvagnargues—closely monitored and instructed by a special Western group of four-power experts that
met usually in Washington or Bonn and was in turn guided by the
four governments (Germany sitting in with the three Western Allies, of course). If the machinery was cumbersome, it was necessary and effective. Sensing a major change in orientation of
Soviet policy toward Berlin, the Western Allies were not about to
make undue concessions or bargain away their rights, after all the
years of standing firm, simply to get an agreement in a hurry. So
the talks wound on slowly through 1970 and well into 1971.

By mid-1971 it was the Russians who at last were showing
signs of being in a hurry. They wanted a European Security Conference, and they wanted their treaty with West Germany ratified.
The Western Allies steadfastly refused to move forward on either
until a Berlin agreement securing the Western position in the city
once and for all, ending the harassments and threats of the Cold
War, was settled, signed, sealed and delivered. The end finally
came in August.

A session of the talks in late July had produced little movement, and the Western ambassadors had prepared vacation plans
when word came that the Russians wanted a meeting in mid-
August. Once again I took a plane for Berlin. At the American
Mission, where General Clay had fought the battle of the airlift, I
found an old acquaintance, a Russian-speaking American Foreign
Service officer whom I had known in Geneva and at other conferences. He could not, he said, tell me much about the substance of
what remained to be decided; it involved such mundane issues as
whether West Berliners were going to have some special type of
passport—but what he could say was that the negotiations were really at the end of the road. "From my experience with the Russians, I think you can take a fair bet that if the meeting goes into a
second day it will mean that we are on our way to a final agree-

ment," he said, "but if it breaks up after one day, then it will
mean that we've hit a major impasse from the Russians, maybe a
dead end or failure." His guidance was enough, as far as I was
concerned, to be able to write confidently when the meeting went
into a second day that agreement seemed to be in sight, while
others were writing gloomily about deepening deadlock and no
progress.

The talks went into a third day, dragged on through the afternoon, and then, as delegates worked into the summer evening,
food was delivered to the Allied Control Council Building, while
the press kept watch in the courtyard outside. The building, a kind
of Prussian baroque style, had housed the infamous Nazi Peoples
Court, where the plotters against Hitler had been tried and sentenced in 1944 and then taken away to be hung by piano wire
from meat hooks, in the most hideous end the Gestapo could de-
vise for them. It had been the scene of the Big Four conference in
the bitter-cold February of 1954, when John Foster Dulles battled
with Vyacheslav M. Molotov. Darkness came, and lights blazed
from the big second-floor room with its large french windows open
onto the courtyard. Suddenly, waiting below well after midnight,
we heard a burst of prolonged applause through the open windows. Berlin's long ordeal was over.

It was after 1 A.M. when the four ambassadors came out of
their meeting on August 19, 1971—ten years to the week after the
Wall had been thrown up in the center of Berlin. They were tired
after fourteen hours of continuous talking in that last session, but
smiling and satisfied. They had an agreement. A bright moon filled
the warm clear Berlin summer sky as I drove back to my hotel to
write and telephone a story to Los Angeles.

I had first flown into Berlin on an airlift cargo plane with a load
of coal in March of 1949, when the blockade was still at its
height, and I had then been on the first train into the city when the
blockade was lifted, two months later. Now I knew that I would
be saying, "Good-bye, Berlin," after nearly a quarter of a century
covering its bizarre happenings and ups-and-downs. By the luck of
assignments, I had been in and out of the city at almost every decisive turn or upheaval. It was like taking leave of a vast open-air
theater after the play is ended. "All the world's a stage, And all

the men and women merely players"—certainly Berlin. As a theatrical production, it had everything: Colorful uniforms of soldiers and officers of four armies deployed against a backdrop of the worst destruction of any city in Europe. Hundreds of airplanes filling the skies, tanks and jeeps and parades galore. Gunfire and sudden death, brave Scarlet Pimpernel escape-runners, student riots and cultural festivals. Opera singers, one of the world's greatest symphony orchestras, comedians, weird nightclubs, pompous publicity seekers at the Wall, politicians of every stamp and interest. A city full of characters out of Bertolt Brecht, George Grosz, Christopher Isherwood, Carl Zuckmayer, Thomas Mann. It had been high drama and low comedy. It had been heroic, pathetic, banal and tragic. It had been a mass morality play on the biggest stage in history, with the world watching. It was over, but it had been a great show while it lasted.

Two months after the Berlin negotiation was concluded, it was announced from Oslo that Willy Brandt would receive the Nobel Peace Prize for 1971—certainly one of the most widely acclaimed choices in the long and controversial history of the award. He had made *Ostpolitik* a part of history. He was at that time the most widely known, respected and popular leader and statesman in Europe, received and welcomed everywhere from Moscow to Washington. As a person, as a human being, he remained the same Willy Brandt of Lübeck and Norway and Sweden and Berlin. He walked with kings but never lost the common touch.

After the four-power agreement, the rest of the diplomatic jigsaw puzzle of *Ostpolitik* fell into place fairly quickly. Negotiations were rapidly concluded between the two Germanies on rail, road and waterway traffic and permanent arrangements for West Berliners to visit East Berlin. The agreement included a lump-sum annual payment for use of the Berlin autobahn, in place of individual car tolls, as Brandt had proposed to Abrasimov nearly four years before. Ratifications of the various treaties moved forward in 1972. The following year, the two German states joined the United Nations, and the Western powers began establishing embassies in East Berlin, granting the East German regime its long-sought diplomatic recognition. Respect, however, was another matter.

But, behind this record of success for *Ostpolitik* and Brandt's worldwide reputation as a statesman and democratic leader, things were not going well on the home front. Brandt was not the strongest or most efficient head of government, nor very deeply interested in economic problems, which inevitably spilled over into cabinet and domestic politics. His troublesome Minister of Economics and Finance, Karl Schiller, resigned from the cabinet in July of 1972, which was a relief and a blow in equal proportions. Brandt decided to go to the country a year earlier than the normal four-year Bundestag mandate, in order to renew and, he hoped, reinforce his victory of 1969.

On November 19, 1972, a record 91 percent of the German voters turned out at the polls, and Willy Brandt carried the Social Democratic Party to the front as the strongest party in Germany. Admittedly it was very narrow: 45.9 percent of the vote, against 44.8 percent for the Christian Democrats, with the Free Democrats holding the balance. But this translated into a forty-eight-seat coalition majority in the Bundestag. It was a solid victory for the moderate left-of-center social and economic policies of the SPD originating in the Bad Godesberg reform program of 1959, in which Brandt had a guiding hand, and a victory for the statesmanship, integrity, courage, vision and pragmatism of the party leader. Unhappily, Brandt did not enjoy it for very long.

At some point early in 1974, the West German counterintelligence service uncovered an East German spy in Brandt's personal entourage—a man named Günter Guillaume, whose assignment in the Chancellery was liaison officer between Brandt and SPD party headquarters. He had "escaped" to the West back in 1956 but had been an officer in the East German Army. He joined the SPD in Frankfurt and energetically worked his way into and up through the organization. A rather jovial, earthy character, he gained Brandt's confidence as a party man, and when the affair finally broke there were hints that an element of blackmail in Brandt's private life had figured in Guillaume's operation. In any case, Brandt was informed by his secret service but asked to play a double game and keep Guillaume in place while he was watched for his East German contacts. This cat-and-mouse affair went on for some time, apparently several months. But when the case finally broke with the arrest of Guillaume and his wife, it was a political disaster for Brandt. It came at a time, moreover, when party dissatisfaction with his internal leadership was mounting, and the charisma of *Ostpolitik* and his external leadership was fading. Suddenly it was time to go—and messy as it all was, Brandt went with dignity. There was much contrast in May of 1974 between Brandt's exit and the Nixon Watergate affair, which was then mounting to its agonizing climax.

Willy Brandt resigned as Chancellor of West Germany on May 7, 1974. He was succeeded ten days later by the SPD's powerful and pugnacious Hamburg leader, Helmut Schmidt. Brandt continued in the post of SPD chairman, the party's elder statesman. The spy Guillaume and his wife were given long jail sentences, and the East German Government was told forcefully not to try to bargain for their release. It was the ultimate irony that the man who had done more than any other political leader in West Germany since the war to stabilize relations with the communist world, gain the confidence of its leaders, and move Europe out of the Cold War through *Ostpolitik* and *détente* should in the end fall victim to that eternal, relentless, cheap crudity of the communist system: a spy in his private office.

Willy Brandt never complained and never explained. He was sixty-one years old, and he had lived a full and often turbulent political life of intense personal commitment and lonely effort. His place in history was established, and there was little he would have been likely to add to what he had already achieved. He had already spoken a suitable epitaph to his political journey in his typically simple and unadorned language when he went to Oslo to accept the Nobel Peace Prize in the Norway he loved, which had meant so much in his life:

"Germany has become reconciled with itself. It has returned to itself, just as this exile has been privileged to rediscover the peaceful and humane characteristics of his native land."

15
Edward Heath

EDWARD HEATH, THE PRIME MINISTER WHO FINALLY TOOK GREAT
Britain into Europe, was the first Conservative Party leader of
completely plebeian origins to occupy No. 10 Downing Street. His
father was a carpenter and his mother was a parlor maid. He was
a Conservative self-made man who devoted himself entirely to
politics and went to the top in a steady, determined and unremarkable rise, the way other men go up in the insurance business or a
military career or dentistry. From his schoolboy beginnings, Ted
Heath did everything well, but not brilliantly. His qualities were
thoroughness, toughness, dependability, hard work and single-
mindedness. He applied himself carefully and diligently to every
task at hand along the way, and he did not make mistakes. Nor
did he take chances. He did not encumber himself with friendships
or indulge in luxuries either material, temperamental or emotional. His progress to the top was as if on an up escalator instead
of scrambling up a ladder or even climbing stairs. There were no
great dramas or challenges or adventures or turning points or ups-
and-downs in Heath's political life—only ups, of methodical mechanical progress until the end, in 1975, when the Tory Party got
tired of his leadership after two election losses and unceremoni-
ously dumped him.

He practiced politics with devotion, but without passion. A
lifelong bachelor, apart from politics his only other interests
have been music and sailing. He won a musical scholarship to Oxford for his competence as an organist, and all his life he has conducted choirs and chamber and symphony orchestras. When he
was able eventually to buy a yacht, he became a skilled and determined sailor, competing and winning in top-category ocean yacht

racing. Yet these avocations seemed a reflection of his political
style and personality. He liked to direct, rather than lead—the detached hand waving the baton above the musicians, or moving the
tiller behind the yacht crew, no messing about, no doubt who's in
charge.

But Heath was the right man in the right place at the right time,
however brief his moment on the stage of history turned out to be.
Early in his political life (he entered the House of Commons in
1950, when Winston Churchill was still leading the Conservative
Party), he reached a firm conviction that Britain had to join
Europe. From his Westminster vantage point, he then watched the
halfhearted fumblings of his party, the bogus attempts, the compromises, mistakes and waverings, and during Macmillan's prime
ministership he was given the job of heading the negotiations in
Brussels in 1961–62 that ended when President de Gaulle barred
the way. But Heath came back from Brussels more determined
than ever that Britain must advance and was not to be kept permanently out. He succeeded to the Conservative Party leadership
in 1965, and when he then became Prime Minister, after a surprising election victory in 1969, he was in no doubt at all as to the first
priority of his government. There would be no fumbles this time.
From Downing Street, he monitored and guided the negotiations in
Brussels with a firm hand to a prompt and successful outcome. His
signature is on Britain's treaty of accession, and the British took
their place at last in the European Common Market in January of
1973, exactly ten years after de Gaulle's veto.

Heath was less successful in negotiating his way through the issues and problems of the British home front, the eternal debilitating struggle with the trade unions and the soggy economy. Nor,
for all his lifetime devotion to Tory party politics, did he ever really catch fire as a party leader. Heath did not spring from the
party inner circle, and there were deep doubts and disquiet in
Tory hearts as to whether he was indeed a true-blue "gut" Conservative. After the preeminent patriarchal establishment figures of
Churchill, Sir Anthony Eden, Harold Macmillan and Sir Alec
Douglas-Home in Downing Street over thirteen years of continuous Conservative rule, a change in leadership to the plebeian

Heath made political sense in 1965, when the country had swung to Labour. But Heath and the party had problems.

He was a liberal Conservative, determined to endow the party with a modern, forward-looking image and a new governmental approach to national problems. While this kind of political stance is neither unusual nor contradictory among Tories, the party still expects it to be accompanied and accomplished with reassuring old-fashioned right-wing rhetoric and feeling. Harold Macmillan was a supreme practitioner of the Tory art of playing up to the right wing while moving to the left. But Heath didn't bother to try. It was not his kind of politics. He had his own inner circle of young advisers, and he was bored by the Tory old guard. He seldom went to their clubs to listen to them sound off and give them the feeling that they had the Prime Minister's ear. He moved them to one side in the party machinery. While he was an indefatigable worker himself for the Tory party, Heath was a loner, without cronies or real friends, no capacity or taste for political small talk, any kind of small talk, and hence he was not in the end a very reassuring figure of a leader for those who regarded themselves as the heart and soul of conservatism. For all his success in riding to the top of the escalator, his party power base was not as solid and secure as it seemed. He held the party leadership for ten years, and when the end came it was abrupt and bitter. Heath seems to have been so far out of touch with the party's right wing that he never saw it coming.

Edward Richard George Heath was born at Broadstairs, on the coast of Kent, on July 9, 1916. The First World War was at its height, and the guns of the battle for Ypres could be heard in Broadstairs from across the Straits of Dover. Heath's father, employed by a local building contractor, was assigned to wartime construction work in his trade instead of being drafted into military service. After the war, in 1920, a second son was born, and by this time the father had risen to a position of "outside manager" with his employer and was supporting the family on an income of five pounds (about twenty dollars) a week. But the Heaths were better off than the average working-class family in England in the 1920s.

Within their limited means, the Heaths did well by their two sons, with a comfortable little home on a tight budget and no vacations except the seaside in front of them, but small extras like piano and violin lessons. In 1926, when young Teddy was ten, he won a small scholarship, worth twelve pounds a year, which enabled him to go on from primary school to a grammar school, Chatham House, at Ramsgate, along the coast from Broadstairs. There he remained for nine years, with a solid scholastic record always in the upper third of his class but never gaining any honors. He worked hard, but contrary to what is always expected of English schoolboys, he took no interest in sports. At the local church in Broadstairs, he sang in the choir every Sunday and began taking organ lessons from the church organist. At fifteen he was conducting the school orchestra and directing a town choir that competed in various local festivals. One of his schoolmates at that time later told a biographer: "He was anything but popular, but he never tried for popularity. He wasn't actively liked or actively disliked. He was respected and accepted, though a little bit intolerant." But at the end of his years at Chatham House, he did receive the school's highest award, established in memory of two brothers killed in the 1914–18 war, and given by votes of the upper-class students "for character."

Heath had set his sights on Oxford University, and chosen Balliol College, where Harold Macmillan had studied, because, he told his father, Balliol "was intellectually distinguished without being snobbish." Money was a major problem. His father had managed to buy out the building firm for which he worked when the owner died, but although in business for himself he was neither secure nor well off with Britain descending into the depth of the depression. Heath got a private loan from a Kent County educational fund of ninety pounds a year, and then in an open competition he won a Balliol organ scholarship worth another one hundred pounds. His family squeezed out another fifty pounds to see him through the school year.

When Heath arrived at Oxford in 1935, age nineteen, he had an unusual interview with the admissions officer, Charles Morris: "I have a clear recollection of his coming to see me, and when I asked him what he wanted to do in life after leaving Oxford, he

replied that he wanted to be a professional politician. I do not
think that I ever heard any other schoolboy answer a similar question in these terms." In fact, Oxford in 1935 was burgeoning with
budding politicians—among them Harold Wilson, later Labour
Prime Minister; Denis Healey, future Labour Chancellor of the
Exchequer; Roy Jenkins, who became president of the Common
Market Commission; Hugh Fraser, Christopher Mayhew and
others. Heath, majoring in the traditional course of philosophy,
politics and economics, of course quickly gravitated also to the famous Oxford Union debating society. The summit of his university
career came when he was elected president of the Union in his
final year. He distinguished himself in particular with a series of
rousing debate attacks on the appeasement policies of the government of Neville Chamberlain. But there was no doubt about where
his political bent lay. He had also joined the University Conservative Association, revitalizing its activities after some moribund
years, and at the same time putting his feet firmly on the starting
tread of the political escalator. Roy Jenkins recalled Heath in
those years as "grave, courteous, perfectly agreeable, not sparkling, old for his years, a thoroughly successful well-established
Balliol figure." And one of his senior Balliol professors, Lord Fulton, gave this assessment: "He was probably disappointed by his
school results, but then he had done a lot of other things. There
was solid virtue and steadiness about him, industry applied to the
right points, sensible and self-controlled use of his time. He was
not academically brilliant but he knew what he wanted to get out
of Oxford."

Each summer of those doom-laden years of the late 1930s,
Heath traveled to the Continent. He spent several weeks in the
summer of 1937 in Nazi Germany, staying first in Düsseldorf and
then with a retired professor and his wife at a Bavarian cottage
near the Austrian frontier. The professor was an old-school German liberal who hated the Nazis and unburdened himself to Heath
on tramps through the Bavarian countryside. He urged Heath to go
to Nuremberg for the annual summer Nazi Party rally and see what
it was like. He did, and it was this experience which then fired his
attacks on appeasement in the Oxford Union debates. The following summer, he traveled with an Oxford student delegation to re-

publican Spain, where the Civil War was at its height, visited the British battalion on the Catalonian front, and was bombed in his Barcelona hotel and machine-gunned on the road to Tarragona. When he graduated, in 1939, he set out with an Oxford friend on "what we knew would be our last long vacation." They crossed the Channel to Brussels, took a train to Hanover and then on to Berlin, and from there to the Free City of Danzig, which was to be the match head of World War II. Traveling third class on hard benches with rucksacks and staying at youth hostels, they went on to Warsaw and then hitchhiked back through Silesia, where Heath had arranged to meet the anti-Nazi professor with whom he had stayed two years before.

"He came with us to Leipzig, and we climbed up to the top of a hill and there we parted," Heath later recounted. "He went east. We knew very well we'd never meet again. It was the date of the Ribbentrop pact with Russia. I remember we heard a paper boy shouting it at the Leipzig railway station. We realized that this would make it bad for us and we ought to get out. German troops were mobilizing and moving west. In the middle of the night we got a train out of Leipzig for Frankfurt and next morning got down to Kehl, on the Rhine, where we crossed over the bridge into Strasbourg. French troops were now mobilizing. We hitchhiked to Paris and got a train to the Channel Coast, and got home two days before war was declared."

A few days after war was declared, Heath volunteered for the Army, and the Oxford Recruiting Board recommended him for the Artillery Corps. But, in the meantime, it had already been arranged that he was to make a tour of universities in the United States that autumn of 1939 in his capacity as president of the Oxford Union, along with another student debater. The recruiting authorities told him that he would not be called up for duty before January, and the Foreign Office and Ministry of Information were anxious for the Oxford Union debaters to proceed with their American tour anyway. But the outbreak of war had obviously changed the atmosphere in which the tour would take place. Heath and his fellow debater were called to the Foreign Office and told that whatever they wound up discussing privately in the United States, when on the platform they were to remember that the official American position was neutrality and they were not to discuss the war.

So Heath set off on his first trip across the Atlantic, a visit to twenty-six universities from Maine to Chicago, down to New Orleans, across to Florida and back up the East Coast. They had sent over a series of debating topics of a safe and nonwarlike nature, but when they got to the University of Pittsburgh the sponsors informed them that they were discarding all the proposed subjects and asking them to discuss "Should America enter the war on the side of the Allies?" In a quandary, in view of the Foreign Office caution, Heath telephoned the British embassy in Washington, got the ambassador, Lord Lothian, on the phone, and asked him what to do. Lothian, with Olympian calm, said there was no need to run away from the subject—but that the two Oxford men should trade off the pro-and-con arguments and each in turn take opposite sides of the question. On this sage advice, they debated their way through the minefields of American neutrality and returned safely to wartime Britain.

It was not, however, until August of 1940 that Heath was finally called up for service in the Royal Artillery—by which time France had fallen, Dunkirk had been evacuated and the Battle of Britain was nearing its climax. After basic training, he moved on to an officer course, and when he got his commission as a second lieutenant he was assigned to an anti-aircraft regiment defending Liverpool, then under heavy air attack as a key port in the convoy operation from the Atlantic. The next three years were filled with a series of postings with his artillery regiment to various stations around Britain, and slow promotion to the rank of captain, when his outfit finally embarked for Normandy after the invasion of the Continent in June 1944. He fought with his regiment all across northern France and Belgium, and then it was thrown into the relief of the ill-fated airborne operation against Arnhem in September of 1944. They then settled down for the winter in the Ardennes, interrupted by the Battle of the Bulge that December. Early in 1945, Heath got command of the regiment when his superior was transferred. He crossed the Rhine with Montgomery's 21st Army Group in March 1945, and was in Hanover when the war ended, where he had visited in the summer of 1939, before the war began. By this time he had been promoted to lieutenant colonel, awarded a medal and been "mentioned in dispatches" for his handling of his outfit. Like his academic record, his military performance had been solid, satisfying but not brilliant.

He was approaching thirty when he was demobilized, in 1946, well after the war in Europe had ended. Sticking to his earliest career goal, he decided to try to get into the House of Commons, never doubting his choice of the Conservative Party, despite the Labour landslide of 1945 that swept Churchill out of office and Clement Attlee into power. But he had to do something in the meantime, so he decided that a post in the Civil Service would be a good way to earn a living and learn at the same time about government machinery from the inside.

He came out at the top in a civil service administrative test and was promptly assigned to a job of better-than-average interest under an exceptionally brilliant chief. He joined the long-term-planning staff of the Ministry of Civil Aviation, which was headed by Peter Masefield, who was one of the guiding geniuses of British aviation. For the next two years, Heath worked on such projects as moving from propeller aircraft to the jet age in civil transport, airport planning and development, and production and design problems. But he had made it clear that he was in the Civil Service only to gain experience and mark time while his name was passed by the Conservative Central Office from one constituency to another for adoption as a prospective parliamentary candidate. Finally, in October of 1947, the local Conservative leaders in the constituency of Bexley, in Heath's home county of Kent, liked his qualifications. They had decided that they wanted a local man who had made good, well educated but from an "ordinary family." On top of that, Heath had a suitable war record, and although he was a bachelor who would be campaigning in a constituency of middle-class family people, it was evident that he would work hard to win. When he was adopted as Bexley's Tory candidate, under the law he resigned from the Civil Service. He then found another "on-the-job-training" post with an old London merchant banking establishment, Brown, Shipley and Co., to earn a living while waiting for a general election. It finally was called by Attlee in February of 1950, as the Labour government neared the end of its five-year mandate after its postwar victory in July of 1945.

There were four candidates in Bexley, and happily for Heath one of them was a Communist. Some 56,000 ballots were cast, and the count was so close that a recount was ordered immediately. At last, in the early-morning hours of February 24, 1950, the result was declared. Heath had won over the Labour Party candidate by 25,854 against 25,721—a plurality of 133. The Communist had polled 481 votes and certainly cost Labour the seat. But Edward Heath was now a member of Parliament.

In the old tradition of the House of Commons, Heath, as a new member, waited four months before rising to "catch Mr. Speaker's eye" and deliver his "maiden speech." His subject, prophetically, was Britain and Europe—specifically, the British response to the Schuman Plan for creating a European Coal and Steel Community, which Jean Monnet had devised and French Foreign Minister Robert Schuman had proposed to Europe that year, on May 9, 1950. The reaction of the Labour government had been one of irritation, followed by lofty rejection. But, at the end of May, during a spring parliamentary recess, Heath had made his first postwar visit to Germany to discuss the Schuman Plan in Bonn. A House of Commons debate on the matter was then scheduled for the last week of June, and Heath rose from the back benches to attack the Labour government for its brusque decision to stand aside and have nothing to do with the negotiations.*

"It is said we should be taking a risk with the whole of our economy. By standing aside we may be taking a very great risk with our economy in the coming years—a very great risk indeed. We all realize the importance of the Empire, and we on this side certainly think it must be supported, but what are the views of the Empire on this matter? Have there been discussions? As far as we can ascertain, they have not protested against this scheme. . . .

"The Chancellor of the Exchequer [Sir Stafford Cripps] spoke all the time as though this were to be a restrictionist plan. Surely

* See also Chapter 6, "The Schuman Plan."

the object is to be one of expansion. That is to be the task of the High Authority, rather than restriction. . . .

"There are seeds of conflict in these negotiations between France and Germany, and I submit that this is a very strong reason why we should take part in these discussions—in order that we may balance out the difficulties which are bound to arise on the economic side. I appeal to the Government that magnanimity in politics is not seldom the truest wisdom—follow that dictum and go into the Schuman Plan to develop Europe and coordinate it in the way suggested."

It was a good speech, even an impressive speech by House of Commons back-bench standards, for Heath had not only hit out at the Labour government on an important subject in a reasoned and well-thought-out diagnosis; he was also out in front of his own Conservative Party leadership, which was as suspicious of Jean Monnet's ideas of supranationalism as the Labour Party. But, of course, since the Tories were not in power, they did not have to show any true, hard position.

Oddly enough, it was almost the only speech Ted Heath made in the Commons for eight years. Eight months after that speech, his diligence and devotion to parliamentary duties as a back-bencher had impressed the chief whip of the Conservatives, who was looking for a new assistant whip from among the influx of new younger members. He offered the job to Heath, who accepted on condition that he would leave after eighteen months if he did not like the work. By tradition in the House of Commons, the whips do not make parliamentary speeches. Their function is to listen, not talk, and to avoid taking positions on intramural party arguments in order to maintain the role of impartiality and confidence of individual members. Their job is to filter and relay party opinion up to the leadership, and then in the end to deliver the votes when the debates are over. As it turned out, it was a function that suited Ted Heath to a T. He loved the dogged grind and the constant attendance at the House of Commons, the foot in the door of power that the job gave him, and the opportunity to expand and enlarge his influence and importance and authority while at the same time enlarging acquaintances without taking on friends.

That October of 1951, Attlee was forced to go to the country again (he had held on after the 1950 election with a majority of only six seats), and the Conservatives returned to power under Winston Churchill. For Heath, the election campaign was overshadowed by the death of his mother, of cancer, two weeks before the polling date, but he sailed back into the House with a solid majority of more than sixteen hundred votes. The Conservative majority, however, was only eighteen seats.

He continued in his job as an assistant whip, now more important than ever, with the Conservatives in power but a narrow majority to be husbanded on every House of Commons vote. He moved up to become deputy chief whip in 1952, and then Churchill finally retired as Prime Minister, in April 1955, in his eighty-first year. Sir Anthony Eden moved into Downing Street, after nearly three decades' waiting in the wings, and promptly called a general election the following month. He increased the Tory majority handsomely to fifty-nine seats, and then reshuffled the government later that year, with Heath taking over as government chief whip—just in time for the acute internal parliamentary crisis of the Suez War.

The Suez War was a prime example of the reasoning behind the rule that whips never make House of Commons speeches. The affair split the party wide open, a nightmare situation for the whips, whose job above all is not to take sides but hold the party together. The main burden fell on Heath, but he has steadfastly refused ever to discuss his own view of the Suez affair. He did everything he could, of course, to sustain Eden and the government, and by his effectiveness he almost certainly made Tory support for Eden seem more solid than it really was. Though he has never said so, he must have been appalled at the political disaster and parliamentary nightmare, and therefore opposed to the blundering policy. But he functioned with complete and tireless loyalty, like a strong chief of staff under a commander in chief collapsing from battle fatigue.

When Eden gave up office, in January of 1957, Heath, although supposedly impartial in his post of chief whip, certainly preferred Harold Macmillan to R. A. Butler, the only other candidate. When Macmillan came back from Buckingham Palace with the

Queen's commission to form a government, he took Ted Heath to dinner, the two of them alone, oysters and champagne at the Turf Club, to talk about Cabinet choices. Heath continued as chief whip but was clearly marked for bigger things.†

Not even the most sanguine of the Tories foresaw in the wreckage of Suez that Macmillan was embarking on a remarkable tenure of more than seven years as Prime Minister. The chief whip's office is at No. 12 Downing Street, and an inside corridor connects to the Prime Minister's residence. Heath was with Macmillan almost every day, invaluable in the first months in helping to steady things and calm the political seas. Macmillan's private secretary has described the relationship of the two men: "Heath was tremendously loyal and tremendously frank with the Prime Minister. He regarded himself as a conduit for channeling information to the Prime Minister about what the party was thinking of him. He was both practical and intellectual. He was totally pragmatic. He knew what he was doing all the time—no messing about."

As Suez receded and Macmillan's political fortunes rose, he called a general election in 1959 and for the third time in a row the Tory Party, remarkably, increased its parliamentary majority over Labour, while Heath doubled the majority in his own Bexley constituency. When the new government was formed, Heath entered the Cabinet at last, as Minister of Labour. But he was there only eight months. In the spring of 1960, Macmillan at long last decided that the time had come to take the plunge and apply to join the Common Market. But there was general surprise when he chose Edward Heath to take charge of the British negotiating team, with a Cabinet appointment as Lord Privy Seal and an office in the Foreign Office, where he would coordinate European policy as deputy to the Foreign Secretary, the Earl of Home. The actual start of negotiations was still some months away, but Macmillan's choice of Heath was shrewd. Heath was thorough and driving, and he believed in the job he was given to do. Moreover, in the end it would be a problem of "political sell" with the Tory party and in the country, when Heath's long and intimate knowledge of the House of Commons would be an asset. But, unhappily for Mac-

† See also Chapter 8, "The Suez War."

millan, as well as Heath, that moment didn't come until ten years
later.

When President de Gaulle lowered the boom on Britain's entering Europe with his press-conference veto of January 14, 1963,
much of the political head of steam went out of Macmillan's administration. The great objective had been refused, and there was
no new political grand design to take its place. Moreover, a series
of scandals—spies and sex—began unraveling in the spring and
summer of 1963, none of them damaging to Macmillan personally
but highly damaging to the government's image. In the end, it was
illness that forced Macmillan's retirement—but, from his hospital
bed in September 1963, he managed a last burst of feverish political activity in order to name his own successor. He was determined to block R. A. Butler from Downing Street. To do this, he
persuaded the Earl of Home to give up his peerage and become Sir
Alec Douglas-Home. A somewhat surprised, confused and bitterly
divided Tory party then dutifully followed Macmillan's last bidding
and adopted the defrocked fourteenth Earl as party leader and
Prime Minister.

The affair was decisive for Heath's political future for two reasons. First, he supported Macmillan's choice of Douglas-Home,
while his two principal young rivals for the future leadership, Iain
Macleod and Reginald Maudling, went down the line for Butler.
In politics, it pays to back a winner. But the main fallout from the
affair was a strong demand in the Conservative Party for a change
in procedure for selecting its leader. Times were changing, and it
could no longer be left to a smoke-filled-room Tory oligarchy to
decide in secret. The obvious way was to elect a party leader by
votes of the Conservative members of Parliament, the way the
Labour Party has always chosen its leader.

Meanwhile, the new Prime Minister took Heath into the Cabinet as Secretary of State for Industry and President of the Board
of Trade. It was going to be only a short-lived government anyway. That comfortable 1959 parliamentary majority would expire
in 1964, and Douglas-Home held out to the end. The election
finally came in October, and Tories watched in anguish as the
Labour Party, under Harold Wilson, squeezed back into power by
a tiny margin of only six seats.

Unbroken Tory rule for thirteen years in Britain was over, but with such a wafer-thin House of Commons majority, every politician knew that Wilson would be bound to call a quick election the first good chance he saw to improve Labour's fortunes. Accordingly, on the Tory side pressure built up to decide the future leadership question promptly, before another election. Sir Alec Douglas-Home was a man of quiet integrity and strong qualities, who had been quite content with life as the fourteenth Earl. He was no man to stand in the way if the party wanted a change. In February of 1965, he promulgated new rules of procedure for electing a party leader, and then, six months later, he stepped down. (Later he returned to the House of Lords as a life peer, at the bottom of the pecking order, plain Lord Home, no longer an earl. An oddly flexible system, the British.)

At the end of July, on the first round of balloting for a new leader, Heath came out on top, but he failed to win by a majority of at least 15 percent, which was required under the new rules. He topped Reginald Maudling 150–133 votes, which was pretty solid evidence that he did not have solid appeal for the Conservative Old Guard. Nevertheless, Maudling announced at once that he would withdraw from the race, and since nobody else wanted to stick his neck out and challenge Heath on a second ballot, he won by votes and default. Edward Heath, carpenter's son and grammar-school boy, had risen to the top with remarkably little on the public record to show what he stood for or how he had done it. He was formally proclaimed leader of the Conservative Party on August 2, 1965, at forty-nine the youngest party leader since the office was created, for Disraeli, in 1868.

Heath's tenure as Conservative leader had a rough start. In March of 1966, Wilson found his moment to call a general election, and slammed the Tories with a landslide Labour victory, winning an overall majority of ninety-seven seats. Neither Heath nor the party had really expected that they were going to reverse national trends and turn Labour out of office in 1966, but the size of the defeat was pretty devastating. It meant a long slog in opposition—something most of the Tory members of the House of Commons had never experienced. Moreover, it was rough for Heath personally in

his regular duels from the opposition front bench with Harold
Wilson. It was here that Heath seemed to suffer from the fact that
in all his years in the House of Commons he had mainly been a silent participant in proceedings. Wilson was a master of rough-and-
tumble, quick-thrust repartee, particularly in the regular question-
and-answer sessions, which are so much the focal point of House
of Commons business. Heath, on the other hand, came on as
pedantic, stodgy and dull. He lacked Macmillan's urbanity under
fire, and too often he rose too quickly to some goading provocation from Wilson with a sputtering answer.

Moreover, the hard-core Tories wanted strong right-wing opposition, but Heath was bending constantly, and logically, to maintain a political posture of liberal, forward-looking Conservative alternative positions to Labour's rule. He felt deeply and sincerely
that it was the duty of responsible leadership not to polarize British politics but to find the democratic middle ground. He was right
in terms of the country, but he was wrong in terms of what his
party expected of him. On such issues as immigration, trade-union
power, the Rhodesian problem, the role of government in the
economy and industry, public spending, and social issues and
problems, Heath was regularly caught between Harold Wilson
firing from the front and his own backbenchers firing from the
rear. Still, he was tough and determined, and he was the elected
party leader.

Heath's basic approach to Britain's future had been formulated
by a series of working parties under a coordinating committee that
he chaired to prepare an election manifesto for 1966. He liked an
orderly, committee approach to decisions. The goals that emerged
were honorable and estimable but also wholly predictable and
anodyne: "Open up new opportunities for merit, talent and individual enterprise . . . change the tax system to provide new incen-
tives . . . more competitive climate in industry . . . an entirely
new approach to manpower problems . . . trade-union responsibility to be redefined and restrictive practices eliminated . . .
more humane social and community services better geared to people's real needs . . ." and finally: "Britain's future lies in
Europe."

A critic of Heath's leadership has since written: "Edward

Heath could never be accused of failing to take cognisance of the ideas of others. Indeed, that is not the charge that his severest critics have levelled at him. They have consistently accused him of having none of his own. More deeply disturbing to some in the party was the fear that he might fall prey to the soft center, to the cultivation of the amorphous middle ground of politics, which they were convinced would be pandering to the enemy and bound to alienate the party's best supporters."

What probably saved Heath as Conservative Party leader, as the Labour government stumbled and fumbled toward 1970, was the growing public evidence of the mendacious and tawdry quality of Prime Minister Harold Wilson. Whatever was wrong with Ted Heath as a personality or a party leader, he did have some standards and he did have integrity and he was not a trimmer or compromiser. Wilson, on the other hand, was utterly uninhibited by principle of any kind, except the principle of staying in power. This was not the Labour Party leadership of either Clement Attlee or Hugh Gaitskell. There was a squalid quality about Wilson, a veneer of cheap success to his premiership, in place of integrity, courage or statesmanship.

Mesmerized by his own unprincipled adroitness as a politician and exhilarated by his constant successes over Heath in verbal jousting in the House of Commons, Wilson decided on a surprise early election, in June of 1970, when his mandate of 1966 still had fifteen months to run. Heath, who was at his best in the dogged work of active campaigning, fought with everything he had, up and down the country, against heavy public-opinion-poll odds, realizing no doubt that his own future as Conservative Party leader was at stake, as well as victory over Labour. It was an election unlike any other in British history, for *all* the public-opinion polls flatly predicted a Labour victory, and all got it wrong. When the campaign opened, the Conservative *Daily Mail* gave Labour an astounding twelve-percentage-point lead over the Tories, and although this dropped in the next three weeks, Labour was still leading solidly in the headlines when the country went to the polls, on June 18. No one will ever know precisely what caused a switch of the voters to the Tories in the final days. There were some bad trade figures, which hurt Labour, and Wilson found himself

stoutly asserting—not for the first or last time—that he would not
devalue the pound. Maybe the electorate voted against another
Wilson promise. Whatever it was that turned things around, a
stunned and utterly dumfounded Harold Wilson moved out of
No. 10 Downing Street, and a triumphant Ted Heath moved in.

Edward Heath's prime ministership lasted only three years and
nine months. It began boldly and positively. The door to Europe
was already ajar, with Pompidou in power in France and Willy
Brandt in Germany, and Heath promptly and effectively set out to
show that he was a worthy, sincere and straightforward European
partner of loyalty and integrity. Not only did he speed the Brussels
negotiation to a successful conclusion; he also deliberately moved
British foreign policy away from its Anglo-American orientation
to an Anglo-European wavelength. Heath had a certain secret admiration for General de Gaulle.

It was on the domestic front where Heath eventually ran into a
dead end, and analysts are still wondering if the Prime Minister
was responsible for his own disaster, or whether he was a victim
of forces and problems in British politics and its trade-union
structure that were impossible to resolve—at any rate, not in the
conditions of Heath's time in power and not in the fashion in
which he went about trying to solve them. Perhaps a more flexible
Prime Minister could have maneuvered and survived. However,
not only was Heath not a very flexible leader, but there had been
so much maneuvering and twisting and sacrifice of principle to political expediency in the Wilson government that Heath was more
determined than ever to stand firmly and unyieldingly on what he
believed was right and necessary for the country, no matter how
dead-ended it might turn out to be.

He had a belief, which all men in power have in one degree or
another, that his logic and persuasion backed by his authority
could produce a wide consensus and resolve problems. He
believed in the ultimate reasonableness of responsible men when
faced with irrefutable facts. But, in strife-ridden, class-ridden Britain, no facts are ever regarded as irrefutable, and responsibility
and reasonableness were not the order of the day with the Labour
Party opposition or the trade-union movement. Across the table,

Heath faced men whose primary objective was to harass and hound the Conservatives out of power. Heath was right in his objectives. He sought, simply, to achieve for Britain what others were doing in West Germany, France, Holland, Scandinavia, almost every industrialized nation on earth: an expanding but stable economy, higher productivity with controlled inflation, wage increases related to production increases, a better investment climate for industry. There was nothing new in this, and God knows Britain's ills and permanent woes have been examined, debated and analyzed to death. Heath wanted to do something positive about it, but the trade unions certainly didn't. They wanted Labour back in power.

Heath probably made a basic misjudgment by sticking to an election commitment to "go for growth," in an effort to emulate the economic performance in France and Germany as Britain prepared to join the Common Market. But the trouble was that this party objective had been fixed by his policy planners three or four years before the election, and economic conditions had changed. By the time Heath came to power, he should have made price stability and holding down inflation his economic priority, instead of growth. So his basic policy wound up boosting wage/price demands, and then the situation became hopelessly aggravated, at the end of 1973, by the Arab-Israeli War, the oil embargo, and the ensuing permanent energy crisis.

To hold down wages, Heath finally resorted to a statutory wage-control act, which was resented by Labour and Tory free-enterprise stalwarts alike. To try to bring the country's trade unions under some kind of rules of fair play for the country, he introduced an Industrial Relations Act, which was a great deal milder than labor laws in the United States, but simply poured more oil on the fires of trade-union militancy. The end came for Heath when the coal miners went out on strike for a second time in two years, in December of 1973, for a massive pay claim that would have breached the statutory guidelines. It was the worst possible time for a coal strike, in winter on the heels of the Arab oil embargo. Perhaps the Prime Minister should have made the miners a "special case" (they were earning less than Spanish coal miners), but he stood firm, arguing that 16 million union members had accepted pay restraints and he wasn't going to knuckle under to one militant union holding the country up to economic blackmail.

Twelve days before Christmas, Heath declared a state of national emergency and put industry on a three-day week to conserve coal stocks. His advisers began urging him to go to the country, but Heath held that a modern Conservative Party should not fight an election mainly against the trade unions. He wanted to settle the strike and then call an election. He still hoped that reason and a sense of national interest would prevail. But not with the British coal miners, one of whose leaders was a Communist. The situation drifted in deadlock until the end of January, when the miners held a national ballot and by a vote of 81 percent decided to stick to their strike. Heath was now at the dead end, and he called an election for the last day of February, 1974.

It turned out to be very close to a replay of Sir Alec Douglas-Home's election, ten years before. The Labour Party nosed out the Conservatives by only five seats—but the Liberals held a balance. The Conservatives, moreover, were well out in front in total popular vote. Heath spent an awkward, and many felt undignified, forty-eight hours in Downing Street trying to patch together a coalition or a working agreement with the Liberals, until finally he accepted defeat and moved out to allow Harold Wilson to move back in.

But, as was the case a decade earlier, it was obvious that Wilson would again have to go for an early election to reinforce his House of Commons majority. First of all, of course, the new Labour government gave the coal miners everything they were asking for, thereby starting the country galloping toward a 24 percent annual inflation rate. Then Wilson sprang an election, in October of 1974, and this time Heath and the Tories lost by forty-three seats.

When the 1965 leadership election procedure was promulgated by Sir Alec Douglas-Home, it was not made clear whether there should be a new election with every new Parliament, or whether the party leader would simply stay until he decided to go. Douglas-Home preferred the latter, which was why he left it vague, but the party now felt otherwise.

Heath had lost three out of four elections as party leader. As far as the Tories were concerned, his "middle ground" was turning out to be quicksand. Between Tories and Labour, it seemed, there was no middle ground—only battleground. Everybody acknowledged that he had been an efficient Prime Minister. Like a good yacht captain, he ran a tight ship. But, as a political leader, he singularly failed to communicate, to rouse, to strike any chords of inspiration or popular appeal—"a conductor tone-deaf to life," as one critic put it. Does anybody remember a Heath speech, or even Heath speaking? Coupled with this, there was a vindictive streak in Heath, a brusqueness and even plain rudeness in the way he handled people of his own party. He had no capacity for being magnanimous or generous with those who did not wholeheartedly endorse or support him. His own little band found him very different to work with, but his display of charm, humor and warmth was certainly confined to a limited inner circle.

The demand within the party for another leadership election after the convening of the new Parliament at the end of 1974 could not be ignored, and Heath promulgated a new set of rules, more complicated and precise than those laid down by Douglas-Home. He knew, of course, that he would be challenged, but he seems largely to have taken his reelection for granted. He was misled by soundings of strong support away from Westminster, out in the party hinterlands. The old government chief whip who used to pride himself on sensing the "feel of the House" was singularly out of touch as the voting neared. It certainly escaped his comprehension completely that he would be ousted from his citadel of masculinity by a woman: Margaret Thatcher, a true-blue "gut" Conservative if there ever was one, a woman who makes no concessions to masculinity and asks no intellectual or political quarter due to her sex.

On February 3, 1975, the results of the first ballot were announced, and Mrs. Thatcher had polled 130 to Heath's 119. Within two hours, Edward Heath stepped down and retired to the back benches of the Conservative Party in permanent bitterness and growing self-isolation. He refused to serve under the new party leader, rejected various olive branches of understanding that Mrs. Thatcher held out to him, and apart from continuing to work his own constituency dutifully and successfully, his service to the party pretty much came to an end. He was no more magnanimous in defeat than he had been in victory.

Edward Heath, in the words of Henry Kissinger, was "a formidable character," utterly disciplined in the exercise of power, strong and dominant, clear-thinking and efficient—lacking very simply the human touch, so varied in men of power but so essential to successful leadership. By now he probably would be a forgotten figure on the list of British Prime Ministers of the twentieth century if he had not been the Prime Minister who took Britain into Europe, and that central, vital historic achievement cannot be taken from him. Indeed, if there was one passion in his political makeup it was Britain's place in Europe, the fulfillment of a role that for too long his nation had rejected or ignored.

He did more than simply take Britain into Europe. For a few brief years, from 1970 to 1974, Europe moved forward under a strong and harmonious triumvirate: Heath in Britain, Pompidou in France and Brandt in Germany. Not only was membership of the European Community enlarged in this period from six nations to nine; a new level of political consultation and cooperation was added to the cumbersome economic machinery of the Treaty of Rome. Common Market summit meetings, which began in those days as occasional affairs, have now become institutionalized as part of the European machinery. The first half of the 1970s, the Heath period, was the most expansive and important time of European development since the Treaty of Rome in 1958.

By an unparalleled convergence of politics and fate, all three leaders disappeared abruptly from the scene within weeks of each other. The first week of March, 1974, Heath left Downing Street after his election defeat. The first week of April, 1974, Pompidou died tragically and painfully of cancer. The first week of May, 1974, Willy Brandt resigned as a result of there being a Communist spy in his private office. Never before had all three major European nations changed top leaders in such a short time span. But they had done their work well, building where Jean Monnet and Robert Schuman had begun, as the new leaders found on moving into place.

16

Britain into Europe

"This royal throne of kings, this scepter'd isle,
This earth of majesty, this seat of Mars,
This other Eden, demi-paradise;
This fortress built by Nature for herself
Against infection and the hand of war,
This happy breed of men, this little world,
This precious stone set in the silver sea,
Which serves it in the office of a wall,
Or as a moat defensive to a house,
Against the envy of less happier lands.
This blessed plot, this earth, this realm, this England. . . ."

King Richard II.
Act II, Scene 1

ALL THAT HAS BEEN GREAT IN GREAT BRITAIN SINCE SHAKE-speare's time militated in the postwar period against Britain's joining Europe and finally surrendering herself openly to a destiny that is no longer hers to control. It scarcely seemed to accord with the prestige of victory after World War II. It was against the grain of a long and glorious history which had been built on the outlook and mentality of a secure island. It was abandonment of the luxury of insularity, with its freedom of choice of when and how to intervene in the affairs of the European continent. It required painful acknowledgment that the Commonwealth and Empire were becoming irrelevant to Britain's future. It ran counter to the orientation of the British economy. It touched to the quick the vital abstract of sovereignty, something the British probably felt was more precious to them than to anybody else, because they had never lost it through invasion, occupation or defeat in their own realm since 1066. At bottom, the idea of joining some embryo European confederation simply never figured in the education, upbringing, mental outlook or historic traditions of British diplomats, civil servants, trade-union leaders, bankers, shopkeepers, industrialists or political leaders who had to steer Britain into the second half of the twentieth century when the war was over.

Of course the British had been sending armies to fight on the continent of Europe for over two centuries, from Marlborough to Churchill. But the very success of these interventions and excursions—an in-and-out policy, with avoidance of any permanent commitment—had served constantly to reinforce the offshore mentality of the scepter'd isle and the envy of less happier lands. It gave the British a satisfying sense of being the ultimate arbiter of Europe's affairs without being a part of Europe. There was great advantage in remaining aloof and apart, free to intervene at a moment of British choosing, then to retire to insularity when European peace and order had been restored. In Palmerston's lofty phrase: "England has no permanent friends and no permanent enemies—only permanent interests."

All the same, the British leaders who fought World War II were acutely aware when the war ended that the world had changed. Six years of conflict, from 1939 to 1945, had dramatically shifted the center of world power from London to Washington. It was the United States that would now have to fill the global role that Britain, the Royal Navy, and the Empire and Commonwealth had effectively discharged for a century and a half. Ernest Bevin knew this, and so did Attlee, Churchill, Eden, the Foreign Office, the British establishment. This was the global picture—yet at the same time there was not much in this view of the world at large to alter Britain's traditional insular approach to the continent of Europe, beyond the Straits of Dover. The secure island had sheltered Europe's governments in exile, inspired its resistance movements, equipped its meager fighting forces, and the British had marched back across the Continent in the vanguard of the liberating armies. Peace and freedom had been restored. The British had again fulfilled the famous valedictorian remark of William Pitt in his London Guildhall speech after the Battle of Trafalgar, in 1805:

"England has saved herself by her exertions, and will, as I trust, save Europe by her example."

But exertion had cost Britain dearly, and she had little to offer the Continent when the war was over but her prestige and her example. British eyes were averted from the problems of the Continent to the problems of the world, and in any case there were problems enough at home. It was an enormous strain for Britain merely to maintain her occupation forces in West Germany, Austria and Berlin—and in 1947 the British found they could no longer carry the relatively marginal but vital burden of economic and military support for Greece in its civil war. When Ernest Bevin renounced this commitment, it was the turning-point decision in postwar history, which abruptly brought the United States to a realization of its responsibilities and produced in rapid order first the Truman Doctrine and then the Marshall Plan. Once European economic recovery got underway, the political recovery of Europe began as well—but Britain's insular approach to European affairs remained unchanged.*

In the face of Europe's postwar destruction and despair, it was as obvious as Newton observing falling apples that Europe should unite to resolve its economic problems and its political future. Eleven centuries after Charlemagne, the time had come at last to create a united Europe. But what form should it take? What kind of united Europe? However obvious the idea, the obstacles were enormous. Germany was defeated and occupied, but could a united Europe be built without Germany? The four occupying powers were committed, at least on paper in the Potsdam Agreements, to treating Germany as an economic whole. Was there to be a peace treaty? Did the unification of Europe have to await solution of the German question? If there was to be an organization, a purely European construction, who would its members be, what would its powers and obligations be? Above all, who would take the lead? In the cold ashes of victory in 1945 and 1946, these were hapless, hopeless questions that were endlessly asked and never answered. It was enough of a problem just to heat houses and find food.

* See also Chapter 2, "The Marshall Plan."

Then, on September 19, 1946, the voice of Winston Churchill was again heard resolutely calling to Europe with historic vision. Six months earlier, Churchill had delivered his famous "Iron Curtain" speech at Westminster College, in Fulton, Missouri, with President Harry S Truman at his side. Now, with his gift of political timing and setting, he chose to address Europe from the University of Zurich, in Switzerland.

"We must build a kind of United States of Europe. The first step in the re-creation of this European family must be a partnership between Western Germany and France. In this way only can France recover the moral and cultural leadership of Europe. There can be no revival of Europe without a spiritually great France and a spiritually great Germany. In this urgent work, France and Germany must take the lead together."

Somewhat paternalistically, Churchill said that Britain assuredly would play a role in this European construction, but he carefully reminded the Europeans of the worldwide commitments of the then still British Commonwealth. Apart from his direct hard-core appeal to France to recover leadership by taking up partnership with West Germany, all was vague and idealistic. Nevertheless, coming from Churchill in 1946 it was dynamic and stirring stuff, a voice of British leadership in drifting, uncertain and increasingly frightening European times. The creation of the Bonn Republic was three years away, yet Churchill was already talking about West Germany as a separate state. When Churchill spoke, not even an embryo of European unity existed. The Zurich speech was a little too visionary for the French, who reacted with resentment at being told by Churchill to grasp Germany by the hand. Still, the public and political reaction everywhere was excited, almost ecstatic. The irony was that when the French did move, four years later, in May of 1950, to follow Churchill's exhortation and create a partnership with West Germany through the Schuman Plan, it was British vision that failed.

Churchill's Zurich speech promptly triggered the latent, leaderless European unity movement into action everywhere. In England, top Conservative Party leaders, with support from the Liberals but virtually no takers from the Labour Party, formed a United

Europe Committee, under Churchill's chairmanship. Similar committees sprang up in France, Belgium, Holland, Italy, the Scandinavian states, and even in West Germany, where the European movement became an early political vehicle for Konrad Adenauer to emerge on the international scene. Through informal and largely personal liaison, these committees gradually came to focus on an organizational objective: creation of a Council of Europe, with a debating assembly and a guiding committee of ministers. Plans were laid to hold a large political congress at The Hague to formalize a popular call upon governments to act. In fact, in many capitals governments were actively encouraging the European movement, anxious to be swept along on a tide of popular demand, looking for a lead and a push from somewhere.

But not at the Foreign Office, in London. Here an attitude had quickly formed of rather sullen resistance and resentment against European unity. In part, this reflected the long-held British suspicion of any continental grouping, or getting involved in any kind of permanent organization that might impinge on sovereignty or freedom of action. In part it also sprang from Ernest Bevin's conviction that Churchill, as leader of the opposition, was simply using the European-unity platform to mount a political flank attack against the Labour government. Bevin had a point; Churchill was certainly no European federalist, and he was out for political gain. All the same, Bevin ignored or misjudged the genuine political aspirations that were at work on the Continent, and instead, with the initial accord of the professionals at the Foreign Office, he established at the very outset a negative attitude toward any and all European political development, which then dogged British foreign policy for the next twenty years.

Bevin's ideas about the postwar organization of Europe, such as they were, seemed largely to have been rooted in Castlereagh, Canning, and the loose, ad hoc diplomatic arrangements by which continental affairs were managed in the nineteenth century following the Congress of Vienna. His first basic step toward Europe after the war was a bilateral treaty of friendship and alliance with France, signed in January of 1947, guaranteeing British military support against any threat to the peace from a revived Germany. This was diplomacy in the old tradition, no doubt useful and necessary in the context of the times, if not very imaginative. Of course Britain wanted to play a role in establishing European peace, stability, cooperation and economic recovery—but without any organization or multinational structure, simply a series of bilateral agreements or arrangements to be activated and orchestrated individually by sovereign powers.

This conservative British approach rapidly surfaced in Bevin's handling of the response to the Marshall Plan offer, in June of 1947. First of all, he did move with commendable alacrity to see that Europe did not muff the chance that was presented by General George C. Marshall's historic offer to underwrite a European economic recovery program. Nobody can take away from Bevin the place in history that that response earned him. But it quickly became apparent that Britain was out to sponsor only a *temporary* Committee of European Economic Cooperation and not a permanent organization, which the United States and many of the Europeans wanted. Under British chairmanship, this committee did its work well as far as preparing a kind of multilateral European shopping list for American aid. But it took a great deal of American arm-twisting and finally some blunt and brutal pressures amounting to a virtual ultimatum, to get the British finally to agree, in 1948, to convert the temporary committee into a permanent, government-constituted Organization for European Economic Cooperation. If Britain didn't want Europe to unite, the United States certainly did. A new ball game was beginning.

Driven finally to accepting that there would be no continuance of American aid without creation of a permanent European organization to coordinate not only the allocation of that aid but general trade and economic policies as well, Bevin finally acceded to the principle "if you can't lick 'em, join 'em." A Briton became the organization's first chairman. The British had wanted almost desperately to continue to deal directly with Washington on a strictly bilateral basis on aid, but Washington was determined that the Europeans get together and cut up the assistance pie themselves by collective negotiation and unanimous multilateral agreement. This argument, fought out in Paris by Ambassador W. Averell Harriman, who was the Marshall Plan aid chief in Europe, was only the first of a long, long series of skirmishes and diplomatic battles in the seemingly endless process of Britain coming to grips at one and the same time with herself, the changed conditions of the world and her place in Europe.

Meanwhile, about the same time that Bevin was being driven to accept the creation of permanent European economic cooperation machinery in Paris, the European Congress convened at The Hague in May of 1948 in an atmosphere of extraordinary exuberance and enthusiasm under an International Committee of the Movements for European Unity. There were 713 delegates from eighteen countries—a glittering list that included more than twenty former prime ministers and premiers, ranging from victorious Winston Churchill to defeated Paul Reynaud, along with such luminaries as philosopher Bertrand Russell and the exiled Spanish historian Salvador de Madariaga. In fact, behind the scenes and largely concealed in the high spirits of the occasion, a considerable battle was fought out between the European federalists of the Continent and the British Conservatives, who, no less than Ernest Bevin, were against creating any European institution with real powers. Nevertheless, Churchill, in a massive and exhilarating speech, called for a European Assembly, and the tide of public opinion for *something* European, some expression of unity, could scarcely be ignored.

Soon after The Hague Congress, Robert Schuman became French Foreign Minister and began a remarkable tenure of nearly five years at the Quai d'Orsay—not only remarkable for the Fourth Republic but also in all French history, exceeded only by Talleyrand in the post-Napoleon period and Maurice Couve de Murville under President Charles de Gaulle. Schuman, of course, was a convinced European, and he moved to translate the resolutions that had been passed at The Hague into government action. In a memorandum to the British and other European states in September 1948, the French proposed that a European Assembly be established with all possible speed—making it clear that "until such time as the nations decide to transfer some part of their sovereign rights to an international European authority, the Assembly could have no legislative or executive powers." This was too much for Bevin and the Foreign Office. Even though it was clear from the French memorandum that such an assembly would be only a debating body, the British bristled at even the hint of a distant possibility of enlarging its powers one day. The Foreign Office replied in a coldly hostile "questionnaire," and Bevin complained about "the prospect of being united with the Continent without taking the Commonwealth into account." In the end the British had little choice but to join a study committee, which began work in Paris in November. Much British foot-dragging now followed—including an incredible proposal that the assembly consist of "an inter-governmental conference of delegates at which all delegates from one country should be nominated by its government and should cast a single bloc vote!" This fortunately died in European consternation. At last, in May of 1949, a Statute of the Council of Europe was formally agreed on in London to develop cooperation through a Committee of Ministers and a Consultative Assembly "through which the aspirations of the European peoples may be formulated and expressed." The British were reluctant to join even powerless organizations. As *The Times* inscrutably commented during this period: "One of the troubles about any form of European Union is that Great Britain can be neither excluded from it nor included in it."

Powerless, toothless, but at least a European body with a voice at last, the Consultative Assembly of the Council of Europe (its members drawn by appointment from national parliaments) convened for the first time in the fine old French city of Strasbourg, on the banks of the Rhine, where it would make its headquarters, on August 10, 1949. Churchill was there, and Belgium's Paul-Henri Spaak was elected the assembly's first president. There was much fanfare about the event, which at the time did genuinely seem to presage the creation of "a kind of United States of Europe." Yet, very quickly, even the assembly voice seemed to strangle. The British had made certain in negotiating the statute that the Committee of Ministers controlled everything—even, initially, the assembly's agenda. Bevin went through the routine of the Strasbourg meetings all but visibly holding his nose. As Paul Reynaud, also an assembly member, commented, "The Council of Europe consists of two bodies, one of them for Europe, the other against it." Nevertheless, it was the first assembly that Europe had ever had, and at least simply by meeting and debating, it succeeded in focusing attention on the great possibilities and the problems.

Although history soon began to pass the Council of Europe by, it still exists and still holds assembly meetings six times a year. It does still do useful work as a pan-European clearinghouse in mundane but important areas such as intergovernmental agreement on common educational standards for recognized European university degrees, the devising of Europe-wide pharmaceutical standards, mutual extensions of social security benefits to each other's nationals, and even a European protocol on traffic offenses so a speeder in one country can be charged when he gets home to his own country. The other important outgrowth of the Council of Europe has been the establishment of the European Court of Human Rights, the only body of its kind in existence anywhere in the world, open to direct appeal by any European citizen.

The British would have been perfectly content if development of Europe had stopped where it was in 1950—with the Organization for European Economic Cooperation, in Paris, to talk about economic problems, and the Council of Europe, in Strasbourg, to talk about political problems. Both institutions had been grudgingly accepted by the British, and their powers and machinery had been well circumscribed to the British Foreign Office point of view. In fact, both of them had really been designed to hold back the development of any truly supranational trends toward European unity—not to encourage things forward. But, by now, European recovery under the spur of Marshall Plan aid was beginning to surge ahead, and however Britain felt about it, Europe would not stand still politically.

Did Robert Schuman and Jean Monnet deliberately set out to trick Great Britain and do the British in when they launched the historic plan for creation of the European Coal and Steel Community, on May 9, 1950? Ernest Bevin certainly felt at the time that there was a strong element of trickery in the fashion in which the French acted. He heard about the Schuman Plan barely an hour before the press conference in Paris at which it was announced. The French had consulted Konrad Adenauer, in Bonn, secretly in advance (which Bevin didn't know) and Dean Acheson on his way through Paris to London (which Bevin did know, to his indignation). They had not consulted him, and he was furious.

To the extent that Schuman and Monnet did move with deliberate calculation from the first secret steps to ensure that their plan would succeed, and not be blocked by the British, they did indeed outmaneuver Bevin and the Foreign Office. By obtaining Adenauer's advance agreement to the plan in secret, they confronted Bevin with something of a *fait accompli*—the key element, the vital principle of a supranational High Authority had already been accepted by West Germany, was not negotiable and would not be watered down. One nation's diplomacy is another nation's trickery.

Probably no Frenchman in this century knew Britain as well as Jean Monnet, who had lived and worked intimately with the British in London in two world wars. Monnet not only knew the British—he *understood* them. He spoke their language with an insight and usage which would do credit to Oxford and Cambridge. He was no phony Anglophile. His admiration and affection for Britain was deep and genuine. So was his acute feel for Europe. Monnet and the French had seen enough of postwar Foreign Office diplomacy in the problems of the Marshall Plan, the OEEC, the Council of Europe, to know perfectly well that Britain's basic attitude toward Europe had not changed. They knew with certainty what the first, knee-jerk reaction of Britain to the Coal and Steel Community proposal would be. To have consulted with Bevin first, before proposing the plan, would have again simply made a French plan hostage to British watering down.

By 1950 it was abundantly clear that Britain would not only always be the slowest ship in the European convoy—if the British had their way the convoy would never sail at all. But Monnet also knew the British well enough to know that in the end they would not, they could not let the convoy sail without them, or if by miscalculation they did, then one day they would certainly catch up and join. In the ensuing three weeks after the Schuman Plan was announced, both Monnet and Schuman spent hours in London in patient explanation, argument, pleading with the British—but never yielding on principle. Monnet was a deeply honorable man, no trickster, open and articulate and profound in analysis and argument. Schuman, if less articulate, had warmth and integrity. Outmaneuvered the British were, but they were not tricked, and they certainly had no grounds to be offended or peeved or angered after the intensive and patient way in which Monnet and Schuman and Ambassador René Massigli labored in those weeks to get Britain to walk through the open door and join the Coal and Steel Community as a founding member.†

Endless elegant and elliptical telegrams flowed from Paris under Monnet's drafting, proposing diplomatic formulations by which Britain could climb on board. But the French would not negotiate the principle of establishing a supranational High Authority with powers of its own to regulate and direct the coal and steel industries, and the British would not accept the principle of a High Authority without knowing exactly what powers it was going to exercise. On this issue Britain parted from Europe—finally to accept all this and far more in finally joining, more than two decades later.

"Experience has taught me that it is not a good thing for the British to obtain special conditions and an exceptional position in their relationships with others, or even for them to cherish such hopes," Monnet wrote in his *Memoirs*. "On the other hand, they are at their best if you firmly offer to work with them on an equal footing. If you stick to your principles, there is every likelihood that the British will sooner or later adapt to the situation and become partners in the full sense of the word. The debate in 1950 contained in embryo all of the many successive attitudes that Britain was to take *vis-à-vis* the European problem during the twenty-five years leading up to the referendum [on remaining in the Common Market] of 1975, when the question was settled once and for all. It revealed in the pure state the way in which the British saw themselves and their national destiny."

For their part, as the French and the Germans, together with the Dutch, the Belgians, the Italians and the Luxembourgers now moved off firmly on their own, the British reacted with sour grapes and ill grace. When negotiations on the Schuman Plan began, a stuffy formal statement by the British embassy in Paris said: "There are precedents of international organizations set up with

† See also Chapter 6, "The Schuman Plan."

fanfares of trumpets which encounter only difficulties and disappointments when the time comes to put them into practice." In their hearts the British simply could not believe that Europe could succeed without them.

When Winston Churchill returned to power, after the general election of October 1951, there was a brief surge of hope that the man who had called in Zurich for the building of "a kind of United States of Europe" would change the British outlook. But Churchill, who was then seventy-seven, had other things on his mind, and Anthony Eden, who returned to the Foreign Office, was, if anything, even less flexible about shaping a British role in Europe than Bevin had been. The Korean War was at its height, and a Commonwealth Division was the largest outside contingent fighting with the Americans in the front lines of Korea. The British were fighting their own Communist guerrilla war in the jungles of Malaya, they still had a major base in the Suez Canal, and the sun still never set on the Union Jack. To this view of the world, Europe was still peripheral.

All the same, the European problem would not go away—particularly since the tireless and fertile Jean Monnet had produced a new plan for the French Government: the Pleven Plan, for creation of a European army. In response to American demands for rearming West Germany so it could fill a much-needed role in the defenses of the North Atlantic Treaty Organization, Monnet proposed extending the supranational idea of the Coal and Steel Community to a European Defense Community. Thus, a reborn German army would not be a national army but part of a European army. It was a pretty awkward device to allay French fears. After all, coal and steel are inanimate industrial products, but men and armies are part of the lifeblood of nations. Still, when the Pleven Plan was proposed, in 1951, it was greeted with another surge of idealistic fervor—from the United States in particular. About the time that the Schuman Plan treaty negotiation was nearing a successful conclusion, negotiations for a Pleven Plan treaty opened in Paris among the same six countries—Britain once again electing to stay out. But, as Eden minuted to Churchill in December 1951: "Now that the Pleven Plan is running into trouble in the countries that put it forward, we are being made the whipping boy."

So Eden came up with an offer, half in and half out, to "link British forces under the direction of the Supreme Allied Commander in Europe with those of the European Defense Community for training, supply and operations by land, sea and air." When Robert Schuman pressed Eden for a formal treaty of mutual assistance with the European Defense Community, he got a dusty answer that "we already have the NATO commitment and I am not convinced that a further engagement is necessary." In any event, after long diplomatic and political wrangling, the French National Assembly finally killed the EDC treaty, refusing to ratify it, in August of 1954. There was a certain satisfaction in London at this collapse of a major European effort at supranationalism, and quiet self-congratulation on British wisdom in having remained outside.

Eden now mounted a triumphant diplomatic rescue operation. In a quick tour of European capitals, circling Paris until the last, he laid the groundwork for bringing West Germany into the Western European Union treaty, which already linked Britain, France, Italy and the Benelux countries. German rearmament with limits and controls would then take place under the WEU treaty, and at the same time West Germany would enter NATO and place her armed forces totally under NATO command. It was indeed a much more straightforward, workable and satisfactory solution than the cumbersome supranational structure of the EDC treaty—and seen from London, it was a setback for the European federalists and a resounding success for the British approach and British diplomacy.

All the same, the Coal and Steel Community was by now a going concern from its headquarters in Luxembourg, where Monnet served as the first president of the High Authority from 1952 to 1955. Britain at least had recognized this reality by establishing the first diplomatic delegation to the High Authority. Monnet next proposed that they go a step further and negotiate a "treaty of association" with the Coal and Steel Community, which was agreed in 1952.

By 1955, when Eden moved up to succeed Churchill as Prime

Minister, the British had pretty much written off European supranationalism and federalism as a spent force. They saw their diplomacy succeeding where French diplomacy had failed. They did
not reckon that the very setback of the EDC treaty would stir
the Europeans to renewed action on the economic front.

In June of 1955, foreign ministers of the six Coal and Steel
Community countries gathered at Messina, in Sicily, to discuss a
series of working papers tabled by various governments, all
addressed to the same theme: what should be done to reanimate
European progress after the setback of the EDC. After three days
of talks, they issued a historic resolution: "We believe that the
time has come to make a fresh advance toward the building of
Europe. . . . This must be achieved first of all in the economic
field. . . . It is necessary to work for the establishment of a
United Europe by the development of common institutions, the
progressive fusion of national economies, the creation of a common market and the progressive harmonization of social policies."

A negotiating committee was promptly formed under Belgium's
Paul-Henri Spaak to get down to work immediately on translat-
ing this resolution first into general proposals and then into a draft
treaty. An invitation immediately went to Great Britain to join in
the work of the committee on the ground floor as a full negotiating
partner.

The reply from London was one of lofty indifference. There
were "special difficulties for this country," the British said, but
they were sending an undersecretary from the Board of Trade,
R. F. Bretherton, economist and amateur entomologist, to sit in.
He was to be neither a delegate nor an observer but a "representative"—neither in nor out.

It soon became apparent from the few spare and critical or hostile remarks that the British permitted him to make in the
course of the Spaak Committee's preliminary work that the Common Market treaty would be a great deal easier to negotiate if the
British stayed out. In any case, when the first round of the Spaak
Committee's work was completed and the shape of what the Europeans were aiming for became clear on paper, the British went
over to open opposition. They withdrew Bretherton from any further sitting in on the work of the Six, and sent a stiff note to

Adenauer, in Bonn, declaring themselves against the creation of a Common Market, which in the British view would "divide" Europe. Instead the British proposed the creation of a wide European Free Trade Area, without any trappings of supranationalism, under the OEEC, in Paris.

Unruffled by this flank attack, the Spaak Committee drove ahead, its portly chairman proving himself to be a remarkably energetic leader as well as a polished technician and negotiator. Jean Monnet, meanwhile, was playing an active role on the sidelines with his Action Committee for a United States of Europe. Britain's back was turned. The year 1956 was the year of Suez and also the year of Hungary. Each of these cataclysmic events in its way played into the hands of the Spaak negotiators. Both Suez and Hungary seemed urgently to underline the need for Europe to unite and move forward.

The Treaty of Rome—an enormous but truly historic document of 248 articles, four annexes, thirteen protocols, four conventions and nine declarations—was signed on March 25, 1957.

By now, Harold Macmillan had succeeded Eden as Prime Minister, in the wreckage of Suez. Early on, at the time of the Council of Europe and the Schuman Plan proposal, Macmillan, in the ranks of the Tory party, had shown himself to be a great deal more sympathetic and open-minded about Europe than Eden. But his first move was to step up pressure for a European Free Trade Area before the Common Market treaty could come into force.

Macmillan named one of the younger potential Tory leaders, Reginald Maudling, to a cabinet post as Paymaster General, with the specific assignment of pushing the Free Trade Area idea around Europe and in the OEEC. Adapting to growing realities, the British now proposed that the Common Market be treated as a single entity within such a free-trade arrangement. At first this idea got a welcome from Monnet and his Action Committee, but when Spaak went to London to talk about the fine print, the British made known that they wanted free trade only for industrial products—not agriculture. Continental enthusiasm promptly cooled. As Maudling made his way tirelessly to Strasbourg and the Council of Europe, to national capitals and to endless OEEC meetings in Paris, the governments of the Six made it clear that as far as they were concerned, the first priority was ratification of the Treaty of Rome.

Then, in the spring of 1958, European affairs ground to a halt while France went through the trauma of the de Gaulle revolution —the end of the Fourth Republic and the return in triumph of General Charles de Gaulle. Dedicated Europeans, within France and outside, greeted the change in France's fortunes with apprehension. From his isolation at Colombey-les-Deux-Églises, de Gaulle had regularly heaped scorn on the idea of supranationalism or surrender of French sovereignty. His opposition to the European Defense Community treaty had been one of the chief factors in its ultimate rejection by the National Assembly. He treated Jean Monnet with something close to contempt.‡

The British embassy in Paris, however, drew momentary heart from all this, and advised London that there was every chance that de Gaulle would sabotage the Common Market treaty, due to its supranational and federalist character. The European Free Trade Area seemed to be an arrangement much more to de Gaulle's taste. The British seemed to have forgotten about agriculture.

Not for the first or the last time, the British misjudged de Gaulle. They did not realize his capacity for extracting every possible advantage for France from the Common Market while simply ignoring or riding roughshod over those treaty obligations he did not like. The British now pushed energetically and hopefully for a decision out of the OEEC on a Free Trade Area. They got it all right. On November 14, 1958, General de Gaulle's Minister of Information simply announced to the press—not even to the OEEC—that "it has become clear to France that it is not possible to set up the Free Trade Area as wished by the British." There were protests and consternation, but that was that. The British retired with wounded pride and patched together a small European Free Trade Area of seven outer-rim states: Britain, Norway, Sweden, Denmark, Austria, Switzerland, Portugal.

‡ De Gaulle had Monnet's phone tapped, but Monnet simply told callers, "What difference does it make—maybe they'll learn something."

Thus, in 1959 Europe divided into the Common Market Six and the EFTA Seven. But it did not take Harold Macmillan long to realize that the convoy had now sailed, and like it or not, Britain had to catch up and join. He circled the problem as if he were dancing a Mozart minuet—advancing, bowing, touching hands, retreating, smiling, but ever hesitating to grab the delicate beauty by the waist for a whirl. What was he waiting for? He vastly improved his domestic power base with an election victory in October 1959. On trips to Washington, he found even the Americans were beginning to ask embarrassing questions about missing the boat and all that. At long last, he made up his mind, toward the end of 1960, to take the plunge.

First he decided on a little bilateral testing with visits to his old comrade from Algiers, General de Gaulle; to Adenauer, in Bonn; to Joseph Luns, in The Hague; to Brussels; to Rome and again to Washington. Finally, in July of 1961, he was ready. But he certainly maneuvered and waffled deliberately to remove any and all sense of change or the dramatic from what he was about to do. First of all he made a great ploy out of the fact that he had "cleared it with Kennedy" and the new American President had no objection. This was not exactly the picture of a Palmerstonian leader deciding where British interests lay and then acting decisively. Moreover, Macmillan insisted on hedging his bets to an exasperating degree by applying *not* to join the European Community but for "a negotiation to see if mutually acceptable conditions could be worked out for British membership." It was the same old British stance that had been adopted at the time of the Schuman Plan. Britain was still refusing to accept the principles of the organization she now sought to join, but wanted to see what kind of a deal she could get. All the same, the Schuman Plan had been only a proposal, while the Common Market was an organization in being. The Europeans had long pleaded with Britain to face this reality and join, and if Macmillan at long last was prepared to make the effort, then his political tactics would have to be accommodated as part of the price of admission.

Sensing trouble in this approach, Monnet issued a formal comment soon after Macmillan's announcement: "The negotiations must move rapidly to avoid creating confusion. It is a mistake to

think that wide-ranging negotiations are necessary. We must not
let ourselves be impressed by the problems of substance; they are
not all that difficult to solve. What counts is the decision to tackle
questions in a forward-looking and constructive manner, rather
than in terms of maintaining the past. That is the fundamental decision which the British Government has now taken. That is what
is historic."

But it was not to be.

Under Edward Heath, the British organized a very strong and
competent European negotiating team of four top-ranking civil
servants—"The Flying Knights" they were soon called, with their
endless aerial shuttling from London and Paris to Brussels and
back. But not only did the British table a list of "special problems" that was endless and complex; the very form of the negotiation was excessively awkward. Due to the kind of application
Macmillan had chosen to make, Britain was negotiating *not* with
the Common Market as an institution but with its six national governments. Thus, for every problem the British raised there was not
one answer but three or four or five or six. The negotiations began
formally on October 10, 1961, and ended fifteen months later,
after General de Gaulle's veto at the most famous of his many
press conferences in Paris, on January 14, 1963. The speed and
dash that Monnet foresaw as essential to success simply was never
there.*

Nobody will ever know when General de Gaulle made up his
mind to bar Britain from Europe. From what he said at the time,
it seems that when the negotiations got underway he was genuinely open-minded about Britain's joining. Nor will anyone ever
know the extent to which his deep-seated vindictiveness over old
slights and slurs at the hands of the British—some real, some imagined, many self-inflicted—figured in de Gaulle's ultimate action.
But the fact remains that the British approach of reluctant willingness, and the tedious, tiresome and nit-picking problems of the negotiation itself, certainly played into the General's hands. There is
little doubt that the negotiation could have succeeded if de Gaulle
had been prepared to see it succeed. All of this has been endlessly

* See also Chapter 7, "Harold Macmillan," and Chapter 10, "The Fifth
Republic."

debated, argued, analyzed and written about. In the final meeting at Brussels, when Couve de Murville made some lofty reference to Britain's being an island, Heath shot back: "We were an island when the negotiation began." But it was like debating a death sentence after the guillotine had done its work.

The end in Brussels was one of those times when Ted Heath's detached, pragmatic, Oxford Union political style served well. He summed up with masterful understatement on a note of disappointment and dismay but not defeat—and he showed great political self-control in avoiding any recriminations against de Gaulle and the French. He left that to Macmillan.

"This is a sad moment for European unity," he told the final negotiating meeting, in Brussels on January 29, 1963. "We told you at the beginning that we wanted to go forward with you in the building of a new Europe. Our words were very carefully weighed. They remain true today. We have been encouraged by the upsurge of support for the fullest British participation in a United Europe which has been demonstrated in so many quarters in these recent weeks. And so I would say to my colleagues: They should have no fear. We in Britain are not going to turn our backs on the mainland of Europe or on the countries of the Community. We are a part of Europe; by geography, tradition, history, culture and civilization. We shall continue to work with all our friends in Europe for the true unity and strength of this continent."

If Britain's first bid to join Europe had ended ignominiously, it was nevertheless all the more certain after the de Gaulle veto that one day Britain would join. The very defeat at de Gaulle's hands was bound to stimulate the European challenge for the British. After the misjudgments and fumbles about Europe for fifteen years in London, Macmillan and Heath had brought about a whole new orientation of British policy, even if it had been brushed off with ill grace by de Gaulle. As one senior British civil servant remarked at the time: "Well, we must now behave like any other rejected lover, and go take a long walk in the country. . . ."

Harold Wilson, when he arrived at No. 10 Downing Street as Labour Prime Minister, in October 1964, had for the previous five years been expending much of his highly touted talent for care-

fully prepared ad libs and polished political epigrams in decrying
the Common Market and deriding Macmillan, Heath and the
Tories for their efforts to drag proud Britain into bed with all
those continental frogs, Wops and Huns. As a political leader,
Wilson performed like a little, round, steel ball in a pinball machine, rolling around and bouncing from one bumper to the next,
making lights flash and the score climb—the more lights and the
higher the score the better. Having rung up all the political points
he could get in opposition to membership in the Common Market,
Wilson now rolled to the next bumper to run up his score as a
"statesman" by launching a new bid to join Europe and succeed
where the Tories had failed. In October 1966, prodded by his
ebullient and unstable Foreign Secretary, George Brown, who at
least *was* obsessed with a genuine conviction about Europe, Wilson
announced that he was going to apply for British membership in
the Common Market "and would not take no for an answer."

Since General de Gaulle was still sitting impassively and immobile in the Élysée Palace, more entrenched and self-satisfied than
ever in pursuit of French *grandeur,* this Wilson *volte-face* on
Europe was not merely mistimed—it was downright embarrassing
in the way it was carried out. Wilson and Brown trailed around
Europe from one capital to the next like Tonio and Canio in
Pagliacci, beating the drum and exhorting the rustics to come to
watch the traveling players at the next performance of their mar-
velous *commedia.* It was all typified by Brown's heartfelt and fervent plea to Willy Brandt, which Brandt said he found "perplexing
and disillusioning": "Willy, you must get us in so we can take the
lead."

All the same, on May 2, 1967, Wilson did sign and deliver to
Brussels and the Common Market capitals a straightforward and
unambiguous letter of British application to join under Article
273 of the Treaty of Rome, and he did declare the hope that
"negotiations will be followed through swiftly on the small number
of really important issues which are to be satisfied." Britain had
thus moved another long step down the road from the Macmillan
application "to see if conditions could be worked out for British
membership." And from the standpoint of British domestic politics, it was of course of inestimable importance that Labour, as

well as the Conservatives, was now committed to joining Europe. But none of this cut any ice with General de Gaulle. He pondered things for three weeks and then called a press conference. Britain, he pronounced, was not yet ready to join Europe. He went over the same litany of commitments to the Commonwealth, commitments to EFTA, and added some new preconditions in the form of a derisory critique of the weakness of the British economy and the state of the British pound. When the Six then met to discuss the British application, the French insisted that they must reach a common position among themselves before negotiating— and since France was able to block ever reaching a common position at all, the British application simply lay on the table and negotiations never even began. *Finita la commedia!*

But, having said that he would not take no for an answer, Harold Wilson kept poking away at the problem from London. De Gaulle's departure from office after his referendum defeat in April 1969 was, for the British, like a stone rolled away. But Georges Pompidou, as de Gaulle's successor, would not be rushed. It was not until a Common Market summit conference at The Hague in December 1969 that the French finally gave a grudging commitment to open negotiations with Great Britain in return for a pledge by the other Common Market heads of state to work out new finance arrangements for agriculture beforehand. Willy Brandt did play the decisive role in opening the door again at last.

Almost certainly, the prospect of opening negotiations to join Europe was one of the elements that contributed to Wilson's decision to go for an early election, fifteen months before one would have been necessary, in June of 1970. But, to Wilson's stunned disbelief and the almost total surprise of the country at large, Ted Heath and the Conservative Party put on a last-minute spurt to squeeze first past the post. All that remained now was for Heath and the British to walk through Europe's open door.

Despite the abrupt change of government, the Foreign Office negotiating team was ready, and Heath knew the problem backwards and forwards. The Common Market, true to its pledge, had scheduled an opening negotiating meeting with the British to take place in Luxembourg on June 30, 1970. Heath, after all the years of waiting, was not about to ask for any further delay. He sent a senior minister, Anthony Barber, to Luxembourg to give full cabinet weight to Britain's opening statement of the negotiation. Inexplicably, after twenty years of fumbling, the British delegation failed to provide the myriad of European journalists who flocked to Luxembourg for the occasion with translations of the Barber statement in French, Italian, German and Dutch—the only official Community languages at that time!

All the same, the remainder is swift to summarize. The British declared themselves ready to swallow the Common Market treaty whole—save for some special arrangements to protect Commonwealth sugar imports into Britain, and New Zealand lamb and butter, plus other technical but on the whole marginal problems of adjustment. Heath, on an important visit to Paris for a long and detailed *tête-à-tête* with Pompidou, managed to reduce the biggest French roadblock, over the question of the strength of the British pound. Of course a treaty of accession to a treaty as long and complex as the Treaty of Rome took endless drafting—at the end it totalled some four hundred pages. Heath went to Brussels for the signing ceremony—marred when an ink bottle was thrown at him and spilled over his Savile Row suit. Britain entered Europe on January 1, 1973.

But this was not the end of the inglorious British saga. After three years of exemplary diplomatic and political leadership to cement the new British relationship with the Continent, Edward Heath was ousted by the electorate, in February 1974. Harold Wilson came bouncing back into Downing Street. The Tories, he promptly proclaimed, had flubbed the negotiation to join Europe, had given far too much away, and now he would have to set it all right. The terms would be renegotiated, he announced. The fact that Britain had signed and ratified a treaty, and that he was calling into question a record of historic British integrity, did not embarrass or inhibit Wilson at all. His tawdry maneuver was such transparent pandering to the anti-Common Market left wing of the Labour Party that it ought to have been thrown in the wastebasket by the other Common Market members. But they swallowed their irritation—perhaps out of sadness and pity for the ignominious political and economic condition into which poor old proud Britain had now fallen. The fatuous Wilson "renegotiation" charade went on for over a year, and endless British capital of Common Market good will and sympathy was expended for some marginal advantages that Wilson could parade before the Tories and his left wing. But this was still not enough. He then decided to put the whole Common Market membership question to a national referendum—two and a half years after Britain had joined! In British constitutional history, Parliament has always been supreme, and never before had there *ever* been a national referendum. Nevertheless, Britain had to go through yet another maneuver to satisfy the political acrobatics of one of the most insufferable Prime Ministers in its history.

Not unexpectedly, when the voice of the people was heard, it was not to the liking of the left wing of the Labour Party. On June 5, 1975, 67 percent voted in favor of honoring Britain's treaty obligation and remaining in the Common Market.

Twenty-five years had elapsed since Jean Monnet went to London to plead with Britain to join the Schuman Plan. In 1950 the British had the highest per capita income in Europe, along with all the other advantages of prestige of victory and pride of leadership. By 1975, Britain was the poor relation, the supplicant problem of Europe, trailing just above Italy in gross national product, third from the bottom of the Common Market per capita income scale. It has been an unhappy story of a scepter'd but blinkered isle, stranded in the silver sea of its own history.

17

Valéry Giscard d'Estaing

VALÉRY GISCARD D'ESTAING, THIRD PRESIDENT OF THE FIFTH Republic and twentieth President of France, is the personification and epitome of the elitist system by which the French are educated and governed.

Born in 1926, a teenager during World War II, he is a postwar graduate of both the *École Polytechnique,* founded by Napoleon in 1802 to create an elite corps of engineers for his armies, and the *École Nationale d'Administration,* founded by General Charles de Gaulle in 1945 to create an elite corps of civil servants to run the government. He is the son of an *inspecteur des finances,* one of the elite corps of financial experts created by King Louis XV in the eighteenth century to run the French treasury. He followed in his father's footsteps by becoming an *inspecteur* himself when he graduated from ENA. Politics is the road to power in most democracies. But in France it is the Civil Service. Giscard d'Estaing was born into the system, educated by the system, used the system to rise spectacularly, and never seems to have doubted that he would go all the way to the top.

The idea of deliberately creating an elite inner circle of civil servants inside a democracy and then handing it vast powers over the levers and wheels of government with scant regard for politicians or the electorate would seem to be something to avoid, shun, abhor and fear. But in France the existence of this elite corps is a matter of national pride and inspiration. To join the elite, if you can make it, is one of the privileges of *liberté, fraternité et égalité* —more or less. Pursuit of elite status is instilled in the French from the moment the six-year-old child dips one of those old-fashioned nib pens into an ink pot and starts out painfully under the baleful eye of a *maîtresse* to write the first letter of the alphabet without a blot. From then on, the French educational system sifts and ruthlessly discards tens of thousands of students. But those who make it into one of the elite *grandes écoles* are secure, protected and vastly rewarded with power.

At the summit of the elitist educational system lies Giscard d'Estaing's alma mater, the École Nationale d'Administration. There is, quite simply, no institution anywhere in the world like this superacademy for training the cream of the French civil servants and its diplomatic corps. There is no great mystery about the school and how it operates and is organized, or how the ENA power structure in France has grown and become all-pervasive since the war. Its doors are open to foreign students (usually including at least one American), and other governments regularly send senior civil servants to Paris to take a look at how it works. But ENA is so quintessentially French, such a reflection of French Government tradition, French logic and mentality and approach to education, that neither the institution nor the system can be transplanted or duplicated in any other national environment. ENA represents the ultimate refinement of the hold the French Civil Service has always exercised on substantive power. Politicians come and go in France, as does crisis, revolution, defeat and victory, but the Civil Service survives and continues and bridges the gaps—for better or worse. Politicians preside and fix temporary priorities, but they are never around long enough to wrest away that residual power of the *hautes fonctionnaires*.

It all began with King Louis XV's creation, the Inspection des Finances, a special "club" of civil servants that was given an original lock hold on state power through authority to approve or reject state spending, including even that of the King himself, if the *inspecteurs* decided that the treasury could not afford to pay. To assure probity and independence of the Inspection des Finances, the Catholic King even staffed it with frugal Huguenot Protestants. They in turn made the Inspection into a kind of self-perpetuating and strongly Protestant oligarchy within the state, choosing those they would admit to power. The *inspecteurs* went right on controlling the French treasury while the guillotine did its work in the Revolution. They were bowing at the door when Na-

poleon walked into power, and they still control the purse strings
of the Fifth Republic.

During World War II, the vast majority of French civil servants
simply sat out the occupation, shuffling their dossiers in the same
routines and trying to pay as little attention as possible to those
who were exercising authority and giving orders. They behaved, in
other words, as they were trained to behave. Was it collaboration?
What *is* collaboration? In any case, when de Gaulle returned to
Paris with the Liberation in 1944, it was manifestly impossible to
purge those who had stayed on the job and worked under Nazi or
Vichy direction. Instead, in the Napoleonic tradition and style, de
Gaulle decided to create a new school to train a new generation of
elite and put an entirely new veneer on the old government machine. And so, the École Nationale d'Administration was born.

De Gaulle picked as its founding director his ardent supporter
Michel Debré, who later helped draft the constitution of the Fifth
Republic and was its first Premier, from 1959 to 1962. Then, to
make certain that the new educational hot-house would take hold,
it was established by regulation that only ENA graduates would in
future be accepted into the Inspection des Finances; the diplomatic service; the Corps des Préfects, the Conseil d'État, where
laws are drafted and reviewed; and other key civil service positions
of power. It's as if in the United States an officer could rise to general in the Army or admiral in the Navy only with a West Point or
Annapolis diploma, or a lawyer could only be admitted to the bar
of the United States Supreme Court with a Harvard or a Yale law
degree.

The intake of students at ENA is extremely small, about one
hundred a year, and competition for places is ferocious. In the
thirty-five years since its founding, it has produced a minuscule
number of graduates: about three thousand. But their hold on positions of power is out of all proportion to their numbers. The
énarques, as they are called, are a formidable "old-boy net" that
makes Harvard Law School and Britain's Oxford and Cambridge
look like mere kindergartens when it comes to the power their
graduates wield over national affairs and government.

The *énarques,* when they have completed three years of intensely competitive schooling, get to pick the particular *corps,* or

branch of government service, where they want to specialize, first choice to those who finish at the top. They usually go for the Inspection des Finances, the Conseil d'État, or the Corps Diplomatique and the Ministry of Foreign Affairs. Once inside, they start out in junior postings of responsibility, but they move quickly. By the age of thirty they can expect to join the personal staff, or *cabinet,* of a government minister, or become a deputy *préfect* in one of the regional departments or a political officer in a French embassy abroad. An ENA diploma guarantees a privileged position within the Civil Service, so it is not competition in the usual sense. Of course some *énarques* are more successful and effective than others, but after the ruthless competition to get inside the system, very few flub it once they are there. Today, as de Gaulle intended, they have infused the entire top echelons of state power.

Starting with the President of France, one quarter of the ministers in the present government are ENA graduates. Most of the French ambassadors have ENA diplomas. Cabinet directors in all the French ministries are ENA men or women. *Énarques* head the Banque de France and most of the major commercial banks, the nationalized Renault Automobile Company, Air France, all nationalized enterprises such as gas, electricity, coal, railroads and aerospace. They are on the boards of private companies in the chemical industry, oil, aluminum, steel and engineering. They run the state economic planning machinery. The two French members of the Common Market Commission, in Brussels, during the 1970s were both ENA graduates. If they decide to leave government service after a requisite number of years, an *énarque* diploma is a certain cachet for success in private business as well. In politics the Gaullist party leader, Jacques Chirac, is an ENA graduate, and so is the No. 2 man and probable future leader of the Socialist Party, Michel Rocard. So it seems a fair bet that Giscard d'Estaing's eventual successor may well turn out to be an ENA graduate also.

There aren't many *énarques,* but this very fact increases their effective power, because they know each other and can get on the telephone and pull levers within the system on behalf of one another. It is arguable in the end whether individually a Frenchman with an ENA diploma is any more brilliant than his opposite in the upper echelons of the British Civil Service, or his German or American counterpart. But the *énarques* are able to *perform* more effectively due to the system and their secure hold on power. Their *grand patron* is Valéry Giscard d'Estaing.

He was born on February 2, 1926, in the German Rhineland city of Coblentz, where his father was attached to the French occupation administration following the First World War. He was one of six children, a comfortable, well-off *famille haute-bourgeoise* with roots in the Auvergne region of France, from which Georges Pompidou also came. The family does not spring from some old or noble line of aristocracy, as is popularly imagined, although of course Giscard d'Estaing is proud to trace his antecedents back for a couple of centuries, as most French families are able to do. But his father simply added the aristocratic prefix of *de* to the family name in 1922—and became Edmond d'Estaing instead of plain Monsieur Estaing. This is frequently the case with aristocratic-sounding French names. At any rate, young Valéry grew up in comfort in Paris and the city of Clermont-Ferrand in south-central France, in an atmosphere of determinedly aristocratic outlook and self-esteem. He was thirteen when war broke out, in 1939, and he did what most other French boys of his age did: He continued in school. He passed the first big hurdle in the French educational sifting, the *baccalauréat* examination, which guarantees admission to university, in 1943, when he was seventeen, having majored in mathematics and philosophy. But of course the war hung over everything.

Waiting for the war to end, he joined a young resistance group at Clermont-Ferrand and planned an escape to England with a couple of friends. But the contact for the operation was caught by the Germans and the plan had to be abandoned. Then, in June of 1944, came the invasion of Normandy, and in August the bulk of the Free French Army, which had been fighting in Italy under the command of General Alphonse Juin, landed on the French Mediterranean coast to drive up the Rhône Valley, liberate southern France and link up with the main Allied Armies, which were advancing on a broad front to the German Rhine. Giscard d'Estaing, a very tall and lanky eighteen-year-old, made his way South from Clermont-Ferrand to enlist as soon as he could contact the advancing French forces. He was assigned to a tank regiment, fought through the winter campaign of 1944–45 around Strasbourg and Belfort, crossed the Rhine, and ended the war in Germany. Awarded the Croix de Guerre, he was demobilized in 1946. Then, on the strength of his *baccalauréat,* his military service and a competitive examination, he got a coveted place in the École Polytechnique.

Although still a military institution run by the Ministry of Defense, with the uniforms and tradition of Napoleon's day, the École Polytechnique is a very modern educational institution with a much wider function than simply training army engineers. It focuses today on mathematics, science, economics, computers, electronics and advanced technologies, and only a small portion of its graduates continue in a military career. Its two-year course is designed, moreover, to fit the competitive requirements for admission on up the ladder into the École Nationale d'Administration. In the upper tenth of his class in 1948, Giscard d'Estaing slid readily into ENA. But, before his courses began, he spent six months in Canada and the United States, teaching and traveling and learning English, which he speaks and reads fluently.

He did well at ENA—not brilliantly, but close enough to the top to be able to become an *inspecteur des finances* at the end of his three years there, in 1952. A classmate remembers him as being extremely quick and facile, brilliant in improvisation, rather than solid or thorough or systematic, in his approach to his courses. Nor was he overly popular, with his rather arrogant and egotistical personality. From the start, he made it clear by his attitude toward his fellow students and associates that he considered himself superior. The elitist system was made for him, and he was not going to waste time being humble in making the most of it.

When he finished his ENA schooling and was preparing for his first assignment at the French treasury, he married Anne-Aymone de Brantes, daughter of a French Army officer in a family of considerable wealth. A grandfather had been one of the founders of the great nineteenth-century Schneider steel manufacturing and industrial concern. Giscard's bride, who was born in 1933, lived in London as a little girl from 1937 to 1939, when her father was assigned there as military attaché, and then in Lisbon in 1941–42. The family returned to France under the occupation, and her father became active in the resistance. He was caught by the Gestapo and deported to Mauthausen concentration camp, where he died in May 1944.

One of Giscard's first assignments as an *inspecteur des finances* was an extended swing through some of what were then still the African colonies of the French Empire, to supervise preparations of budget and financial programs and check the administrative accounts. It is a good example of how the French system works, to put a very young man into a key role in the exercise of power. It also was the beginning of an African association for the ambitious and rising *inspecteur* which later became one of the focal points of his presidency. By 1955, after various other assignments at the treasury, he became deputy cabinet director in the office of Premier Edgar Faure, one of the more successful politicians of the Fourth Republic and one of the few who also played a role in the Fifth Republic.

In the Premier's office, Giscard d'Estaing, not yet thirty years old, was at the center of power, just as Georges Pompidou had been when he joined General Charles de Gaulle's Cabinet after the liberation of Paris in 1944. Now came a chance to add politics to his credentials of an ENA diploma and membership in the Inspection des Finances. His grandfather held what was practically a family seat in the National Assembly from one of the election districts of Clermont-Ferrand. In 1956 he decided to retire, and young Giscard ran to take his place. He was elected handily, left the Civil Service, and took a seat in Parliament as the Fourth Republic lurched to its end. For the ensuing two and a half years, Giscard d'Estaing was a brilliant young man waiting in the wings, serving on the Finance Committee of the National Assembly as governments came and went. Then, in May of 1958, began the political cyclone that brought down the Fourth Republic and swept General de Gaulle back into power. The new, Fifth Republic constitution was adopted by national referendum, and elections were held for a new National Assembly—to which Giscard was returned. In January 1959, the first government of the Fifth Republic was formed, with Michel Debré as Prime Minister under de

Gaulle's presidency. Valéry Giscard d'Estaing became Secretary of State for Finance and No. 2 man at the treasury. At thirty-three he was the youngest man in the government. Three years later, when de Gaulle brought Pompidou in as Prime Minister, Giscard moved up to become Minister of Finance and Economic Affairs, the youngest Finance Minister in French history. He held the post until 1966.

Giscard d'Estaing was an ideal Gaullist minister—as tall as the General himself and similarly cold, brilliant and arrogant. He showed a zest for Gaullist style and positively reveled in all the grandeur and independence of de Gaulle's thunderbolt diplomacy. He took on the protocol mannerism of the Grand Master, such as making sure that he arrived last for meetings of European Common Market Finance Ministers to make a grand entry with the others seated and waiting.

He also showed a Gaullist ruthlessness and taste for political maneuver and intrigue. By mid-1963, following the General's veto of British entry into the Common Market, France was facing economic difficulties. Expansionist policies had worked well in the five years following de Gaulle's return to power, but inflation was now running well ahead of expansion and pushing the country into a weakening position *vis-à-vis* its European partners, Germany in particular. Prime Minister Pompidou was taking a relaxed view of the situation, believing that economic liberalism to encourage investment would result in higher production and an improved competitive position. But the ambitious Finance Minister, behind Pompidou's back or over his head, had captured de Gaulle's ear to urge economic discipline and a deflationary policy of austerity and stability. He used terms that were music to de Gaulle's concepts of leadership and of France.

De Gaulle moved with typical shock tactics against his own government. In August, Pompidou left for St. Tropez and a vacation on the Côte d'Azur. Suddenly, on August 13, he got a summons to return immediately to Paris for an emergency cabinet meeting. Ministers gathered to find de Gaulle in one of his cold, fuming rages, declaiming against the government for inactivity and demanding "decisive measures in two weeks" to halt inflation and impose stability. Moreover, he turned to the Finance Minister and personally charged him with preparing the plan of action. Giscard d'Estaing, from the treasury citadel on the rue de Rivoli, called the *inspecteurs* together and went to work without even consulting Pompidou. When the austerity plan was ready, de Gaulle decided that it would be announced by the Prime Minister and the Finance Minister at a joint news conference. It was painfully obvious— Giscard did nothing to hide it—that the Prime Minister had been rebuffed by de Gaulle and upstaged by his young Finance Minister.

In the intrigue of the Gaullist court, the launching of the 1963 austerity-stabilization program placed Giscard d'Estaing in the running as de Gaulle's potential successor—along with Pompidou. Of course neither man would dare proclaim or even hint to any such ambition, but it soon became known in Élysée Palace gossip that de Gaulle had said to the young man: "When you are President of France one day. . . ." It was part of the game de Gaulle played, but it was pretty heady stuff. Much later it was reported by de Gaulle's intimates that he had also remarked of Giscard: "One day he will betray me. Let's hope that he does it well!" This, indeed, was a remark much in the General's style. Moreover, de Gaulle was right.

Pompidou waited, shrewd and careful as always. The longer he remained in office, close to de Gaulle, the more likely it would be that he would be the next President, whatever Giscard's maneuverings. His moment to strike back came finally after the presidential election of December 1965, when de Gaulle ran for a second term and was forced into an unexpected and humiliating runoff by the Socialist Party leader, François Mitterrand. Pompidou promptly blamed the election setback on Giscard, and found de Gaulle a ready listener: "By prolonging the austerity plan unduly, the Minister of Finance was largely responsible for the failure of the first-round ballot. If we keep him on, we shall run the risk for the same reason of suffering an even more serious setback in the 1967 legislative elections," the Prime Minister argued. So, in January 1966, when Pompidou was renamed to form a new government to start de Gaulle's second term of office, Giscard d'Estaing was dropped from the Cabinet. He was succeeded by the ever-ready Michel Debré, who took over with a mandate to relaunch expansion in place of austerity and get the country in a good mood for the National Assembly elections.

Under the Fifth Republic constitution, Giscard d'Estaing quickly returned to the National Assembly seat that he had given up to become a government minister eight years before. He became chairman of the Assembly's Finance Committee, but, more important, he took over active leadership of the group of centrist Assembly members with whom he had long been associated, the Independent Republicans. They were junior partners with the Gaullists in the government majority in the Assembly. But as the run-up to the 1967 legislative elections began, Giscard d'Estaing sought to give his party more of an identity and position of its own by adopting an ingenious campaign slogan: *"Oui—mais. . . ."* (Yes —but. . . .) This drew infinite scorn from General de Gaulle and the Gaullists, but with the French electorate looking for safe alternatives, the campaign tactic worked well enough to improve the strength of the Independent Republicans and also to give Giscard more of a political image in the country at large.

Then came the events of May 1968, culminating when de Gaulle dropped Pompidou as Prime Minister after the dust began to settle, in July. Pompidou now joined Giscard d'Estaing in exile in the National Assembly, and Giscard quickly showed his adroitness as well as his eye on the future by smoothly setting out to patch up his relations with the former Prime Minister. Both men knew that the time of Gaullist succession could not be long delayed. Pompidou was ready for sympathy, and he got it promptly from Giscard—particularly at the time of the Delon-Markovic affair and the rumors of Madame Pompidou's attending lewd parties, when it seemed that the Élysée Palace was deliberately fostering a campaign of smear and political blackmail. By private and public gestures, Giscard, fifteen years younger than Pompidou, threw his personal support behind the older man in the certainty that the succession would go to Pompidou and that he could afford to secure his own position and wait.

In April 1969, when de Gaulle launched his fatal referendum on constitutional reform, Giscard d'Estaing found his moment to "betray" the General, and he did it well. He came out openly for a

"no" vote and a defeat of the referendum—none of the "yes—
but. . . ." tactic any longer. On the other hand, Pompidou and
the Gaullists had loyally if not very enthusiastically gone through
the motions of support for the General. Giscard's open opposition was therefore certainly of importance to the outcome. At
midnight on Sunday, April 27, 1969, with 53 percent of the French
voters having said no to the referendum, General de Gaulle's resignation as President of France was announced over television by his
Prime Minister, Maurice Couve de Murville. The election process
began almost at once, and Pompidou, in the end, was an easy victor, although it took two rounds of voting to wrap it up. Jacques
Chaban-Delmas became Pompidou's first Prime Minister, and Giscard d'Estaing returned to the treasury as Minister of Economics
and Finance.

General de Gaulle left another *bon mot* behind that has long
dogged Giscard d'Estaing: "The trouble with Giscard is the people." Responding to this in an election broadcast when he was
running for the presidency after Pompidou's death, in 1974, Giscard said of himself: "I am accused of being cold. I think this is
untrue. I think I am reserved because that is my nature, and because I don't much like show. But reserved people feel as strongly
as others do. I want to look France in the eyes, but also appeal to
her heart." Whatever his view of himself, and his hope to appeal
to French hearts, Giscard's basic strength with the French voters
scarcely lies in warmth or emotion. His approach to the French is
that of an aristocratic pedagogue, the appeal of the elitist. It is not
hearts he appeals to, but brains, with the kind of cold intellectual
efficiency and capacity for logical exposition that are expected of
graduates of the École Nationale d'Administration and members
of the Inspection des Finances.

One of his close political associates and cabinet ministers,
Jacques Duhamel, wrote of him: "Giscard d'Estaing embodies the
type of man who is not of popular essence, but who provokes admiration. It is his competence, his authority which can carry him
through a process of reasoning, through an instinct of conservatism, if need be through a reflex of caution. It is not the impression of belonging to the same class as those he asks to vote for

him. It is not a movement of the heart, not a sentimental approval by which he gains his support."

The Ministry of Finance, where he spent thirteen years in all before becoming President of the Republic in 1974, is not exactly a place where the heart is expected to supersede the brain. And in fact, his record as France's treasury minister for so many years was not particularly original or enlivening. Of course he was efficient and impressive and projected himself on the international monetary scene with great style. But he was no innovator. In fact, it was Georges Pompidou himself, with his banker's background, who largely controlled the decision-making process in the economic sphere after de Gaulle's departure. It was Pompidou who decided on a quick devaluation of the French franc after he moved into the Élysée Palace, and Pompidou who guided policy in 1971, when President Nixon abruptly abandoned the Bretton Woods obligations and ended convertibility of the dollar into gold. The key elements in the subsequent package of currency realignment were worked out by Pompidou and Nixon at their 1971 conference in the Azores, which was then taken by Giscard d'Estaing to Washington for negotiation in what became the Smithsonian Agreement. It is therefore difficult to place any political labels or identity or personality on Giscard d'Estaing apart from all-purpose terms such as brilliant, clear-headed, penetrating, analytical, efficient, sure of himself, polished, etc. But, in a world of growing technologic complexity, perhaps that is what people want and government needs.

The end for Georges Pompidou came with great suddenness, in April 1974, despite all the visible evidence for well over a year that he was a sick man. He carried on with incredible willpower and stoic discipline right to the last, and the secret that he had a fatal cancer was well kept. Only two weeks before he died, he flew to the Black Sea to confer with Leonid Brezhnev. When he began his last, painful and agonizing descent to death, not even his closest cabinet associate, Foreign Minister Michel Jobert, was told that the end was near. Pompidou was at his own country home west of Paris when the cancer finally closed in on his remaining strength, and he asked that he be taken to spend his final hours at the apartment where he had lived for more than twenty years in the heart of Paris on the Isle Saint-Louis. Suddenly, without a word of warning, shortly before 9 P.M. on April 2, 1974, radio and television programs were interrupted with the announcement that the President of the Republic was dead.

The machinery of the constitution of the Fifth Republic again took over. There were three principal candidates: The perennial François Mitterrand, who had pushed General de Gaulle into a runoff in the election of 1965 and who this time would have the backing of an ostensibly united Socialist-Communist Confederation of the Left; Jacques Chaban-Delmas, Pompidou's former Prime Minister, who would be the official candidate of the Gaullist Party; and Valéry Giscard d'Estaing, leader of the Independent Republicans. In the meantime, under the constitution, the old government remained in place until a new President was elected, so that Giscard was still the Minister of Finance. From the outset of the campaign, Mitterrand, with the united backing of the Left, led comfortably over the other two in public-opinion polls. Chaban-Delmas proved to be a poor campaigner and a dull speaker. Giscard launched a John F. Kennedy-style political blitz, almost embarrassingly imitative of American campaign methods.

Realizing that, indeed, "the trouble with Giscard is the people," he cooperated fully with his managers and French photographers in an incongruous series of photo "happenings": Giscard playing an accordion in the local bistro in his home town in the Auvergne; Giscard in a pullover sweater riding the Paris Métro with ordinary *citoyens;* Giscard in shorts and a jersey playing football (soccer) with his local team; Giscard chatting over a glass of *vin ordinaire* at a bar; Giscard walking his dogs in the woods; Giscard sliding behind the wheel of his car; Giscard with his wife and four handsome children. It was a bit much, but it worked, and in the first round of voting he finished well out in front of Chaban-Delmas to face Mitterrand in the runoff. To nobody's surprise, Mitterrand led with 44 percent, followed by Giscard with 33 percent and a derisory 15 percent for the Gaullist Chaban-Delmas. Thus, if the combined right-wing vote held, Giscard was in sight of a runoff victory. But it was too narrow for comfort, and after sixteen years of right-wing rule there was little doubt that a strong leftist tide was running.

Then a funny thing happened, after the first-round votes were counted. At the Ministry of Finance, Giscard's office received a telephone call from the Soviet embassy requesting an appointment for Soviet Ambassador Stepan Chervonenko, ostensibly for a talk about Franco-Soviet economic relations and trade matters. It was as obvious as a newspaper headline that the ambassador was acting on instructions from Moscow. He would have been out of his mind to request such a meeting with a presidential candidate at the height of an election campaign on his own initiative. Soviet diplomatic representatives do not do such things on their own. Right out in the open, the Soviet Union was blatantly throwing its support behind Giscard d'Estaing, candidate of the Right, against François Mitterrand and the Socialist-Communist Left.

A dumfounded French Communist Party issued a statement ruefully accusing the Soviet Union of interfering in France's internal affairs! The French Communists declared that "it is all the more regrettable that this initiative has created a pretext for political speculation which represents this as a display of preference for the right-wing candidate." It certainly was—and it may well have been decisive in Giscard's narrow victory, on May 19, 1974.

The outcome was incredibly close. Mitterrand polled 49.2 percent of the votes cast, and Giscard d'Estaing won with 50.8 percent. The total ballot was well over 26 million. Giscard was elected President of France by only 470,000 votes. That, of course, was enough, but a tiny shift, of a mere 235,000—less than 1 percent of the total—would have completely altered the outcome and the outlook for France, for Europe and for the French Communist Party trying on its new, Eurocommunism political garb. Possibly this was why the Soviet ambassador intervened as he did. Had enough Communist voters taken the hint and either stayed at home and abstained or voted to ensure a victory for Valéry Giscard d'Estaing? There is no way of knowing or proving it one way or the other. But this much is certain: In the tiny margin on which the outcome depended, Giscard needed all the help he could get to win, the intervention of the Soviet ambassador included.

Valéry Giscard d'Estaing took up residence in the Élysée Palace at the age of forty-eight, the youngest French President since Casimir-Périer, in 1894. He declared at once on election night that the French people had voted for change and that they would get it. What in fact they have gotten since then is mild reform rather than change—center-right government with a Giscardian style as a kind of icing on a cake that still cuts and tastes the same. But it is successful, stable, and, given the vicissitudes of the world's economy, the French are about as well governed as anybody.

Like General de Gaulle and Pompidou, Giscard d'Estaing governs from the same right-wing power base, even with a number of the same personalities, and with much of the same political slogans of independence, national identity and purpose. But, at the same time, he is certainly more modern in outlook, more open to new ideas, and he has added enough liberal and center-left coloration of reformist measures to keep ahead so far of any leftist shifting of political tides. On his first anniversary in office, he summed up what he was doing very smoothly: "It was easy to brand me as a conservative when I was Minister of Finance. One expects a Finance Minister to be conservative. But since I became President I have not heard much criticism of my conservatism. People are more inclined to say that I carry change too far. I am a traditionalist who likes change."

A sampling of Giscardian reform measures bears this out. He reduced the voting age for French citizens to eighteen years. In a Catholic country, abortion has been legalized (largely the political and parliamentary work of his then Minister of Health, Mme. Simone Veil, who is Jewish). In education, priorities have shifted away from liberal arts and humanities courses to greater emphasis on courses oriented to economic needs: business management, computer training, sciences, engineering, technologies—diplomas that qualify for jobs in business and industry. A company reform law has partially dented the secrecy of French corporations, though this still falls far short of public accountability such as exists in the United States and Great Britain. An ingenious tax break allows every French citizen to deduct five thousand francs from his taxable income every year if he invests it in the stock market. A parallel break on the other side of the capitalist coin requires all companies in France above a certain capital worth to set aside a portion of their stock for free distribution to employees as "worker participation."

Such measures, indeed, are the work of "a traditionalist who likes change." They are evolutionary, rather than revolutionary, government policy. In fact, the real revolutionary change in France in the past quarter of a century has been in the structure of its economy and the way the country lives—not in the way it is governed.

Since General de Gaulle returned to power in 1958, France's gross domestic product has tripled, and France has moved up to become the world's fourth-largest exporting nation, following Japan. Over this period, the amount of money the French spend on food has declined by half, while that spent on health and hygiene has increased threefold. Six times as many young people now pass their *baccalauréat* examinations for automatic admission to free university schooling. Twenty-five years ago, washing machines, television sets and refrigerators were only beginning to come onto the mass market in France, and today seven out of ten households are equipped with these appliances. Where only 8 percent of working-class families owned automobiles in the 1950s, today it is nearly 70 percent. The revolution in French farming has been extraordinary: a drop in the farm labor force from around 18 percent of the total to under 10 percent, which has been accompanied by an increase in farm productivity with a value now totaling some 40 billion dollars a year, making France the world's second-largest agricultural exporter, after the United States. France has more farmland under cultivation than West Germany and Italy combined. She produces 40 percent of all Common Market cereals, 30 percent of its milk, butter, cheese and sugar. One third of Europe's cows graze on French pastures. In industry, France's Renault (a nationalized company) came to the rescue of American Motors and invested heavily in Mack Trucks in the United States, while Peugeot bought out the entire overseas operation of the ailing Chrysler Corporation. The European Airbus, with France the consortium leader, has cracked a virtual American monopoly in the air transport market, and Michelin has caused an upheaval in the American tire market.

France today has a gross national product that is about 60 percent greater than that of Great Britain. Her citizens earn nearly double the annual per capita income of the British. In Europe's oldest and longest economic competition, the French have long since taken the lead, and the eyes of the French economic planners are now fixed on the next target, which is to pull abreast of West Germany in industrial output and gross product. This is a tall order for France, in particular given the fact that there is a population gap of more than 8 million people between the two nations and the French birthrate is about the only statistic which has dropped in the past decade to nearly zero growth. But the task of expansion is not an impossible one. An enormous advantage that France holds over every other country in Europe is the size (and wealth) of her geography. France is a vastly underpopulated land. Germany and Britain crowd 2½ times as many inhabitants onto each square kilometer of national territory as the French. In short, there is ample room for growth in every sense in France.

Giscard d'Estaing took office at a fortunate time with this economic expansion and change at full flood—and he has added his own push to the process in two areas that are decisive for the future: telecommunications and nuclear power. For some reason or other, while everything else pushed ahead in France in the 1960s, the planners did very little to bring the state-owned post-office/telephone system into the second half of the century. In his first year in office, Giscard d'Estaing waved the magic wand of an Inspecteur des Finances turned President of the Republic and ordered a crash investment program of $25 billion in the telephone system, to be spent at a rate of $5 billion a year for five years. As a result, the number of French households with telephones jumped from approximately 30 percent in 1975 to 51.3 percent at the end of the decade, with an even greater and faster expansion ahead, now that much of the basic new infrastructure is in place.

It is in the field of nuclear energy that French *"planification,"* under Giscard d'Estaing's presidency, is showing the world. With only meager resources of natural gas and a negligible amount of coal, France, more than any other major industrial nation in the world except Japan, is dependent on imported oil and fuel supplies. About 70 percent of France's present energy requirements must be met by imported fuel, mainly oil. It does not take a diploma from the École Polytechnique to figure out that it costs the nation an enormous amount of exports to pay this fuel bill, and this in turn means an unacceptably precarious national economic equation. For the French, the clear, irrefutable answer is a major switch to nuclear power. Having faced this logical and elemental fact early in the decade, when the first fuel crisis and wave of oil-price increases struck a complacent world, in 1973, the French have succeeded in making nuclear power an extraordinary national priority in every sense—politically, economically, technologically, financially, an industrial priority, a planners' priority and a public priority to a degree that no other Western nation has yet equaled. Other countries, including the United States, wallow in environmental, legal, safety and technical arguments, in emotional theoretical debates about the nature of society, in endless mirror mazes of red tape and regulatory procedures, in overlapping lines of authority and public and private political battles. But, by a typical national application of logic, while other nations fight about nuclear power the French have embraced it. No antinuclear lobby pollutes the political air, and when the parties of the Left berate the government on this question, it is for not doing *enough*. But nuclear power and the French Government seem to be made for each other. Under Giscard's presidency, the nuclear program is a planner's dream, where the technocrats, scientists, financial experts, engineers and officialdom are joined in a vast, enthusiastic national enterprise.

In 1975, Giscard's first full year in office, France was producing about 8 percent of its electricity by nuclear power. By the end of the decade, this had pushed up to just under 15 percent. But the lead time on nuclear-power stations in France is approximately six to eight years, from inception to the time they begin operating, and the spectacular expansion is now just getting underway. More than thirty nuclear power stations are scheduled to come on stream by 1985—a rate of approximately one *every two months*. By the middle of the decade, France expects to be deriving about 60 percent of its electric power from nuclear stations, the highest percentage of any nation in the world. And every megawatt of nuclear power means a savings of one million barrels of oil per year.

If there is a certain complacency about President Valéry Giscard d'Estaing's outlook on his country, it is perhaps understandable—even though it could prove to be a political Achilles' heel. He has followed the "new French revolution" firsthand in his years at the treasury as well as the presidency, and of his nation today he has written in a slim little volume titled *French Democracy:*

"The very stability of the political system and therefore of the men in office has given an impression of immutability, whereas in fact the country has been shaken to its foundations. The upheaval took place without the trumpet calls of political revolutions, behind people's backs, as it were, and this explains the difficulty they have in measuring and defining it. The French character, however, has remained the same. It is quick to the point of being volatile, instinctively generous but held back by earthly possessions; eager to discuss but sometimes preferring the *fait accompli;* fervently proud of France but poorly informed about what foreigners think; full of all sorts of ideas but conservative about immediate surroundings; witty, decent but fond of easy jokes, feasting and eating. France has ceased to be an archaeological, gastronomic curiosity and become a modern, respected nation in the world."

In foreign policy, France's relations with her European partners and her role in world affairs, Giscard d'Estaing is a true disciple of General de Gaulle. The style, of course, is different: less strident, more realistic, less pretentious and overblown in rhetorical pronouncements and less deliberately anti-American. Again, in *French Democracy* he writes: "To assert independence, France does not need to be cantankerous. And when it practices cooperation, France does not risk being diminished, for it has a vocation to cooperate. A country of world ideas, scene of the greatest political revolution of modern times, possessed of a language and culture that have spread far and wide, democratic France will not retire within itself. It will remain an inventive partner, respected by the modern world; preserving its personality intact but opening its mind and heart to the great changes of our time and the new solidarity which today binds mankind together."

This being said, Giscard d'Estaing is just as determined as de Gaulle ever was about that mystical word "independence." It is a fixation of French behavior and the conduct of French foreign policy that France must *always* act independently. France will always give the blessing of her "cooperation" as an independent act, which must be seen first and foremost to be in the interest of France, not out of any altruistic reasons and certainly not in response to outside pressures or pleading. It is axiomatic that when France is asked to cooperate in some diplomatic or international enterprise, she will first listen skeptically, react with doubts and misgivings, then go away and think it over while the *demandeur* waits nervously, and finally return with an entirely original position and set of analytical reasons designed to demonstrate that France has independently, on her own, decided to cooperate. It's the way the game is played in Paris.

To take one example, back in 1960 General de Gaulle haughtily ended French participation in the disarmament talks in Geneva—partly to show his disdain while building his own independent nuclear force, partly because the talks were chaired jointly by the United States and the Soviet Union. But, by 1978, Giscard d'Estaing had decided that this had become diplomatically counterproductive for France, so he announced with a great flourish that world conditions had changed and France was now ready to play a vital new role in the search for disarmament. But first he insisted that the Geneva disarmament committee be reorganized and enlarged, with a rotating chairmanship instead of Soviet-American cochairmanship. To satisfy the French, this was duly voted in the United Nations, after which France resumed her place at the table. A Gaullist position had been reversed in Gaullist style. Incidentally, the outlook for disarmament has not yet notably altered as a result of France's new enthusiasm.

Giscard also emulates de Gaulle in the use of protocol gestures to demonstrate independence or irritation. When President Ford went to Brussels, in 1975, for a summit conference of the North Atlantic Treaty Organization, Giscard, in line with de Gaulle's well-known anti-NATO attitude, would send only his Foreign Minister to the meeting. But he then flew to Brussels to attend a state banquet given by King Baudouin, of Belgium, for the visiting heads of government—making it clear that he was accepting a personal invitation from the King but not attending any NATO gath-

ering! On another occasion, he stayed away from a dinner at No.
10 Downing Street, in London, given by Prime Minister James
Callaghan on the eve of an international economic summit meeting with President Carter, because Callaghan had also invited
Common Market Commission President Roy Jenkins and the
French President was against giving this kind of recognition and
status to the Commission president. This sort of game is, of
course, pure Gaullism.

Because the French will always tend to be determinedly prickly
and independent in their international relations, it is invariably
easier—even a relief—for other governments to cooperate with a
French initiative, rather than seek French cooperation. This was
the case when Giscard d'Estaing proposed holding a North-South
conference on economic relations between the developed and developing worlds (even though little came of it). It was also the
case when the French President instituted yearly international economic summit meetings with the United States, West Germany,
Italy and Japan (Canada and the Common Market Commission
were added subsequently despite his objections). Had either of
these ideas been proposed by the United States or some other
country, the probability is that France would have refused cooperation or at best gone along grudgingly, but since they were French
initiatives they took on special virtue.

Giscard d'Estaing's most positive and forward-looking acts of
foreign policy have been within Europe. He has fostered substantive progress toward greater unification of Europe in three key directions: First, at his initiative, Common Market summit meetings
have been institutionalized three times a year as a kind of embryo
"Cabinet of Europe" to conduct grand strategy business in both
the economic and political spheres and take decisions at the top
which then filter down through the Council of Ministers and the
Brussels Commission. Secondly, together with West German
Chancellor Helmut Schmidt, he played a key role in launching the
European Monetary System, which links the Common Market
currencies (except the British pound) in a system of stable rates
backed by common reserves. It is a start toward a federal reserve
system for Europe. Finally, he withdrew France's long-held objection to electing members of the European Parliament, in Stras-

bourg, instead of appointing them from national parliaments. The first European election was duly held in June 1979, and the result is another new dynamic in the growing unity of Europe.

Giscard d'Estaing presides over France—and glides from one of his summit conferences to the next—with a kind of lofty serenity that is also Gaullist in emulation. But there is one great difference: De Gaulle always made summit conferences a matter of a long, steep ascent, like climbing some diplomatic Mount Everest to get there. But he did see foreign ambassadors in Paris regularly, by way of preparing summits and propounding his ideas to other governments in the traditional manner of diplomacy. Giscard, on the other hand, prefers to talk only to heads of state and hardly ever sees a foreign ambassador in Paris except the insistent Soviet ambassador. He operates almost entirely in a small, closed circle at the Élysée Palace which is heavily staffed with fellow ENA graduates. He never has to face parliamentary rough-and-tumble of the House of Commons or the Bundestag variety, which the British Prime Minister and the West German Chancellor must attend and dominate along with the rest of government machinery. Giscard is no man for the hurly-burly of democracy. Summitry is his world, and he takes full advantage of hot-line telephones and the jet age to concentrate on direct dealings with his peers. He is secure in this elitist heaven, and scarcely ever leaves it.

On the domestic political front, after his narrow election victory in 1974, with the country split down the middle between the Gaullist-Giscardian Right and the Socialist-Communist Left, it was pretty obvious that in order to consolidate his political hold on France he would have to govern more and more toward the left. But as his book *French Democracy* also shows in one paragraph after another, the ENA graduate and Inspecteur des Finances abhors political ideology and labels both left and right. Instead he is devoted to logical, civil-service analysis of problems and the evolution of polished plans and programs to answer what he perceives to be public concerns—all of which is curiously lacking in any political inspiration or fervor. All the same, move to the left he did.

In the first four years of Giscard's term of office, the Communist Party, in its freshly laundered costume of democratic Euro-

communism, was linked with the Socialist Party in the tightest
political embrace since the depression days of the Popular Front,
in 1936, and the left for a time looked like a certain winner, with
elections for a new National Assembly ahead. A grave constitutional crisis loomed: How could a President of the Republic
elected by a rightist majority run the country with a National Assembly elected by a leftist majority? Despite the urgings of his first
Prime Minister, Jacques Chirac, to call an early election, before
the tide became too strong, Giscard, in what was probably the biggest political decision of his career, opted instead to drop Chirac,
replace him with Raymond Barre, and wait things out until the
Assembly came to the end of its five-year term, in the spring of
1978. The gamble paid off handsomely. The Communists split with
the Socialists on the run-up to the election, turning probable victory into certain defeat. The Giscardian-Gaullist forces romped
home with an increased Assembly majority. No wonder the French
President is serene to a point of complacency as he nears the end
of his first term and heads with confidence toward reelection in
1981.

"The trouble with Giscard is that he does not know that history
is tragic," Raymond Aron, elder statesman of French commentators, has remarked. He has never been touched by tragedy or defeat, and even his setbacks have scarcely been more than rest-
pauses on the way up. He has lived cocooned in security and success with his economic texts and his application of logic, a love of
literature and Mozart at the piano. "In music as in all things I try
my hand at, there is something that can be called perfection," he
has said. "I think Mozart is perfection itself." Summits, Success,
Mozart, Perfection—but one day he may wake up to find that truth
and reality lie not alone in Descartes, Montaigne and Keynes but
also in Shakespeare and Machiavelli.

18
Eurocommunism

OVER THE DECADE OF THE 1970S, INTERNAL POLITICS IN France, Italy, Spain and Portugal revolved around an old ideology that seemed to be surging toward power in a new, democratic garb: Eurocommunism.

In France, it took the form of a Confédération des Gauches, a carefully constructed political alliance between the Communist and Socialist parties, concluded in 1972, for cooperation in fighting ensuing elections at every level. The Left Alliance then came within less than 1 percent of defeating Valéry Giscard d'Estaing for the presidency in 1974. In the next years it continued from strength to strength in municipal and cantonal elections in what seemed to be an irresistible political tide. The very stability that had been achieved under the Fifth Republic was paradoxically creating conditions for the Communists to move back into power for the first time since 1947 through this polarization of French politics between solid blocs on the left and the right.

In Italy, the Communist Party, long independent-minded and subtly led, had risen in steady, solid progression in every election since 1946 to an extraordinary crest of success thirty years later. From 4.3 million votes representing 19 percent of the total, in the first postwar Italian election, Communist strength reached 9 million votes in May of 1972 and then a resounding 12.6 million in June of 1976–34.4 percent of the total and only 4 percent behind the ruling Christian Democrats. In these circumstances, Communist Party leader Enrico Berlinguer negotiated his "historic compromise" with the Christian Democrats, in effect permitting them to go on governing the country, but only on Communist sufferance, with certain agreed lines of policy that the party would support. Thus, the Communists had a foot in the door of power in Italy in 1976, even if they had not yet moved into any offices or sat down yet behind any ministerial desks.

In Portugal in April of 1974, the inheritors of the Salazar dictatorship were toppled in a bloodless revolution plotted by military officers. Communist Party leader Álvaro Cunhal came hurrying back to Lisbon from fourteen years' exile in Prague and Moscow to take charge of the party as it emerged at last from underground. Over the next eighteen months, Cunhal and the Communists fought to the very brink of power in tactics of pure Stalinism, with the assistance of a coterie of leftist officers who virtually controlled the armed forces. But, in the end, free, democratic elections kept Portugal from exchanging one form of dictatorship for another.

In Spain, the death of Franco, in November 1975, ended Europe's last Fascist dictatorship, after nearly forty years. Communist Party leader Santiago Carrillo was waiting in exile in France, where he had demonstrated an early and determined independence of Moscow in such matters as prompt public opposition to the Soviet crushing of the Dubček regime, in Prague, in August of 1968. In Spain nobody really knew how strong the Communist Party would prove to be, but clearly it had the cachet of having led the long underground fight against the Fascist regime. Under King Juan Carlos, the Spanish authorities began moving with caution but firmness and clear purpose to open the political doors gradually and control their own peaceful transition from Fascism to constitutional democracy under a monarchy. Would the Communists try to dislodge the process and start some political avalanche rolling? Carrillo, in his role as a good Eurocommunist, signaled that he intended to play the game by democratic rules. Those in power in Madrid, in good Spanish fashion, took their time. Arrests and harassment stopped, but it was not until 1977 that the Communist Party was legalized. Carrillo returned, and the Communist flower of the Spanish Civil War, Dolores Ibarruri, "La Pasionaria," flew back from Moscow to a rapturous homecoming in Madrid. Spain waited, along with her Mediterranean Catholic neighbors, to see how far this cresting wave of Eurocommunism would carry.

The political upsurge of the Communist parties in Western Europe from roughly 1972 to 1979 was followed in Washington with something close to consternation. Was this to be one of the fruits of East-West *détente* and the relaxation of tensions with the Soviet Union and the Communist world? Even Secretary of State Henry A. Kissinger lost his diplomatic cool—particularly during the Portuguese revolution when he concluded from the other side of the Atlantic, with a blinkered and myopic analysis, that a Communist takeover of a NATO ally looked inevitable. Instead of concentrating on how he might come to the support of democratic forces in Portugal, Kissinger talked cynically about letting the country go down the drain to the Communists as a warning to the rest of Western Europe, a means of "inoculating" the Continent against this spreading Red disease. Fortunately, the Europeans showed better nerve and cooler heads. Of course, it was close in Portugal, but it was no thanks to Kissinger and the United States that the democratic forces prevailed. The nine governments of the European Common Market, acting jointly in Brussels at a crucial juncture, announced a substantial economic aid program for Portugal—but only if it maintained pluralistic democratic government. Then the Socialist parties of West Germany, France, Britain, Austria, Sweden, Norway and Denmark all came discreetly to the aid of the Portuguese Socialist Party with hard cash to build its organization, print its newspaper and fight the election in the front line against the Communists. And so, in Lisbon, the tide was turned.

Then in France, as elections neared for a new National Assembly in March of 1978, the Communist Party suddenly broke its alliance with the Socialists. The election outcome was a sweeping victory for the Giscardian-Gaullist right wing, which will continue to control the Assembly until 1983. French politics is back where it was in the 1960s, with an end, for the foreseeable future, of any prospect of national political success for the Left.

In Spain, in elections for a new Cortes under the new, democratic constitution, in March of 1979, the Communist vote leveled off at just under 10 percent of the total. In Italy, by early 1979 the "historic compromise" arrangement had unraveled, and national elections were again held, in June. For the first time since the war, the Communist vote went down instead of up—skidding back to 29 percent after the big 34.4 percent win of 1976. In Portugal in December 1979, the second national election since the revolution produced a 180-degree turn to the right, and a six-seat parliamentary majority for a coalition of the center-right and conservative parties.

By the end of the decade, Eurocommunism had shot its bolt as a rising political force in the democracies of Western Europe. Whatever novelty the supposed new look of communism might have had, in the crucial tests the Communists were still Communists, and the democratic voters still preferred democratic parties. What was it, then, that produced this upsurge of apparent Communist support in the early part of the decade? What punctured it and brought it back down? What, indeed, is "Eurocommunism"— is it a myth or a reality? What kind of a political force is it likely to be in the 1980s?

The term Eurocommunism was probably the most effective piece of Communist political repackaging to be invented since Marx wrote his *Manifesto*. It was coined, appropriately enough, by a Yugoslav journalist named Frane Barbieri. It was first used by Barbieri in an article he wrote for an Italian political periodical, *Giornale nuovo,* on June 25, 1975, in which he set out to analyze from a Titoist and Yugoslav perspective some of the writings of Carrillo, the Spanish party leader then still in exile, who had already gone farther, more openly, than any other Communist leader in Western Europe in taking his distance from Moscow.

The term "neocommunism" could not be applied to the independent line Carrillo was taking, which of course was also reflected in varying degrees in the other Western European Communist parties as well. So Barbieri hit upon "Eurocommunism," really as an abbreviation for "Western European communism." The term caught on faster than Esso became Exxon. It was quickly embraced by the Communist parties themselves—no doubt in the realization that this was a happy, rejuvenating new label, carrying with it the implication of an emancipation from Moscow and the image of some bright and shining new Western Democratic communism on the political rosters in place of the sinister old revolutionary machine manipulated by Stalin, the Comintern and the KGB.

By coincidence, three weeks after Barbieri first used the term in print, a kind of birth certificate of Eurocommunism was signed in the Italian city of Leghorn (Livorno) at a meeting of Santiago Carrillo and Enrico Berlinguer. On July 12, 1975, the two party leaders issued a joint declaration of ideological principles— overblown and involuted, as Communist policy statements always are, but in essence pledging the Italian and Spanish parties to work "for convergence and agreement with all political forces" in their democracies and develop their internal and international policies "in complete autonomy and independence." There was no mention anywhere in the document of the Soviet Union as the leader of progressive forces in the world or any other such customary accolade to Moscow. Moreover, this was the first time that two Western European Communist parties had independently signed a joint statement of principle on their own. It was followed four months later by a similar joint declaration by the Italian and French Communist parties, signed by Berlinguer and Georges Marchais in Rome on November 15, 1975.

In essence, the intent and thrust of these two declarations was to establish a political image of the Communist parties of Western Europe acting in close cooperation, independent of Moscow, to develop their own political strategies and tactics in the context of the workings of the European democracies. The 1975 declarations were the culmination of a long postwar process of "taking distance from Moscow." Moreover, they coincided (probably not by accident) with the conclusion of the Helsinki Agreements on Security and Cooperation in Europe, signed by thirty-five heads of state in the Finnish capital at the end of July 1975, in the biggest European summit conference since the Congress of Vienna, in 1814.

Ever since Tito's break with Stalin, in 1947, the focal question by which the Communist parties of Western Europe have constantly been examined and assessed has been their subservience to Moscow. Of course, in 1947 all the other European Communists lined up obsequiously, without a murmur of misgiving, behind Stalin the Great Leader when Tito was expelled from the Comin-

tern and cast into the outer darkness of independence/heresy. But
if Eurocommunism really had a beginning it was probably back
then. From that point on, it was possible to follow Tito's example
and be a stalwart Marxist-Leninist without having to prostrate before Moscow every morning. But each of the Western European
parties, differing in qualities of leadership, intellect, organization
and national temperament, had to find its own feet and maneuver
at the end of the tether in its own way.

The Italians, under Palmiro Togliatti, exiled in Moscow during
the 1930s and then back in Rome in undisputed party control
after the war, were the earliest and most successful in displaying
subtle hints of a certain autonomy. Togliatti played a kind of
Levantine versus Byzantine game of maneuver with Stalin, mirac-
ulously without following the rest of the prewar Comintern leadership into liquidation. Somehow he managed early on to master the
art of taking distance without breaking ties. It was Togliatti who
first applied the word "polycentrism" to the process, and Berlinguer built on this.

The leadership of the French Communist Party, on the other
hand, has consistently been more rigid, orthodox and Stalinist,
going back to the 1930s. Its ruling Politbureau has always been a
self-perpetuating oligarchy of determinedly working-class men
with a love of power, worship of discipline and antipathy toward
the party's intellectual fringe. The French Communist leaders
never showed the slightest evidence of trying to find room for maneuver with Stalin the way Togliatti did, and their slavish loyalty
to every Moscow twist and turn really only began to chip away
after the events in Prague in 1968.

As for the two smaller parties—Spain and Portugal—their existence until 1974–75 was of course completely underground, and
their maneuverings vis-à-vis Moscow therefore of only peripheral
importance. Nevertheless, Carrillo and Cunhal ran very different
shows, the Spaniard very much in the style of the Italian party and
the Portuguese more in line with the French Stalinist orthodoxy.
Carrillo had the advantage of being in exile in the freedom of
Paris, while Cunhal waited in Moscow and Prague. Carrillo, above
all, showed very early on a determination to adapt the Spanish
Communist Party to Spanish political conditions post-Franco and

not simply follow a Lenin-Stalin manual on how to make a revolution. In this, Carrillo was almost certainly motivated by the overwhelming determination of the whole Spanish people not to get caught up in the horrors of another civil war when Franco died. Carrillo knew that there would simply be no support in Spain for a violent, revolutionary bid for power—so he began taking distance from Moscow control, trimming political sails accordingly, early on, in order to do what he did, which was to take his place at the head of a Spanish Communist Party working its way legally and peacefully in a Spanish democracy. Cunhal, on the other hand, came roaring back to Lisbon waving the Red revolution texts. His Stalinist tactics of violence, intimidation and ruthless action came perilously close to succeeding.

From the time of the 1947 Tito break onward, the supposedly unshakable faith of the Communist world in Lenin's successors and the Soviet model went through a series of shocks and tremors, each of which had the effect of requiring party leaders at a distance from Moscow to do some thinking on their own and explaining to their followers—even if the end result was still the same old required reflex of unquestioned loyalty. The first big shock came while Europe was still locked in the atmosphere of the Cold War, at the Twentieth Party Congress of the Soviet Union, in 1956. Party leaders from all over the world gathered to listen in stunned astonishment and disbelief to Nikita S. Khrushchev's wild, almost hysterical denunciation of the evils of Stalin. This was followed a few months later by Khrushchev's ordering the Red Army into Budapest to crush the Hungarian uprising, in November. After that, in the early 1960s, relations cooled between Moscow and Peking, resulting finally, in 1962, in the Great Schism, which effectively ended forever the myth of monolithic communism. Then came Khrushchev's abrupt downfall, in 1964, when the rest of the Communist world was expected to send instant congratulations to Leonid Brezhnev and the new Soviet leadership. For the French Communist Party, more confusion followed when President Charles de Gaulle headed for Moscow, in 1966, to launch his own personal campaign of *détente* and got an almost rapturous welcome from the collective leadership of the Kremlin. Moreover, despite the American involvement in Viet-

nam, which peaked about 1968, there were distinct signs of a thaw
between Moscow and Washington as well: The first tentative steps
toward discussions on strategic arms limitations had begun in
1967 under President Lyndon Johnson at his Glassboro, New Jersey, meeting with Soviet Premier Aleksei Kosygin. Tentative arrangements had even been worked out for a Johnson-Brezhnev
summit meeting at the end of the summer of 1968. Then, in August, came the climactic event of the postwar period for the Communist parties of Europe: the Red Army rolled into Prague to
snuff out the regime of Alexander Dubček in Czechoslovakia.

As far as Moscow was concerned, at each of these twists and
turns it was simply the duty of every Communist Party to come to
attention, salute and keep quiet. But Stalin was no longer alive
and it was not the 1930s. The world in which Communist parties
had to operate was not standing still. Even Romania, deep inside
Warsaw Pact geography, still managed to hold out a sympathetic
hand to Mao Tse-tung and Peking when Khrushchev withdrew the
hand of Moscow. In 1968, the Soviet occupation of Prague became the watershed point at which the Western European Communist parties in effect stood up before shocked opinion in the
Communist as well as non-Communist world and were counted.

The Italians were forthright and prompt and clear in their condemnation, and so was Carrillo from Paris. The French party
writhed with its collective conscience, then expressed "surprise
and reprobation" at use of the Red Army to crush a Communist
regime, and subsequently watered this down to "disapproval." But
when the Russians then forced the hapless Czechs to legitimize the
occupation of their country with a new "treaty of friendship," the
French Communist Party at once welcomed this "normalization"
of the situation. A few months later, a French party delegation
visited Moscow to reaffirm "fraternal sincerity and friendship"
with the Soviet Communist Party. All the same, there had been an
important if only brief breach with Moscow, and gradually, in the
face of the realities of French politics, the party began to move
down the path of greater independence and ideological overhaul,
particularly in its growing support for Soviet dissidents. Georges
Marchais succeeded Rochet as party leader, and although he is as
hard as nails and a complete disciplinarian when the chips are

down, the French Communists did begin to take on a new look. Serious negotiations opened with the Socialists, leading to their political compact in 1972. At a party Congress in February 1976, the process reached a peak when Marchais announced to the surprised faithful that he was jettisoning the slogan "dictatorship of the proletariat" and replacing it with "a union of the people of France."

Over the period of the early 1970s, moreover, the Communist parties were having to respond increasingly to established political and economic realities in Western Europe, with which they were living and operating and trying to make political headway but which were unshakable and could no longer successfully be questioned or challenged. One of these was the European Common Market. For years, in slavish obedience to Moscow, the Communists had opposed the Common Market—but if ever there was a success that workingmen were enjoying, it was the economic success of Europe in which the Common Market was a vital engine. Gradually, the Italian Communist Party in the lead, Communist opposition shifted to Communist support—tuned, of course, to the importance of the Market in establishing European independence of the United States. Then, with the Helsinki Agreements and the start of Mutual and Balanced Force Reductions talks in Vienna between the Warsaw Pact and the North Atlantic Treaty Organization, even NATO began to look different to Communist ideologues. This particular evolution of Eurocommunism took final form when Berlinguer gave a remarkable interview, in 1976, to the Italian newspaper *Corriere della Sera,* in which he said:

"I feel that because Italy does not belong to the Warsaw Pact, from this point of view we can proceed along the Italian road to socialism in complete independence." The interviewer then asked the Communist leader if the NATO pact was "a useful shield behind which to build socialism in freedom," and Berlinguer replied: "Yes. It is another reason why I do not want Italy to leave the Atlantic Alliance, as well as because by leaving it we would upset the international balance. I also feel safer being on this side of the fence."

At this point, the ashes of Joseph Stalin must have been stirring in the urn in the Kremlin wall.

Political conditions in Western Europe in the 1970s in fact offered the Communist parties fairly fertile soil in which to plant, cultivate and harvest results for the new Eurocommunism image of independence of Moscow, concern for human rights, support for the Common Market, and devotion to *détente,* stability and the democratic institutions of the West. First of all, there was a whole new, young, postwar generation taking its place in the political spectrum. It was a generation that scarcely had any memory at all of the parlous economic conditions of the Marshall Plan days, of the tensions of the Cold War, of the slugging battles in the trade-union movements between Communists and Socialists of Berlin, of the efforts of sustained leadership that had gone into building economic and political stability in Western Europe.

Moreover, the new generation arrived on stage on a wave of violence—the student uprisings of the 1960s, which culminated in Paris in the events of May 1968. In West Germany and West Berlin, the Baader-Meinhof killer gang of Marxist-anarchist urban terrorists ran wild. In Italy, it was the Red Brigades of kidnapers, murderers, torturers, terrorists. The Palestine Liberation Organization added its multinational operations in airplane hijackings, Carlos and his accomplices grabbing the entire ministerial council of the Organization of Petroleum Exporting Countries in Vienna, and the ghastly gunning down of the Israeli sports teams at the 1972 Munich Olympic Games. There was clear evidence to satisfy police and intelligence services at this period that these terrorist groups were actively supported from Eastern Europe with funds, equipment, training and safe hideaways between jobs. There is nothing inconsistent in the Communist parties cultivating an image of political respectability in Western Europe while at the same time the KGB works to foment instability.

All this violence was accompanied, of course, by the cries and slogans of every age and inspiration for overthrow of established order, upheaval of bourgeois society, changing the world. In Italy and France, the violence had been propelled at least in part by the simple fact that the right wing had been in power virtually continuously since the war. In Italy, the Christian Democrats maintained (and still maintain) unbroken political dominance of the country with occasional cosmetic changes in the direction of the Left for thirty-five years, despite Communist gains at every election up to 1979. In France, there was one period of Socialist Party government after the war, but that was the Suez War period, and it could scarcely be regarded as a swing to the left in the way France was governed. Otherwise the country has been governed since President Charles de Gaulle's return in 1958 firmly from the center-right with occasional liberal moves to the left. Thus, in the two biggest Catholic democracies on the Continent, there has never been a swing of the political pendulum since the war such as has taken place in Britain from Conservatives to Labour and back, or in West Germany from Christian Democrats to Social Democrats. It was this immobilism of politics which led Jean-Paul Sartre and others to give their dubious spiritual philosophical blessing to violence from 1968 on, youth taking to the streets to storm police barricades, urban terrorism as a justifiable recourse necessary to produce change. Sartre even went to pay a comforting visit to the Baader-Meinhof terrorists in jail in Stuttgart.

To add to the rising political prospects for Eurocommunism, the Arab-Israeli War of 1973 with the subsequent Arab oil embargo against the West and the takeoff of wild, OPEC-engineered oil-price increases abruptly turned the economies of the West into slowdown and recession after those years of maximum growth. Unemployment returned as a permanent economic and social problem of the 1970s.

Finally, it was obvious and inevitable that the Communists would gain a political boost and be seen as a major dynamic force on the European scene when the Fascist dictatorships in Spain and Portugal came to an end. Whatever the real or imagined strength of communism among the Spanish and Portuguese peoples, the party was bound to come out from underground proclaiming maximum victory for the forces of revolutionary change. This in turn would bring an impact of additional forward political momentum for Eurocommunism in Italy and France—the wave of the future, as the left would have it. When the Salazar remnant was overthrown and Franco died, the political pendulum could only swing to the left. The question was how far, how fast and how controlled.

As these elements all gradually converged to produce the most notable upsurge of Communist political strength in Western Europe since 1947, what was the Soviet attitude toward rising Eurocommunism? Moreover, where did the ultimate loyalties of the Eurocommunist parties really lie? Was this independence from Moscow merely a tactical façade? When the chips were down, how democratic were the Communist parties in their new garb? Indeed, was Moscow still somehow orchestrating and controlling the whole face-lift, as a means of destabilizing Western Europe in the name of *détente?*

There are no categorical answers to any of these questions, but there are general answers—or conclusions to be drawn from the fashion in which events ran their course to the end of the 1970s. First, from reactions and behavior in the Soviet Union, Moscow was prepared to live with a certain amount of "independence" on the part of its sibling European parties for the sake of tactical political advantages in the democratic process. Besides, there was the uncomfortable fact that not much could be done about it. But when Moscow judged that things were going too far—as in the case of Santiago Carrillo and the Spanish—denunciation followed as a warning to the others.

Secondly, the Soviets made it abundantly clear, particularly in France in the run-up to the decisive National Assembly elections of 1978, that they had no wish to see the Communists come to power. The Russians openly showed their backing of Valéry Giscard d'Estaing and his government against the Communist-Socialist Left. It is less clear if or how the Russians might have intervened against power-sharing by the Italian Communist Party, but the end result was much the same as in France. One way or another, in both countries forward momentum of Eurocommunism stopped before either party gained power.

Willy Brandt noted much earlier, after the Berlin Wall went up and he began shaping his diplomatic strategy of *Ostpolitik,* that the two superpowers since 1945 had consistently "respected the spheres of influence broadly agreed at Yalta" and that "the Soviet Union had done little to support the Communist parties of Italy or

France in their efforts to gain power." Enrico Berlinguer echoed that conclusion in the 1976 interview with the *Corriere della Sera* in which he endorsed Italian membership in NATO. "You can argue that the Soviet Union aspires to hegemony over its allies," he said, "but there is not a single action to suggest that it intends to go beyond the frontiers fixed at Yalta."

In any case, it does not require deep political analysis to conclude that Soviet interest would not be well served by Eurocommunism taking power in Western Europe. The Russians are better off with Communist parties confined to acting as political pressure forces inside the Western democracies in support of Soviet ends, rather than by any advent of independent-minded Communist parties in power. From earliest Bolshevik times, through Trotsky, Tito and Mao Tse-tung, the Soviet Union has always sought to crush independence anywhere in the Communist movement. It has had to live with a certain amount of this in the form of Eurocommunism, which it clearly has not enjoyed. But, by the end of the decade, the movement in Western Europe was back about where Moscow wanted it to be.

In the late years of the Salazar regime and of his successor, Marcello Caetano, I was back and forth to Portugal on various reporting assignments and was always struck by the innate decency and simple human dignity of the Portuguese people. Lisbon is one of Europe's most attractive and interesting cities, and I always came away feeling a sadness for a people and a country that surely deserved a better break and a better system of government than its suffocating, spiritless, intellectually insulting dictatorship. When the revolution of April 25, 1974, finally sent Caetano packing off to exile in Brazil, I was again soon back, and for the next eighteen months was in and out of Lisbon at various times as the country teetered on the brink of a postrevolution Communist takeover. The real turning point came when the revolutionary regime honored its pledge to hold free parliamentary elections within one year, in April 1975, despite Communist pressures to have the voting called off. Books have been written reconstructing the tortuous course of events in Portugal and the mishmash that Henry Kissinger succeeded in making of America's response to what was happening. There is one, simple personal story for me to recount, which somehow cut through all of the emotions and confusions and violence and political swirl that were going on and reduced it all to simple basic truths that did indeed prevail.

Just before Portugal's first free election in half a century, I headed to the North of the country to see what was happening in the city of Porto and its surrounding region, where two basic industries were concentrated: port wine and textiles. I spent the evening of my arrival at dinner with the American and British consuls in the city, who more or less agreed on a very gloomy assessment of the election outlook. Two days before, a Communist street gang had burned Socialist Party headquarters in Porto, and fear and intimidation, the two consuls told me, almost certainly would annul the election process.

The American even talked about sending his wife and children out of the country in the next days in the fear that his residence might well become a target for some mob. His British counterpart, an older hand in the business, visibly stiffened his upper lip at this: "I wouldn't do that, old boy. Know what you feel you're up against, of course, but it wouldn't help with the locals, you know."

Next morning, I had arranged with a young Portuguese medical student who spoke English to drive out into the country in his car to try to get some feel of what was happening at the local level. We headed for the city of Guimarães, a twelfth-century fortified strongpoint on the approaches to Spain where Portugal's first king had ruled. We found the headquarters of the Socialist Party, up a flight of stairs over a store, some rickety chairs and a battered typewriter and two friendly young men. The local party leader, they told us, was a lawyer who at that moment was defending a client at the Municipal Court House, but if we went there we could probably see him when the case was over. A helpful court official carried messages, and a rendezvous was arranged at a bistro near the old city walls an hour or so later.

António Mota Prego was small and wiry, like most of his countrymen, friendly, serious and intense, in his mid-thirties, exuding restless energy and determined confidence in his country's democratic future. He spoke English, helped out from time to time by my student-interpreter. A bottle of cold rosé wine was brought, and in the next forty-five minutes I suddenly felt that I had at last come to the truth and reality of what was happening in the country. As I wrote it immediately after, here is what he had to say:

"We used to be afraid in Portugal that the Fascist dictatorship would end one day in civil war and bloodshed, and now we Portuguese are living with the effects of civil war but fortunately without the bloodshed.

"When I say we are living with the effects of civil war, I mean that we are torn by the problems which civil war brings in agreeing about the country's political future. But I keep saying to our people: you must not be pessimistic, you must be optimistic. I remind them of how much worse we used to expect that the post-Fascist period would be. You know, it is very, very difficult to build political parties and create democratic understanding in people out of practically nothing, starting from zero.

"I am a Marxist. I have read Marx and Lenin, and I believe completely that the best future for Portugal lies in its people owning the basic means of production and controlling the main elements of the economy. But I joined the Socialist Party immediately after the revolution because I differ with the Communist Party since I also believe that we can have a political pluralism in this country, and the Communists do not believe in that. I want Portugal to arrive in a political condition where there is full national agreement on the creation of a socialist state, which all the political parties would support.

"I do not believe in the Western European type of social democracy, because it is not Marxist enough for conditions in Portugal. I make a difference between social democracy as it is practiced in Western Europe and democratic socialism, which is what we need in Portugal. Our Socialist Party is the natural leader, and I believe that we will be the majority party in the country after the April 25 election. [It did come out the strongest party.]

"We are very, very strong here in the North. I doubt that the Communists will get more than 5 percent of the vote here in Guimarães—maybe 10 percent for the combined vote of all the leftist parties, the Maoists and the Trotskyites and the rest. [Again he hit it about on the nose.] At our big rallies we have filled the biggest movie house in town to overflowing every time, and our smaller rallies out in the villages always draw well, several hundred people.

"Textiles are the biggest industry all over the North, something like five hundred mills, big and small. Nationalize the textile industry? Well, perhaps one day in the future, but the textile workers do not want nationalization now. They know they are not yet ready for it. They say that they have to know more about running industry before the people can take control of it, and that is why they are strongly Socialist here, rather than Communist. Under Socialist Party policy, we may come to the people owning the textile industry one day, but not until the people want it and are ready for it.

"The Communists are better organized than we are, and have more money to spend, but we are growing—almost too fast for our party organization. It's funny, but it's the Communists who create the most interest at all of our political meetings. They do not cause trouble or violence for us, the way they have in Lisbon or Porto, because they know that we are the most popular with the people and it would only do their own party harm if they tried to break up our meetings. But they do always send people to ask questions, and it is the debate between our speakers and the Communist questioners which makes our meetings interesting and lively. Our speakers can give good democratic answers, and they always win the arguments and the support and applause.

"Since the first of the year, Socialist Party membership here in Guimarães has jumped in three months from two hundred to more than a thousand. We do not have the organization to fill in the necessary forms and make out the file of name, occupation, age, address, place of work and all that. The more we grow the more it costs to send out material to members. But we are feeling the real democratic enthusiasm of the people. Even if the Communists are better organized and have more money, we know that we are stronger and are growing.

"I dislike the useless, bourgeois-democratic atmosphere of elections. All these posters are a waste of money—but we have to put them up because the people expect it, they think it is a sign of political strength and activity. But you will notice that in Guimarães we do not have as many Socialist Party posters as you'll see in other cities, and that is because I have tried to spend our money and energy in other ways. I get the supporters to buy their own party badges and the stickers for their automobiles.

"Intimidation at the polls? Absolutely not. This is Portugal's first free election in the lifetime of practically all our people, and of course they will turn out to vote. Nobody is going to be intimidated. Everybody takes this election very, very seriously. You will see."

I wished that Henry Kissinger had been there to listen to António Mota Prego, leading the Socialist Party of Guimarães out of nowhere into battle against a hardened Communist organization. But Kissinger, instead, was listening to the American consul in Porto who was thinking of evacuating his family, as intimidated as he believed the Portuguese voters to be. On election day, more than 6 million Portuguese went to the polls—an astounding 91 percent of the voters—in conditions of total order and tranquillity, almost, it seemed, as if they were going to Mass. The Communist Party polled barely 15 percent (less in the North), and Communist hopes for a Red Revolution were completely dashed. They did not give up, and with the support of leftist officers high in power and control of the armed forces, they still tried to impose Communist rule, which the ballot box had rejected. But, in the end, a handful of willful Reds could not reduce the democratic majority that had been built out of faith and hard work by António Mota Prego and other unsung heroes of democracy like him all over the country.

In France, following the 1972 political compact between the Communists and the Socialists, the Confédération des Gauches forged steadily upward in combined percentage strength from one election to the next and in public opinion polls in between. But there was an important and largely unanticipated aspect to this leftist upsurge—and that was the fact that the Socialist Party was making the gains. At the outset, in 1972, the Communist Party was about where it had been stuck almost consistently since the war, 20 percent of the French vote, with the Socialist Party dragging along at around 14 percent. The Communists went into the alliance convinced, apparently, that they stood to gain the most with their superior organization, this new cachet of democratic respectability cooperating with the Socialists, and their increasing show of independence from Moscow. Instead, the Socialist tail was soon wagging the Communist dog.

At the outset, there was the near victory that the Left Alliance brought to the Socialist Party leader, François Mitterrand, in the presidential race against Giscard d'Estaing in 1974. After that came cantonal elections in which the Left continued to forge ahead, and then a really sweeping success in municipal elections throughout the country, in March 1977. Together, the Socialist and Communist parties captured control of nearly two thirds of all the local councils in France. But, astoundingly, the Communists were still stuck at approximately 20 percent of the vote, while the Socialists had now soared to 32 percent. This was a clear, combined national majority, with National Assembly elections in the offing in April 1978. It looked as if nothing could stop the Left at last from wresting power from the Right. But, by June of 1977, there were the first signs of fraying Communist nerves over the second-place position in which they found themselves. A revision of the 1972 joint platform was needed to fight the 1978 election, but at an initial meeting in July, difficulties began to show. The talks then broke off, by agreement, until after the traditional French August vacation.

During this period, President Giscard d'Estaing and his government managed to maintain a certain equanimity in the face of the leftist trend, while the Gaullist Party leader, ex-Prime Minister Jacques Chirac, seemed at times to be in a state of near hysteria. He had wanted an early election to head off what now seemed to be happening. Instead, he had been dropped by Giscard d'Estaing and replaced by Raymond Barre, on whom the burden of winning the election now rested. Toward the end of August, Barre invited a small group of American correspondents to lunch for one of his periodic background talks, and we were all a little surprised when he flatly predicted to us that the Left Alliance would break apart "probably before the election." He gave no explanation for this assessment, and it seemed to most of us at the time an effort to put a brave front on a difficult political problem he was facing.

But, about a week after this talk with Barre, I had arranged a lunch alone with a high French official, a friend who best remains anonymous. When our discussion turned to the political outlook, he told me the following story. Soon after the municipal elections in March of 1977, he said, he had received a request for an appointment from a Soviet journalist who was visiting Paris. The man duly arrived at his office and introduced himself as working as a special correspondent for Victor Louis—a well known Soviet journalist in Moscow who is frequently used by the KGB and the Soviet Government to plant well-informed leaks in the world press. After a rather pro forma discussion of Franco-Soviet relations and the prospects for the visit to Paris of Leonid Brezhnev that was due to take place that May, the journalist suddenly switched the conversation to the French political situation. My French friend related:

"He talked about the big gains of the Left in the municipal election, and then said to me, 'There will be no Left victory in your National Assembly elections. The Politbureau has already decided that this is not the time for the Communist Party to come to power in France.'

"I said to him that this was all very interesting, but it was surely a matter of French internal politics and nothing for the Politbureau to decide. He then said: 'But I have not made myself clear. This is a decision of the French Politbureau of which we have been informed. There will be no victory of the Left in your national election.'"

My friend went on to say that he had written an immediate confidential memorandum of the conversation for limited top-level internal circulation. Somewhat taken aback by the story, I simply asked him whether there appeared to have been any other point to the journalist's visit. "None whatsoever," he said. It was self-evident that the journalist (if that's what he was) had been sent from Moscow on instructions, as a kind of unofficial nondiplomatic channel to pass an important piece of political intelligence to the French Government. It also showed that Moscow still had a clear pipeline into the French Politbureau. It accounted for Prime Minister Barre's apparent certainty that there would be a Communist-Socialist split before the election. It also helped explain why it was that Leonid Brezhnev had gone out of his way when he visited Paris in May to go and call on Jacques Chirac but did not meet with Georges Marchais. There was no question how the Soviet Government wanted the French election to turn out.

The split then came rapidly—barely a week, in fact, after my talk with the French official. In early September, before talks with the Socialist Party were due to resume, *L'Humanité* came out with a six-page special spread of signed articles by various Politbureau members from Marchais on down that laid out a set of clearly impossible demands for future cooperation with the Socialists—for example, an agreed program of wholesale nationalization of major corporations and all the banks, and a social program that would have cost $100 billion to implement.

A dumfounded François Mitterrand, who was basing everything on an I-can-handle-the-Communists image, struggled with Marchais to patch up some kind of agreement, but it was hopeless. Mitterrand did not dare give in to the Communists without losing his own credibility, and Marchais was determined on a break anyway. True to the prediction that the Soviet "journalist" had passed to the French six months before, the Left Alliance fell apart in October 1978, thus ensuring that there would be no victory of the Left in April. It was all over but the hand-wringing and the counting. Giscard d'Estaing's party, together with the Gaullists, sailed back with an increased National Assembly majority of nearly one hundred seats, and will control the legislature, unless there is a surprise early election, until 1984.

In the aftermath in the French Communist Party there was bitter disillusion by the party intellectuals—in particular a leading party writer, Jean Ellenstein. But Marchais showed his disdain for his dissenters by refusing to allow any of the postelection inquest in the party to foul the pages of *L'Humanité,* so Ellenstein spread his anguish and outrage in a series of articles for the readers of *Le Monde.* Whatever the supposed liberalizing effects of Eurocommunism, in the end Communist Party discipline was as tight under Marchais as it ever was under those old Stalinists Waldeck Rochet and Maurice Thorez.

And so, as France headed into its 1981 presidential election maneuvering, François Mitterrand was still mournfully and rather pathetically chasing the political rainbow of a new pact with the

Communists on which to challenge Valéry Giscard d'Estaing. Marchais had succeeded not only in splitting the Confederation of the Left, but in splitting the Socialist Party as well. French politics was more or less back to where it had been at the start of the decade of the 1970s—and the Communist Party under Marchais clearly intends that it will stay that way.

By the end of the decade, Eurocommunism was a spent force, and the Communist parties of France, Italy, Spain and Portugal no longer presented anything like an image of a new movement taking its distance from Moscow, some kind of Western European Titoism on the upsurge in the democracies. After the defeat of the Left in France, in April 1979, Italy held national elections in June and the Communist vote skidded by nearly 5 percent. Party hard-liners had not been very happy with Berlinguer's strategy of power sharing with the bourgeois Christian Democrats, preferring a return to the orthodox politics of the class struggle. Berlinguer accordingly walks a new tightrope of seeking to satisfy his hard-liners while at the same time trying to maintain pressures to obtain a power-sharing status which means compromises to the moderates.

The Soviets then administered their own *coup de grâce* to Eurocommunism with their invasion of Afghanistan two days after Christmas 1979. In an obvious repeat of the tactic they used in Prague in 1968, a phony "call for assistance" had been prearranged and fooled nobody. Nevertheless, Georges Marchais rushed off to Moscow to a bear-hug welcome by Leonid Brezhnev after giving the full and unquestioning backing of the French Communist Party to this Soviet aggression against an independent Third World state. In Rome and Madrid, Berlinguer and Carrillo —more sensitive to Italian and Spanish public opinion than Marchais bothered to be about French public opinion—both condemned the Soviet action, as they had the invasion of Prague, twelve years before. But the common front of Eurocommunism was broken, and from the standpoint of the Kremlin it was far more important to have the French Communist Party back in line. The Soviet Union has gotten used to living with independence in the Italian and Spanish parties, and as long as they are not joined by the French there is little the Kremlin needs to fear about some major schism or runaway Eurocommunist movement out of control.

Shortly before the Soviet forces moved into Afghanistan, the Kremlin pronounced its ideological death sentence on Eurocommunism. Boris Nikolaevich Ponomarev, the seventy-four-year-old secretary of the Central Committee of the Communist Party of the Soviet Union and director of its International Department, in charge of relations with Communist parties not in power (including, of course, the parties in Western Europe), delivered a long ideological speech on the subject of Eurocommunism in which he said:

"So-called Eurocommunism is opposed to real socialism and rejects the historic and universal role of Soviet achievements. Eurocommunism can only bring harm to the international Communist movement as well as to the parties which adhere to it. The leaders of Eurocommunist parties are beginning to understand that this policy is meeting with growing disapproval from the party rank and file, as well as from the militant cadres of their parties. The Central Committee of the Soviet Communist Party will do all it can in the future to eliminate all deviations from Marxism-Leninism and from proletarian internationalism."

Stripped of its dialectical jargon, the Ponomarev speech was an unvarnished order to the Communist Party leaders of Western Europe to curb this Eurocommunism fallacy and get back in line or face the consequences. Georges Marchais, Enrico Berlinguer, Santiago Carrillo and Álvaro Cunhal no doubt listened to the Kremlin speech with varying enthusiasm, but they all have the message.

19

Helmut Schmidt

KONRAD ADENAUER WAS THE POSTWAR BUILDER OF THE BONN Republic, and Willy Brandt was its innovator in foreign policy. Since 1974, Chancellor Helmut Schmidt has been West Germany's great consolidator—the economic prowess of the Federal Republic and its political stability, its vital role in the security of the West in the North Atlantic Treaty Organization, its predominant place in the European Common Market, the steady diplomacy of its relations with the Communist world, and its growing if carefully modulated influence in global affairs. Schmidt's role has therefore been less dramatic or history-making than that of the Chancellors of the formative years in Bonn. But, in many ways, he has emerged as the superior of both Adenauer and Brandt, intellectually as well as politically, and in the long run the effectiveness of his contribution in the stability and solidarity of his country and its position in the heart of Europe may well turn out to be the superior achievement of historic statesmanship also.

"A statesman is in general a man of common opinions and uncommon abilities," wrote Walter Bagehot, the great English constitutional essayist. Certainly the first striking quality of Helmut Schmidt is his no-nonsense, down-to-earth, uncluttered, commonsense approach to Germany's problems and his view of the world from Bonn. His uncommon ability can be summed up in one of those mouthful German words: *fingerspitzengefühl,* a finger-tip intuition and feel for politics and leadership. He has grown visibly as a political leader at home and a statesman of commanding presence in the world since he acceded to the chancellorship when Willy Brandt resigned. He is a trained economist with a keen intellect and an enormous capacity for work. He has an organized mind, reads voraciously, absorbs and analyzes rapidly, and has great clarity of expression (in English as well as German, written or spoken) in citing his conclusions. He has force, he has a clear sense of direction, he has vision, and he has style.

Above all, Helmut Schmidt is a political animal. Politics has been his profession and his life since he graduated from university after World War II. He loves the combat of politics, as well as the rewards of achievement and accomplishment it can bring. Because he is a political realist, there is nothing abstract or theoretical about his approach to problems. He is rooted in "the art of the possible," and he also knows that "power begets power." He is a political fighter and does not leave it to others to fight his battles for him. He has been called *"Schmidt die Schnauze"* since his early days in the Social Democratic Party—roughly "Schmidt the Lip"—for his pugnacious way of always telling people off. But he is also known as *"Schmidt der Macher"*—Schmidt the doer and fixer. Since he became Chancellor, with the growing experience of office and the multiplicity of his international dealings and face-to-face meetings with other world leaders, his well-known combativeness has become more controlled and his style has matured, even mellowed. So, too, has his effectiveness increased. He is less of a *schnauze* and more of a *macher*. He is not beset by any egotism of power. On the contrary, he instinctively tries to avoid the image or impression of West Germany throwing its weight around, trying to dominate or play too powerful or dynamic a role in Europe or in NATO or in international affairs generally. Since national self-effacement and personal pugnaciousness do not exactly go hand in hand, Schmidt has reined himself in, no matter how impatient he becomes of Jimmy Carter, Margaret Thatcher or Valéry Giscard d'Estaing.

Still, there is no reining in of the sheer economic force of the West German Federal Republic in the Common Market, in East-West trade, on the oil market, on the world monetary and banking system, on problems of currency stability, on growth rates and inflation, and in the military sphere on the security of Europe. Schmidt presides over the most dynamic political-economic-military force in Europe, and he knows it.

He knows too that he presides over a divided Fatherland,

with all of the potential political, emotional and diplomatic problems this entails. He knows that in Eastern Europe there are also dynamisms of history at work that must be guided, channeled and contained if they are not to become explosive. He knows that in Western Europe—France in particular—there is always latent nervousness about Germany, about German power or too much German "independence." The French play their own game constantly with the Soviet Union, but they will not give up—they do not want to give up—the fear of Germany playing it, the fear that Willy Brandt's *Ostpolitik* might one day turn out to be some Hitlerian *Drang nach Osten* which would dislodge the stability of Europe.

What, then, are Helmut Schmidt's common-sense policies in the face of these concerns, and his statesman's answers? First, he is utterly rooted in the Konrad Adenauer fundamental of West Germany's commitment and place in the West: the closest possible Franco-German ties and membership in the European Common Market and in the front-line security bastion of the West through the NATO Alliance. But he also knows that beyond the Elbe there are not just Communist governments but people: Silesians, Pomeranians, East Prussians, Poles, Czechs, Slovaks, Hungarians and all the rest. In spite of the tragic history of the past fifty years, there are still ties of culture and history and literature and language that are transcendental and that may well become more important in the rest of this century than they have been for a hundred years. Schmidt means to see that West Germany nurtures these ties of civilization prudently and carefully, without propaganda or politics, but with understanding and hope.

Yet, for every move he makes to water the garden of *Ostpolitik*, he will also see to it at the same time that West German feet are planted firmly in the Atlantic Community and the West.

Because there is nothing particularly novel about such policies for West Germany, Schmidt is not likely to be perceived as making any new or original contribution to history. Simply to build and consolidate policies inherited from Adenauer and Brandt may not seem to take imagination or vision. But the Federal Republic today is an entirely different dynamic than it was thirty years ago, in Adenauer's time, when it was still flat on its back in the ruins of

World War II and had no military forces and was not even permitted to have much of a foreign policy. Even since Willy Brandt's chancellorship, the political, economic and military dynamics have continued to change for West Germany—not the least as a result of Brandt's own openings to the east through *Ostpolitik*. How is the latent power and the new dynamism of the Federal Republic to be steered, directed, controlled? That is the problem facing Helmut Schmidt, and it is a far different problem from that which faced Adenauer or Brandt.

To take a prime example, where would NATO and Western Europe be if Helmut Schmidt were not persevering in a strong military posture? Suppose West Germany had decided to say no to plans to station a new generation of upgraded tactical nuclear missiles on her territory in the 1980s: the Pershing-II rockets and the land-based cruise missiles with enough range to strike targets in the Soviet Union? If Schmidt had bowed to Soviet pressure over the missile program or trimmed his sails to satisfy certain left-wing urgings in his own party, then indeed France and the rest of Western Europe would have cause to be nervous and jittery about the implications of West German *Ostpolitik*. But he did not, and it is a vital example of Schmidt's policy of ensuring Germany's leading role in the stability of the West while at the same time offering trade and harmony in relations with the East. With each passing month, the pivotal importance of the Federal Republic at the divided center of Europe grows—and so does the statesman's role of Helmut Schmidt.

He is a stocky, solidly built man only five feet eight inches tall. But, with his strong and striking features and his thick iron-gray hair, he always seems to be physically taller than he really is, and he exudes power when he enters a room. He smokes too much, and on top of that he is fond of taking snuff, making it fashionable in Germany once again, but he scarcely drinks at all, except Coca-Cola. He is a glutton for work, fourteen to sixteen hours a day every day he is on the job in Bonn. Then, on weekends, he tries to turn off, get away to his own home in a middle-class suburb of his native Hamburg and switch to twelve hours of sleep to recharge his physical and mental batteries. The Schmidts also have a little cottage on a lake in Schleswig-Holstein north of Hamburg, which they acquired shortly after the war, and this is their vacation spot. He likes sailing but otherwise takes no particular exercise. He is a passionate chess player. He is also very musical, plays the organ with accomplishment, loves Bach and enjoys symphony or opera when he can find time to attend. He is utterly unpretentious in his living habits and life-style. He is a very private man, with his wife, Hannelore, or "Loki," whom he married during the war, in 1943, and their only child, an adult daughter who works in the economics department of a bank in Frankfurt. His Hamburg home is two houses knocked together: his father's house and one he bought next door. Only a few yards separate his home from neighbors on either side, but there is enough garden for a small swimming pool in the back. He also added a little pavilion wing after he became Chancellor to provide a little more room for meetings and entertaining. It is a far cry from the Château Rambouillet or Camp David or Chequers or the Soviet *dachas* at Pitsunda, on the Black Sea coast—but here Schmidt has entertained Giscard d'Estaing, Jimmy Carter, James Callaghan, Leonid Brezhnev and other selected statesmen. It is his home, where he is comfortable and relaxed, and it is a quiet demonstration that power has not altered his tastes, habits or personality.

Helmut Schmidt was born in Hamburg on December 23, 1918, barely one month after the end of the First World War, when Red revolutionaries and Spartacus demonstrators were running riot in Berlin and the other big cities and towns of the Reich. Both his parents were schoolteachers, strong Lutheran Protestants, and very strict at home in the traditional German way, but largely apolitical in outlook. He attended Litchward School, in Hamburg, which was avant-garde in its teaching methods but sharp on discipline. Here he met his future wife, who was studying to be a teacher. He also joined the Hitler Jugend, which he regrets, and in 1937 he graduated as valedictorian of his class. Schmidt, along with his love of music, also had a bent for sketching and painting (which he still does on his vacations) and wanted to become an architect and go into city planning. But, by then, the Nazis had reinstituted national service, and when he came out of school he was promptly swept up by the Reich Labor Service, the Todt-Organisation, run by the infamous Robert Ley, which was responsible for public works, autobahns, planning and construction all over Germany including building the concentration camps. At the outbreak of war, in 1939, Schmidt was transferred into the Wehrmacht and commissioned an anti-aircraft artillery officer.

He never talks about his wartime experiences, but he served first in the West and then in the Russian campaign. By 1944, he was on a tour of Berlin headquarters staff duties. He was in Berlin when the Nazi regime was rocked by the July 20, 1944, plot on Hitler's life. The Nazi People's Court was then convened to try and sentence not only the immediate plotters but hundreds of others whom the Gestapo flushed out of its files from all over Germany. Schmidt was required to attend the court for two days, along with other young headquarters officers, to stiffen their ideological spines. But instead, he says, he found the mad-dog hectoring of the tortured defendants by the presiding Nazi judge simply repulsive.

Late in 1944, he returned to the fighting on the Western Front. In the Ardennes Forest, following Hitler's last military gamble— the Battle of the Bulge—he was captured and spent the next six months in a British prisoner-of-war camp in Belgium. It was there, with the Third Reich collapsing, that Schmidt's political awareness really began. Inevitably talk among the prisoners centered on the ruin of their nation and what the future would hold. Some of the older officers who had been Social Democrats before the Nazis suppressed all political parties in Germany were now at last free again, in the PW cages, to speak their minds and discuss their ideas and idealism. It was in these conversations, Schmidt has said, that he began to think about politics and Germany's future.

Out of the PW camp at last, and back in Hamburg, where his wife and mother and father had all survived the war, Schmidt, at the age of twenty-seven, enrolled in a course in economics at Hamburg University. One of his professors was Karl Schiller, a brilliant if rather egotistical and pompous teacher, whom Schmidt would succeed twenty-five years later as federal Minister of Economics, in Bonn. An old Hamburg friend of Schmidt's says of those early university days that despite the appalling destruction of the city and the university buildings and the lack of fuel, food and the simple means of life, there was an extraordinary intellectual fervor. "It was an unusual situation because most of the students were older men like Schmidt, active minds and mature with their lives ahead of them but denied university education because of the war. And they were dealing with an older generation of teachers, too old for the war but with roots going back before Hitler's time. The result was a very open, active, searching, probing intellectual atmosphere of debate and discussion about the nature of society, economics, politics, Germany's future, and what each now hoped to do with his own life. They didn't have much to eat, and in winter it was bitter cold in those damaged buildings, but a lot of thinking and talking made up for it."

Hamburg has always been a Socialist political stronghold in Germany, with its predominantly working-class population, its vast harbor and industry. Socialist influence and Social Democratic doctrine quickly resurfaced at the university after the years of Nazi suppression. Schmidt from the outset was much more of a political activist than political ideologue. But, at the same time, he had come to feel as a matter of plain practical politics and economic logic that a Social Democratic approach to government would serve postwar Germany far better than old-fashioned conservatism. Without much doubt, he was also influenced by the simple fact that the Social Democrats already dominated politics and power in postwar Hamburg, and if you wanted to get anywhere in politics you joined the SPD. At any rate, Schmidt entered the German Socialist Student League at Hamburg University, and by the time he graduated, in 1949, he was the chairman of its National Executive Committee and thus working in close proximity to the SPD party organization and political leadership.

He came out of university, age thirty, just as the Berlin airlift ended, the Bonn constitution was approved, and West Germany's first free national election in sixteen years was held to launch the new government of the Federal Republic. It was, of course, a victory (although a narrow one) for Konrad Adenauer and the Christian Democrats with their Bavarian wing, the Christian Socialists. Among most young adults Schmidt's age at this period of postwar history, the prevailing attitude toward politics and the new government was "*ohne mich*" (without me)—a kind of turned-off political nihilism. But Schmidt had opted firmly for a life in politics, and he moved into the SPD-controlled Hamburg city-state administration. Due to its size and its Hanseatic origin and traditions of a free city, Hamburg (as well as Bremen) had the status of one of the twelve separate *Länder,* or states of the Federal Republic under the Bonn constitution. By 1953, Schmidt was heading the Hamburg Economics and Transport Department.

In West Germany's second federal election, in 1953, Schmidt entered the Bundestag as a deputy from Hamburg. These were the years of Adenauer's triumphs and complete dominance of German politics. Schmidt worked at his parliamentary duties and rose in the SPD ranks to become a member of the party's parliamentary steering committee and then a member of the SPD National Executive. But he showed his independence of mind in one particular action. The party, then drifting under the uninspired leadership of Erich Ollenhauer, sought to make political capital out of tactical opposition to German rearmament and the building of the new Bundeswehr. Schmidt took a much more realistic view of the necessity for German rearmament. To demonstrate his position, he volunteered, as a former German officer, for a special tour of reserve training duty, in 1958. He came in for a lot of party grumbling and criticism, which he simply ignored. Then, in 1959, the party's unhappiness with Ollenhauer's leadership and its continuing slide with the voters resulted in a palace-guard revolt by Willy Brandt and others, including one of the parliamentary leaders, Herbert Wehner. A rewriting of the SPD political platform followed, moving the party well away from old dogmas about nationalization of industry, the class struggle, etc., and broadening the electoral appeal to the middle class as well as the working class. Schmidt, within the National Executive, was firmly in the camp of the nondoctrinaire moderates and worked on much of the preparation and drafting of what became known as the Bad Godesberg Compromise—on which Brandt then went on to fight the 1961 election.

However, by this time Schmidt had grown tired of the routines of a Bundestag opposition member and saw little chance of the party's wresting power from Adenauer. So he elected to return to a more active life in Hamburg. Instead of the Bundestag again, he got elected to the Hamburg Senate and quickly took over the key post of the Internal Affairs Department in the city-state administration. In this job, he got an unexpected break, propelling him into headlines, from, of all things, the weather.

In the late spring of 1962, a North Sea gale with torrential rains and high tides suddenly burst up the Elbe River, broke through the protective dikes outside Hamburg, and brought raging floods and widespread damage, with more than three hundred deaths. Hamburg's minister-president was a rather ineffectual SPD figurehead, and Schmidt der Macher quickly took over. He literally told his boss to stay away from the office and let him handle it. He called in the press to inform Hamburg of the full extent of the disaster, and then turned the conference around by telling the assembled journalists: "If you have any ideas about what to do, I want them now—not criticism in the newspapers tomorrow morning; that will be too late." From then on, for the ensuing crucial days, he was all over the place, mobilizing and directing the police and fire departments, the transport and utility services, relief organizations and hospitals and social services, the schools and public works departments, galvanizing the whole city into one big disaster-relief operation. He even ordered out the new German Army on his own, quite probably illegally, to get troops into action to mend the dikes. Technically the Army takes orders only from the federal authorities, in Bonn, not state administrations. But the Hamburg State Senator for Interior Affairs simply called the regional commander of the Bundeswehr in Hamburg: "There are three hundred people dead, the dikes have gone; get your men out there and help." The Army did. From the role of a backroom boy and a rather anonymous ex-Bundestag member, Helmut Schmidt suddenly became a headline figure and public personality on the German scene. He told friends later, with unabashed satisfaction: "What a relief to be really doing something instead of sitting and debating in Bonn."

Unlike many other men of power, Helmut Schmidt was never motivated on his way up by any glittering ambition, but simply by a love of hard work and challenges. He never set out to become federal Chancellor, and when he gave up his Bundestag seat and went back to Hamburg, he had more or less written himself out of a future in national politics, as far as he could see. He loved his city and he enjoyed his job. But his sheer abilities propelled him onward and upward. About this time, as a side interest, he spent some months in London at the International Institute for Strategic Studies. The result was one of the first original postwar military studies to emerge in West Germany, a treatise titled *Defense or Retaliation,* which added another dimension to Schmidt's growing stature.

But, by 1965, with Bundestag elections again in the offing, the political climate had altered greatly. Konrad Adenauer had at last been nudged into grumpy retirement, and his immediate successor, Ludwig Erhard, was having a difficult time convincing the German public that he was really filling the old man's shoes. Erich Ollenhauer had died, and the SPD was now fully under Willy Brandt's leadership, finding real political momentum at last, twenty years after the war. And Schmidt by now was the strongest SPD personality in Hamburg. So he headed back to the national scene. He returned to the Bundestag in the 1965 election, rejoining the SPD parliamentary steering committee. He was then one of the inner circle in Bonn that urged Brandt to seize the opportunity in January 1967 to form a "grand coalition" with the CDU/CSU. Brandt at first was reluctant to leave Berlin and did not like the idea of a coalition, but he could not in the end refuse the judgment of his party colleagues in Bonn. The coalition was duly formed with Kurt Georg Kiesinger as Chancellor and Brandt Vice-Chancellor and Minister of Foreign Affairs. In the ensuing division of posts, Schmidt was left out of the Cabinet but got exactly what he wanted. He became SPD floor leader in the Bundestag.

Schmidt's political talents as a parliamentarian and combative debater, along with his intellectual qualities, now began to come into full public flower. Moreover, given the inherent political difficulties and awkwardness of making the grand coalition work at the cabinet level, the real strength and success of the government lay increasingly on the floor of the Bundestag. Schmidt, working with the CDU floor leader, Rainer Barzel, saw to it that the legislative machinery functioned smoothly and effectively, on the whole more successfully than the Cabinet was functioning.

While Willy Brandt, the SPD party leader, operated in the upper reaches of diplomacy, devoting himself mainly to *Ostpolitik* and the international scene, Schmidt became more and more the operative leader of the party, with his influence and strength growing enormously through his hold on the parliamentary leadership. In tandem with Brandt, this was vital to the ultimate success of the SPD in the Bundestag election in 1969.

At last the breakthrough came for Willy Brandt and the Social Democrats—just under 43 percent of the total vote, a solid bloc of 224 Bundestag seats, and enough strength to put together by fast political footwork a coalition with the small, liberal Free Democratic Party, which had squeezed home with 5.8 percent of the vote, to add thirty seats and produce a majority in the Bundestag. Brandt formed a government, and Helmut Schmidt became Minister of Defense.

When Schmidt took over direction of the West German armed forces, he inherited a force that had expanded to nearly half a million officers and men since its beginnings, in 1956. But much of the growth had been uncoordinated and wasteful, and Schmidt set out at once to impose more efficiency and cohesion on the overall structure, as well as a more modern and flexible organization of the combat units. The Army was grouped into three corps of twelve divisions, with a divisional structure based on thirty-three strengthened brigades. Schooling and training were reorganized, and expenditure shifted toward development and production of new equipment. A decade later, Schmidt's reorganization of the German forces remains intact.

The fashion in which Schmidt grabbed hold and retuned the sprawling German defense effort was one of the successes of the early period of Social Democratic government. On the international scene, among his fellow defense ministers in the North Atlantic Treaty Organization, Schmidt was not merely effective but intellectually outstanding. Within the government, Brandt had other problems—in particular his Minister of Economics and Finance, the difficult prima donna Karl Schiller, Schmidt's old professor from Hamburg. Schiller did not work well with other people and was tiresomely ambitious. He got on badly with his opposite number in Paris, French Finance Minister Valéry Giscard d'Estaing, and he had a habit of going his own way, with scant regard for the responsibilities of cabinet government. By July of 1972, even the patient Brandt had had enough of Schiller. He was dropped in a cabinet reshuffle, and Schmidt became federal Minister of Economics and Finance and the undisputed No. 2 in the SPD government.

All the same, Schmidt still took a pragmatic, unambitious view of his own future. Willy Brandt decided on an early election in 1972 instead of waiting until the Bundestag came to the end of its normal, four-year term a year later. He came sweeping back into power with the SPD increasing its vote to nearly 46 percent of the total. Brandt was then sixty, and Schmidt was fifty-five. Schmidt told intimates quite flatly that, as far as he could see, Brandt was popular and secure for the indefinite future and that when the SPD eventually did have to look for another leader it would look for a much younger man. Schmidt and Brandt had a good working relationship and mutual appreciation and understanding, although there was no closeness of friendship between the two men. Schmidt, in fact, does not have many close friends, although he has a wealth of admirers and is a convivial man who is a good listener and enjoys company. But then he quickly retires into his own privacy and detachment and self-reliance.

Schmidt appreciated Brandt's ability with people, his stature, and his inherent warmth and qualities of statesmanship. But he was impatient of Brandt's rather disorganized and vague working habits, his inability to keep things focused in cabinet meetings and his vagaries while he pondered and reflected and made up his own mind. The things in Brandt that charmed and attracted people were on the whole things that irritated Schmidt, a man with a crisp, organized, no-nonsense approach to problems of government and decision-making. All the same, both men were intelligent and each respected the other and knew that he needed the other—qualities that were mutually complimentary.

Still, Schmidt fretted and grew more and more choleric about Brandt's inefficiency and lack of focus or concentration on the growing economic problems following the 1973 Israeli-Arab war and the onslaught of the oil blockade and price rise. One result of this period, almost certainly, was a physical problem for Schmidt:

a thyroid deficiency, which resulted in some disturbing ups and downs of health. The details are as private as the rest of Schmidt's private life, but he was taking thyroid treatment, and he did spend periods in the hospital. Yet, after he became Chancellor, the thyroid problem seems to have faded away, and his health has been stable and uncomplicated. A close acquaintance in Hamburg thinks that the problem was induced at least in part by his frustrations and worries over Willy Brandt's governing leadership, and that when he became Chancellor himself he calmed down, in a way, and his thyroid with it.

In any case, neither Schmidt nor anybody else in Bonn could have guessed or foreseen that less than two years after his sweeping 1972 election victory, Willy Brandt would be dislodged from power as a result of a security risk, the planting of a Communist spy in his office by the East Germans under control of the Soviet KGB.

Gunter Guillaume crossed the border from East Germany in 1956 as a "refugee" and worked his way into the Social Democratic Party organization and up through the machine to become a trusted aide in Brandt's private office. In late 1973 or early 1974 he was finally spotted as a Communist agent by the West German security service. But, in total secrecy, Brandt was asked to play along as if nothing were known while Guillaume was watched, to uncover his contacts. Almost certainly, the charade that Brandt had to carry out, continuing to show confidence and normal friendship with a spy in his office, was a contributing factor to the growing weakness in his leadership of the government over the months while the cat-and-mouse play went on. When the case finally broke, in May 1974, and Guillaume and his wife were arrested, it came as a disastrous political blow to the architect of *Ostpolitik*. Moreover, there had been growing party disenchantment with Brandt, led by Herbert Wehner, himself an ex-Communist from the 1930s but a power in the party rank and file. Wehner wanted a leadership change. But there was no plotting against Brandt on the part of Helmut Schmidt—on the contrary, as Brandt felt the pressure for his resignation growing, Schmidt argued with him for hours alone on a last evening to hang in, face the storm and brazen it out. After all, Brandt himself had done no wrong, and it was not Schmidt's way to run away from a fight, and he genuinely believed that Willy Brandt should do the same. But Brandt had a different psychological makeup, and the Guillaume affair, with all of its complexities, had taken the charge out of his political batteries. Despite Schmidt's pleading, he had decided to go, and he went with dignity. Almost certainly, Brandt was encouraged in his decision by the fact that he had such a strong, able, intelligent and experienced associate, who could take over without dislocation to the party or the country and with a maximum of efficiency and support. So Helmut Schmidt became the fifth Chancellor of the Bonn republic, on May 16, 1974.

By a coincidence of history, three days after Schmidt became West German Chancellor, in Bonn, Valéry Giscard d'Estaing was elected President of the French Republic for a seven-year term. There is every political probability, moreover, that these two men will continue to lead their respective countries and dominate the affairs of Europe to the middle of the new decade and beyond. When they arrived, simultaneously, at the summit of national power, in 1974, they had already come to know each other well and had a warm working relationship, as fellow finance ministers in meetings of the European Common Market, the International Monetary Fund, the Organization for Economic Cooperation and Development, and other, ad hoc sessions to cope with the financial turbulence in Europe and the world following the 1973 oil embargo and the world-shaking takeoff of fuel-price increases that followed. As trained economic experts in the field of policy making, which was the most urgent and vital, it was natural that they should act quickly to cement their relationship on taking high office. Moreover, as far as the direction of the Common Market was concerned, Harold Wilson had returned to No. 10 Downing Street for a second tour of office after dislodging Edward Heath in the 1974 election. Wilson was putting Britain through another of its flip-flops about Europe after the brief years of Heath's European enthusiasm. Wilson had proclaimed that Heath's terms of entry into the Common Market would have to be renegotiated by Labour—so with Britain sulking on the sidelines, Schmidt and Giscard d'Estaing slid into gear to keep the Common Market motor running smoothly ahead.

"I was brought up as an Anglophile, to some degree emerged into an Americanophile, and in the ten years that I first spent in government I turned into a Francophile," Schmidt once told an interviewer. "Still, I've not forgotten my youthful leaning towards England. I've not so far been satisfied by England's role in Europe and I hope that there's going to be greater satisfaction in future."

Schmidt and Giscard d'Estaing are Europe's odd couple—the tall, aristocratic Frenchman with his lofty elegance, his love of protocol and the trappings of power, the elitist born to the purple and cocooned in success; the stocky, down-to-earth Hamburg proletarian politician, ex-prisoner of war, who is anybody's equal in intellectual clarity and the exercise of power and is more concerned about showing restraint than showing off. They converse and work in English—to the carping criticism of French linguistic purists; the French must be the only people in the world who think it is a disgrace if their President speaks a second language. Although Giscard and Schmidt have few common tastes or interests, they do have a strong intellectual rapport and mutual respect, and that is more than enough. They have a common feel for the future of Europe and the immense importance of Franco-German amity as the essential underpinning of European success and stability. They understand and trust each other in a deep sense, and that is as fundamental as any form of friendship.

Schmidt, at the same time, demonstrates his *fingerspitzengefühl* instinct in his relations with Giscard and the French by constantly ensuring that France takes the lead and gets the major credit for European diplomatic, political and economic initiatives. He knows full well that results are more readily obtained in Europe by following France, rather than trying to push, pull, persuade or lead the French. As a prime example, the creation of the European monetary system, in 1978–79, was overwhelmingly the work of Helmut Schmidt, buttressed and largely bankrolled by the German monetary reserves and the strength of the deutsche mark. But Schmidt did not take the initiative by a long shot: he first sold the plan carefully to Giscard d'Estaing and got France to take the lead, while Germany characteristically played the polite, supporting role. This *"Après vous, mon cher Valéry"* tactic seems to suit both Schmidt and Giscard d'Estaing very well.

In shaping German policies, Schmidt lives—at times seems to be obsessed—with the preoccupation that the success of his nation merely rouses fears and apprehensions and resentments instead of admiration and emulation. Of course it does to an extent, but not overwhelmingly any longer. There are many important leaders outside Germany who are critical of Schmidt on this point and feel that much too often he uses this as an excuse for German inaction, that he carries the supposed virtue of German restraint too far. Perhaps this will change in the 1980s as Schmidt finds himself propelled more and more into situations in which Germany will clearly have a duty and a responsibility to show initiative and act. But when a questioner once asked him how long Germany must go on living with its past, he replied: "As long as I live, and a little longer. The greater the relative success of Germany, the longer the memory of Auschwitz will last." Schmidt is not a man with a guilt complex. But he is a political realist who prefers to err on the side of caution, building into the conduct of affairs of the Bonn republic a permanent reflex of restraint to ensure that when Germany does take an initiative it will not be misjudged or misunderstood or misrepresented.

"A number of things have led to a situation in which the political weight of my country has become a little greater than it was in the 1970s or the late 1960s," he says. "I don't like that development too much, but it was more or less unavoidable. *Ostpolitik* has given us greater freedom of action. There is our economic success. There is our domestic stability. But if Germany's weight has grown, it has mostly been due to a better performance, relatively speaking, in comparison with others. Others had a chance to perform much more effectively than they have done. I hope they will do better."

As a head of government and trained economist, Schmidt does enjoy one great political-economic advantage over practically all other leaders—and that is the phobia of the German nation about inflation. While others worry about growth rates, unemployment, money supply, balance of payments, capital flows, investment rates, etc., Germany is obsessed with only one economic indicator: the rate of inflation. It all goes back, of course, to the appalling experience of the 1920s, when Schmidt was a little boy and inflation was so terrible that it took basketfuls of paper reichsmarks to buy a loaf of bread. There was a near repeat after World War II until the Allied currency reform of 1948 successfully wiped out a second postwar inflation and set the Western occupation zones (soon to become the Federal Republic) on a sound monetary footing and the road to national recovery. Indeed, it has often seemed that Germans are more fearful of a revival of inflation than of any political revival of Nazism—perhaps rightly so, since inflation has been a more likely danger, and if it did happen it could induce the other. In any case, the German fixation on inflation has meant that governments, whatever their political complexion, have enjoyed a ready-made, built-in national consensus on economic policy. The whole people, from the trade unions to the steel barons, have been ready to sacrifice any marginal advantages of wage increases or profits for the sake of fighting inflation. No other government operates in this kind of political-economic atmosphere, although heaven knows they all wish that they could. The result, of course, has been the foundation of one of the world's outstanding examples of overall economic success. In the decade of the 1970s, the worst inflationary period of this century, the German rate has consistently been about half the OECD average, never above 8 percent and usually below 5 percent, while others have been in double digits.

West Germany's economic predominance in Europe thirty-five years after the war is almost awe-inspiring. The country has a population, swollen by refugees from East Germany, of more than 61 million, compared to 56 million each in Great Britain and Italy and 53 million Frenchmen. The gross national product of the Federal Republic at the end of the 1970s was close to $600 billion annually, against above $400 billion in France, $250 billion in Britain and $200 billion in Italy. German per capita income was approximately $8,800 annually, with France at $7,400, Britain at $4,500 and Italy at $3,600. German exports amounted to a towering $120 billion annually, about the same as United States world exports, followed in the world by Japan at $81 billion, France at $64 billion and Britain with $58 billion. German currency reserves, in excess of $42 billion, were nearly three times as great as United States reserves.

The German lesson, which *Schmidt die Schnauze* will occasionally unload when somebody has the temerity to suggest that Germany "ought to be doing more to lead the world out of recession," is that if you take care of your inflation problem, most other problems will take care of themselves. It may be an oversimplification, but fortunately for the Bonn government, the German nation believes it, and it has worked.

Against this backdrop of economic success and diplomatic restraint, Helmut Schmidt's worst domestic headache of his first four years of office was urban terrorism—primarily the mindless killers of the Baader-Meinhof gang. From 1972 to 1978, Germany was subjected to a wave of killings, kidnapings, bombings, assassinations and shoot-outs, all in the name of some invented ideology that lay between Marxism and anarchy. It reached its climax in October 1977 with the hijacking of a Lufthansa airliner over the Mediterranean, which was then flown to the Somalian capital of Mogadishu, below the Red Sea. Here the hijackers issued their demand: The lives of the hostages in return for the release of leaders of the Baader-Meinhof gang in German jails. But the outcome was a triumph for Schmidt.

Taking personal charge from a crisis-center command post in Bonn, Schmidt went four days and nights with virtually no sleep while negotiations were strung out with the hijackers and a specially trained antiterrorist squad was secretly airlifted to the scene. Landing after dark on the blacked-out airfield, the unit stormed the aircraft with lightning surprise, knocked out the hijackers with flash and concussion grenades, shot and killed two, wounded and captured the others, and freed the hostages. So great was the risk and so tense the political situation surrounding the operation that Schmidt had made up his mind to resign as federal Chancellor if it went wrong and the hostages were killed as a result of his orders. Instead, it made him a national political hero. Within hours of the news that the hijackers were dead or captured and the hostages freed, three of the Baader-Meinhof leaders serving long-term jail sentences committed suicide in their cells. But this messy end did not take much luster from Schmidt, and from that moment on, terrorism in West Germany began to peter out. Like most crimes, the affair has little to do with history, but it had a great deal to do with the stability of West Germany and the leadership image of Helmut Schmidt.

The people of West Germany today are living in greater affluence, comfort and contentment than Germans have ever enjoyed in their history. Materially, socially, culturally, politically, there is little they can ask for that is not within their grasp. For the first time in centuries, Germany is largely at peace with itself, as well as with its neighbors. Yet, at the same time, there is an indefinable lack of one essential ingredient about the Federal Republic, which can be described only as the lack of a sense of nationhood. There is no "Fatherland" and the word itself is neither popular nor used, but the Federal Republic is not truly a nation-state in the eyes of its contented citizens.

"If I think of Germany at night, I cannot sleep," said the poet Heinrich Heine in a famous phrase a hundred and fifty years ago. The great unanswered German question—dream or nightmare—is, of course, the reunification of the German nation. It does not keep anybody awake today, let alone tempt the wildest German politician to beat the drums for action. Germans visit back and forth across the East-West border by the millions every year. But West Germans are not ready to put at risk all that they have gained in thirty-five years in security and material and political comforts for the dubious values that their East German relatives enjoy. As for East Germany, it is inconceivable, so far, that the Soviet Union would countenance any relaxation of its grip on its most productive satellite, or make a reunification of the two Germanies even theoretically possible. Nevertheless, it remains the ultimate German question—which Helmut Schmidt looks at with his usual unvarnished straightforwardness.

"I always say the same thing, whether on German television or in conversation with Leonid Brezhnev. I always remind people of the Polish example. Historically there have been four divisions of Poland. After the third division, at the end of the eighteenth century, there was nothing left of Poland. All the Polish nation was divided among the three great European powers of that time:

Russia, Prussia and Austria. But the Polish nation came back. Then again, in 1939, there was a fourth division of Poland, between Stalin and Hitler, and it ceased to exist. But, over a period of two hundred years now, Poles have not given up the will, did not give up the hope of getting together one day in the future. They didn't know when. The first line of the Polish national anthem since the early-nineteenth century has been "Poland is not lost as yet"—and so far they have been proven right.

"I do not foresee under what auspices and conditions the Germans will get together again, but they will. Maybe only in the twenty-first century—I do not know. But it would obviously be wrong for any European nation to believe that the nation-state is normal for any nation but not for the Germans.

"I do not think that the present alliances will last for centuries. For the time being, the NATO alliance is totally indispensable for maintaining peace in Europe. Therefore the alliance is good for the Germans and they'll stick to it. There is no need and indeed no reason for philosophizing about Germany's adherence to the alliance.

"But the Poles waited for two centuries. Nevertheless the matter was very vital, very deep in their souls. It's not necessary that you advertise it every Sunday. One Germany is not something which anybody thinks of as being right around the corner, or even the corner after the next. It's some way in the future, but it does exist. It's a real desire in the soul of the German nation, whether in the West or the East."

When it does begin to happen, the best that Europe can hope for will be that a Helmut Schmidt, "of common opinions and uncommon abilities," is around to preside with restraint over what will be a dynamic and volatile process for all concerned.

20

To the Helsinki Station

On the afternoon of Tuesday, July 29, 1975, a day of hot and cloudless brilliance under the crystalline blue of the northern sky, a special train from Moscow pulled into the Helsinki Station, and Leonid Brezhnev descended heavily to the platform to be greeted by President Uhro Kekkonen, of Finland.

The Soviet leader had traveled to the Finnish capital for the greatest conclave of heads of state that Europe has seen in this century—a gathering, moreover, for which he was largely responsible. President Ford flew in from Washington, and government leaders came from every capital in Europe, East and West, including Liechtenstein, San Marino, Monte Carlo and the Vatican. Only Albania stayed away. Thirty-five chiefs of state in all arrived in Helsinki to make speeches for two days and then affix their signatures to a unique diplomatic document which had taken three years to negotiate and seven decades of history to achieve: the Final Act of the Conference on Security and Cooperation in Europe.

Interpretations and assessments of these Helsinki Agreements and their real usefulness and worth vary greatly. They have no legal or binding character and have not been ratified by any legislature. They read largely like 115 pages of pious principles, platitudes, legalisms and statements of the obvious. To the United States, they are almost exclusively noteworthy for their extensive provisions on respect for human rights. For the Western Europeans, they are a broad *modus vivendi* for the conduct of diplomatic, economic and cultural relations with the Communist half of Europe. For Brezhnev and the Soviet Union, the Helsinki Agreements were a crowning achievement of *détente* diplomacy, with the

Final Act an affirmation and acceptance by the West of the
boundaries of Europe and spheres of influence that had been
loosely agreed on by Roosevelt, Churchill and Stalin at Yalta in
February of 1945.

Whatever value or utility or importance governments and peoples today assign to the Helsinki Agreements, they do constitute a
watershed in European history. The real worth of what was signed
at the Helsinki summit is a great deal more implicit in its
significance than explicit in the texts. The thirty-five-nation summit gathering, thirty years after the end of the Second World War,
brought East and West in Europe together after the cold war and
a long history of relentless Communist conflict with the capitalist
democracies—neither side fully accepting or trusting either the motives or the pledges of the other, but in the end putting signatures
to a negotiated document on cooperation which amounts to a
truce or an armistice, the closest equivalent to a pan-European
peace treaty that is likely ever to be achieved.

The impetus behind the Conference on Security and Cooperation in Europe came from the Soviet Union and Leonid Brezhnev—not, it can be assumed, from motives of altruism or virtue,
and not without much ideological argument in the Kremlin about
the class war, leadership of the revolution and the sacred texts of
Lenin. In reality, Brezhnev's train journey from Moscow to the
Helsinki Station for the signing ceremony closed out a cycle of
Communist history that began in another European railroad station fifty-eight years before.

Vladimir Ilich Lenin set out at three-ten on the afternoon of Monday, April 9, 1917, from the main railroad station in the Swiss city
of Zurich, where he was living in exile, to return to the Russian
capital of St. Petersburg on perhaps the most famous train journey
in history.

It was a journey that completed the disintegration of the old
order of Europe established at the Congress of Vienna in 1815,
and marked the beginning of a new, permanent division of the
Continent into Communist and non-Communist worlds.

"They transported Lenin in a sealed train like a plague bacillus
from Switzerland to Russia," Winston Churchill wrote in a famous

phrase. The journey was secretly promoted, organized and financed by the German Government of Kaiser Wilhelm II and the German General Staff at the height of the First World War. By returning Lenin to his homeland, the Germans set about deliberately to foment a revolution in order to obtain peace on their Russian front, so they could concentrate their full military strength against the French, the British and the Americans now coming into the war in the West. In this they succeeded. But the move was one of the colossal misjudgments of all history, and a divided Germany today continues to pay the price.

On March 15, 1917, with the Czarist armies mired in mud and military disaster, the first shock of revolution erupted in St. Petersburg, and Czar Nicholas abdicated in favor of his brother Michael, who declined. A government of liberal social-democratic complexion took over under Kerensky, supported at the outset by both Bolsheviks and Mensheviks. It was a government of reform rather than Marxist-Communist revolution, and it was also committed to continuing the patriotic war against the German enemy. It was scarcely a government to Lenin's taste, and when news of the uprising reached Zurich he began agitatedly trying, that very evening, to arrange somehow to get back to Russia. Lenin was then a vigorous forty-seven years old.

In Berlin, in the secrecy of the Wilhelmstrasse, the Germans for some months had been contemplating exactly this same possibility, and already had an entire secret section working on funding antigovernment activity in Russia, as well as secret agents in Lenin's entourage. The offer to Lenin of safe-conduct passage across Germany was passed by one of these agents, from the German minister in Berne, Baron Gisbert von Romberg, acting on an urgent instruction from Berlin on March 26 that had been personally approved by the Kaiser before transmission.

Lenin had hoped to avoid both the onus and the risk of traveling across enemy territory to return home, but in the end he could wait no longer and had no other choice. To protect himself as far as possible from the charge of treason and the risk of arrest when he arrived at the Russian border, it was he who insisted on the "sealed train." From the Zurich station on the afternoon of April 9, Lenin traveled on a regular Swiss train with a party of thirty-two revolutionary comrades—men, women and two children—to a tiny German border village called Gottmadingen, near the Swiss city of Schaffhausen. There the sealed train for the journey across Germany was waiting.

It consisted of only an engine and two cars—a passenger car with three second-class compartments (upholstered seats) and five third-class compartments (hard seats), plus a baggage car. Lenin and his wife shared one of the second-class compartments. With doors locked and two German escort officers plus a Swiss intermediary guarding and supervising the journey, the train left, in the early-morning hours Tuesday and wound north through Stuttgart, Karlsruhe, Frankfurt and then Berlin, where it arrived on Wednesday, April 11.

There the train was held unexpectedly for nearly twenty hours at the Potsdam Station, in the heart of the city—a delay that still tantalizes historians today. Were there any direct secret contacts between Lenin and the German Foreign Ministry during that night layover? Nobody knows, but the probability seems strong. What has emerged from Wilhelmstrasse archives captured by the Western Allies at the end of World War II is clear documentary historic evidence of the enormous German funding of the Bolshevik cause through intermediaries in Copenhagen and Stockholm—more than $2 million at 1917 exchange rates, which would then have been worth at least ten times what it could buy today. Whatever transpired in Berlin, the sealed train moved off on Thursday to the little port town of Sassnitz, on the Baltic, where Lenin and his party left German territory and boarded a Swedish ferry for a rough crossing to Trelleborg.

They arrived by train in Stockholm on the morning of Friday the thirteenth, and in between endless, nonstop sessions with revolutionary faithful who were flocking from other points in exile to get ready for the big show, Lenin went shopping and bought new trousers and shoes. His party left that night for the Swedish-Finnish border at the northern end of the Gulf of Bothnia, where they would meet their first Russian officials—Finland then still being a Russian duchy.

The initial border crossing was tense (unknown to Lenin, a Russian-speaking British officer took part in the proceedings), and the examination of the party was rigorous, but they were Russian subjects entering a Russian province and there were no arrests. Lenin described his profession as "journalist." Across the border on Easter Sunday, from the Finnish town of Tornio, he sent a triumphant telegram to his sister in St. Petersburg: ARRIVING MONDAY 11 P.M. INFORM PRAVDA.

On Monday, April 16, 1917, almost exactly one week to the hour after crossing the Swiss frontier into Germany, Lenin crossed the Finnish border into Russia proper. At the border point, Lenin's younger sister and a party of comrades from St. Petersburg boarded the train to bring him up to date on what had been happening. But when at last the train puffed to a final halt, more than half an hour late, in the Finland Station at St. Petersburg, Lenin was astounded at the throng gathered to greet him. The private waiting room of the departed Czar was hung with red banners, and an honor guard of the Imperial Army was drawn up to present arms as if the Czar himself were returning. A military band broke into a stirring welcoming rendition of the "Marseillaise." It had not yet had time to learn the "Internationale."

Lenin's arrival at the Finland Station triggered into action the twentieth century's great latent revolutionary force. Karl Marx and Friedrich Engels had written *The Communist Manifesto* back in 1848, and since then, revolutionaries of every character and description, every intellectual quality and criminal mediocrity, had been flocking to the red banner in inchoate confusion. But the results in terms of real substantive power anywhere until 1917 had been nil. Lenin now transformed theory into action, aspiration into force, confusion into iron discipline, and revolution into Communist power.

But Marx had laid down that a backward country of serfs and agriculture such as Russia would be one of the last places for world revolution—not a starting point. Writing his theories in the British Museum library from the perspective of the dark, satanic mills of the England of Charles Dickens, Marx foresaw revolution beginning in industrial society, where workers could be organized to seize the means of production and transfer power into their own hands.

Lenin then astounded Party workers in his very first speech, before his first night's sleep back in St. Petersburg, by brushing this Marxist theory aside. In two hours of flaming oratory, he rejected the idea that Russia was not yet ready for revolution, lashed out at any policy of gradualism and cooperation with Kerensky and the reform government under the Czar's brother, and called for "all power to the Soviets." Still, it took Lenin another six months, with vital help from Trotsky, to batter the Kerensky government into oblivion and finally install a true Red revolution in power in those November 1917 "ten days that shook the world."

Under Lenin's driving force, communism first triumphed in a backward, nonindustrial state, but this did not change Marxist doctrine. Viewed through Marxist eyes in 1917–18, a war of imperialism was aggravating the contradictions of capitalism. Revolutionary conditions were ripening everywhere. World revolution was beginning, Russia was in the vanguard, and Lenin was the new prophet and leader.

Indeed, when the Red mutiny broke out in the Kaiser's fleet, at Kiel, Germany, in October 1918, followed by the Spartacus uprising in Berlin, it looked as if both Marx and Lenin were going to be right. By that time, the gamble in returning Lenin to Russia in the sealed train no longer looked so good to the German General Staff. But the abdication of the Kaiser, the rapid conclusion of an Armistice to end the First World War, and the gradual containment of the Reds by German conservatives and Social Democrats brought things back under control in Germany, more or less. Still, in Marxist terms, the "objective conditions" for communism remained favorable. There was appalling inflation, and Communist activity in the Weimar Republic was stronger and more effective than anywhere else in Western Europe. The Communist heroine was Rosa Luxemburg.

In Moscow, where Lenin now ruled the Soviet Union from the Kremlin, the Comintern was formed, with Trotsky as its first director, to weld the Communist International movement under Russian leadership. Money, organization, discipline and secrecy— these were the weapons of the revolutionary struggle, inside the trade union movements, in a growing network of secret agents and espionage, in Communist publications that blossomed in every language, in the Communist parties which now had the means and the example for the struggle to bring down the capitalist system.

The Wall Street crash of 1929, taking the world into the Great Depression, heightened Marx's "objective conditions" for revolution. Coupled with this came the rise of Fascism in Mussolini's Italy, Hitler's Germany, and then the climactic Spanish Civil War, in which the Communists practically swallowed up the Republican cause. As democratic governments in Western Europe floundered under conservative leadership, unable to come up with either economic or political policies or ideals to solve the human plight of peoples while Fascism seemed to thrive, Communism took on the appeal of a clear answer.

Communist recruitment was brightened by stars such as André Gide, Louis Fischer, Ignazio Silone, Stephen Spender, Arthur Koestler, Pablo Picasso—and at Oxford University the enlistment of Guy Burgess, Donald MacLean, Kim Philby and Anthony Blunt, who were to perform the most damaging operation of espionage and treason in British history. George Bernard Shaw and Lady Astor trooped off to Russia with Beatrice and Sidney Webb to applaud the wonder that was being wrought. The veteran American liberal Lincoln Steffens made the pilgrimage to Moscow and came out to pronounce: "I have been over into the future, and it works."

Meanwhile, Stalin had replaced Lenin, exiled Trotsky and eventually arranged his murder, and embarked on his infamous campaign of famine and purges to subdue his people to his own paranoia. In Western Europe, he shifted the Comintern line in the mid-1930s to a flank attack on political democracy. It was now the Popular Front, to align with the Social Democrats and liberals with the dual aim of giving the Communist parties a better chance of boring from within against democratic capitalist society, and at the same time divert attention from the realities of Communist rule in the Soviet Union.

Then came World War II—which began, of course, when Stalin astounded the Communists as well as the democracies by his deal with Hitler to divide Poland under the guise of a nonaggression pact. Overnight, in August of 1939, the Communist parties in the

West had to flip-flop on the party line. Instead of calling for a
solid front against Fascism, they now did all they could to oppose
and sabotage another "war of imperialism." But when Hitler then
invaded the Soviet Union, on June 20, 1941, they had to change
back overnight. The "war of imperialism" now became "the great
patriotic struggle against Fascism." Despite the disasters of his
own miscalculations, which very nearly brought about Russia's defeat, for Joseph Stalin the war was the great historic opportunity to
consolidate and spread Soviet Communism, and he made the most
of it.

With epic heroism and appalling losses, and the assistance of
the capitalist Allies, the invading Nazi armies were slowly contained and then driven back to defeat. Four years after the Nazis
marched into Russia, Stalin sat down in the Berlin suburb of Potsdam, in July 1945, with Winston Churchill and Harry S Truman,
to divide up the spoils. The Red Army had reached the European
dividing lines that had been agreed on at Yalta. Apart from finally
granting Austria its promised independence in 1955, they have not
yet retreated by one meter.

For Stalin, the wartime alliance with the capitalist powers never
required any abandonment of the goal of world revolution. By the
time the victorious leaders got home from Potsdam, the political
struggle was being reactivated by the Communist parties in Western Europe all over again. Waves of Communist-led strikes hit
France, Italy, Belgium, even Britain and Holland in the difficult,
postwar years. In Greece, the Communists fought an open civil
war to try to bring that country into Stalin's orbit. The Comintern,
which had been suppressed by Stalin during the war as an act of
solidarity with the Allies, was soon replaced by the new Cominform. The snuffing out of bourgeois democratic parties in the satellite countries of Eastern Europe got underway with all the
methods perfected in the Russian great terror of the 1930s. The
blockade of Berlin was ordered. The cold war began.

But, as these pages have shown, Western Europe was not lacking
in resources of men of power and the ideals and the means to
meet the postwar challenges of politics, economics and society.
There was none of that vacuum of leadership that followed the

First World War in Europe and the United States (Harding and Coolidge, Bonar Law and Baldwin, Poincaré and Briand).

Moreover, out of the Great Depression, there had come a revolution in capitalist economic theory. John Maynard Keynes had taught the capitalist system how to save itself. On top of Keynesian economics, the entire problem of managing the war effort in Great Britain and the United States had been one vast experience in economic planning and the administration of government controls, in socialism and social democracy without any political label. The days of *laissez-faire* democratic government were over. From managing the war effort, governments moved on automatically to managing peacetime economies by democratic means. Of course some governments and political parties were more militant and left than others, but, broadly speaking, every political party in Western Europe, from Right to Left, was now committed to governing with broad social aims and responsibilities: full employment, social security, higher living standards, more-even distribution of wealth, greater opportunity, better education, medical care, wider sharing of culture, leveling out of class structures, social justice, expansion of trade, open borders for Europe's peoples. No longer did communism have any monopoly, real or supposed or theoretical, of answers to the future.

From Moscow, Stalin responded by orchestrating a fight by the Communists everywhere, every step of the way, to hamstring, obstruct, thwart, derail postwar European recovery, European unity, European security, as Europe's leaders, together with the United States, pulled to solve the prodigious problems and challenges. The Communists opposed the Marshall Plan, they opposed the Schuman Plan, they opposed the North Atlantic Treaty. But at least there was political compensation in the fashion in which Stalin consistently overplayed his hand. The Communist parties in Western Europe were so blatantly obstructive of obvious national interests that it made it easy to dislodge them from participation in government, and after that, their opposition to basic measures or policies often provided the clarifying political push to getting vital treaties or acts approved.

The five years from 1947 to 1952 was the great formative period for postwar Western Europe—roughly from the time that

President Truman came to the rescue of Greece and Turkey until the ratification of the Schuman Plan and the establishment of the European Coal and Steel Community. To a remarkable degree, the solid foundation that was put into place at that time continues to be the base for the security and the political and economic stability of Western Europe. The structure has been progressively enlarged and expanded, but the foundations have never basically changed or been undermined—not even by President Charles de Gaulle's pullout from military cooperation with France's allies in the North Atlantic Treaty Organization and the subsequent transfer of NATO headquarters from Paris to Brussels.

By the time of Stalin's death, in 1953, the postwar Communist challenge had been contained and Western Europe was well on the road to the most peaceful and prosperous and expansive era in its long history. At the end of the decade, Stalin's successor, Nikita S. Khrushchev, renewed the cold war by reactivating the Berlin threat all over again and then going on to challenge the United States directly by planting nuclear missiles in Cuba. Not only were these ventures met by Alliance solidarity, including General de Gaulle; in the final showdown, the relative inferiority of the Soviet Union in conventional naval forces as well as strategic nuclear forces had been harshly exposed. Khrushchev recoiled in the opposite direction, and quickly changed course by seizing President Kennedy's offer of a treaty to ban nuclear testing in the open atmosphere above ground. But at some point the Politbureau decided that it had had enough of the ebullient, erratic Khrushchev, and he was deposed in favor of Leonid Brezhnev in 1965.

Under Brezhnev, a sustained pursuit of a policy of *détente* with Western Europe now began. The ideological blessing for this shift away from world revolution, the class struggle and war against capitalism was conveniently provided by the Politbureau's longtime chief interpreter of Marxist-Leninist-Stalinist holy writ, Mikhail Suslov, who made it all very simple: "*Détente* is the application of Leninist principles of peaceful coexistence in the practice of international relations, against the fierce resistance of opponents of peaceful development led by the military-industrial complex of the United States of America." *Détente,* in other words, was a new way of targeting the United States as the chief enemy and seeking to isolate it from its European allies.

So much for the ideological window dressing. Lenin, in fact, had gone through a similar tactical shift back in the early 1920s when he proclaimed his New Economic Policy (NEP) and invited in Western capitalists (Henry Ford was one of them) to develop industrial production which was beyond Soviet means. Lenin called it a policy of "one step backward, two steps forward," and justified it all by declaring that the capitalists would provide him with the rope by which he would eventually hang them.

Forty years after Lenin's NEP period, the Soviet Union was still far behind the capitalist world. By the 1960s, the postwar period was proving to be an extraordinary runaway economic success for Western capitalism, particularly in comparison with the achievements of Communist planning and management in Eastern Europe. When it came to forecasting the historic course of capitalism and the problems of its contradictions, Karl Marx was a dead loser and John Maynard Keynes was the winner. While Stalin and Khrushchev battered away at Western Europe in twenty years of futile ideological struggle, a whole revolution of industrial technology had left the Soviet Union with more catching up to do than ever.

Almost certainly, another element in Moscow's switch to the *détente* line toward Western Europe was the final schism with Red China, which developed in 1961–62. Coupled with the Cuban missile crisis, this produced and continues to produce what at times seems to be near hysteria in Russia at the prospect of military conflict on this vast Asian frontier, possibly a two-front war. Military and political prudence therefore logically lay in seeking to ease tensions and stabilize relations with Western Europe.

Thus, *détente,* for Brezhnev, offered practical breathing space for the Soviet Union, just as the NEP period had for Lenin. Russia needed credits, trade, high-technology equipment, new industrial complexes, the overspill of Western capitalism, to bail the Communist system out of its mismanagement and planning disasters and productive torpor. Even the Kremlin could see that it scarcely made sense to conduct a cold war against Western Europe and at the same time try to borrow capitalist wealth. By the end of the decade of the 1970s, *détente* had worked so well that the Communist bloc was $65 billion in debt to the West.

At the same time, when Brezhnev took over Soviet leadership, strong *détente* overtures had come from the West as well. General de Gaulle set out deliberately, from 1963 on, to worsen French relations with the United States and detach himself from the Atlantic Alliance and at the same time seek closer relations with the Soviet Union. In Bonn, the first stirrings of *Ostpolitik* had begun, to be taken up and given concerted diplomatic drive from 1966 on by Willy Brandt, although for very different reasons and in a very different style from the rather malevolent impulses that drove de Gaulle. From Washington, too, President Lyndon B. Johnson had proposed a Soviet-American negotiation to limit strategic nuclear weapons. And in 1968, Richard M. Nixon was elected President of the United States, proclaiming the opening of a new era in which negotiation would replace confrontation.

If Leonid Brezhnev had any difficulty in selling the policy of *détente* to the hard-liners in the Kremlin collective leadership, they were either reassured or bought off by two decisive parallel actions. First, there was a long-term commitment to maintain the most prodigious and sustained arms-production drive that any nation has ever mounted in all peacetime history. One way or another, around 20 percent of the entire gross national wealth of the Soviet Union has been devoted every year of *détente* on armaments, equipment and maintenance of military forces. It needs little cataloguing: a new, blue-water navy, a formidable increase in both strategic and tactical nuclear forces, a complete modernization of conventional equipment from tanks to communications, and the development of a long-distance airlift and supply capacity. *Détente* would provide the great political cover for the Soviet Union to catch up and overtake the West in general and the United States in particular in those military fields where its weakness had been exposed by the Cuban missile crisis.

The second reassurance to the hard-liners was Brezhnev's decisive action to use military force to wipe out the Prague experiment by Alexander Dubček of "communism with a human face" in August of 1968. Brezhnev acted on that occasion in the best Stalinist tradition, as Khrushchev had acted in Budapest in 1956 and Stalin had acted against every Eastern state in his grasp from 1945 to 1953.

How outraged, how impotent, was the Western reaction to Prague! And how relatively brief the interruption to the *détente* process! General de Gaulle was one of the first to regain his *sang-froid*. Willy Brandt had to put the Czechs at the bottom of his *Ostpolitik* normalization list. Lyndon Johnson was almost as astonished as President Carter was twelve years later, when Brezhnev ordered the Red Army into Afghanistan. Richard Nixon was furious about it right up to Election Day 1968. There is an old Arab saying: Dogs bark, but the caravan moves on.

In the aftermath of Prague, Brezhnev and the Soviet Union wanted and needed *détente* with the West more than ever. The use of military force against an ally had violently shattered the peace-loving, trustful image Brezhnev had sought to build up. Moreover, within the Warsaw Pact the repercussions had been disastrous for the Kremlin: a massive swelling of anti-Russian feeling everywhere. The brutal crushing of a liberal Communist regime by Soviet troops remained, and still remains, a live, sensitive, volatile issue in Warsaw Pact countries, long after it took place.

To counter this anti-Soviet feeling in both East and West, and to get back on its chosen diplomatic track, the Soviet Union needed some kind of new diplomatic "grand design" for *détente*. It needed a new initiative. This began to emerge in an unexpected way. One year after Prague, in August of 1969, I suddenly received a telephone call from a Polish Press Agency correspondent in Paris, inviting me to go to Warsaw on short notice to take part in "a conference which the Polish Press Institute is organizing of East-West journalists to discuss the origins of the Second World War on the thirtieth anniversary of its beginning." The Poles had not been generous with visas for American journalists in the months following the Prague operation, and I made a quick telephone call to Los Angeles and got an immediate okay to accept. As it happened, I was the only American who managed to turn up, but a number of friends were there. Every NATO country was represented, along with the Swedes, the Swiss, and of course solid ranks from the Soviet Union and the Eastern bloc. It was a lively and interesting four days in Warsaw—but it quickly developed that the real purpose of the conference was simply to use a discussion of the origins of World War II in order to launch a proposal by the Polish Foreign Ministry to convene a European security conference. "The time has come," the theme ran, "for us all to eliminate the danger of World War III by recognizing the status quo in Europe."

When I got back to Paris after some pretty blunt and outspoken East-West exchanges in Warsaw about events in Prague and the usefulness of a European security conference under these circumstances, I made the rounds of various friends and contacts to see if the proposal was being floated on a diplomatic level as well, whether it seemed to have any real official weight behind it. In fact, it was not a new idea. It was first tried out, at a Berlin Big Four conference, in February of 1954, which I had covered. Soviet Foreign Minister V. M. Molotov had proposed it to John Foster Dulles, as a transparent move to try to head off the rearming of West Germany. It had cropped up occasionally in Soviet speeches or statements, and Brezhnev had tried it out on General de Gaulle when they met in Moscow in June of 1965. Diplomats with whom I talked were not surprised that the Russians would use the Poles to float it again, but they were skeptical as to how serious it was and certainly wary of giving it any encouragement. All the same, about two months later it became clear that it *was* a serious Soviet-backed diplomatic move when a formal proposal to the West to join in a European security conference was included in a communiqué on a meeting of Foreign Ministers of the countries of the Warsaw Pact.

Meanwhile, by this time the Soviet Union was also about to open talks with the United States in Helsinki, in November of 1969, to negotiate an agreement on strategic arms limitation. So a double diplomatic *détente* campaign was underway from the Kremlin—one line of approach on a bilateral basis to the United States, another line of multilateral approach to Western Europe. All that brief messy business in Prague was supposed to be forgotten.

Llewelyn E. Thompson, twice the U.S. ambassador in Moscow, of that wonderful American diplomatic trio of Soviet experts that included Charles E. Bohlen and George Kennan, once remarked to me that "when the Soviet Union fixes a new strategic objective in its policy, it will then make all kinds of concessions which seemed impossible the day before in order to get there as quickly as possible."

By 1970 it was clear that a European Security Conference had become a major strategic objective of Soviet foreign policy. The Western response, orchestrated largely through NATO, was properly cool and cautious. At the Big Four level—the United States, Great Britain, France and West Germany—it was promptly laid down that there was no point in going to any European security conference until agreement first was reached with the Soviet Union on a final settlement of the twenty-five-year-old Berlin problem. In Washington, Dr. Henry A. Kissinger, in his role as President Nixon's national security adviser, was completely skeptical. He and Nixon wanted to keep the *détente* process with the Soviet Union in their own hands. For them, bilateral superpower diplomacy was the best way of arranging the world, and things would simply become needlessly cluttered up if some big, multilateral conference now brought the Europeans into the act. As a diversionary tactic, the United States proposed that NATO first engage the Russians in East-West talks on conventional military force reductions in Central Europe as a kind of corollary to the SALT negotiations and forerunner to an eventual security conference. All these moves and countermoves were tossed back and forth in a kind of "battle of communiqués" after successive meetings of NATO and Warsaw Pact foreign ministers.

All the same, in fulfillment of Tommy Thompson's observation, the Soviet Union began making tactical moves in order to get to the strategic objective. After all those years of harassment and blockade of the Western Allies, serious negotiations opened in Berlin with the Russians in 1970 on an agreement on access and the status quo of the city, and was concluded in August 1971. By this time, the first SALT agreement was also beginning to take shape, and Willy Brandt had completed *Ostpolitik* agreements in Poland, Hungary, Romania and the Soviet Union in which recognition of existing frontiers by West Germany was the key element.

The SALT Treaty was then signed in Moscow by President Nixon, on May 26, 1972.

Henry Kissinger still wanted to focus next on a NATO-Warsaw Pact negotiation on conventional force reductions, but Brezhnev wanted his security conference. Finally a deal was struck. Kissinger agreed to go along with preliminary discussions on a security conference to begin in Helsinki in September 1972, and Brezhnev agreed to preliminary discussions on mutual, balanced force reductions beginning in Vienna in January 1973. Fifty-five years after Lenin arrived back at the Finland Station to launch the Communist revolution that irrevocably divided Europe, Leonid Brezhnev was on his way to the Helsinki Station in pursuit of capitalist cooperation and a truce.

"When the Russians are not involved in ideological or Communist political objectives in their foreign policy, they remain basically very conservative, traditional, cautious and legalistic in their behavior and their aims," a British diplomat with long experience in Soviet affairs said to me as preparations for Helsinki got underway at the Foreign Office.

"They have little or no respect for law within their own system, but they can become extremely legalistic in international affairs when law can be put to their use. Getting something on paper is always very important for the Russians. We can see clearly that they have now formed a basic foreign-policy objective of getting every country in Europe plus the United States and Canada to sign an international agreement which will legitimize their grip on Eastern Europe. In the same way, it was very important for us to get their signature on a legal document covering our presence in Berlin. In fact, the documents may not change the existing situation very much, but it is that cachet of legality and legitimization which has become of some overriding importance to the Russians. That's what they want out of the conference. The question is, what do we get out of it?"

The price that Western diplomats of every nationality agreed instinctively and unanimously had to be extracted from the Russians and the Communist bloc was a commitment to common humanitarian principles and the fundamental rights of people no matter what their system of government. With this in view, one of the first Western moves was to insist that it should not be just a "security" conference but a conference about cooperation as well. The Russians then sought, in effect, to limit cooperation to freer movement of trade. The West demanded a commitment to freer movement of peoples, information, ideas. It is a measure of the difficulty that it took three years of endless discussion and prolonged, sustained, patient diplomacy to wear the Russians down on this head-on clash of simple fundamentals to finally produce an agreement. But, as the British diplomat also remarked to me: "There is one basic rule in dealing with the Russians, and that is that you must always be prepared to sit at the table one day longer than they are."

This enveloping diplomatic enterprise began in almost casual simplicity. Once it was clear that the major powers were in agreement to have a conference, the Finnish Government dispatched invitations to every capital from Moscow to Ottawa and Malta to Oslo, inviting governments to send representatives to what was known as "the tea-party stage" of proceedings in Helsinki. Most governments sent their ambassadors resident in Helsinki. This series of meetings was brief, with a decision to convene a preparatory conference to work out an agenda and the outlines of an agreement—its chapter headings and principles—for a full-scale negotiation. The preparatory stage was vital, and special diplomatic teams now converged on Helsinki to work for five months, from November of 1972 through the following April. After that, the heavy negotiation on the text of the final act got underway in Geneva in September 1973 and lasted twenty-two months.

At no time in my commuting to conference sessions across over three years in Helsinki and Geneva, and later at the first Review Conference, in Belgrade in 1977–78, did I ever find any Western diplomat to be naïve or starry-eyed about what could be achieved with the Soviet Union in the field of human rights, or anything but realistic and ultimately cynical about the workings of the Communist system. They were fully aware that whatever they extracted from the Russians in the way of paper commitments, in the end the system would go on and the Soviets would always blandly behave toward their captive peoples however brutally they liked. But

Western diplomats did firmly believe that it was still worth all the struggle and effort of those endless months of negotiation to get that human rights "code of conduct" signed by Brezhnev and enshrined as an international agreement so that the Communist system could then be judged by a common standard on how it was living up to pledges to its own people and the world at large.

The instinctive intellectual commitment and solidarity of all Western diplomats behind this simple fundamental objective, and the sustained effort that they all put into seeing it through, were remarkable. What was startling and indefensible was the fashion in which Henry A. Kissinger very nearly sold the whole effort down the river.

Kissinger's interest or sympathy in the Conference on Security and Cooperation in Europe had never been high. Not only was he bored by arcane arguments over platitudinous texts that he judged would have little practical or historical meaning; in 1974 he was also up to his neck in the enveloping problems of Watergate. In June of that year, President Nixon seized a last opportunity to organize one more spectacular trip abroad to try to recapture public opinion, first to the Middle East and then to Moscow.

In Moscow, Kissinger and Nixon elected to try to enlist Russian help to speed up the Geneva negotiations, already well behind early target dates, and rush through an agreement so that Nixon could then go to a big summit signing ceremony in Helsinki before the end of the summer of 1974. Only the human-rights provisions seemed to be holding things up. Soviet Foreign Minister Andrei Gromyko was more than sympathetic and cooperative. It could all be wrapped up in a matter of weeks, he said, "if you can persuade your allies to be more reasonable in their demands on us on all those provisions on human rights." Grasping at this offer, Kissinger returned to Washington and drafted fresh instructions for the U.S. delegation at Geneva, telling them in effect to reduce the human-rights provisions to a handful of simple declarations of principle and ignore all the detailed commitments on things like family reunification and the right to marry nationals of other states, which the Soviet Union was not likely to pay any attention to anyway.

But the United States could not act alone. A special meeting of the NATO Council was then convened in Brussels to review the common Western negotiating position. After much discussion, Kissinger's new approach was rejected outright by a vote of fourteen to one. A French diplomat present at the meeting later told me with much satisfaction that it was the first and only time that NATO had ever been fourteen to one against anybody but France. The Western European governments insisted on standing firm on their demands for a detailed bill of human rights in return for the political and economic agreements the Soviets wanted. Kissinger had no choice but to retreat. And so the humanitarian provisions were saved. A few weeks later, Nixon was out of office, but it took another full year before the Russians finally caved in, gave the West more or less what it wanted, and cleared the way at last for the Helsinki summit.*

Leonid Brezhnev, Gerald Ford, Valéry Giscard d'Estaing, Helmut Schmidt, Harold Wilson, Marshal Tito, Nicolae Ceausescu, Archbishop Makarios, Pierre Elliot Trudeau, Olof Palme and all the other thirty-five heads of state met in the newly completed Finlandia Hall, in the center of Helsinki, an austerely lovely concert auditorium and complex of meeting halls in glistening white marble set like some graceful architectural swan in a park of trees with a lake in the background. The signing ceremony took place on the morning of August 1, 1975.

The Final Act of the Conference on Security and Cooperation in Europe begins with the customary preamble of principles, followed by a section on political and security agreements, a section dealing with cooperation in the economic field, and a section of cultural and humanitarian provisions in which the commitments to improvements in human rights and the flow of information are contained.

In the political undertakings, the key passage declares quite simply that all parties recognize the frontiers of all states of Europe to be "inviolable"—a carefully chosen word that does not mean either permanent or unchangeable. The document goes on

* When President Ford took over, Kissinger changed his mind about the utility of the Helsinki Agreements and toughened his instructions to the U.S. delegation considerably in support of the human-rights provisions.

to pledge the signatory nations "to refrain from the threat or use of force against the territorial integrity of any state," but adds that "frontiers can be changed, in accordance with international law, by peaceful means and by agreement." Finally in this section, the Western powers also extracted from the Soviet Union, after long political argument and negotiation, a declaration that spells out that "all peoples always have the right, in full freedom, to determine when and as they wish their internal and external political status, without external interference, and to pursue as they wish their political, economic, social and cultural development."

As far as Moscow is concerned, these passages in the Helsinki Final Act, taken collectively, constitute de facto acceptance by the West of the borders where the Red Army halted after World War II, the final legitimization of Soviet control over everything east of the Elbe River where there is ample Soviet power to insure against change. As far as the Western powers are concerned, the agreement does no more than record a status quo while keeping the door open at the same time for changes in the map of Europe or changes in the political system of any country, as the West has always sought to do, no matter how remote such possibilities may presently seem to be. Short of never having negotiated the Helsinki agreements at all, it is difficult to conceive of any wording of an agreed text on East-West political understanding that would have given away any less or obtained any more.

In a broad, general sense, the Helsinki Final Act has had a stabilizing influence, and it is this which gives it a historic quality. After two world wars and six decades of conflict between the Communist and capitalist systems, the Final Act is *the* document which recognizes and records the European stalemate—the hollow inability of the Communist system to make any headway in Europe beyond rifle range of the Red Army, and the total failure of the Soviet Union to compete with the capitalist world economically; the inability of the Western Powers to force the Red Army out of Eastern Europe, or to be able to bring about any evolution of political change in the region where the Soviet Union exercises ruthless control. Instead of going on with a pretense of either side's ever being likely to penetrate fundamentally the position of the other, they came together to sign a kind of live-and-keep-hope-alive agreement between Europe's two competing systems. Or, as the French would say, *"Plus ça change, plus c'est la même chose."*

In the five years following the Helsinki summit, it was indeed remarkable how things had changed but how they still remained the same. Once the ink was finally dry on the signatures on the Final Act, the Soviet Union began its crackdown on political dissidents, who had been allowed a little bit of a free run while the human-rights provisions were still being negotiated. Czechoslovakia slavishly followed the Soviet example. Meanwhile the pace of the Soviet armament program never faltered, whether the Helsinki Agreements constituted a truce, an armistice, or a de facto peace agreement. And in Vienna, the much-publicized Mutual and Balanced Force Reductions talks, between NATO and the Warsaw Pact, on which Henry Kissinger once seemed to place such importance, bogged down in the longest-running nonproductive negotiation in all diplomatic history. At the end of the decade, after seven years of talks in Vienna, not one single sheet of paper had yet been signed or agreed to about anything.

Nevertheless, throughout the second half of the 1970s, East-West relations did move forward in a more relaxed, normal political climate and atmosphere. Trade jumped considerably, largely on the strength of overgenerous Western credit terms, as the Soviet Union and all the other countries in its orbit came rushing to buy much-needed machine tools, industrial plant, computers, know-how, in order to fulfill their lagging production targets and economic plans. The more detectable results of Helsinki were to be seen not in the behavior of the Soviet Union but in that of the smaller countries of the Warsaw Pact. There the Communist regimes moved very gingerly but positively toward some implementation of some of the human-rights and other agreements. Practically all the Eastern European countries except Czechoslovakia quietly but steadily eased up on the abominable restrictions on relatives' leaving to rejoin families in the West. It became easier for journalists to obtain visas, and officials seemed to be more readily available for interviews and talked more candidly.

The flow of travel increased from Eastern Europe to the West, and in the smaller countries, unlike the Soviet Union, a much greater atmosphere of freedom of speech (not, of course, the press) and discussion and thought became apparent—in particular, much greater freedom and devotion to religion. If ever there seemed to be a crowning act of East-West *détente,* it was the election of a Polish Pope in the Vatican in 1978.

Some things were changing—but the Communist system still remained the same.

The *détente* decade of the 1970s ended with a bang when the Red Army rolled into Afghanistan, on December 27, 1979. At the same time, to underline his contempt for the human-rights provisions of the Helsinki Agreements, Brezhnev ordered that Russia's longtime leading dissident, nuclear physicist and Nobel Peace Prize winner Andrei Sakharov, be transported from Moscow to forced exile in the town of Gorky, off limits to foreigners.

By the end of the decade, Brezhnev's *détente* policy had paid off with maximum advantage for the Soviet Union: Good relations and stability in Europe contributing enormously to solving the economic and production problems of the Communist bloc, costing little in return apart from minimal cordiality and negotiated good behavior, while the arms buildup had gone on unchecked. With no major security or political concerns on its western front, the Soviet Union had already reached out to obtain footholds and assert its power in Africa: Angola, Mozambique, Ethiopia; and on the Arabian peninsula: Aden and South Yemen. Meanwhile the Shah of Iran had been forced out of his country, which plunged into Islamic revolutionary turmoil. There was no longer any power to intervene or prevent a Soviet strategic push in the direction of the warm water of the Indian Ocean and the Persian Gulf. Afghanistan, Iran's neighbor, was there on the map for all to see. This time there was no Marshall Plan to combat "hunger, poverty, desperation and chaos," no leadership to be rallied, no coalition to be built. There was only the savage, primitive, raw Afghan courage in those wild and desolate mountains and passes.

It was a Soviet foreign minister, Maxim Litvinov, who stood before the League of Nations in Geneva in the appeasement year of 1936 to wave an accusing, warning arm at the Great Powers of Western Europe and declare that "Peace is indivisible." As the

1980s begin, Western Europe faces the same stark question all over again: Is not *détente* indivisible?

In the thirty-five years since the end of World War II Western Europe has been a favored region of the world. Protected by the United States, it has made truly enormous achievements for itself and its peoples. The Europeans have sloughed off with relief the nineteenth-century role of imperialism, set their colonies free and built for themselves the most stable, secure, well-governed and productive area of the world, with living standards, social benefits, educational standards and a way of life for its citizens that is unrivaled anywhere in culture, depth and variety. Western Europe is more prosperous and content, more trouble-free and united than it has been in all its history.

But it is a little too content, too smug, too secure for its own good. Western Europe has done well for itself, but the question for the 1980s is, What is it now going to do for the security and well-being of a troubled and endangered world?

Further Reading

(IN CHAPTER ORDER)

Bevin, by Trevor Evans (George Allen & Unwin, London, 1946)

Ernest Bevin; Portrait of a Great Englishman, by Francis Williams (Hutchinson, London, 1952)

Life and Times of Ernest Bevin, by Alan Bullock (Heinemann, London, 1960)

Ernest Bevin and the Foreign Office, by Sir Roderick Barclay (privately printed, London, 1975)

Home and Abroad, by Lord Strang (Andre Deutsch, London, 1956)

The Semblance of Peace, by John W. Wheeler-Bennet and Anthony Nicholls (Macmillan, New York, 1972)

The Fifteen Weeks, by Joseph Jones (Harcourt, Brace, New York, 1955)

The Marshall Plan and Its Meaning, by Harry Bayard Price (Cornell University Press, Ithaca, N.Y., 1955)

Present at the Creation, by Dean Acheson (Norton, New York, 1969)

Witness to History, by Charles E. Bohlen (Norton, New York, 1973)

Memoirs, by George Kennan (Hutchinson, London, 1969)

Years of Trial and Hope; the Truman Memoirs, by Harry S Truman (Doubleday, Garden City, N.Y., 1956)

Crisis and Conflict; the Truman Presidency, 1945–1948, by Robert J. Donovan (Norton, New York, 1977)

The Adenauer Memoirs, by Konrad Adenauer (Weidenfeld & Nicolson, London, 1966)

Adenauer, His Authorized Biography, by Paul Meymar (Dutton, New York, 1957)

Adenauer, A Study in Fortitude, by Terence Prittie (Cowles Books, London, 1971)

Germany, 1866–1945, by Gordon A. Craig (Oxford University Press, New York, 1978)

Divided Berlin, by Hans Speier (Frederick A. Praeger, New York, 1961)

Decision in Germany, by General Lucius D. Clay (Doubleday, Garden City, N.Y., 1950)

Berlin Command, by Brigadier General Frank Howley (Putnam, New York, 1950)

Bridge Across the Sky, by Richard Collier (McGraw-Hill, New York, 1978)

Diplomat Among Warriors, by Robert Murphy (Doubleday, Garden City, N.Y., 1964)

Memoirs, by Jean Monnet (Doubleday, Garden City, N.Y., 1977)

Jean Monnet and the United States of Europe, by Merry and Serge Bromberger (Coward-McCann, New York, 1969)

Sketches from Life, by Dean Acheson (Harper & Bros., New York, 1959)

The United States and the Unity of Europe, by Max Beloff (Brookings Institution, Washington, 1963)

Twentieth-century Europe: Paths to Unity, by Richard Vaughan (Barnes & Noble, New York, 1979)

The Recovery of Europe, by Richard Mayne (Harper & Row, New York, 1970)

The Macmillan Memoirs, by Harold Macmillan, 5 vols. (Macmillan, London, 1965–73)

Macmillan: A Study in Ambiguity, by Anthony Sampson (Allan Lane: The Penguin Press, London, 1967)

British Prime Ministers of the Twentieth Century, ed. John P. Macintosh (Weidenfeld & Nicolson, London, 1978)

Suez 1956, by Selwyn Lloyd (Jonathan Cape, London, 1978)

Dulles over Suez, by Herman Finer (Quadrangle Books, Chicago, 1964)

Full Circle; the Eden Memoirs, Vol. III, by the Right Honorable Sir Anthony Eden (Cassell, London, 1960)

Story of My Life, by Moshe Dayan (Weidenfeld & Nicolson, London, 1976)

The Real Suez Crisis, by Jacques Georges-Picot (Harcourt Brace Jovanovich, New York, 1978)

The Middle East in Revolution, by Humphrey Trevelyan (Macmillan, London, 1970)

The Game of Nations, by Miles Copeland (Weidenfeld & Nicolson, London, 1969)

The Road to Suez, by Erskine B. Childers (MacGibbon & Kee, London, 1962)

Nasser; the Cairo Documents, by Muhammad Heikal (New English Library, London, 1970)

The Rise and Fall of Sir Anthony Eden, by Randolph S. Churchill (MacGibbon & Kee, London, 1959)

War Memoirs, by Charles de Gaulle, 3 vols. (Collins and Weidenfeld & Nicolson, London, 1955–59)

De Gaulle, by Aidan Crawley (The Literary Guild, London, 1969)

An Explanation of De Gaulle, by Robert Aron (Harper & Row, New York, 1966)

Two Men Who Saved France: Pétain and De Gaulle, by Major General Sir Edward Spears (Eyre & Spottiswoode, London, 1966)

Assignment to Catastrophe, by Major General Sir Edward Spears, 2 vols. (Heinemann, London, 1954)

Pétain and De Gaulle, by Jean Raymond Tournoux (Heinemann, London, 1966)

No Laurels for de Gaulle, by Robert Mengin (Farrar, Straus & Giroux, New York, 1966)

The de Gaulle Revolution, by Alexander Worth (Robert Hale, London, 1960)

The Death of the Fourth Republic, by Ronald Matthews (Eyre & Spottiswoode, London, 1954)

De Gaulle's Republic, by Philip M. Williams and Martin Harrison (Longmans, Green, London, 1960)

The New French Revolution, by John Ardagh (Secker & Warburg, London, 1968)

A Savage War of Peace, by Alastair Horne (Viking Press, New York, 1977)

The French Communist Party Versus the Students, by Richard Johnson (Yale University Press, New York, 1972)

The Almost Revolution, by Alain Priulax and Sanford J. Ungar (Dell, New York, 1969)

The Duel: de Gaulle and Pompidou, by Philippe Alexandre (Houghton Mifflin, Boston, 1972)

Willy Brandt, Portrait of a Statesman, by Terence Prittie (Schocken, New York, 1974)

My Road to Berlin, by Willy Brandt (Peter Davies, London, 1960)

People and Politics, by Willy Brandt (Little, Brown, Boston, 1978)

The Ides of August; the Berlin Wall Crisis, by Curtis Cate (Weiden-feld & Nicolson, London, 1978)

Edward Heath, by George Hutchinson (Longmans, Green, London, 1970)

Heath and the Heathmen, by Andrew Roth (Routledge & Kegan Paul, London, 1972)

An End to Promises, by Douglas Hurd (Collins, London, 1979)

A State of England, by Anthony Hartley (Hutchinson, London, 1963)

The Challenge of the Common Market, by U. W. Kitzinger (Basil Blackwell, Oxford, 1961)

Great Britain or Little England, by John Mander (Penguin, London, 1963)

Atlantic Crisis, by Robert Kleiman (Norton, New York, 1964)

The General Said No, by Nora Beloff (Penguin, London, 1963)

From Commonwealth to Common Market, ed. Pierre Uri (Penguin, London, Atlantic Institute, 1968)

Decline or Renewal? France Since the 1930s, by Stanley Hoffman (Viking, New York, 1974)

French Democracy, by Valéry Giscard d'Estaing (Doubleday, Garden City, N.Y., 1977)

The Totalitarian Temptation, by Jean-François Revel (Doubleday, Garden City, N.Y., 1977)

An Economic History of Modern France, by François Caron (Columbia University Press, New York, 1979)

The Myth of France, by Raymond Rudorff (Hamish Hamilton, London, 1970)

Eurocommunism: Its Roots and Future, ed. G. R. Urgan (Maurice Temple Smith, London, 1978)

Eurocommunism: Myth or Reality, ed. Paolo Filo della Torre (Penguin, New York, 1979)

From Stalinism to Eurocommunism, by Ernest Mandel (Schocken, New York, 1979)

The God That Failed, ed. Richard Crossman (Hamish Hamilton, London, 1950)

Eurocommunism: Implications for East and West, by Roy Godson and Stephen Haseler (Macmillan, London, 1978)

Germans, by George Bailey (World Publishing, New York, 1972)

Detente Diplomacy: the United States and European Security, by Timothy W. Stanley and Darnell M. Whitt (University Press of Cambridge, London, 1970)

Europe's Futures, Europe's Choices, ed. Alastair Buchan (Institute for Strategic Studies, London, 1969)

The Unhinged Alliance, by J. Robert Schaetzel (Council on Foreign Relations by Harper & Row, New York, 1976)

The Diplomacy of the Great Powers, by Sir William Hayter (Hamish Hamilton, London, 1960)

Europe Between the Super-Powers: the Enduring Balance, by A. W. DePorte (Yale University Press, New Haven, 1979)

A Continent Astray; Europe 1970–78, by Walter Laqueur (Oxford University Press, New York, 1979)

The Sealed Train, by Michael Pearson (Putnam, New York, 1975)

To the Finland Station, by Edmund Wilson (Farrar, Straus & Giroux, New York, 1940 and 1972)

Index